Counseling
American
Minorities

A CROSS-CULTURAL PERSPECTIVE

Counseling
American
Minorities

A CROSS-CULTURAL PERSPECTIVE

FOURTH EDITION

Donald R. Atkinson
UNIVERSITY OF CALIFORNIA - SANTA BARBARA

George Morten
LOYOLA MARYMOUNT UNIVERSITY

Derald Wing Sue
CALIFORNIA STATE UNIVERSITY - HAYWARD

WCB Brown & Benchmark
PUBLISHERS

Madison, Wisconsin • Dubuque, Iowa • Indianapolis, Indiana
Melbourne, Australia • Oxford, England

Book Team

Editor *Michael Lange*
Developmental Editor *Sheralee Connors*
Production Coordinator *Carla D. Arnold*

A Division of Wm. C. Brown Communications, Inc.

Vice President and General Manager *Thomas E. Doran*
Executive Managing Editor *Ed Bartell*
Executive Editor *Edgar J. Laube*
Director of Marketing *Kathy Law Laube*
National Sales Manager *Eric Ziegler*
Marketing Manager *Carla Aspelmeier*
Advertising Manager *Jodi Rymer*
Managing Editor, Production *Colleen A. Yonda*
Manager of Visuals and Design *Faye M. Schilling*

Production Editorial Manager *Vickie Putman Caughron*
Publishing Services Manager *Karen J. Slaght*
Permissions/Records Manager *Connie Allendorf*

Wm. C. Brown Communications, Inc.

Chairman Emeritus *Wm. C. Brown*
Chairman and Chief Executive Officer *Mark C. Falb*
President and Chief Operating Officer *G. Franklin Lewis*
Corporate Vice President, Operations *Beverly Kolz*
Corporate Vice President, President of WCB Manufacturing *Roger Meyer*

Cover and interior design by Elaine G. Allen

Copyedited by Mary Palmborg

Photo research by Kathy Husemann

Part Openers
Part Opener 1: © David Grossman; Part Opener 2: © James L. Shaffer; Part Opener 3: © Lisa Law/The
Image Works, Inc.; Part Opener 4: © James L. Shaffer; Part Opener 5: © Bob Daemmrich/The Image Works,
Inc.; Part Opener 6: © James L. Shaffer.

CONTENTS

v

PART 4
The Asian American Client

PART 5
The Latino Client

PART 6
Implications for Minority Group/Cross-Cultural Counseling

PREFACE

This fourth edition of *Counseling American Minorities: A Cross-Cultural Perspective,* like the first three, is designed to help counselors and mental health practitioners maximize their effectiveness when working with a culturally diverse population. A major thesis of this book is that culturally sensitive counselors can establish the necessary and sufficient conditions of a helping relationship with many clients who come from cultural backgrounds different from their own. While similarity of race/ethnicity and culture between the counselor and client may be highly correlated with counseling success, we believe that other attributes (ability to share a similar world view, knowledge of the client's culture, use of appropriate counselor roles, etc.) also contribute to a productive counseling relationship and may help overcome barriers that can result from cultural differences.

The purposes of this edition remain the same as those of the earlier editions. First, the book is intended to sensitize counselors to the life experiences and within-group differences of four racial/ethnic minority groups. A second major purpose is to examine how counseling has failed to meet the mental health needs of racial/ethnic minorities in the past. A third purpose is to suggest new directions for the counseling profession when serving racial/ethnic minority in the future.

This edition represents the most extensive rewriting of the book since it first appeared in 1979. Chapters 1, 2, 3, and 16 have been completely revised to reflect the recent theoretical and research advances in cross-cultural counseling. Many new developments and trends have appeared since the 1989 edition and we have tried to synthesize contemporary thinking and current data for the reader. In addition to changes in the four chapters that we wrote, eleven of the twelve readings included in this edition are new (one retains the same title but the chapter has been rewritten).

When we selected readings for parts 2 through 5 of the current edition, we tried to maintain our original design of beginning each part with a historical/sociological overview of the racial/ethnic group followed by two readings that discuss the pragmatics of counseling members of the group. In selecting new readings, we attempted to identify articles that reflect the latest theory and research regarding the ethnic group discussed. We feel that the new readings reflect the most recent thinking and the increasing sophistication of publications on cross-cultural counseling.

In place of the APA Division 17 Position Paper on cross-cultural competencies included in the appendix of earlier editions we have substituted a position paper by the Professional Standards Committee of the Association for Multicultural Counseling and Development. The latter position paper expands upon many of the principles included in the earlier publication and generally reflects current thinking with respect to training counselors for cross-cultural counseling.

A number of individuals contributed to this edition as reviewers. We'd like to thank Chris Kleinke, University of Alaska; Colleen L. Gift, Highland Community College; and Dr. Les Parrott, Seattle Pacific University.

The current edition can be used in conjunction with a variety of courses related to counseling and mental health service. The book has served as both a primary text and as supplemental reading for such courses as cross-cultural counseling, multicultural counseling, diversity issues in mental health, counseling techniques, theories of counseling, community psychology, and mental health outreach. Parts 2 through 6 conclude with a number of hypothetical cases which require the reader to assume he or she is interacting with a racial/ethnic minority client. Each case is followed by several questions designed to induce the reader to examine his/her own biases and stereotypes, and to explore potential obstacles to minority group/cross-cultural counseling. The most effective use of these cases and questions will probably occur when they serve to stimulate group discussion, preferably in settings where the participants represent several different racial/ethnic groups.

It is a sad commentary on our times that we can conclude this Preface by paraphrasing the concluding statement from the Preface to the third edition. It would be pleasing if we could report that oppression of minorities had become a thing of the past in the thirteen years since the first edition of *Counseling American Minorities: A Cross-Cultural Perspective* first appeared in print. Unfortunately, such is not the case. Legislative and judicial achievements with respect to nondiscrimination and affirmative action of the 1960s and 1970s came under attack in the 1980s and early 1900s. Racial/ethnic minorities continue to experience discrimination in employment, housing, and education. Physical harassment and abuse of minorities is actually on the rise and has been for a number of years. The income gap between the very wealthy (largely European Americans) and the very poor (disproportionately composed of racial/ethnic minorities) has grown considerably since our first edition. The need for counselor knowledge of, and sensitivity to, the experiences of racial/ethnic minority clients is greater now than it has been at any time in the past three decades. We hope this text contributes to the knowledge and sensitivity the counselors and other mental health workers will need when working with racial/ethnic minority clients.

D.R.A.
G.M.
D.W.S.

PART 1

Racial/Ethnic Minorities and Cross-Cultural Counseling

1
Defining Populations and Terms

The Diversification of the United States

Earlier writers have referred to the "greening" (Reich, 1970) and the "graying" (Sheppard, 1977) of America to identify the impact large segments of the population have had on the United States. The current population trend might well be referred to as the "diversification" of the United States. This trend started in the late 1960s and is a function of two major forces: (a) current immigration patterns; and (b) differential birthrates among racial/ethnic groups.

The current immigration wave, which consists of documented immigrants, undocumented immigrants, and refugees, is the largest in U.S. history. Unlike earlier immigrations which originated primarily in Europe and whose members were readily assimilated into the mainstream culture, the current wave consists primarily of Asian (34 percent), Latin American (34 percent), and other visible racial/ethnic groups who historically have not been so readily assimilated. When combined with the higher birthrates among these and other ethnic groups already in residence (Caucasian American = 1.7, African American = 2.4, Mexican American = 2.9, Vietnamese = 3.4, Laotians = 4.6, Cambodians = 7.4, and Hmong = 11.9 per mother), the current immigration wave is resulting in dramatic increases in the non-White populations. During the 1980s alone the Asian American population increased by 79.5 percent, the Latino population by 38.7 percent, the American Indian population by 21.6 percent, and the African American population by 14.4 percent (U.S. Census Bureau, 1990). With the Caucasian Americans increasing by only 7.0 percent during this time period, the result is a changing complexion of the U.S. populace. This is particularly evident in California, the state that serves as the bellwether of national trends. In 1990, African Americans, Asian Americans, and Latinos made up 40 percent of the California population; these groups are expected to comprise over 50 percent of the citizenry by the year 2000 (Jones & Clifford, 1990). At the national level, the U.S. Census Bureau projects a population of over 280 million by the year 2000, consisting of

200 million Whites, 37 million Blacks, 31 million of Spanish origin, and 12 million Asians and other racial/ethnic minority groups (U.S. Bureau of the Census, 1986). The National Coalition of Advocates for Students (1988) estimates that by the year 2050, one in three U.S. residents will be non-White.

The diversification trend will have a significant impact on a number of U.S. institutions. For example, the number of African Americans in the labor force is expected to increase over 29 percent between 1986 and 2000 (Kutscher, 1987). Similar figures for Latino and Asian Americans are 75+ percent and 70+ percent, respectively. Education will be significantly impacted by the changing demographics. In California the number of Caucasian American students dropped below 50 percent of the public school enrollment for the first time in 1988. By 1990, one in every four students in California lived in a home in which English was not spoken and one in every six was foreign born.

The diversification of the U.S. population has important implications for professional counselors and other mental health service providers. Counselors need to increase their cultural sensitivity, knowledge of cultures, and culturally-relevant counseling skills in order to meet the needs of a culturally diverse client population. Mental health services need to be structured to optimize utilization by and effectiveness for racial/ethnic populations. And professional organizations need to press for policy and legislation at the local, state, and national level that will address discrimination against culturally diverse groups. This book is intended to facilitate the development of counselors and mental health service providers who can meet these needs. In order to discuss the experiences and counseling-related needs of the racial/ethnic populations that make up a growing proportion of the U.S. population, it is necessary to begin with a common terminology.

Defining Terms

It is particularly important for counselors to become familiar with terminology relevant to cross-cultural counseling because the misuse of some terms may be interpreted by some clients as cultural insensitivity. It is also important for counselors to recognize that not all terms are universally accepted across or within racial/ethnic populations.

Culture, Race, and Ethnicity

There is a great deal of confusion in both the general public and the counseling profession about the meaning of the terms culture, race, and ethnicity. Moore's (1974) attempt to resolve the confusion is often cited in any discussion of these three terms:

Sometimes we tend to confuse race and ethnic groups with culture. Great races do have different cultures. Ethnic groups within races differ in cultural content. But, people of the same racial origin and of the same ethnic groups differ in their cultural matrices. All browns, or blacks, or whites, or yellows, or reds are not alike in the cultures in which they live and have their being. The understanding of the culture of another, or of groups other than our own, demands a knowledge of varied elements within a culture or the variety of culture components within a larger cultural matrix (p. 41).

We have some difficulty with this discussion of culture, race, and ethnicity. First of all, we are not sure what is meant by "great races" (are some races "greater" than others?). Also, we are not convinced that ethnicity is a classification schema that should be subsumed under race, as seems to be implied in Moore's (1974) statement. In fact, we have some difficulty with the concept of race itself (as will become evident). In our own attempt to shed some light on these issues we offer the following discussion.

Numerous definitions of culture have been developed by anthropologists over the years, including Kroeber and Kluckhohn's (1952) attempt to synthesize many of them:

Culture consists of patterns, explicit and implicit, of and for behavior acquired and transmitted by symbols, constituting the distinctive achievement of human groups, including their embodiments in artifacts; the essential core of culture consists of traditional (i.e., historically derived and selected) ideas and especially their attached values; culture systems may, on the one hand, be considered as products of action, on the other as conditioning elements of further action (p. 181).

Needless to say, the myriad of confusing definitions that Kroeber and Kluckhohn set out to eliminate was only augmented by their earnest efforts. The most succinct and useful definition, for our purposes, is that offered by Linton (1945), who defined culture as, ". . . the configuration of learned behavior and results of behavior whose components and elements are shared and transmitted by the members of a particular society" (p. 32). Thus, culture is not, as an Andy Capp cartoon suggests, something that "my crowd has and yours doesn't have." Every society that shares and transmits behaviors to its members has a culture.

According to the *Oxford Dictionary of Words,* the term race first appeared in the English language less than three hundred years ago. Yet in that brief time race has come to be one of the most misused and misunderstood terms in the American vernacular (Rose, 1964). Race has been defined in two ways. The first definition is based solely on physical or biological characteristics. "To the biologist, a race, or subspecies, is an inbreeding, geographically isolated population that differs in distinguishable physical traits from other members of the species" (Zuckerman, 1990, p. 1297). Some social scientists also have adopted a biological definition. For example, Krogman (1945) defined race as ". . . a subgroup of peoples possessing a definite combination of physical characters, of genetic origin, the combination of which to varying degrees distinguishes the subgroup from other subgroups of mankind" (p. 49). Basic to a biological definition of race is the view that humans can be divided into a set number of genetic groups on the basis of physical characteristics. Physical differences involving skin pigmentation, head form, facial features, and the color, distribution, and texture of body hair are among the most commonly applied criteria assumed to distinguish races of people.

As Anderson (1971) points out, however, this system is far from ideal, in that not all racial group members fit these criteria precisely. While three basic racial types—Caucasoid, Mongoloid, and Negroid—are commonly accepted, a great deal of overlapping occurs among these groups. When we look beneath the superficial characteristics, we find there are more similarities between groups than differences (owing to the fact that all humans originate from a single genus species, homo sapiens), and more differences within racial groups than between them (Littlefield, Lieberman, & Reynolds, 1982). Race as a biological concept can be questioned on other grounds. For example, the concept of races resulting from common gene pools can be questioned. As Schaefer (1988) points out, "given frequent migration, exploration, and invasions, pure gene frequencies have not existed for some time, if they ever did" (p. 12). Paradoxically, in the United States an individual is commonly identified as Black if he/she has any African American blood, as American Indian if he/she has at least one grandparent who is American Indian. In these cases racial designation has little to do with an isolated gene pool. Also, there is no biological explanation for why some physical features (e.g., skin color) have been selected to determine race while others (e.g., eye color) have not. As Zuckerman (1990) suggests, "many of the features are not correlated and none by themselves could furnish an indisputable guide to the anthropologists' definitions of racial groups" (p. 1298). Furthermore, the fact that scientists cannot agree how many races there are, with estimates ranging from three to 200 (Schaefer, 1988), suggests that there is little agreement about the criteria defining race.

Unfortunately, this biological definition of race has given rise to ideological racism, an ideology that links physical characteristics of groups of people to psychological and/or intellectual characteristics (Feagin, 1989). Ideological racism has provided the basis for discrimination and oppression of certain groups of people who are assumed to be inferior and undesirable. As Mack (1968) points out, although race in the biological sense has no biological consequences, what people believe about race has very profound social consequences. For example, anyone who has physical characteristics associated with African Americans is identified as Black, ignoring the fact that the majority of his/her ancestors may be European

American. On the other hand, the federal government requires that to be classified as American Indian, the person must have at least 25 percent Indian "blood." And the consequences are not limited to what others think about a particular group of people. Through subtle yet effective socializing influences, group members are taught and come to accept as "social fact" a myriad of myths and stereotypes regarding skin color, facial features, and other physical characteristics.

A second definition of race includes both a biological and a social component. Cox (1948) was among the first to provide a social perspective by defining race as "any people who are distinguished or consider themselves distinguished, in social relations with other peoples, by their physical characteristics" (p. 402). The social component is dependent on group identity, either evolving within the group or assigned by those outside the group. It should be noted, however, that the term race has been applied to cultural groups whose members share little or no unique physical characteristics. As Hughes (1958), points out:

> . . . (Jews) . . . are not a biological race because the people known as Jews are not enough like each other and are too much like other people to be distinguished from them. But as people act with reference to Jews and to some extent connect the attitudes they have about them with real and imagined biological characteristics, they become a socially supposed race (p. 67).

Regardless of its biological validity, the concept of race has taken on important social meaning in terms of how outsiders view members of a "racial" group and how individuals within the "racial" group view themselves, members of their group, and members of other "racial" groups. In other words, the concept of race has taken on important dimensions in terms of how individuals identify who they are. The concept of racial self-identification is one about which we will have more to say in Chapter 3.

A review of the literature on ethnicity reveals that this term also has two different interpretations, one broad and one narrow (Feagin, 1989). In the broad sense, ethnicity is determined by physical or cultural characteristics. Because this broad definition includes physical characteristics, ethnicity is often used interchangeably with race. This position is expressed by Glazer (1971):

> Thus one possible position on ethnicity and race, and the one I hold, is that they form part of a single family of social identities—a family which, in addition to races and ethnic groups, includes religions . . . , language groups . . . , and all of which can be included in the most general term, ethnic groups, groups defined by descent, real or mythical, and sharing a common history and experience. (p. 447)

The more narrow definition of ethnicity is taken from the Greek root word *ethnos*, originally meaning "nation" (Feagin, 1989). In this narrow sense ethnicity distinguishes groups on the basis of nationality or cultural characteristics, and physical characteristics are not necessarily a part of ethnic differences. Thus, Rose (1964) defined an ethnic group as a group in which the members share a unique social and cultural heritage passed on from one generation to the next. Similarly, Schaefer (1988) identifies ethnic groups as "groups set apart from others because of their national origin or distinctive cultural patterns" (p. 9). According to the narrow definition of ethnicity, ethnic differences involve differences in nationality, customs, language, religion, and other cultural factors; physical differences are not necessarily germane to ethnic differences. If one accepts the view that ethnicity is the result of shared social and cultural heritage, then Jews, for example, are an ethnic group but not a racial group.

What can be concluded from this examination of the various definitions of culture, race, and ethnicity? Well for one thing, the validity of the concept of race is called into question. We are not convinced that race is a valid term, although it may be useful, as Johnson (1990) has suggested, to document the effects of racism and the progress in eradicating it. As Zuckerman (1990) points out, "geographical isolation may have been a significant factor producing inbreeding in the distant evolutionary past, but now the barriers that separate populations are political, cultural, and religious rather than geographic" (p. 1297). Ethnicity seems to be a much more useful term since it is descriptive (with regard to nationality and/or culture) but without the problems associated with defining race. The difficulty is that the concept of race is so pervasive in the United States that it contributes significantly to how most (if not all) of us identify ourselves. In other words, some of us choose to identify ourselves racially and counselors must recognize the important role that race plays in self-identification.

In recognition of the role that both race and ethnicity play in self-identification, we use the term race/ethnicity to signify groups of people who share a common ancestry and cultural heritage. It is important to recognize, however, that due to the process of acculturation, individuals of the same ancestry may or may not share the same cultural values and behaviors. As Sue and Zane (1988) point out, it is important for counselors to "avoid confounding the cultural values of the client's *ethnic group* with those of the *client*" (p. 41).

Before leaving this discussion of culture, it is important to dismiss two terms, "culturally deprived" and "culturally disadvantaged," that have been widely used in the past in conjunction with racial/ethnic groups. The term "culturally deprived" implies the absence of culture, a (perhaps hypothetical) situation that has no relationship to the groups addressed in this book. Notwithstanding the effects of the larger society's culture on racial/ethnic groups through the mass media, the groups discussed in this book clearly possess and transmit their own cultures.

The term "culturally disadvantaged" suggests the person to whom it is applied is at a disadvantage because she/he lacks the cultural background formed by the controlling social structure. The use of "disadvantaged" rather than "deprived" is intended to recognize that the individual possesses a cultural heritage, but also suggests it is not the *right* culture. While less noxious than "culturally deprived," "culturally disadvantaged" still implies a cultural deficiency, whereas the real issue is one of ethnocentrism, with the values of the majority culture viewed as more important than those of ethnic cultures. A person may be economically disadvantaged because he/she has less money than the average person, or educationally disadvantaged due to inferior formal education. We seriously object, however, to any inference that racial/ethnic groups have less culture.

Even the more accepted terms "culturally different" and "culturally distinct" can carry negative connotations when they are used to imply that a person's culture is at variance (out-of-step) with the dominant (accepted) culture. The inappropriate application of these two terms occurs in counseling when their usage is restricted to ethnically diverse clients. Taken literally, it is grammatically and conceptually correct to refer to a majority client as "culturally different" or "culturally distinct" from the counselor if the counselor is a minority individual.

Melting Pot, Acculturation, Assimilation, and Cultural Pluralism

Throughout the early stages of its development, the United States projected an image of the cultural melting pot, a nation in which all nationalities, ethnicities, and races melted into one culture. Many Americans took pride in the melting pot image and a play by British playwright Israel Zangwill, entitled *The Melting Pot,* enjoyed widespread popularity in this country when it was first performed in 1908. Inherent in the melting pot concept was the view that a new and unique culture would continually emerge as each new immigrant group impacted upon the existing culture (Krug, 1976).

Not everyone in the United States, however, subscribed to the melting pot theory and philosophy. The Chinese Exclusion Act passed by Congress in 1882 was the first of a number of federal and state laws established to ensure that certain immigrant groups would have minimal impact on the emerging American culture. In 1926 Henry Pratt Fairchild, a noted American sociologist of the time, wrote that the melting pot philosophy and unrestricted immigration were "slowly, insidiously, irresistibly eating away the very heart of the United States" (Fairchild, 1926, p. 261). According to Fairchild and others, the "heart of the United States," was an (equivocally defined) American culture that was based primarily on the values and mores of early immigrants, principally English, Irish, German, and Scandinavian groups. Instead of melting all cultures into one, opponents of the melting pot philosophy argued that an effort should be made to culturally assimilate ("Americanize") all immigrant groups. To reduce the effects of the melting pot phenomenon and increase the probability of cultural assimilation, immigration quotas were developed for those countries whose culture diverged most from the American culture. Public education, with its universal use of the English language, was viewed as the primary institution for perpetuating the existing American culture (Epps, 1974).

Before moving on to a discussion of cultural pluralism, an alternative to the melting pot and assimilation philosophies, it is helpful to distinguish between assimilation and acculturation. Gordon (1964) has identified acculturation as one of seven different types of assimilation. Acculturation refers to cultural assimilation or the acquisition of the cultural patterns of the core or dominant society. However, assimilation implies more than the adoption of the dominant culture. In addition it requires that structural assimilation be achieved, or, as suggested by McLemore (1983), that "members of the two groups interact with one another as friends and equals and that they select marriage partners without regard to ethnic or racial identities" (p. 35). Even though some immigrants (and their descendants) may desire to become acculturated and may make every effort to adopt the culture of the dominant society, total assimilation may be beyond their grasp since it requires acceptance by members of that society. Thus, for some racial/ethnic persons, assimilation may be a desired but unachievable goal.

For others, assimilation may not be a desired goal. Many members of racial/ethnic groups find the cultural assimilation philosophy objectionable because it calls for relinquishing their traditional racial/ethnic values and norms in favor of those of the dominant culture. With the civil rights movement of the 1960s and 1970s came a growing interest in cultural pluralism. According to the theory of cultural pluralism, individual racial/ethnic groups maintain their own cultural uniqueness while sharing common elements of American culture (Kallen, 1956). Cultural pluralism is often likened to a cultural stew; the various ingredients are mixed together, but rather than melting into a single mass, the components remain intact and distinguishable while contributing to a whole that is richer than its parts alone. Cultural pluralism enjoyed some popularity and acceptance during the 1970s as evidenced by the passage of the Ethnic Heritage Studies Bill by Congress in 1973 and the implementation of bilingual, bicultural education in many metropolitan school districts. Some of the gains in bilingual, bicultural education made in the 1970s were lost in the 1980s; by pure force of numbers, however, the current immigration trend presents a strong argument in favor of continuing or re-instituting such programs in the future.

Ethnocentrism, Racism, Prejudice, Stereotypes, and Oppression

Individuals who advocate the acculturation of racial/ethnic groups into American culture can be said to share a characteristic with individuals who seek to exclude these groups from American society altogether; both are ethnocentric. Sumner (1960) defined ethnocentrism as the "view of things in which one's own group is the center of everything, and all others are scaled and rated with reference to it" (p. 27–28). Individuals who expect racial/ethnic groups to acculturate are in essence saying that the existing U.S. culture is superior to any culture or mix of cultures that could result from the melting pot or cultural pluralism philosophies.

Believing other cultures and ethnicities are inferior to your own is also a characteristic of racism. J. Jones (1972) has defined three types of racism: individual, institutional, and cultural. Individual racism involves the personal attitudes, beliefs and behaviors designed to convince oneself of the superiority of one's race/ethnicity over other races/ethnicities. Institutional racism involves the social policies, laws, and regulations whose purpose it is to maintain the economic and social advantage of the racial/ethnic group in power. And cultural racism involves society beliefs and customs that promote the assumption that the products of the dominant culture (e.g., language, traditions, appearance) are superior to other cultures.

Ethnocentrism and racism inevitably result in prejudice, which refers to negative attitudes, thoughts, and beliefs toward an entire category of people (Schaefer, 1988). Allport (1958) defined prejudice as:

> an antipathy based upon a faulty and inflexible generalization. . . . It may be directed toward a group as a whole, or toward an individual because he [or she] is a member of that group. (p. 10).

Since prejudice is an attitude or belief, it is not always evident in a person's behavior. Prejudice may manifest itself in subtle, covert ways. Counselors who unconsciously treat clients differently based on their racial/ethnic background may be doing so as the result of their unrecognized prejudices.

A stereotype is an over-generalization about a group of people. Some authors define stereotypes as a function of prejudice (Schaefer, 1988) while others conclude that it is an inevitable and necessary coping mechanism for avoiding cognitive overload (Brown, 1965). Stereotypes in general have been criticized for being incorrect generalizations, generalizations of unspecified validity, products of faulty thought processes characterized by rigidity, and conditioned beliefs based on limited experience (Brigham, 1971). Stereotypes can be negative or positive but, as McCauley, Stitt, and Segal (1980) point out, all stereotypes can have negative repercussions if they are used to make predictions without gaining more information about a person. For example, a positive stereotype of Asian Americans is that they are high achievers who experience few emotional/social problems. However, a school counselor who assumed on the basis of race/ethnicity that an Asian American student needed no personal (only academic and career) counseling without knowing the student's socioeconomic background, peer relationships, past performance record, etc. would be, in effect, discriminating against the student on the basis of a racial/ethnic stereotype.

Oppression is a state of being in which the oppressed person is deprived of some human right or dignity and is (or feels) powerless to do anything about it (Goldenberg, 1978). Oppression can manifest itself in many ways. European Jews during World War II, and both African Americans and American Indians throughout much of U.S. history, are examples of groups that have experienced oppression in its most extreme form, genocide. Insidious forms of oppression that continue to plague groups of Americans in the 1990s include political, economic, and social oppression. Examples of oppression currently experienced by racial/ethnic groups include underrepresentation in the 1990 census, sub-minimum wages paid to undocumented workers, the racial/ethnic slurs that permeate written and oral communication, and physical attacks upon individuals by racist perpetrators.

Minority, VREG, and Third World

As Cook and Helms (1988) suggest, social scientists are looking for words with which to refer to non-Caucasians in the U.S. population. Several terms have been used by authors in the counseling literature; each has one or more drawbacks. Some authors have used the term minority to refer to physically or behaviorally identifiable groups that make up less than 50 percent of the U.S. population. Included in this definition are racial/ethnic minorities, the aged, and disabled persons.

In common usage, however, numerical size alone does not determine minority status. Over 80 percent of the population of South Africa is non-White, yet this group is frequently referred to as a minority by individuals within and outside South Africa (Rose, 1964). Wirth (1945) has offered a definition of minority based on the concept of oppression that is preferred by the present authors and is employed in this book. According to Wirth (1945), a minority is:

> . . . a group of people who, because of physical or cultural characteristics, are singled out from the others in society in which they live for differential and unequal treatment, and who therefore regard themselves as objects of collective discrimination (p. 347).

Since we have already established culture as characterized by shared and transmitted behavior, this definition allows us to accept all those groups included in the racial/ethnic and numerical definitions, plus other groups that are oppressed by society *primarily because of their group membership* as minorities. Most importantly, this definition allows us to include women, a group of oppressed individuals who constitute a numerical majority in the United States, as minorities. Racial/ethnic minority, then, refers specifically to groups of people who, because of physical characteristics or ancestry, are singled out for discrimination.

Some authors prefer the phrase "visible racial, ethnic group" (VREG) over the term racial/ethnic minority when referring to persons of color or linguistic diversity (Cook & Helms, 1988). However, this designation emphasizes the use of visible physical characteristics as acceptable criteria for determining a racial/ethnic group, a concept that we questioned earlier in the discussion of race. Also, some individuals may self-identify as a member of a racial/ethnic minority group based on ancestry even though they are not visibly members of the group.

Another term that sometimes is used interchangeably with the words racial/ethnic minority is Third World. The term Third World enjoys international acceptance as a means of describing the nonindustrialized nations of the world that are neither Western nor Communist (Miller, 1967). Many of these countries are located in Africa, South America, and Asia, primarily non-White portions of the world. It has also been used as a symbol of comradeship among all oppressed people. In the United States, therefore, non-White individuals are sometimes referred to as Third World persons. The term is used less frequently now than it was in the 1960s and 1970s to identify U.S. minorities, perhaps because this U.S. interpretation is at odds with international usage.

Wirth's (1945) definition notwithstanding, many people object to the term minority because it implies "less than." We are sensitive to this issue but have elected to continue using the term at this point because: (1) minority continues to be widely used to describe groups subjected to oppression; (2) no other more appropriate and equally descriptive term has emerged; and (3) we are reluctant to change the title of our book until a more positive term has gained acceptance.

Terms Associated with Specific Racial/Ethnic Groups

Just as there is disagreement about the terms to refer collectively to all non-Whites, there is a lack of unanimity about the best terms to use when referring to specific racial/ethnic groups. Some terms may be accepted in some regions or by some generations within a racial/ethnic minority group but not by others. Furthermore, terms associated with specific racial/ethnic groups are problematic because they fail to recognize ethnic and cultural differences within a larger racial/ethnic group.

As the current edition of this book was being revised, African American, American Indian, Asian American, and Latino were emerging as the standard, although by no means universally accepted, references for the four major racial/ethnic minorities in the United States. As suggested, however, some individuals object to these terms because they are too broad and fail to recognize important ethnic differences that exist within the groups. For example, the term Asian American technically includes all Americans who can trace their ancestry to the continent of Asia (including such disparate cultural groups as Iranians, Asian Indians, Koreans, etc.), although common usage is restricted to descendants of Eastern Asia parentage. To recognize these distinctions, many researchers and writers refer to the specific country of origin, particularly when discussing Asian American and Latino populations (e.g., Japanese American, Vietnamese American, Mexican American, Cuban American). Similarly, American Indians point to the fact that, depending on how one categorizes tribal affiliations, there are as many as 500 tribes in the United States, as evidence that any single term glosses over the cultural variation within their population.

Other objections have been raised to these general terms. Some individuals who can trace their ancestry to Africa prefer the terms Black or Afro American to African American, perhaps due to historical usage. Latino is generally preferred over Hispanic by most people who trace their ancestral lineage to Central and South America because the former emerged from the group itself while the latter was created by the U.S. Bureau of Census. However, this preference is far from universally accepted, as evidenced by professional articles that have appeared recently arguing for and against each term (Hayes-Bautista & Chapa, 1987; Trevino, 1987). Also, some individuals object to the use of Latino for the same reason that they find Hispanic offensive; both Latin and Hispanic refer to countries that conquered and oppressed the indigenous people of Central and South America. Further, an increasing number of people prefer to self-identify as biracial/ethnic, bicultural, multiracial/ethnic, or multicultural.

In view of these disagreements about terminology, it is important that the counselor is sensitive to the client's preferred term for self-identification. If the issue of race/ethnicity emerges in counseling, the counselor may want to ask the client how he/she self-identifies. In other situations, the terms African American, American Indian, Asian American, and Latino are generally acceptable, although every effort should be made to acknowledge specific ethnic groups and to recognize individual preferences. We use these four terms for the purpose of organizing our discussion of cross-cultural counseling in this book, but we readily acknowledge that such groupings are an oversimplification, and we apologize to readers who find any of them offensive.

We also prefer the term European American to the terms White, Caucasian American, and Anglo. Although they are descriptive and at times we fall back on them, we find White and Caucasian American objectionable because they assume racial differences that, as we suggested earlier, we feel are questionable. We feel Anglo is the least appropriate term to use because technically it refers to people of English descent (or more distantly, of Germanic descent). People who trace their ancestry to Italy, France, and the Iberian peninsula, for example, often object to being called Anglo American. Further, the term European American is more congruent with the emerging trend of identifying the region (or more specifically, country) of ancestry (e.g., African American, Asian American, Chinese American).

Cross-Cultural Psychology, Cross-Cultural Counseling, Multicultural Counseling, and Minority-Group Counseling

Cross-cultural psychology is sometimes confused with cross-cultural counseling. Cross-cultural psychology refers to "the systematic study of behavior and experience as it occurs in different cultures, is influenced by culture, or results in changes in existing cultures" (Triandis, 1980, p. 1). A major purpose of cross-cultural psychology is to determine which psychological laws have universal application and which are culture specific. The terms etic and emic have been used to describe phenomenon that have, respectively, universal application or culture-specific application.

Cross-cultural counseling refers to any counseling relationship in which two or more of the participants are culturally different. This definition of cross-cultural counseling includes situations in which both the counselor and client(s) are minority individuals but represent different racial/ethnic groups (African American counselor—Latino client; Asian American counselor—American Indian client, and so forth). It also includes the situation in which the counselor is a racial/ethnic minority person and the client is European American (African American counselor—European American client, Latino counselor—European American client, and so on). Multicultural counseling is often used interchangeably with cross-cultural counseling.

Minority group counseling, by way of contrast, can be defined as any counseling relationship in which the client is a member of a minority group, regardless of the status of the counselor (who may be a member of the same minority group, a different minority group, or the majority group). To date much of the writing on minority group counseling has dealt exclusively with racial/ethnic minorities and has examined the majority counselor-minority client relationship to the exclusion of other possibilities. This limited view of minority group counseling has fallen into some disfavor, perhaps because it ignores the special conditions of a counseling relationship in which the counselor is also a racial/ethnic minority person. Further, there is concern that the term minority group counseling suggests a minority pathology; this is perceived as analogous to "Black pathology," an attempt to explain Black behavior in terms of White norms.

This book is primarily concerned with counseling situations in which the client is a member of a racial/ethnic minority group and is culturally different from the counselor. Since the intention is to include counseling relationships defined as minority group counseling *and* cross-cultural counseling, the editors have elected to identify this focus as *minority group/cross-cultural counseling.*

References

Allport, G. (1958). *The nature of prejudice* (abridged ed.). New York: Doubleday, Anchor Books.

Anderson, C. H. (1971). *Toward a new sociology: A critical view.* Homewood, IL: The Dorsey Press.

Brigham, J. C. (1971). Ethnic stereotypes. *Psychological Bulletin, 76,* 15–38.

Brown, R. (1965). *Social psychology.* New York: Free Press.

Cook, D. A., & Helms, J. E. (1988). Visible racial/ethnic group supervisees' satisfaction with cross-cultural supervision as predicted by relationship characteristics. *Journal of Counseling Psychology, 35,* 268–274.

Cox, O. C. (1948). *Caste, class, and race.* Garden City, NY: Doubleday.

Epps, E. G. (1974). *Cultural pluralism.* Berkeley, CA: McCutchan.

Fairchild, H. P. (1926). *The melting pot mistake.* Boston: Little, Brown.

Feagin, J. R. (1989). *Racial & ethnic relations.* Englewood Cliffs, NJ: Prentice-Hall.

Glazer, N. (1971). Blacks and ethnic groups: The difference, and the political difference it makes. *Social Problems, 18,* 447.

Goldenberg, I. I. (1978). *Oppression and social intervention.* Chicago: Nelson-Hall.

Gordon, M. M. (1964). *Assimilation in American life.* New York: Oxford University Press.

Hayes-Bautista, D. E., & Chapa, J. (1987). Latino terminology: Conceptual bases for standardized terminology. *American Journal of Public Health, 77*(1), 61–68.

Johnson, S. D. Jr. (1990). Toward clarifying culture, race, and ethnicity in the context of multicultural counseling. *Journal of Multicultural Counseling and Development, 18,* 41–50.

Jones, C., & Clifford, F. (1990, August 28). Census puts state near 30 million. *Los Angeles Times,* pp. A1, A18.

Jones, J. M. (1972). *Prejudice and racism.* Reading, MA: Addison-Wesley.

Kallen, H. M. (1956). *Cultural pluralism and the American idea.* Philadelphia: University of Philadelphia Press.

Kroeber, A. L., & Kluckhohn, C. (1952). *Cultural: A critical review of concepts and definitions.* New York: Vintage Books.

Krogman, W. M. (1945). The concept of race. In R. Linton (Ed.), *The science of man in the world crisis* (pp. 38–62). New York: Columbia University Press.

Krug, M. (1976). *The melting of the ethnics.* Bloomington, IN: Phi Delta Kappa Education Foundation.

Kutscher, R. (1987, September). Projections 2000: Overview and implications of the projections to 2000. *Monthly Labor Review.* Washington, DC: U.S. Department of Labor.

Linton, R. W. (1968). *The cultural background of personality.* New York: Appleton-Century.

Littlefield, A., Lieberman, L., & Reynolds, L. T. (1982). Redefining race: The potential demise of a concept in anthropology. *Current Anthropology, 23,* 641–647.

Mack, R. W. (1968). *Race, class & power.* New York: American Book Co.

McCauley, C., Stitt, C. L., & Segal, M. (1980). Stereotyping: From prejudice to prediction. *Psychological Bulletin, 87,* 195–208.

McLemore, S. D. (1983). *Racial and ethnic relations in America* (2nd ed.). Boston: Allyn & Bacon.

Miller, J. D. B. (1967). *The politics of the third world.* London: Oxford University Press.

Moore, B. M. (1974). Cultural differences and counseling perspectives. *Texas Personnel and Guidance Association Journal, 3,* 39–44.

National Coalition of Advocates for Students. (1986). *New voices: Immigrant students in U.S. public schools.* Boston: Author. (ERIC Document Reproduction Service No. ED 297 063)

Reich, C. A. (1970). *The greening of America: How the youth is trying to make America livable.* New York: Random House.

Rose, P. I. (1964). *They and we: Racial and ethnic relations in the United States.* New York: Random House.

Schaefer, R. T. (1988). *Racial and ethnic groups* (3rd ed.). Glenview, IL: Scott, Foresman.

Sheppard, H. L. (1977). *The graying of working America: The coming crisis in retirement-age policy.* New York: Free Press.

Sue, S., & Zane, N. (1987). The role of culture and cultural techniques in psychotherapy: A critique and reformulation. *American Psychologist, 42,* 37–45.

Sumner, W. G. (1960). *Folkways.* New York: Mentor Books.

Thompson, E. T., and Hughes, E. C. (1958). *Race: Individual and collective behavior.* Glencoe, IL: Free Press.

Trevino, F. M. (1987). Standardized terminology for Hispanics. *American Journal of Public Health, 77*(1), 69–72.

Triandis, H. C. (1980). Introduction to Handbook of cross-cultural psychology. In H. C. Triandis & W. W. Lambert (Eds.), *Handbook of cross-cultural psychology: Perspectives, Volume 1* (pp. 1–14). Boston: Allyn & Bacon.

U.S. Bureau of the Census. (1986). *Statistical Abstract of the United States: 1987* (107th ed.). Washington, DC: U.S. Government Printing Office.

Wirth, L. (1945). *The problem of minority groups.* In R. Linton (Ed.). *The science of man in the world crisis.* New York: Columbia University Press.

Zuckerman, M. (1990). Some dubious premises in research and theory on racial differences. *American psychologist, 45,* 1297–1303.

2
Within-Group Differences among Racial/Ethnic Minorities

In Chapter 1 we discussed how the United States is being diversified by the immigration and high birthrate of ethnic minority groups. This process of diversification, while accelerated at the current time, is not new to the United States. American Indians and immigrants from Africa, Asia, and Latin America have always found it difficult to assimilate into the dominant culture and many individuals and families chose to maintain their distinct cultural identification, at least in part. By the third decade of the twentieth century, social scientists began to recognize that the assimilation process was not always a smooth, predictable one, even for those who chose to adopt the dominant culture. It also became evident that not all ethnic groups were equally successful in attaining educational and economic goals.

In order to explain the differential success rates of the various racial/ethnic groups, researchers began to examine intergroup differences. For the most part, research prior to 1970 compared scores of racial/ethnic minority subjects to those of European American subjects on a variety of psychological and behavioral measures. Whether intended or not, implicit in this practice was the assumption that European American performance on these measures represented the norm or desired performance since they were not successful in achieving ''the American dream.'' Deviations from the norm could be used to explain why some racial/ethnic minority groups were not ''succeeding'' in the United States. Several hypotheses were offered to explain this phenomenon, including the hypothesis that some racial/ethnic groups are inferior to others and the hypothesis that some cultures are inferior to others.

By the 1970s, however, critics of this research methodology and the genetic and cultural deficit theories were arguing that comparative data have limited usefulness, can be misleading, and, in some cases (e.g., use of standardized IQ tests to measure intelligence), can be destructive. Rather than comparing the scores of racial/ethnic minorities on behavioral and psychological measures to those of European Americans, these critics argued, social scientists should examine ethnic minority performance within the context of their own culture. For example, tests should be normed for each racial/ethnic groups and individual performance should be contrasted with ethnic group norms, rather than to European American norms. In the counseling and mental health literature, this resulted in a shift from studies that compared subjects' reactions to counseling across racial/ethnic groups to studies that described reactions to counseling within a specific racial/ethnic group.

Studies that described reactions to counseling by a single racial/ethnic minority population were useful in that they pointed out the need for ethnically similar counselors, culturally sensitive counselors, and culturally compatible counseling strategies. However, they too were misleading in that normative responses of the participants often were generalized to an entire racial/ethnic minority group. Reviewers of this cross-cultural counseling research began pointing out by the late 1970s and early 1980s the need to include within-group differences as variables of interest in future research with racial/ethnic minorities. An underlying thesis in these reviews was that counselors need to recognize diversity within racial/ethnic groups as well as diversity between racial/ethnic groups when working with a racial/ethnic minority client; in particular, the counselor needs to understand both the client's cultural heritage and the degree to which the client identifies with his/her cultural heritage.

By the 1980s research reports began to appear in the counseling literature that included within-group differences as independent variables. Ponterotto (1988) reviewed the cross-cultural counseling research published in the *Journal of Counseling Psychology* from 1976 to 1986 and found that all of the studies that included intragroup differences as independent variables (28.6 percent of those reviewed) were published after 1980. Furthermore, the results of a recent survey of experts in cross-cultural counseling suggest that more studies in the future will include within-group differences as independent variables. Heath, Neimeyer, and Pedersen (1988) conducted a Delphi poll fifty-three experts to predict the future of the field for a ten-year period. With respect to theoretical and empirical publications, the panel predicted a 35 percent increase in publications related to being bicultural, a 32 percent increase related to acculturation, and a 30 percent increase related to racial-ethnic identity.

We agree with those reviewers who have argued in favor of including intragroup differences as independent variables in future cross-cultural counseling research. Each of the major racial/ethnic populations in the United States manifests great diversity, including but not limited to diversity of attitudes, values, behavior, education, income, acculturation, and racial/ethnic identity. By ignoring within-group diversity, researchers promote the view that the group is homogeneous and that model data from a single sample can be generalized to an entire racial/ethnic group.

While it is undeniable that each minority group has a unique cultural heritage that makes it distinct from other groups, this fact has erroneously been interpreted as evidence of cultural conformity—a monolithic approach which views all African Americans, American Indians, Asian Americans, and Latinos as possessing the same group attitudes and behaviors. Clearly, uniformity of attitudes and behaviors is no more true for minority individuals than it is for members of the dominant culture. With regard to the very issue of cultural distinction, racial/ethnic minority attitudes may vary from desire for total assimilation into the dominant culture to total rejection of the dominant culture and immersion in the minority culture (Parham & Helms, 1981).

S. Due and D. W. Sue (1971) provide evidence of the disparate ways in which Chinese Americans respond to cultural conflict. Some reject their Chinese background entirely and try to assimilate into the dominant society. Others adhere to traditional cultural values and attempt to resist assimilation. Still others stress pride in their racial identity while refraining from the conformity inherent in both the traditional Chinese practices and assimilation into the mainstream culture. Similarly, Ruiz and Padilla (1977) suggest there is a danger inherent in trying to isolate the "true nature" of the Hispanic character since each person's attitudes and behaviors are a function of his/her degree of acculturation. Furthermore, these writings suggest that not only do intra-group differences exist, but attitudes and behaviors within individuals can fluctuate greatly as their identification with one culture or another changes.

In this chapter we examine two within-group variables, acculturation and racial identity development, that the cross-cultural counseling experts surveyed by Heath et al. (1988) predict will play an increasingly important role in future theory and research publications. A number of studies have already focused on the effects of acculturation on counseling process and outcome with American Indian, Asian American, and Latino clients. Similarly, a growing body of research has examined the relationship between Black racial identity development and counseling variables. We conclude the chapter with a discussion of our own Minority Identity Development Model.

Acculturation as a Within-Group Variable

According to Olmedo (1979), acculturation is "one of the more elusive, albeit ubiquitous, constructs in the behavioral sciences" (p. 1061). Keefe (1980) suggests that "acculturation is one of those terms all social scientists use although few can agree upon its meaning" (p. 85). However, there is general agreement that acculturation is a process of change that occurs when two or more cultures come in contact with each other (Redfield, Linton, & Herskovits, 1936).

The assimilation model developed by Park and Burgess (1921), among the first to describe the process of acculturation, was widely accepted by social scientists until recently. Basically, this model implies that the United States is a melting pot in which immigrant groups contribute elements of their own culture to an evolving U.S. culture. As suggested in Chapter 1, however, many contemporary social scientists take issue with the melting pot theory. According to the model, complete assimilation usually occurs within three generations after immigration (Neidert & Farley, 1985). These critics point out that total assimilation has been limited in the past to European immigrants and that people of color are expected to acculturate, but never allowed to completely assimilate (Novak, 1972). Also, most contemporary social scientists describe acculturation in the United States as a unilateral process in which immigrant groups are expected to adopt the dominant culture but contribute little or nothing to it (Keefe, 1980).

Another criticism of the early assimilation model has to do with the negative and positive effects of acculturation. Park (1928) coined the term "marginal man" (person) to describe the negative effects of being caught between two cultures. According to Park (1950), the marginal person lives in a permanent state of crisis due to an internalized cultural conflict; he suggested that some of the psychological manifestations are "intensified self-consciousness, restlessness, and malaise" (p. 356). Stonequist (1961) has expanded upon this theme, suggesting that "the marginal situation produces excessive self-consciousness and race-consciousness" and " 'inferiority complexes' are a common affliction" (p. 148). The fact that some individuals function well in two or more cultures, however, has lead some critics to question the marginal person concept (Valentine, 1971). Also, many of the psychological problems that are concomitant with acculturation may be the result of discrimination rather than cultural conflict per se (DeVos, 1980).

Although anthropologists and sociologists have studied acculturation for many decades, psychologists have only recently examined the process. Padilla (1980) defines acculturation as "a critical psychological process about which little is yet known" (p. 2). He suggests that while the acculturation process may be somewhat unique to every immigrant group, "many of the psychological processes underlying acculturation are probably similar" (p. 3).

Some controversy also exists about whether acculturation is a unidimensional or bidimensional process. The unidimensional model conceptualizes acculturation as a single continuum, with the indigenous culture on one end and dominant U.S. culture on the other. According to this model, cultural traits (e.g., attitudes, values, behavior) of the indigenous culture are gradually lost while cultural traits of the dominant society are gradually adopted over time.

The bicultural socialization model, however, assumes a dual socialization process for racial/ethnic minority individuals. Racial/ethnic minorities simultaneously experience enculturation within their own racial/ethnic group culture while also being exposed to socialization forces within the dominant culture (Valentine, 1971). Bicultural socialization can be conceptualized as two continua, one representing low to high levels of commitment to the indigenous culture and one representing low to high levels of commitment to the dominant culture. Oetting and Beauvais, (in press) have expanded this concept into a multidimensional model of acculturation. The multidimensional model conceptualizes acculturation along multiple continua, with each dimension representative of the cultures to which a person is exposed. For example, a Mexican American may have been socialized at home to a traditional Mexican culture but socialized in school to the dominant culture and exposed through friends to American Indian culture.

According to the bidimensional model of acculturation, the bicultural person and the marginal person respond differently to their socialization in two cultures. The marginal person feels caught between the conflicting values of two cultures and consequently feels little commitment to either. In contrast, the bicultural individual feels committed to both cultures and selectively embraces the positive aspects of each culture. According to De Anda (1984), six factors contribute to the development of a bicultural rather than a marginal perspective: (a) degree of cultural overlap between the two cultures; (b) the availability of cultural translators, mediators, and models; (c) the amount and type of corrective feedback regarding attempts to produce normative behaviors; (d) the compatibility of the minority individual's conceptual style with the analytical cognitive style valued by the dominant culture; (e) the individual's degree of bilingualism; and (f) the degree of dissimilarity in physical appearance between the individual and those representative of the dominant culture.

Although the acculturation and biculturalism concepts can be applied to all racial/ethnic minorities, acculturation as a process of adopting the dominant culture seems most applicable to American Indians, Asian Americans, and Latinos. Recent research has begun to document the relationship between acculturation and counseling process and outcome variables for these racial/ethnic groups. Acculturation among Latinos has been found to be related to preference for an ethnically similar counselor (Sanchez & Atkinson, 1983), perceptions of counselor trustworthiness (Pomales & Williams, 1989), expectations for counseling (Kunkel, 1990), and willingness to self-disclose in counseling (Sanchez & Atkinson, 1983). Similarly, a relationship has been documented between acculturation and attitudes toward counseling among Asian Americans. A survey of Chinese,

Japanese, and Korean American college students revealed that, as hypothesized, the most acculturated students were (a) most likely to recognize personal need for professional psychological help, (b) most tolerant of the stigma associated with psychological help, and (c) most open to discussing their problems with a psychologist (Atkinson & Gim, 1989). The results of a subsequent survey of Asian American students, however, suggested an inverse relationship between acculturation and both the severity of problems they experienced and their willingness to see a counselor about those problems (Gim, Atkinson, & Whiteley, 1990). In a survey assessing preferred help providers, less acculturated students ranked counselors/psychologists highest, followed by medium acculturated and finally more acculturated students (Atkinson, Whiteley, & Gim, 1990). Gim, Atkinson, and Kim (1991) found that less acculturated subjects consistently gave their lowest credibility ratings to a culture-blind Caucasian American counselor, supporting the hypothesis that ethnic similarity and cultural sensitivity are important issues to less acculturated Asian Americans. A study involving cultural commitment in which Native Americans served as the subject population also found that students with a strong commitment to Native American culture expressed a stronger preference for an ethnically similar counselor and they expected more nurturance, facilitative conditions, and counselor expertise than did respondents with a weak commitment to their indigenous culture (Johnson & Lashley, 1989).

Although few in number, these studies provide consistent documentation that acculturation is related to how racial/ethnic minority clients perceive and respond to counseling services. In general, they suggest that less acculturated racial/ethnic minorities are more likely to trust and express a preference for and a willingness to see an ethnically similar counselor than are their more acculturated counterparts. For Asian Americans the findings to date suggest a direct relationship between acculturation and willingness to see a counselor for concerns perceived as ''non-psychological'' in nature (e.g., academic or career problems, financial problems, relationship problems). Less acculturated Asian Americans may also prefer a racially/ethnically similar counselor who is culturally sensitive over other types of counselors.

In summary, acculturation is a measure of within-group diversity that has been found to be related to a number of counseling process variables. It seems evident that counselors working with an ethnic minority client should be aware not only of the client's ethnic background but the extent to which the client identifies with and practices the culture of his/her ancestors.

Ethnic Identity Development as a Within-Group Variable

One of the most promising approaches to the field of cross-cultural counseling has been the renewed interest in racial/ethnic/cultural identity development. When we first published our Minority Identity Development Model in the original (1979) edition of this book, we were aware of only five precursor models, three of Black identity development (Cross, 1971; Jackson, 1975; Vontress, 1971), one of Chinese American personality development (S. Sue & D. W. Sue, 1971), and one of Japanese American political types (Mayovich, 1973). Since our original edition, however, we have become aware of numerous earlier and subsequent models for Black (Gay, 1984), Latino (Ruiz, 1990), White (Helms, 1985b, 1990; Ponterotto, 1988), female (Downing & Roush, 1985), homosexual (Cass, 1979; Troiden, 1989), biracial (Poston, 1990), ethnic (Ford, 1987), racial/cultural (D. W. Sue & D. Sue, 1990) and general minority identity development (Highlen et al., 1988; Myers et al., in press). In her recent book on Black and White racial identity, Helms (1990) lists eleven identity development models for African Americans alone.

Some of the early attempts at describing racial identity development models took the form of simple typologies in which a particular minority group was divided into smaller subcategories or types, often based on their political views. As Hall, Cross and Freedle (1972) point out, these subgroups generally included both ''conservative'' and ''militant'' types and one or two categories in between. In terms of their implications for counseling, Helms (1990) refers to these as CAP (Client as Problem) models, since each type was assumed to present a different problem for counselors.

As an example of any early typology, Vontress (1971) theorized that Afro Americans conformed to three distinct subgroups: (1) Colored, (2) Negro, and (3) Black. Briefly, these subcategories represented decreasing levels of dependence upon White society and culture as the source of self-definition and worth, and an increasing degree of identification with Black society and culture. As another example, Mayovich (1973) typed Japanese Americans according to four separate categories: (1) Conformists, (2) Anomic, (3) Liberal, and (4) Militant. Mayovich (1973) hypothesized that as a result of their acceptance or rejection of traditional values and their involvement or detachment from social issues, all Japanese Americans (at least those of the Sansei generation) fell into one of these four types.

This method of ''typing'' racial/ethnic minorities has been heavily criticized, however (Parham & Helms, 1981; Helms, 1985; Atkinson & Schein, 1986; Ponterotto & Wise, 1987). Banks (1972), for instance, contended that these theorists have mistakenly proposed labels that attribute certain fixed personality traits to people, when in fact their behavior is a function of a specific situation. Others (Cross, 1970; Hall, Cross, & Freedle, 1972; Jackson, 1975) suggested that any attempt to define minority "types" must acknowledge movement of individuals across categories. Helms (1985) also pointed out that these models may (a) place too much emphasis on individual rather than system change; (b) become obsolete as the societal forces on which they are based change; (c) assume erroneously that identity development follows a linear and continuous course; and (d) contribute to a view of the "stages" as static and fixed rather than dynamic and evolving. In spite of such criticisms, it is important to recognize the early topologies as pioneering attempts that paved the way for more sophisticated models of identity development.

A second major approach has viewed racial/ethnic minority attitudes and behavior as a product of an identity development continuum. This approach differs from topologies in that minority attitudes and behaviors are viewed as flexible and a function of the individual's state of identity development. Rather than type the individual, stages of development through which any minority person may pass are described. Attitudinal and behavioral attributes, therefore, are not viewed as fixed characteristics but as related to identity development.

These early attempts to define a process of racial/ethnic identity development were almost exclusively the work of Black scholars who were obviously influenced in their thinking by the impact of social, psychological, and cultural events in the 1960s. Hall, Cross, and Freedle, (1972) describe how these events highlighted the process of Black identity transformation:

> We have seen a change in the nature of black-white relations in America. To be sure, this change has produced many consequences, one of which has been an identity transformation among American blacks. The transformation has been an older orientation whereby most blacks viewed themselves as inadequate, inferior, incapable of self-determination, and unable to cope with the intricacies of life in a complex society, to one of feeling adequate, self-reliant, assertive, and self-determinative (p. 156).

Helms (1990) cites the Cross (1970, 1971, 1978, 1991) model of Black racial identity development as "the primary means of investigating racial identity in the counseling and psychotherapy process" (p. 19). Cross originally described his model as a "Negro-to-Black Conversion Experience" (1971) and later as a process of psychological nigrescence (1978). Basically, the model consists of four stages: Preencounter, Encounter, Immersion, and Internalization. According to the model, Blacks at the Preencounter stage are "programmed to view and think of the world as being nonblack, anti-black, or the opposite of Black" (Hall, Cross, & Freedle, 1972, p. 159). At the next stage, the Encounter stage, the Black individual becomes aware of what being Black means and begins to validate him/herself as a Black person. During the Immersion stage, the Black person rejects all nonblack values and totally immerses him/herself in Black culture. Finally, in the Internalization stage, the Black person gains a sense of inner security and begins to focus on ". . . things other than himself and his own ethnic or racial group" (Hall, Cross, & Freedle, 1972, p. 160).

Janet Helms and Thomas Parham have been largely responsible for the application of the Cross model to research in counseling. Together they developed the Black Racial Identity Attitude Scale (RIAS-B) to measure the first four stages of Cross' (1971) model (Parham & Helms, 1981). They have used the RIAS-B to examine the relationship between Black identity development and counseling-related variables. Parham and Helms (1981) found that Preencounter attitudes were associated with a preference for White counselors while Encounter and Internalization attitudes were associated with a preference for Black counselors and a rejection of White counselors. In a subsequent study, Parham and Helms (1985a, 1985b) found that proWhite-antiBlack (Preencounter) attitudes and proBlack-antiWhite (Immersion) attitudes were inversely associated with mentally healthy self-actualizing tendencies. Encounter attitudes, on the other hand, were directly related to self-actualization tendencies and inversely related to feelings of inferiority and anxiety. Ponterotto, Alexander, and Hinkston (1988) found that the relationship between racial identity development categories and preferences for counselor characteristics were not as hypothesized. However, Black students' value orientations (Carter & Helms, 1987) and cognitive styles (Helms & Parham, 1990) have been found to be related to Black racial identity development.

In summary, there is empirical support for the concept of Black Racial Identity Development and the stages of BRID have been found to be related to counseling process and outcome variables.

Minority Identity Development (MID) Model

Although the Black identity development models pertain specifically to the African American experience, the editors of the present text believe that some of the basic tenets of these theories can be generalized and applied to other minority groups, due to their shared experience of oppression. Although each of the ethnic groups discussed in this book has a unique culture (indeed, within these broad groupings are a number of unique cultures), the fact that they have been subjected to various forms of physical, economic, and social discrimination suggests that they share a common experience that affects how they view themselves and others. Some earlier writers (Stonequist, 1937; Berry, 1965) have also observed that minority groups share the same patterns of adjustment to cultural oppression.

Based on views expressed by earlier writers and our own clinical observation that these changes in attitudes and subsequent behavior follow a predictable sequence, we developed a five-stage Minority Identity Development (MID) model. The MID model we describe on the following pages is not presented as a comprehensive theory of personality development, but rather as a schema to help counselors understand minority client attitudes and behaviors within existing personality theories. The model defines five stages of development that oppressed people may experience as they struggle to understand themselves in terms of their own minority culture, and the oppressive relationship between the two cultures. Although five distinct stages are presented in the model, the MID is more accurately conceptualized as a continuous process in which one stage blends with another and boundaries between stages are not clear.

It is our observation that not all minority individuals experience the entire range of these stages in their lifetimes. Prior to the turbulent 1960s—a decade in which the transition of many individuals through this process was accelerated and, therefore, made more evident—many people were raised and lived out their lives in the first stage. Nor is the developmental process to be interpreted as irreversible. It is our opinion that many minority individuals are socialized by their parents to hold the values associated with level five, but in coming to grips with their own identity, offspring often move from level five to one of the lower levels. Further, it does not appear that functioning at lower levels of development is prerequisite to functioning at higher levels. Some people born and raised in a family functioning at level five appear never to experience a level-one sense of identity.

At each level we provide examples of four corresponding attitudes that may assist the counselor to understand behaviors displayed by individuals operating at or near these levels. Each attitude is believed to be an integral part of any minority person's identity, or of how he/she views (a) self, (b) others of the same minority, (c) others of another minority, and (d) majority individuals. It was not our intention to define a hierarchy with more valued attitudes at higher levels of development. Rather, the model is intended to reflect a process that we have observed in our work with minority clients over the past three decades.

Stage One—Conformity Stage

Minority individuals in this stage of development are distinguished by their unequivocal preference for dominant cultural values over those of their own culture. Their choices of role models, life-styles, value system, etc., all follow the lead of the dominant group. Those physical and/or cultural characteristics that single them out as minority persons are a source of pain and are either viewed with disdain or are repressed from consciousness. Their views of self, fellow group members, and other minorities in general are clouded by their identification with the dominant culture. Minorities may perceive the ways of the dominant group as being much more positive, and there is a high desire to "assimilate and acculturate." The attitudes which minorities may have about themselves in this stage are ones of devaluation and depreciation on both a conscious and subconscious level. For example, Asian Americans may perceive their own physical features as less desirable and their cultural values and Asian ways as a handicap to successful adaptation in the dominant society. Their attitudes towards members of their own group tend to be highly negative in that they share the dominant culture's belief that Asian Americans are less desirable. Stereotypes portraying Asian Americans as inarticulate, good with numbers, poor managers, and aloof in their personal relationships are accepted. Other minority groups are also viewed according to the dominant group's system of minority stratification (i.e., those minority groups that most closely resemble the dominant group in physical and cultural characteristics are viewed more favorably than those less similar). Attitudes towards members of the dominant group, however, tend to be highly appreciative in that the members are admired, respected, and often viewed as ideal models.

It is quite obvious that in the Conformity stage of development Asian Americans and other minorities view themselves as deficient in the "desirable" characteristics held up by the dominant society. Feelings of racial self-hatred caused by cultural racism may accompany this type of adjustment (S. Sue & D. W. Sue, 1971).

A. *Attitude toward self: Self-depreciating attitude.* Individuals who acknowledge their distinguishing physical and/or cultural characteristics consciously view them as a source of shame. Individuals who repress awareness of their distinguishing physical and/or cultural characteristics depreciate themselves at a subconscious level.

B. *Attitude toward members of same minority: Group-depreciating attitude.* Other members of the minority group are viewed according to dominant-held beliefs of minority strengths and weaknesses.

C. *Attitude toward members of different minority: Discriminatory attitude.* Other minorities are viewed according to the dominant group's system of minority stratification (i.e., those minority groups that most closely resemble the dominant group in physical and cultural characteristics are viewed more favorably than those less similar).

D. *Attitude toward members of dominant group: Group-appreciating attitude.* Members of the dominant group are admired, respected, and often viewed as ideal models. Cultural values of the dominant society are accepted without question.

Stage Two—Dissonance Stage

The movement into the Dissonance stage is most often a gradual process but as Cross (1971) points out, a monumental event such as the assassination of Martin Luther King may propel the Black person into the next stage. Denial is a major tool used by persons in the Conformity stage; minorities in the Dissonance stage begin to experience a breakdown in their denial system. A Latino who may feel ashamed of his/her cultural upbringing may encounter a Latino who seems proud of his/her cultural heritage. An African American who may have deceived himself/herself into believing that race problems are due to laziness, untrustworthiness, or personal inadequacies of his/her group, suddenly encounters racism on a personal level.

A. *Attitude toward self: Conflict between self-depreciating and self-appreciating attitudes.* With a growing awareness of minority cultural strengths comes a faltering sense of pride in self. The individual's attitude toward distinguishing physical and/or cultural characteristics is typified by alternating feelings of shame and pride in self.

B. *Attitude toward members of same minority: Conflict between group-depreciating and group-appreciating attitudes.* Dominant-held views of minority strengths and weaknesses begin to be questioned, as new, contradictory information is received. Cultural values of the minority group begin to have appeal.

C. *Attitude toward members of different minority: Conflict between dominant-held views of minority hierarchy and feelings of shared experience.* The individual begins to question the dominant-held system of minority stratification and experiences a growing sense of comradeship with other oppressed people. Most of the individual's psychic energy at this level, however, is devoted to resolving conflicting attitudes toward self, the same minority, and the dominant group.

D. *Attitude toward members of dominant group: Conflict between group-appreciating and group-depreciating attitude.* The individual experiences a growing awareness that not all cultural values of the dominant group are beneficial to him/her. Members of the dominant group are viewed with growing suspicion.

Stage Three—Resistance and Immersion Stage

In this stage of development, the minority individual completely endorses minority-held views and rejects the dominant society and culture. Desire to eliminate oppression of the individual's minority group becomes an important motivation of the individual's behavior.

D. W. Sue and D. Sue (1990) believe that movement into this stage seems to occur for two reasons. First, the person begins to resolve many of the conflicts and confusions in the previous stage. As a result, a greater understanding of societal forces (racism, oppression, and discrimination) emerges, along with a realization that he/she has been victimized by it. Second, the individual begins to ask him/herself the following question: "Why should I feel ashamed of who and what I am?" The answers to that question will evoke both guilt and anger (bordering on rage): guilt that he/she has "sold out" in the past and contributed to his/her own group's oppression, and anger at having been oppressed and "brainwashed" by the forces in the dominant society.

A. *Attitude toward self: Self-appreciating attitude.* The minority individual at this stage acts as an explorer and discoverer of his/her history and culture, seeking out information and artifacts that enhance his/her sense of identity and worth. Cultural and physical characteristics which once elicited feelings of shame and disgust at this stage become symbols of pride and honor.

B. *Attitude toward members of same minority: Group-appreciating attitude.* The individual experiences a strong sense of identification with, and commitment to, his/her minority group, as enhancing information about the group is acquired. Members of the group are admired, respected, and often viewed as ideal models. Cultural values of the minority group are accepted without question.

C. *Attitude toward members of different minority: Conflict between feelings of empathy for other minority experiences and feelings of culturocentrism.* The individual experiences a growing sense of camaraderie with persons from other minority groups, to the degree that they are viewed as sharing similar forms of oppression. Alliances with other groups tend to be short-lived, however, when their values come in conflict with those of the individual's minority group. The dominant group's system of minority stratification is replaced by a system which values most those minority groups that are culturally similar to the individual's own group.

D. *Attitude toward members of dominant group: Group-depreciating attitude.* The individual totally rejects the dominant society and culture and experiences a sense of distrust and dislike for all members of the dominant group.

Stage Four—Introspection Stage

In this stage of development, the minority individual experiences feelings of discontent and discomfort with group views rigidly held in the Resistance and Immersion stage, and diverts attention to notions of greater individual autonomy.

What occurs at this stage is very interesting. First, the minority individual may begin to feel progressively more comfortable with his or her own sense of identity. This security allows the person to begin to question some of the rigidly held beliefs of the Resistance and Immersion stage that all "Whites are bad." There is also a feeling that too much negativism and hatred directed at White society tends to divert energies from more positive exploration of identity questions. This stage is characterized by greater individual autonomy. During this stage the person may begin to experience conflict between notions of responsibility and allegiance to his/her own minority group, and notions of personal autonomy. There is now a belief that perhaps not everything in the dominant culture is bad and that there are many positive as well as negative elements within it.

A. *Attitude toward self: Concern with basis of self-appreciating attitude.* The individual experiences conflict between notions of responsibility and allegiance to minority group and notions of personal autonomy.

B. *Attitude toward members of same minority: Concern with unequivocal nature of group appreciation.* While attitudes of identification are continued from the preceding Resistance and Immersion stages, concern begins to build up regarding the issue of group usurpation of individuality.

C. *Attitude toward members of different minority: Concern with ethnocentric basis for judging others.* The individual experiences a growing uneasiness with minority stratification that results from culturocentrism and placing a greater value on groups experiencing the same oppression than on those experiencing a different oppression.

D. *Attitude toward members of dominant group: Concern with the basis of group depreciation.* The individual experiences conflict between an attitude of complete distrust for the dominant society and culture, and an attitude of selective trust and distrust according to dominant individuals' demonstrated behaviors and attitudes. The individual also recognizes the utility of many dominant cultural elements yet is uncertain whether or not to incorporate such elements into his/her minority culture.

Stage Five—Synergistic Stage

Minority individuals in this stage experience a sense of self-fulfillment with regard to cultural identity. Conflicts and discomforts experienced in the Introspection stage have been resolved, allowing greater individual control and flexibility. Cultural values of other minorities as well as those of the dominant group are objectively examined and accepted or rejected on the basis of experience gained in earlier stages of identity development. Desire to eliminate *all* forms of oppression becomes an important motivation for the individual's behavior.

A. *Attitude toward self: Self-appreciating attitude.* The individual experiences a strong sense of self-worth, self-confidence, and autonomy as the result of having established his/her identity as an individual, a member of a minority group, and/or a member of the dominant culture.

B. *Attitude toward members of same minority: Group-appreciating attitude.* The individual experiences a strong sense of pride in the group without having to accept group values unequivocally. Strong feelings of empathy with the group experience are coupled with an awareness that each member of the group is an individual.

C. *Attitude toward members of different minority: Group-appreciating attitude.* The individual experiences a strong sense of respect for the group's cultural values coupled with awareness that each member of the group is an individual. The individual also experiences a greater understanding and support for all oppressed people, regardless of their similarity or dissimilarity to the individual's minority group.

D. *Attitude toward members of dominant group: Attitude of selective appreciation.* The individual experiences selective trust and liking for members of the dominant group who seek to eliminate repressive activities of the group. The individual also experiences an openness to the constructive elements of the dominant culture.

Implications of the MID Model for Counseling

As suggested earlier, the MID model is not intended as a comprehensive theory of personality, but rather as a paradigm to help counselors understand minority client attitudes and behaviors. In this respect, the model is intended to sensitize counselors to (1) the role oppression plays in a minority individual's identity development, (2) the differences that can exist between members of the same minority group with respect to their cultural identity, and (3) the potential that each individual minority person has for changing his/her sense of identity. Beyond helping to understand minority client behavior, the model has implications for the counseling process itself.

The general attitudes and behaviors that describe minority individuals at the Conformity stage (e.g., denial of minority problems, strong dependence on and identification with dominant group, etc.) suggest that

TABLE 2.1

Summary of Minority Identity Development Model

Stages of Minority Development Model	Attitude toward Self	Attitude toward Others of the Same Minority	Attitude toward Others of Different Minority	Attitude toward Dominant Group
Stage 1— Conformity	Self-depreciating	Group-depreciating	Discriminatory	Group-appreciating
Stage 2— Dissonance	Conflict between self-depreciating and appreciating	Conflict between group-depreciating and group-appreciating	Conflict between dominant-held views of minority hierarchy and feelings of shared experience	Conflict between group-appreciating and group-depreciating
Stage 3— Reisistance and Immersion	Self-appreciating	Group-appreciating	Conflict between feelings of empathy for other minority experiences and feelings of culturocentrism	Group-depreciating
Stage 4— Introspection	Concern with basis of self-appreciation	Concern with nature of unequivocal appreciation	Concern with ethnocentric basis for judging others	Concern with the basis of group depreciation
Stage 5— Synergetic Articulation and Awareness	Self-appreciating	Group-appreciating	Group-appreciating	Selective appreciation

clients from this stage are unlikely to seek counseling related to their cultural identity. It is more likely that they will perceive problems of cultural identity as problems related to their personal identity. Clients at this stage are more inclined to visit and be influenced by counselors of the dominant group than those of the same minority. Indeed, clients may actively request a White counselor and react negatively toward a minority counselor. Because of the client's strong identification with dominant group members, counselors from the dominant group may find the conformist client's need to please and appease a powerful force in the counseling relationship. Attempts to explore cultural identity or to focus on feelings may be threatening to the client. This is because exploration of identity may eventually touch upon feelings of racial self-hatred and challenge the client's self-deception (''I'm not like other minorities''). Clients at the Conformity stage are likely to present problems that are most amenable to problem solving and goal-oriented counseling approaches.

Minority individuals at the Dissonance stage of development are preoccupied by questions concerning their concept of self, identity, and self-esteem; they are likely to perceive personal problems as related to their cultural identity. Emotional problems develop when these individuals are unable to resolve conflicts which occur between dominant-held views and those of their minority group. Clients in the Dissonance stage are more culturally aware than Conformity clients and are likely to prefer to work with counselors who possess a good knowledge of the client's cultural group. Counseling approaches that involve considerable self-exploration appear to be best suited for clients at this stage of development.

Minority individuals at the Resistance and Immersion stage are inclined to view all psychological problems (whether personal or social in nature) as a product of their oppression. The likelihood that these clients will seek formal counseling regarding their cultural identity is very slim. In those cases when counseling is sought, it will tend to be only with an ethnically similar counselor, and generally in response to a crisis situation. Therapy for Stage Three clients often takes the form of exposure to, and practice of, the ways and artifacts of their cultures. Clients at this stage who do seek counseling are likely to prefer a group setting. In addition, approaches that are more action-oriented and aimed at external change (challenging racism) are well received. D. W. Sue and D. Sue (1990) believe that most counselors find minorities at this stage difficult to work with. A counselor (even if a member of the client's own race) is often viewed by the culturally different client as a symbol of the oppressive establishment. A great amount of direct anger and distrust may be expressed toward the counselor. The counselor will be frequently tested and challenged as to his/her own racism and role in society.

Clients at the Introspection stage are torn between their preponderant identification with their minority group and their need to exercise greater personal freedom. When these individuals are unable to resolve mounting conflict between these two forces, they often seek counseling. While Introspective clients still prefer to see a counselor from their own cultural group, counselors from other cultures may be viewed as credible sources of help if they share world views similar to those of their clientele and appreciate their cultural dilemmas. Counselors who use a self-exploration and decision-making approach can be most effective with these clients.

Clients at the Synergistic stage of identity development have acquired the internal skills and knowledge necessary to exercise a desired level of personal freedom. Their sense of minority identity is well balanced by an appreciation of other cultures. And, while discrimination and oppression remain a painful part of their lives, greater psychological resources are at their disposal in actively engaging the problem. Attitudinal similarity between counselor and client becomes a more important determinant of counseling success than membership-group similarity.

While the MID model makes good intuitive and clinical sense, it has yet to be adequately tested empirically. Morten and Atkinson (1983) did find evidence of a relationship between level of MID and preference for counselor race among African Americans but we are not aware of any attempt to replicate these results with other racial/ethnic populations. As authors of the model we are perhaps negligent for not submitting it to empirical verification but each of us has been occupied with research and writing in other areas. However, we hope the model will stimulate much-needed research with regard to minority identity development and that the model will help the reader distinguish and comprehend intra-group differences that are evident in the readings to follow. The development of an instrument that can measure identity development across minority groups would be a major first step to researching the relationship between MID stages and counseling process and outcome. We encourage readers interested in minority identity development to pursue this avenue of research.

References

Atkinson, D. R., & Gim, R. H. (1989). Asian-American cultural identity and attitudes toward mental health services. *Journal of Counseling Psychology, 36,* 209–212.

Atkinson, D. R., & Schein, S. (1986). Similarity in counseling. *The Counseling Psychology, 14,* 319–354.

Atkinson, D. R., Whiteley, S., & Gim, R. H. (1990). Asian-American acculturation and preferences for help providers. *Journal of College Student Development, 31,* 155–161.

Banks, W. (1972). The Black client and the helping professional. In R. I. Jones (Ed.), *Black psychology.* New York: Harper & Row.

Berry, B. (1965). *Ethnic and race relations.* Boston: Houghton Mifflin.

Carter, R. T. (1990). The relationship between racism and racial identity among White Americans: An exploratory investigation. *Journal of Counseling and Development, 69* (1), 46–50.

Carter, R. T. & Helms, J. E. (1987). The relationship between Black value-orientation and racial identity attitudes. *Measurement and Evaluation in Counseling and Development, 19* (4), 185–195.

Cass, V. C. (1979). Homosexual identity formation: A theoretical model. *Journal of Homosexuality, 4,* 219–235.

Cross, W. E. (1970, April). *The black experience viewed as a process: A crude model for black self-actualization.* Paper presented at the Thirty-fourth Annual Meeting of the Association of Social and Behavioral Scientists, Tallahassee, FL.

Cross, W. E. (1971). The Negro-to-Black conversion experience: Toward a psychology of Black liberation. *Black World, 20* (9), 13–27.

Cross, W. E., Jr. (1978). The Cross and Thomas models of psychological Nigresence. *Journal of Black Psychology, 5* (1), 13–19.

Cross, W. E., Jr. (1991). *Shades of Black: Diversity of African-American identity.* Philadelphia: Temple University Press.

de Anda, D. (1984). Bicultural socialization: Factors affecting the minority experience. *Social Work, 29,* 101–107.

DeVos, G. (1980). Acculturation: Psychological problems. In I. Rossi (Ed.), *People in culture.* New York: Praeger.

Downing, N. E., & Roush, K. L. (1985). From passive acceptance to active commitment: A model of feminist identity development for women. *The Counseling Psychologist, 13,* 695–709.

Ford, R. C. (1987). Cultural awareness and cross-cultural counseling. *International Journal for the Advancement of Counselling, 10* (1), 71–78.

Gay, G. (1984). Implications of selected models of ethnic identity development for educators. *The Journal of Negro Education, 54* (1), 43–52.

Gim, R. H., Atkinson, D. R., & Kim, S. J. (1991). Asian American acculturation, counselor ethnicity and cultural sensitivity, and ratings of counselors. *Journal of Counseling Psychology, 38,* 57–62.

Gim, R. H., Atkinson, D. R., & Whiteley, S. (1990). Asian-American acculturation, severity of concerns, and willingness to see a counselor. *Journal of Counseling Psychology, 37,* 281–285.

Hall, W. S., Cross, W. E., & Freedle, R. (1972). Stages in the development of Black awareness: An exploratory investigation. In R. I. Jones (Ed.), *Black psychology* (pp. 156–165). New York: Harper & Row.

Heath, A. E., Neimeyer, G. J., & Pedersen, P. B. (1988). The future of cross-cultural counseling: A Delphi poll. *Journal of Counseling and Development, 67,* 27–30.

Helms, J. E. (1984). Toward a theoretical explanation of the effects of race on counseling: A Black and White model. *The Counseling Psychologist, 12,* 153–165.

Helms, J. E. (1985). Cultural identity in the treatment process. In P. Pedersen (Ed.), *Handbook of cross-cultural counseling and therapy.* Westport, CT: Greenwood Press.

Helms, J. E. (1990). *Black and White racial identity: Theory, research, and practice.* Westport, CT: Greenwood Press.

Helms, J. E. & Parham, T. A. (1990). The relationship between Black racial identity attitudes and cognitive styles. In J. E. Helms (Ed.) *Black and White racial identity: Theory, research, and practice* (pp. 119–131). Westport, CT: Greenwood Press.

Highlen, P. S., Reynolds, A. L., Adams, E. M., Hanley, C. P., Myers, L. J., Cox, C. I., & Speight, S. L. (1988). *Self-identity development model of oppressed people: Inclusive model for all?* Paper presented at the meeting of the American Psychological Association, Atlanta, Georgia.

Jackson, B. (1975). Black identity development. *MEFORM: Journal of Educational Diversity & Innovation, 2,* 19–25.

Johnson, M. E. & Lashley, K. H. (1989). Influence of Native-Americans' cultural commitment on preference for counselor ethnicity and expectations about counseling. *Journal of Multicultural Counseling and Development, 17,* 115–122.

Keefe, S. E. (1980). Acculturation and the extended family among urban Mexican Americans. In A. M. Padilla (Ed.), *Acculturation: Theory, models and some new findings* (pp. 85–110). Boulder, CO: Westview Press.

Kunkel, M. A. (1990). Expectations about counseling in relation to acculturation in Mexican-American and Anglo-American student samples. *Journal of Counseling Psychology, 37,* 286–292.

Mayovich, M. H. (1973). Political activation of Japanese American youth. *Journal of Social Issues, 29,* 167–185.

Myers, L. J., Speight, S. L., Highlen, P. S., Cox, C. I., Reynolds, A. L., Adams, E. M., & Hanley, T. C. (1991). Identity development and world view: Toward an optimal conceptualization. *Journal of Counseling and Development, 20,* 29–36.

Morten, G., & Atkinson, D. R. (1983). Minority identity development and preference for counselor race. *Journal of Negro Education, 52,* 156–161.

Neidert, L. J., & Farley, R. (1985). Assimilation in the United States: An analysis of ethnic and generation differences in status and achievement. *American Sociological Review, 50,* 840–850.

Novak, M. (1972). *The rise of the unmeltable ethnics.* New York: MacMillan.

Oetting, E. R., & Beauvais, F. (in press). Orthogonal cultural identification theory: The cultural identification of minority adolescents. *International Journal of the Addictions.*

Olmedo, E. L. (1979). Acculturation: A psychometric perspective. *American Psychologist, 34,* 1061–1070.

Padilla, A. M. (1980a). *Acculturation: Theory, models and some new findings.* Boulder, CO: Westview Press.

Parham, T. A., & Helms, J. E. (1981). The influence of black students' racial identity attitudes on preference for counselor's race. *Journal of Counseling Psychology, 28,* 250–257.

Parham, T. A., & Helms, J. E. (1985). Attitudes of racial identity and self-esteem of Black students: An exploratory investigation. *Journal of College Student Personnel, 26* (2), 143–146. (a)

Parham, T. A., & Helms, J. E. (1985). Relation of racial identity attitudes to self-actualization and affective states of Black students. *Journal of Counseling Psychology, 32,* 431–440. (b)

Park, R. E. (1928). Human migration and the marginal man. *American Journal of Sociology, 33,* 881–893.

Park, R. E. (1950). *Race and culture.* Glencoe, IL: Free Press.

Park, R. E., & Burgess, E. W. (1921). *Introduction to the Science of Sociology.* Chicago: University of Chicago Press.

Pomales, J., & Williams, V. (1989). Effects of level of acculturation and counseling style on Hispanic students' perceptions of counselor. *Journal of Counseling Psychology, 36,* 79–83.

Ponterotto, J. G. (1988). Racial consciousness development among White counselor trainees: A stage model. *Journal of Multicultural Counseling and Development, 16,* 146–156. (a)

Ponterotto, J. G. (1988). Racial/ethnic minority research in the Journal of Counseling psychology: A content analysis and methodological critique. *Journal of Counseling Psychology, 35,* 410–418. (b)

Ponterotto, J. G., Alexander, C. M., & Hinkston, J. A. (1988). Afro-American preferences for counselor characteristics: A replication and extension. *Journal of Counseling Psychology, 35,* 175–182.

Ponterotto, J. G., & Wise, S. L. (1987). Construct validity study of the racial identity attitude scale. *Journal of Counseling Psychology, 34,* 13–131.

Poston, W. S. C. (1990). The biracial identity development model: A needed addition. *Journal of Counseling and Development, 69,* 152–155.

Redfield, R., Linton, R., & Herskovits, M. (1936). Memorandum on the study of acculturation. *American Anthropologist, 37,* 149–152.

Ruiz, A. S. (1990). Ethnic identity: Crisis and resolution. *Journal of Multicultural Counseling and Development, 18,* 29–40.

Ruiz, R. A., & Padilla, A. M. (1977). Counseling Latinos. *Personnel and Guidance Journal, 55,* 401–408.

Sanchez, A. R., & Atkinson, D. R. (1983). Mexican-American cultural commitment, preference for counselor ethnicity, and willingness to use counseling. *Journal of Counseling Psychology, 30,* 215–220.

Stonequist, E. V. (1937). *The marginal man.* New York: Charles Scribner's Sons.

Stonequist, E. V. (1961). *The marginal man: A study in personality and culture conflict.* New York: Russell & Russell.

Sue, D. W., & Sue, D. (1990). *Counseling the culturally different: Theory and practice.* New York: John Wiley.

Sue, S., & Sue, D. W. (1971). Chinese-American personality and mental health. *Amerasia Journal, 1,* 36–49.

Troiden, R. R. (1989). The formation of homosexual identities. *Journal of Homosexuality, 17,* 43–73.

Valentine, C. A. (1971). Deficit, difference, and bicultural models of Afro-American behavior. *Harvard Educational Review, 41,* 135–157.

Vontress, C. E. (1971). Racial differences: Impediments to rapport. *Journal of Counseling Psychology, 18,* 7–13.

3
Counseling Racial/Ethnic Minorities: An Overview

In Chapter 1, we described how the United States is becoming increasingly culturally diverse as a result of the current wave of immigrants from Latin America and Asia and the higher birthrate among racial/ethnic minority populations than among the European American population. The diversification of the population suggests that counselors will need to be prepared to work with a variety of racial/ethnic populations. In Chapter 2, we described the diversity within racial/ethnic minority groups that is often overlooked by mental health professionals. In order to work with racial/ethnic minority clients, counselors need to understand the variables that contribute to individual differences within ethnic minority populations. In this chapter, we discuss how racial/ethnic minorities have responded to the mental health profession, examine some of the reasons that racial/ethnic minorities over- and underutilize mental health services, and explore the possibility that professional psychology has failed to meet the mental health needs of racial/ethnic minorities. We begin by providing some of the evidence that documents this failure, data on racial/ethnic minority overrepresentation in inpatient psychiatric hospitals and underutilization of community mental health services. We conclude the chapter by suggesting that barriers to cross-cultural counseling can be overcome and that there may actually be benefits to cross-cultural counseling for both clients and counselors.

Ethnic Minority Utilization of Mental Health Services

A number of researchers have examined archival data from psychiatric hospitals, outpatient mental health clinics, and university counseling centers to determine if racial/ethnic minorities utilize these facilities at the same rates as European Americans. In general, the utilization patterns for inpatient services is quite different than those for outpatient services. In reviewing research on the relationship between race and use of inpatient mental health services, Snowden and Cheung (1990) found a history of

Black overrepresentation in mental hospitals dating back to 1914. They also reviewed 1980 and 1981 survey data from the National Institute of Mental Health and found that: (a) both African Americans and American Indians are more likely than Whites to be hospitalized; (b) African Americans are more likely to be diagnosed as schizophrenic and less likely to be diagnosed as having an affective disorder than are Whites; and (c) Asian Americans/Pacific Islanders are not as likely to be hospitalized as Whites, but when they are they remain in the hospital for a longer period of time (p. 347). African American overrepresentation may be particularly acute in public psychiatric hospitals (Cannon & Locke, 1977; Krammer, Rosen, & Willis, 1972). Examining only involuntary hospitalization (which constitutes 29 percent of all psychiatric hospitalization), Rosenstein, Milazzo-Sayre, MacAskill, and Manderscheid (1987) found that non-Whites are 3.53 times more likely than Whites to receive involuntary criminal commitment and 2.41 times more likely to receive involuntary noncriminal commitment. Snowden and Cheung (1990) suggest that racial differences in public hospitalization may be due to socioeconomic differences, cultural differences in seeking help, and diagnostic biases on the part of referring psychologists and psychiatrists.

On the other hand, there is evidence that at least some racial/ethnic minorities are underrepresented as clients of community mental health services and university counseling services. Based on a review of national data, the Special Populations Task Force of the President's Commission on Mental Health concluded in 1978 that racial/ethnic minorities ''are clearly underserved or inappropriately served by the current mental health system in this country'' (Special Populations, 1978, p. 73). More recently, Cheung and Snowden (1990) reviewed data from community-based surveys of mental health utilization and concluded that compared to Whites: (1) Asian Americans and Latinos are underrepresented; (2) African Americans are underrepresented in some studies and overrepresented in others; and (3) little is known about Native American utilization rates. When racial/ethnic minorities do make an initial contact with a mental health service, there is evidence that they are less likely to return for subsequent counseling than their European American counterparts. For example, Sue and McKinney (1975) found that up to 50 percent of the Asian clients did not return to a mental health clinic after an initial contact, compared to a 30 percent drop-out rate for Caucasian clients.

Similarly, there is evidence that racial/ethnic minorities underutilize college counseling services. In a survey of university counseling services across the country, Magoon (1988) found that Black students were underrepresented as clients in 40 percent of the small schools and 46 percent of the large schools. For Hispanic clients, 32 percent of the small schools and 37 percent of the large schools reported underrepresentation. In a separate study of a single campus, only 7 percent of the Mexican

American students made use of the counseling services in a one year period compared to 14 percent of the White students (Sanchez & King, 1986). There is reason to believe that for Asian Americans, utilization rates may be linked to the stigma of psychological problems; Sue and Kirk (1975) reported that when compared to non-Asian American students, Asian American students underused university psychiatric services but overused university counseling center services. As a result of data like these, Stone and Archer (1990) described the provision of counseling services to ethnic minority students as one of the major challenges facing college and university counseling centers in the 1990s.

Not all reviews of ethnic minority utilization patterns have lead to the conclusion that they are underrepresented as clients of community mental health. Lopez (1981) reviewed utilization studies for Mexican Americans and concluded that this subgroup of Hispanics used mental health services on a parity with Anglo Americans. Lopez suggests, however, that these studies may have overestimated Mexican American utilization because they did not take the level of need into account, nor did most of them take termination patterns into account.

Discrepancies in utilization studies may be due to research design differences and type of population sampled. Atkinson (1985) reported that while archival studies of mental health outpatient clinics tend to support the hypothesis of underutilization, survey and analogue studies on university campuses often do not. Overall, however, the data continue to suggest that ethnic minorities are overrepresented in psychiatric hospitals and underrepresented as clients of community mental health services and university counseling services.

Explanations for Underuse of Community Mental Health Services

The obvious question arises, why are there differential utilization patterns across ethnicities? With respect to hospitalization, Snowden and Cheung (1990) cite socioeconomic differences as the primary factor; Whites are more likely to have the resources to prevent hospitalization. With respect to use of outpatient counseling services, three explanations have emerged in the professional psychology literature. The first explanation is that ethnic minorities have less need for mental health services than do European Americans, i.e., they have fewer mental health problems. A second view is that values indigenous to minority cultures discourage the use of mental health services by racial/ethnic minorities. The third view is that mental health services have failed to adequately meet the needs of racial/ethnic minorities. In the following sections we explore these explanations for the underutilization of mental health services by racial/ethnic minorities in greater detail.

Mental Health Needs of Ethnic Minorities

Although it would be a mistake to suggest a cause-and-effect relationship between ethnicity (or even culture) and mental health problems (King, 1978), there is reason to believe that, rather than having less need for mental health services than European Americans, racial/ethnic minorities may actually have more need for mental health services. The primary reason for this conclusion is that psychological disorders are most common and severe among the lowest socioeconomic classes (Korchin, 1980), and racial/ethnic minorities are overrepresented among the low income population. Ogbu (1987) points out that those racial/ethnic groups that became minorities in the United States involuntarily through slavery, conquest, or colonization (e.g., American Indians, African Americans, native Hawaiians) are among the very lowest socioeconomic groups in this country. The negative effects of poverty, which include anxiety, depression, low self-esteem, aggression, poor school achievement, and loneliness have been documented for various ethnic minority populations (Canino, Earley, & Rogler, 1980; Chin, 1983; Torres-Matrullo, 1976).

Malgady, Rogler, and Costantino (1987) suggest there may be other factors operating that explain why racial/ethnic minorities are identified as having a higher incidence of mental health problems:

> Psychiatric epidemiological studies reveal distressing statistics suggesting that the prevalence of mental health problems in the Hispanic American population is disproportionately high relative to that in other ethnic groups. Nevertheless, the veracity of such studies of prevalence rates must be questioned when one considers Hispanics' linguistic and cultural variance with respect to the majority culture, which serves as the reference against which mental health status is judged (p. 232).

Thus, the figures on mental health problems among language/cultural minorities may be inflated by misdiagnosis due to language and cultural differences between mental health practitioner and client.

Nonetheless, overrepresentation in the poverty and near-poverty income levels appears to be the major reason epidemiological studies report a higher incidence of mental health problems among racial/ethnic minorities than among European Americans. Smith (1985) reviewed the literature on race and psychopathology and concluded that "overall, this review has found that Black Americans in particular and ethnic minorities in general have more psychological disorders than whites; but when class is taken into account, the differences become minimal" (p. 548). However, she also concluded that when investigators do control for class, there is still evidence that Blacks and other racial/ethnic minorities are subjected to more stress than their White counterparts. She concluded that prejudice, discrimination, and hostility are stressor stimuli experienced by African Americans and other racial/ethnic minorities that contribute to their mental health problems.

Immigration also can be a particularly stressful experience (Atkinson, 1986; Atkinson & Juntunen, in press; Cheung, 1987; Esquivel & Keitel, 1990). For example, several recent research reviews (Leong, 1986; D. W. Sue & D. Sue, 1990) have found evidence that the stresses associated with immigration have contributed to the mental health problems of Asian Americans. In addition to the stress associated with the physical act of relocation, immigrants may experience stress as a result of war and violence in their native land, cultural conflict between the culture they are leaving and the U.S. culture, racial/ethnic tension and discrimination in their new community, and economic disadvantages in a society unwilling to recognize their training and skills (Cheung, 1987; First, 1988; Nguyen & Henkin, 1983; Rumbaut, 1985; Smalley, 1984).

Malgady et al.'s (1987) suggestion of diagnostic bias notwithstanding, it is evident that racial/ethnic minorities experience as many mental health problems as European Americans. The hypothesis that they underutilize outpatient mental health services and university counseling services because of lesser needs is clearly unjustified.

Cultural Values Inherent in Ethnic Minority Cultures

A number of values inherent in the cultures of African Americans, American Indians, Asian Americans, and Latinos have been cited as the reason for their underutilization of university counseling and community mental health services. One hypothesis is that in some cultures, acknowledgement of mental health issues may be suppressed because of cultural values. Esquivel and Keitel (1990) point out that "in some cultures it is a dishonor for the family to have a child with an emotional problem" (p. 215). In some cultures, denial of psychological problems may produce somatic symptoms and/or physical solutions. For example, there is some evidence that Asian Americans are more likely than European Americans to attribute mental illness to a biological cause (Sue, Wagner, Margullis, & Lew, 1976), thereby suggesting a medical rather than a psychological solution. After reviewing research on counseling and psychotherapy with Asian Americans, Leong (1986) concluded that Asian Americans tend to express psychological symptoms via somatization and "to exhibit lower levels of verbal and emotional expressiveness than do whites" (p. 197).

When psychological problems do interfere with functioning, racial/ethnic minorities may prefer to use help providers within the ethnic community rather than conventional mental health services. For example, it has been suggested that racial/ethnic minorities prefer to use intrafamilial support systems to resolve psychological problems and that racial/ethnic minorities use folk therapies to deal with mental health problems (Esquivel & Keitel, 1990). Sue et al. (1976) also found that many Asian Americans feel they can control their mental health by exercising willpower and avoiding morbid thoughts.

Although cultural values within an ethnic minority community may contribute to underutilization of outpatient mental health services, we object to singling out cultural values as the primary cause. A more valid explanation, in our opinion, is that values within an ethnic culture may conflict with values inherent in conventional counseling strategies. This hypothesis of conflicting values will be discussed in a forthcoming section.

Professional Psychology's Failure to Meet the Mental Health Needs of Racial/Ethnic Minorities

Perhaps the most salient explanation of ethnic minority underutilization of mental health services is that psychology as a profession has failed to meet the mental health needs of racial/ethnic minorities. Two major categories of criticism have emerged: (1) psychology has failed to recognize the special needs of racial/ethnic minorities, and (2) even when special needs are recognized, psychology has failed to provide culturally relevant forms of treatment.

Failure to Recognize Special Needs

Until the mid-1960s, the counseling profession demonstrated little interest in or concern for the status of racial, ethnic, or other minority groups. Counseling and guidance, with its traditional focus on the needs of the "average" student, tended to overlook the special needs of individuals who, by virtue of their skin color, physical characteristics, cultural background, or socioeconomic condition, found themselves disadvantaged in a world designed for White, middle-class people. Psychologists in private practice, with their clientele primarily limited to middle- and upper-class individuals, also overlooked the needs of ethnic minority populations.

The events of the 1960s can probably be credited with stimulating the American Psychological Association (APA), the American Personnel and Guidance Association (APGA, now called the American Association for Counseling and Development—AACD), and other professional organizations to begin addressing the needs of ethnic minorities within their organizational structure. Both AACD and APA now have divisions which focus on racial/ethnic minority issues. According to McFadden and Lipscomb (1985), the first formal step toward forming the current AACD Association for Multicultural Counseling and Development (AMCD) was taken in 1969 when the APGA Senate adopted a resolution establishing a salaried National Office of Non-White Concerns as part of the APGA central office. The Association for Non-White Concerns in Personnel and Guidance became a reality in 1972 and was renamed the AMCD in the mid-1980s.

Casas (1984) has documented that APA interest in ethnic minority issues moved from an ad hoc committee level in the 1960s to the granting of divisional status to ethnic psychologists in 1987. The first formal sign of interest in racial/ethnic minority issues within the APA structure was the establishment of an Ad Hoc Committee on Equal Opportunity in Psychology in 1963. The purpose of this committee was to examine problems experienced by racial/ethnic minorities who seek training and employment in psychology. This ad hoc committee was made a standing committee (Committee on Equality of Opportunity in Psychology—CEOP) in 1967 and was charged with the formulation of policy regarding the education, training, employment, and status of minority groups in psychology. In 1970 their charge was broadened to include, among other things, women's issues, advocacy for victims of racism, affirmative action efforts, and Project Impact (the precursor of the current Minority Fellowship program).

In 1971 APA established the Board of Social and Ethical Responsibility for Psychology (BSERP) to examine ways in which social responsibility can be integrated as a dominant theme in the science and profession of psychology. The CEOP was one of three committees assigned to BSERP. The scope of the CEOP was narrowed to focus only on racial/ethnic minority issues in 1974. The APA Office of Cultural and Ethnic Affairs was established in 1978, and the Board of Ethnic Minority Affairs was established in 1980. An important step was taken in 1981 when the APA revised the organization's ethical guidelines and mandated that psychologists receive training in cultural differences. The APA also amended accreditation standards to include the requirement for formal training in cross-cultural issues (Mio & Morris, 1990). The Society of Psychological Study of Ethnic Minority Issues (Division 45) was formally established by APA in January 1987.

The increased attention to ethnic minority issues within AACD and APA can be attributed in part to the political activities of racial/ethnic minority members and their nonminority supporters. For example, in 1969, the Black Student Psychological Association presented a number of demands to the APA Council of Representatives that directed attention to the underrepresentation of ethnic minorities in professional psychology. Also, advocates for racial/ethnic minority issues were active at the 1973 Vail Conference, the 1975 Austin Conference, and the 1978 Dulles Conference, all of which addressed at some level the need to expand the roles of culturally diverse people in psychology (Sue, 1990). The establishment of Division 45 was the direct result of an intense lobbying effort by ethnic minority members of APA.

Although the AACD, APA, and other professional organizations have given increased attention to ethnic minority issues, many of the same problems that affected counseling services for diverse groups in the 1960s have persisted. The Dulles Conference, for example, documented in 1978 the underrepresentation of ethnic minorities among psychologists, university faculty, APA members, and APA governing bodies. The Dulles Conference report also cited continued racism in the profession and in society as reasons why inadequate mental health services are still accorded racial/ethnic minorities. The Special Populations Task Force of the President's Commission on Mental Health (1978) similarly concluded that racial/ethnic minorities "are clearly underserved or inappropriately served by the current mental health system in this country" (p. 73). More recently, several reviews of research published in the 1980s conclude that racial/ethnic minorities still may be receiving differential and inferior forms of treatment from counselors and psychologists (Abramowitz & Murray, 1983; Atkinson, 1985).

In examining these historical events, it is clear that professional psychology has moved from a position of ignoring the special needs and experiences of racial/ethnic minorities to a current position of increased sensitivity and activity. It is also clear, however, that the profession has been largely reactive (to the political pressures of constituent groups) rather than proactive in its response and that many inequities still remain.

Failure to Provide Culturally Relevant Counseling

The fact that various racial/ethnic minorities are underrepresented in community mental health services, despite the fact that they experience as much or more stress than do nonminorities, suggests these groups perceive conventional counseling as irrelevant to their needs. According to Sue and Zane (1987), "the single most important explanation for the problems in service delivery (for ethnic minorities) involves the inability of therapists to provide culturally responsive forms of treatment" (p. 37). It seems reasonable to assume that ethnic minority clients, particularly those who maintain some of the values from their ancestral culture, will prefer to see counselors and other mental health practitioners who are sensitive to and knowledgeable about their cultural background.

There is some evidence to support this assumption. African American, American Indian, Latino, and Filipino American university students who had never sought the assistance of a counselor in dealing with a personal problem ranked "counselors who value and respect cultural differences" highest of eleven suggestions for improving university counseling services (Atkinson, Jennings, & Liongson, 1990). Pomales, Claiborn, and LaFromboise (1986) found that Black college students rated White counselors who were portrayed as culture-sensitive more culturally competent than those who were portrayed as culture-blind. Similarly, Asian American college students rated the counselor as a more credible source of help and more culturally competent when portrayed as culture-sensitive than when portrayed as culture-blind, regardless of the counselor's ethnicity (Gim, Atkinson, & Kim, 1991).

Language and cultural differences between clients and counselors, lack of diversity among counselors, lack of training in cultural sensitivity for counselors, and failure to confront racism have been cited as evidence that psychology has failed to provide culturally relevant and responsive forms of treatment.

Language and Cultural Differences Scott and Borodovsky (1990) point out that in cross-cultural counseling, "language differences become barriers when (a) the participants misconstrue the statements of one another, (b) negative prejudgments by participants of one another are based on these differences, and (c) such differences are not experienced or appreciated as expressions of the client's cultural heritage and/or identity" (p. 167). The heavy reliance by counselors on verbal interaction to build rapport presupposes that the participants in a counseling dialogue are capable of understanding each other. Yet rapport building may be impossible when counselors fail to understand the client's language and its nuances (Romero, 1985; Vontress, 1973; Wilson & Calhoun, 1974). Uneducated clients may lack the sophisticated verbal skills needed to benefit from "talk therapy" (Calia, 1966; Tyler, 1964), especially when confronted by a counselor who relies on complex cognitive and conative concepts to generate client insight. Furthermore, counselors may incorrectly or negatively interpret statements from clients who speak with an accent, or who do not use standard English to express themselves (Padilla, 1991; D. W. Sue & D. Sue, 1990).

D. W. Sue and D. Sue (1977) have pointed out that the use of standard English with a lower income or bilingual client may result in misperceptions of the client's strengths and weaknesses. Furthermore, Vontress (1973) suggests that counselors need to be familiar with minority group body language lest they misinterpret the meaning of postures, gestures, and inflections. For example, differences in nonverbal behavior are frequently seen between African Americans and European Americans. When speaking to another person, European Americans tend to look away from the person (avoid eye contact) more often than do African Americans. When listening to another person speak, however, African Americans tend to avoid eye contact while European Americans make eye contact. This may account for statements from teachers who feel that Black students are inattentive (they make less eye contact when spoken to) or feel that Blacks are more angry (intense stare) when speaking (D. W. Sue, 1990; D. W. Sue & D. Sue, 1990).

Even when the counselor and client share a common language, cultural differences between them may create a barrier that renders counseling ineffective. According to Wilson and Calhoun (1974), ". . . the values inherent in two different sub-cultures may be realistically as diverse as those of two countries." While the major concern with this issue, in the final analysis, centers on the counselor's influence upon the client, culture-bound value differences can also impede rapport building. Cayleff (1986) suggests that "cultural misunderstandings . . . may precipitate difficulties in communication, obscure expectations, affect the quality of care dispensed, and dramatically alter a patient's willingness or ability to maintain a therapeutic program" (p. 346).

Lack of Ethnic Diversity among Counselors Theoretically, language and cultural differences would not be an issue if clients always had access to a linguistically and culturally similar counselor. Unfortunately, however, racial/ethnic minorities are severely underrepresented in professional psychology and the chances of achieving parity with their representation in the population in the near future is highly unlikely. In the most extensive study of ethnic minority representation to date, Russo, Olmedo, Stapp, and Fulcher (1981) found that ethnic minority psychologists comprised only 3 percent of the American Psychological Association membership in 1979. For the three major applied specializations in the APA, the percentage of the membership who were racial/ethnic minorities was 2.8 percent for counseling psychology, 3.1 percent for clinical psychology, and 3.6 percent for school psychology. Of the 4,112 counseling psychologists in APA, forty-six were Black, twenty-nine Asian American, and thirteen American Indian.

In order to determine the number of racial/ethnic minority psychologists that might be "in the pipeline," Russo et al. (1981) examined data on new Ph.D. graduates in psychology from 1972 up to 1980. They found that in 1972, 6.7 percent of the new Ph.D.s were racial/ethnic minorities; by 1980 this figure had only increased to 8 percent. In 1980, 8.4 percent of the new Ph.D.s in clinical psychology were ethnic minorities compared to 7.8 percent in counseling psychology and 2.9 percent in school psychology. These data confirm the findings of earlier as well as subsequent studies that consistently document underrepresentation of ethnic minorities as students and faculty in psychology and counseling programs. African Americans, American Indians, Asian Americans, and Latinos have been found to be underrepresented as students and faculty for clinical psychology programs (Bernal & Padilla, 1982; Boxley & Wagner, 1971; Kennedy & Wagner, 1979; Padilla, Boxley, & Wagner, 1973), counseling psychology programs (Parham & Moreland, 1981), and counselor education programs (Atkinson, 1983; Young, Chamley, & Withers, 1990). Further, a recent article in the *APA Monitor* (Moses, 1990) indicated that the percent of psychology Ph.D. recipients who are racial/ethnic minorities has not changed in the last decade.

Training programs will need to actively recruit and support ethnic minority students if ethnic parity is ever to be achieved in psychology and counseling. However, there is reason to believe that few training programs make any significant effort to recruit and retain ethnic minorities. A survey of counselor education programs revealed that while efforts were made to recruit ethnic minority students, many training programs continued to rely on traditional admissions criteria that tended to overlook the strengths of underrepresented applicants (Atkinson & Wampold, 1981). More recently, Moses (1990) reported that APA estimates only fifteen or twenty training programs have been proactive in recruiting and retaining ethnic minority students.

When given a choice between an ethnically similar counselor and an ethnically dissimilar counselor, many ethnic minority clients (or potential clients) do prefer a counselor who is similar to them ethnically. This has been found to be true for African Americans (Atkinson, 1983; Harrison, 1975; Sattler, 1977), American Indians (Haviland, Horswill, O'Connell, & Dynneson, 1983), Asian Americans (Atkinson, Maruyama, & Matsui, 1978; Gim, Atkinson, & Kim, 1991; Wu & Windle, 1980), and Latinos (Keefe, 1978; LeVine & Padilla, 1980; Padilla & Ruiz, 1973; Ponce & Atkinson, 1989).

Racial/ethnic minority underrepresentation in psychology and counseling combined with studies of preference for counselor ethnicity provide strong support for the hypothesis that minority underutilization of mental health services is due, at least in part, to the lack of racial/ethnic minority counselors.

Failure to Confront Racism among White Trainees In an earlier section, we pointed out that professional psychology has been slow in responding to the special needs of racial/ethnic minority population. Carney and Kahn (1984) suggest that the tendency on the part of White mental health professionals to ignore or minimize the importance of ethnic/cultural differences "is based on the belief that persons who are racially and culturally different are also culturally and/or genetically deficient" (p. 111). Even those psychologists and counselors who consciously try to promote ethnic equality may unconsciously commit racist acts. Casas and Atkinson (1981) pointed out that university counselors who attempt to be sensitive to the needs of racial/ethnic minority students sometimes base their counseling services on stereotypes that are not supported by research.

There are data that can be interpreted as evidence that European American (or White) psychotherapists are biased in their treatment of racial/ethnic minorities. When minorities do bother to seek treatment there is evidence that they are diagnosed differently and receive "less preferred" forms of treatment (Abramowitz & Murray, 1983). Differential diagnoses and treatment of minorities is presumably a function of stereotypes held by counselors. Analog studies have generally not provided evidence that counselors hold biased views of racial/ethnic minorities, presumably because the purpose of such studies is usually self-evident. However, several studies employing an illusory correlation paradigm have found that counselors hold stereotypic views of racial/ethnic minorities. Atkinson, Casas, and Wampold (1981) found that university counselors tend to group student characteristics into constellations reflective of common ethnic stereotypes. Wampold, Casas and Atkinson (1982) found that nonminority counselor trainees are more likely to be influenced by stereotypes when assigning characteristics to racial/ethnic groups than are minority counselor trainees.

Clearly, racism takes many forms, ranging from unconscious stereotyping by someone consciously committed to egalitarianism, to those individuals who commit acts of violence against racial/ethnic minorities. European American counselors probably represent a range of racist attitudes. Sabnani, Ponterotto, and Borodovsky (1991) point out that White counselor trainees enter training at different levels of White Identity Development and that a developmental approach is needed to raise their awareness of ethnic issues. We will have more to say about this in Chapter 16. For our purposes here, however, we conclude that the (conscious and/or unconscious) racist attitudes held by European American counselors has been a factor in deterring many racial/ethnic minority individuals from seeking or remaining in counseling.

Conflict of Values Inherent in Counseling Process and Ethnic Minority Cultures Psychology may have failed racial/ethnic minorities in the past because the profession did not recognize that values inherent in the counseling process may conflict with the cultural values of racial/ethnic groups. Instead of blaming the values in the minority culture for underutilization of services, the problem can be reframed as a conflict between values inherent in the counseling process and those inherent in the culture of the client.

There are a number of values inherent in the counseling process that may come in conflict with values inherent in ethnic minority cultures. For example, one of the first and most obvious value differences encountered by the middle-class counselors and the low-income, racial/ethnic minority clients involves the willingness to make and keep counseling appointments. As D. W. Sue and D. Sue (1977) point out, ". . . lower-class clients who are concerned with "survival" or making it through on a day-to-day basis expect advice and suggestions from the counselor . . . (and) . . . appointments made weeks in advance with short weekly 50 minute contacts are not consistent with the need to seek immediate solutions" (p. 424).

Many professionals argue that self-disclosure is a necessary condition for effective counseling. However, self-disclosure may be contrary to basic cultural values for some minorities. D. W. Sue and S. Sue (1972) have pointed out that Chinese American clients, who are taught at an early age to restrain from emotional expression, find the direct and subtle demands by the counselor to self-disclosure very threatening. Similar conflicts have been reported for Chicano (Cross & Maldonado, 1971) and Native American (Trimble, 1976) clients. Poor clients, of whatever racial/ethnic background, frequently resist attempts by the counselor to encourage client self-exploration and prefer to ascribe their problems, often justifiably, to forces beyond their control (Calia, 1966). In addition, racial/ethnic minorities have learned to distrust European Americans in general and may "shine on" a majority counselor, since this has proven to be adaptive behavior with Whites in the past. D. W. Sue and D. Sue (1977) suggest that self-disclosure is itself a cultural value and counselors who ". . . value verbal, emotional and behavioral expressiveness as goals in counseling are transmitting their own cultural values" (p. 425).

Often, in order to encourage self-disclosure, the counseling situation is intentionally designed to be an ambiguous one, one in which the counselor listens emphatically and responds only to encourage the client to continue talking (D. W. Sue & S. Sue, 1972). This lack of structure in the counseling process may conflict with need for structure that is a value in many cultures. Racial/ethnic minority clients frequently find the lack of structure confusing, frustrating, and even threatening (Haettenschwiller, 1971). Atkinson, Maruyama, and Matsui (1978) found that Asian Americans prefer a directive counseling style to a nondirective one, suggesting the directive approach is more compatible with their cultural values. Similar results were found in a replication of the Atkinson et al. (1978) study with Japanese American young adults (Atkinson & Matsushita, 1991), American Indian high school students (Dauphinais, Dauphinais, & Rowe, 1981), and Mexican American community college students (Ponce & Atkinson, 1989). Black students also were found to prefer a more active counseling role over a passive one (Peoples & Dell, 1975).

Differences in attitudes toward sexual behavior often enter the counseling relationship between a counselor and client representing different socioeconomic classes. For the most part, open acceptance of sexual promiscuity differs from one socioeconomic level to another, although other factors (e.g., religious beliefs) play heavy roles. Middle-class counselors, whether consciously or unconsciously, often attempt to impose middle-class sexual mores on lower- and upper-class clients.

Minorities have criticized contemporary counseling approaches which they contend have been developed by and for middle-class European Americans (Edwards, 1982; Jackson, 1985; Katz, 1985; S. Sue & Zane, 1987). Katz (1985) suggests that the counseling profession "has at its core

an inherent set of cultural values and norms by which clients are judged"
(p. 615) and that these cultural values and norms are the product of
European American cultures. In order to make counseling more responsive
to ethnic minority needs, these critics argue, we must develop strategies,
theories, and models that are appropriate to specific populations. Using
treatment approaches developed for White, middle-class Americans with
ethnically diverse clients is illogical and possibly even dangerous
(Edwards, 1982).

The issue is perhaps best represented semantically by the emic-etic
dichotomy, which was first presented by the linguist, Pike (1954). Draguns
(1976) offers the following definition of these two terms:

> Emic refers to the viewing of data in terms indigenous or unique to the culture
> in question, and etic, to viewing them in light of categories and concepts
> external to the culture but universal in their applicability. (p. 2).

The criticisms relevant to the current discussions, then, focus on what can
be called the "pseudoetic" approach to cross-cultural counseling (Triandis,
Malpass, & Davidson, 1973): culturally encapsulated counselors assume
that their own approach and associated techniques can be culturally
generalized and are robust enough to cope with cultural variations. In
reality, minority critics argue, we have developed emic approaches to
counseling that are designed by and for middle-class European Americans.

However, there is disagreement about the need to provide culturally
responsive forms of treatment. At one extreme are authors who contend
that the constructs from several existing counseling theories and strategies
are universally applicable (Fukuyama, 1990; Vontress, 1979). At the other
extreme are authors who urge counselors to adopt the helping strategies
from the client's indigenous culture (Cayleff, 1986; Heinrich, Corbine, &
Thomas, 1990; Torrey, 1970). In between these two extremes are a number
of other positions, including the views that conventional counseling
theories and strategies can be matched with (Majors & Nikelly, 1983;
Ponterotto, 1987), adapted to (Toldson & Pasteur, 1972; Ruiz & Casas,
1981; Wilson & Calhoun, 1974), or combined into eclectic approaches
compatible with (Harper & Stone, 1974; McDavis, 1978; Stikes, 1972) the
client's culture. Furthermore, even those individuals who identify with their
ethnic culture may not feel that counselors need to employ helping
strategies from that culture. Atkinson, Jennings, and Liongson (1990)
reported that "counselors who use helping methods from my culture" was
ranked last (mainstream-identified respondents) or second to last
(bicultural-identified and ethnic-identified respondents) by African
American, American Indian, Filipino American, and Latino college students
who had never sought counseling assistance for a personal problem when
they were asked to rate eleven suggestions for improving counseling
services.

Lack of Training in Cultural Sensitivity There is a growing recognition that graduate training programs must not only overcome racism in their students, they must proactively prepare their students to serve racial/ethnic minority clients. Ridley (1985) describes five imperatives for the development of training programs that promote cross-cultural competence. In a position paper that resulted from the APA-sponsored Vail Conference, it was strongly recommended that it be considered unethical for psychologists not trained in cultural diversity to provide services to ethnically diverse groups. Also, both the APA and AACD (American Association for Counseling and Development) have incorporated knowledge of cultural diversity into their training standards.

Although the need for culturally knowledgeable and sensitive counselors is reflected in the APA and AACD ethical guidelines, mandated by the APA accreditation requirements, and supported by research, there is evidence that doctoral programs still may not be providing formal training in this area. Bernal and Padilla (1982) surveyed clinical psychology training programs and found that none of the respondents required a course on racial/ethnic minority issues and that only 20 percent offered a course on the topic. Moreover, Bernal and Padilla (1982) reported that only 41 percent (thirty-one of seventy-six) of the clinical psychology programs responding to their survey offered one or more courses "that might [even] contribute to the student's understanding of minority or other cultures" (p. 782). Similarly, a recent survey of counselor education programs found that only one third of the responding programs require courses or practicums in cross-cultural counseling (Ibrahim, Stadler, Arredondo, & McFadden 1986). Mio and Morris (1990) acknowledge that the situation may have improved in recent years but suggest that from their own experience, "there still seems to be much resistance against the inclusion of cross-cultural issues as part of the standard curriculum" (p. 435). Their perception is confirmed by the fact that the Committee on Accreditation currently cites diversity issues in about 75 percent of its program reviews (Moses, 1990).

For the most part, psychology programs are reluctant to change their curriculum (Moses, 1990). Cultural influences affecting personality, identity formation, and behavior manifestations frequently are not a part of the training psychologists and counselors receive. When minority group experiences are discussed, they are generally seen and analyzed from the "White, middle-class perspective." Unimodal counseling approaches are perpetuated by graduate programs in counseling that give inadequate treatment to the mental health issues of minorities (Ponterotto & Casas, 1987). As a result, counselors who deal with the mental health problems of minorities often lack understanding and knowledge about cultural differences and their consequent interaction with an oppressive society.

While there is general agreement that training programs must prepare students to work with racial/ethnic minority populations "there is little agreement on what organized psychology can and should do to help programs improve their records in this field (Moses, 1990). Some authors have suggested that APA, AACD, and other organizations have not been specific enough about the training that counselors and psychologists should receive with respect to culturally diverse groups. As Ponterotto and Casas (1987) suggest, "the [counseling] profession has not yet defined culturally competent training" (p. 433). Others argue that professional organizations have not pushed curriculum change forcefully enough through their accreditation procedures (Wyatt, quoted in Moses, 1990).

Although professional mental health associations have not included specific cultural competencies in their training standards, models of cross-cultural competencies do exist. The APA Division 17 Education and Training Committee developed a position paper identifying cross-cultural counseling competencies that was published in *The Counseling Psychologist* (D. Sue, Bernier, Durran, Fienberg, Pedersen, Smith, & Vasquez-Nuttall, 1982). More recently, the Professional Standards Committee of the Association for Multicultural Counseling and Development developed a position paper that expands upon some of the principles put forth in the Division 17 paper. The AMCD paper is reprinted in Appendix A. Models for achieving competence in cross-cultural counseling are also discussed in a number of recent journal articles (e.g., LaFromboise & Rowe, 1983; Lopez et al., 1989; Mio & Morris, 1990; S. Sue, Akutsu, & Higashi, 1985). These models will be discussed at greater length in Chapter 16.

Intrapsychic Etiology Model Counseling in this country has grown out of a philosophy of "rugged individualism" in which people are assumed to be responsible for their own lot in life. Success in society is attributed to outstanding abilities or great effort. Likewise, failures or problems encountered by the person may be attributed to some inner deficiency such as lack of effort or low aptitude (D. W. Sue, 1978). For the minority individual who is the victim of oppression, the person-blame approach tends to deny the existence of external injustices (racism, sexism, age, bias, etc.). A number of authors have criticized the counseling profession for accepting this intrapsychic view of client problems.

To some extent, the assumption of an internal etiology is inherent in all conventional counseling approaches. According to Smith (1985):

> What has become known as the traditional model of counseling is, in reality, a set of principles that has been extracted from various counseling theories and that is seen to cut across theoretical counseling formulations. Such principles tend to stress that (1) clients' problems are located within the individual (intraphysically based), rather than in the conditions to which minorities adjust; (2) clients' problems should be resolved internally; (3) clients are

familiar with the roles of client and counselor; and (4) talk rather than direct action is the more desirable counseling technique (p. 568).

Katz (1985) also is critical of conventional psychotherapy. She and others urge counselors to look at the extrapsychic causes of client problems. Proponents of this view argue that the counselor should change the environment, rather than simply changing individual behavior, when working with disfranchised groups.

The intrapsychic model assumes client problems are the result of personal disorganization rather than institutional or societal dysfunctioning (Bryson & Bardo, 1975). Counselors, critics argue, should view minority clients as victims of a repressive society and rather than intervene with the victim, counselors should attempt to change the offending portion of the client's environment (Banks, 1972; Katz, 1985; D. W. Sue, 1978; D. W. Sue & D. Sue, 1990; Williams & Kirkland, 1971).

Pedersen (1976) has suggested that the counselor can help the minority client either adopt, or adapt to the dominant culture. Vexliard (1968) has coined the terms autoplastic and alloplastic to define two levels of adaption; the first, ". . . involves accommodating oneself to the givens of a social setting and structure and the latter involves shaping the external reality to suit one's needs" (Draguns, 1976, p. 6). Thus, critics of the conventional counseling role see cultural adoption and the autoplastic model of adaption as repressive but predictable outcomes of the intrapsychic counseling model. The counseling roles they advocate can be viewed as directed toward the alloplastic end of the auto-alloplastic adaption continuum, and will be discussed in some detail in the final chapter of this book.

Recently, some authors have expressed concern that by stressing environmental causes of psychological problems experienced by racial/ethnic minorities too much, counselors relieve their clients of personal responsibility for bringing about change in their lives. Parham and McDavis (1987—see Chapter 5) advise counselors to work toward changing both oppressive external environments and destructive personal behavior when counseling African American men. Parham and McDavis (1987) point out that

> restricting intervention to external factors alone, however, implies that Black men have no part in alleviating their predicament as a population at risk and that they lack the mental fortitude to deal effectively with adverse conditions in society. . . . Black men must simultaneously shoulder some of the blame for their predicament and some of the responsibility for developing personal intervention strategies that will ultimately better their condition. Counseling professionals can assist Black men in developing such strategies. (p. 24).

Parham and McDavis' point is well taken; an overemphasis on external causes of mental health problems could lead to a denial of responsibility on the part of clients for either causing or resolving the problems. However, we also feel that since most counselors have been trained to view client problems as having an internal etiology and to treat mental health problems with strategies that assume an intrapsychic cause, the threat of misdiagnosing an external cause is greater than that of misdiagnosing an internal cause.

Summary

This review of the explanations for underutilization of community mental health services by racial/ethnic minorities suggests that lack of mental health problems is not a valid reason. Racial/ethnic minorities experience the same psychological problems as European Americans; due to the added stress associated with oppression, they may actually experience a greater threat to mental health than do most European Americans. Also, blaming underuse on values inherent in the racial/ethnic minority culture fails to recognize that there are European American values inherent in conventional psychotherapy therapy. Hence, a more accurate representation is that a conflict exists between the values inherent in the client's culture *and* in conventional psychotherapy, a conflict the counselor can resolve by providing a more culturally relevant form of help.

Although professional organizations have moved a long way since 1969, it is evident that professional commitment to such efforts as providing ethnically diverse counselors, training in cross-cultural counseling, and alternative ways of conceptualizing client problems is still lacking. Thus, we feel the mental health professions must accept a major share of the responsibility for underutilization of services by racial/ethnic minorities.

Barriers to Minority Counselor-Minority or Majority Client Counseling

As used in the counseling literature, minority group counseling frequently implies that the counselor is a member of the dominant culture and the client a minority group member, suggesting that this combination is of greatest threat to effective counseling. A few authors have referred to the problems encountered in counseling when the client and counselor are from the same racial/ethnic group. Virtually none have discussed the difficulties experienced when the counselor is from a different minority group than the client. Lest the impression be given that culturally related barriers only exist for the majority counselor-minority client dyad, we now turn briefly to difficulties experienced by minority counselors and their clients.

Intra-Minority Group Counseling

Several authors have identified problems that the racial/ethnic minority counselor may encounter when working with a client from a cultural background similar to that of the counselor. Jackson (1973) points out that the minority client may respond with anger when confronted by a minority counselor. The anger may result from finding a minority person associated with a majority controlled institution. Some clients may experience anger, on the other hand, because they feel a majority counselor would be more competent, thus enhancing the probability of problem resolution. Or the client's anger may reflect jealousy that the counselor has succeeded through personal efforts in breaking out of a repressive environment. In the case of a minority counselor, the counselor may also be seen as

> . . . too white in orientation to be interested in helping, as less competent than his colleagues, as too far removed from problems that face the patient, or as intolerant and impatient with the patient's lack of success in dealing with problems (Jackson 1973, p. 277).

The minority counselor may respond to minority client anger by becoming defensive (Jackson, 1973), thus impeding the counseling process. Minority counselors may also either deny identification with or overidentify with the client (Gardner, 1971). Sattler (1970) has suggested that minority counselors may have less tolerance and understanding of minority clients and view the contact as low status work compared with counseling a majority client.

Calnek (1970) points out that the danger exists that minority counselors too often adopt stereotypes that Whites have developed concerning how minority clients think, feel and act. The counselor may deny that the client is also a minority person, for fear the common identification will result in a loss of professional image for the counselor. Over-identification, on the other hand, may cause the counseling experience to degenerate into a gripe session. Calnek also refers to the danger of the counselor projecting his/her own self-image onto the client because they are culturally similar.

Sue (1988) points out that "ethnicity per se tells us very little about the attitudes, values, experiences, and behaviors of *individuals*" and that "ethnic matches can result in cultural mismatches if therapists and clients from the same ethnic group show markedly different values" (p. 306).

Inter-Minority Group Counseling

Counselors representing one racial/ethnic minority group who find themselves working with a client representing a different racial/ethnic minority group often face the problems associated with both the majority counselor-minority client and the intra-minority group counseling situations. Although the camaraderie of racial/ethnic minorities that results from awareness of shared oppression helps to bridge cultural differences on college and university campuses, in the nonacademic world these differences are often as intense or more intense than those between the dominant and minority cultures. One need only observe Mexican American students and parents in East Los Angeles, or Black students and parents in Bedford-Stuyvesant to gain an appreciation of ethnocentrism and the difficulty which culturally different minority counselors can perceive in these situations. Furthermore, the counselor representing a different racial/ethnic minority than the client may be suspect to the client, for the same reasons counselors of similar minority backgrounds would be suspect.

Potential Benefits in Cross-Cultural Counseling

Almost no attention has been given in the counseling literature to identifying the benefits of cross-cultural counseling. In reference to the minority counselor-majority client dyad, Jackson (1973) suggests that the client may find it easier to, ". . . share information that is looked on as socially unacceptable without censor from the therapist" (p. 275), suggesting self-disclosure, at least of some materials, may be enhanced. Students who are rebelling against the Establishment, for instance, may prefer a minority counselor, feeling that the counselor's experience with oppression qualifies him/her to acquire empathy with the client (Gardner, 1971). Gardner (1971) also suggests majority clients may prefer minority counselors if they are dealing with material that would be embarrassing to share with a majority counselor. Jackson (1973) points out that there is a tendency in this situation to perceive the counselor more as another person than as a superhuman, notwithstanding those cases where the counselor is perceived as a "super-minority." In the latter case, the client may view the minority counselor as more capable than his/her majority counterpart, owing to the obstacles the counselor had to overcome. The net effect in this case may be a positive expectation. The possibility that minority counselors are less likely to let secrets filter back into the client's community is also cited by Gardner (1971) as a positive variable in cross-cultural counseling.

Several authors (Draguns, 1975, 1976; Trimble, 1976), while referring in part to national cultures, have suggested that cross-cultural counseling is a learning experience to be valued in and of itself. The counseling process, with its intentional provision for self-disclosure of attitudes, values and intense emotional feelings, can help the counselor and client gain a perspective on each other's culture, frequently in a way never experienced outside of counseling. Cross-cultural counseling also offers an opportunity to both counselor and client to expand their modes of communication, to learn new ways of interacting. Rather than being viewed as a deficit, client (and counselor) bilingualism should be viewed and treated as a strength.

It seems evident that further research and discussion are needed regarding both the barriers and benefits of cross-cultural counseling. Those discussed above, along with several proposed by the current authors, are outlined in table 3.1. In addition to citing positive and negative aspects of cross-cultural situations, the authors have attempted to identify their counterparts when counselor and client are culturally similar.

Table 3.1
Culturally Relevant Barriers and Benefits in Inter- and Intra-Cultural Counseling

Inter-Cultural Counseling	
Barriers	*Benefits*
—client resistance	—client's willingness to self-disclose some material
—client transference	—client less likely to view counselor as omniscient
—client cultural restraints on self-disclosure	—client expectation for success may be enhanced
—client expectations	—potential for considerable cultural learning by both client and counselor
—counselor countertransference	—increased need for counselor and client to focus on their own processing
—counselor maladjustment to the relationship	—potential for dealing with culturally dissonant component of client problem
—counselor misdirected diagnosis	
—counselor patronization of client's culture	
—counselor denial of culturally dissonant component of client problem	
—counselor "missionary zeal"	
—language differences	
—value conflicts	

Intra-Cultural Counseling	
Barriers	*Benefits*
—unjustified assumption of shared feelings	—shared experience may enhance rapport
—client transference	—client willingness to self-disclose some materials
—counselor countertransference	

Editors' View

The editors of this book are in agreement with those earlier writers who have suggested that cross-cultural counseling can not only be effective for resolving client difficulties, but can also serve as a forum for a unique learning experience. That barriers to cross-cultural counseling exist is not at issue here. Clearly, cultural differences between counselor and client can result in barriers that are, in some instances, insurmountable. As suggested earlier, however, we believe cross-cultural counseling can actually involve benefits to both client and counselor that may not be possible in intra-cultural counseling. No one has yet offered conclusive evidence that differences in status variables (e.g., race, ethnicity, sex, sexual orientation) alone create barriers to counseling. The fact that one person in a counseling dyad is born Black and one White, for instance, should not negate the possibility of their working together effectively. From our perspective, it is how we perceive and experience our and our client's Blackness and Whiteness that creates barriers to constructive communication. For the most part, our perceptions and experiences are shaped by a socialization process that begins at birth. We feel that the conventional counseling role (nonequalitarian, intrapsychic model, office-bound, etc.) often helps to perpetuate the very socialization process that creates a barrier between culturally different individuals.

The results of several recent studies support the hypothesis that cultural sensitivity on the part of the counselor can help overcome some of the barriers that exist when the counselor and client are ethnically different. Pomales, Claiborn, and LaFromboise (1986) found that Black college students rated a White counselor who acknowledged and showed interest in the role of culture in the client's problem more positively than they did a "cultural blind" (one who minimized the importance of culture and shifted the conversation to other factors) White counselor. A replication of the Pomales et al. (1986) study with Asian American students found that the counselor was rated more credible and culturally competent when portrayed as culturally sensitive than when portrayed as culturally blind, regardless of ethnicity (Gim, Atkinson, & Kim, 1991). These findings suggest that cultural sensitivity can enhance the counselor's credibility (and presumably effectiveness) with a culturally different client. Furthermore, a series of studies employing a paired-comparison technique for assessing preferences for counselor characteristics suggests some counselor characteristics may be more important to clients than racial/ethnic similarity per se (Atkinson, Furlong, & Poston, 1986; Atkinson, Poston, Furlong, & Mercado, 1989; Ponterotto, Alexander, & Hinkston, 1988; Bennett & Big Foot-Sipes, in press).

There is also reason to believe that it can be helpful in counseling if the counselor and client are at different stages of racial identity development. Helms (1984, 1990) has developed an Interaction Model of Counseling based on the Black and White racial identity development theories described briefly in Chapter 2. Based on the counselor and client stages of racial identity development, four types of relationships are possible: parallel, crossed, progressive, and regressive. These relationships are present in both racially similar and dissimilar dyads. When counselors and clients are of the same race and are at the same stage of racial identity development, a parallel relationship exists. A crossed relationship exists when a racially similar counselor and client are at diametrically opposite stages of racial identity development, i.e., they have opposing attitudes (e.g., Preencounter/Immersion or Reintegration/Autonomy). A progressive relationship for a racially similar dyad is one in which the counselor's stage of racial consciousness is at least one stage more advanced than the client's (e.g., Reintegration/Contact or Immersion/Encounter). And a regressive relationship is one in which the client's stage of development is at least one stage more advanced than the counselor's.

When the counselor and client are racially dissimilar, parallel dyads are those in which counselors and clients share similar attitudes about Blacks and Whites (e.g., Autonomy/Internalization). Crossed dyads are those characterized by opposing attitudes toward Blacks and Whites (e.g., Immersion/Reintegration).

The effects of parallel, crossed, progressive, and regressive dyads on counseling outcomes is complex and the reader is referred to Helms (1990) for a more extended discussion. For our purposes, the model is useful because it suggests that some crossed dyads, particularly those involved in progressive relationships, can result in positive counseling outcomes.

Some critics will argue that differences in experiences are paramount, that a counselor who experiences being African American will understand the African American client's perspective better than any European American counselor ever can. We agree to a point. There is simply no conclusive evidence, however, that a counselor must experience everything his/her client does. Carried to the extreme, the similarity of experience argument suggests that all counseling is doomed to failure since no two individuals can ever fully share the same life experiences. Furthermore, while cultural differences do result in unique experiences for both the client and the counselor, our experiences as human beings are remarkably similar. This view—that we are more alike than different—is perhaps best expressed by the sociobiologist De Vore (1977):

> Anthropologists always talk about crosscultural diversity, but that's icing on the cake. The cake itself is remarkably panhuman. Different cultures turn out only minor variations on the theme of the species—human courtship, our mating system, child care, fatherhood, the treatment of the sexes, love, jealousy, sharing. Almost everything that's importantly human—including

behavior flexibility—is universal, and developed in the context of our shared genetic background (p. 88).

References

Abramowitz, S. I., & Murray, J. (1983). Race effects in psychotherapy. In J. Murray & P. R. Abramson (Eds.), *Bias in psychotherapy* (pp. 215–255). New York: Praeger.

Atkinson, D. R. (1983). Ethnic minority representation in counselor education. *Counselor Education and Supervision, 23*, 7–19.

Atkinson, D. R. (1983). Ethnic similarity in counseling psychology: A review of research. *The Counseling Psychologist, 11*(3), 79–92.

Atkinson, D. R. (1985). A meta-review of research on cross-cultural counseling and psychotherapy. *Journal of Multicultural Counseling and Development, 13*, 138–153.

Atkinson, D. R. (1986). Cultural issues in school and family. In L. Golden & D. Capuzzi (Eds.), *Helping families help children: Family interventions with school-related problems.*

Atkinson, D. R., Casas, J. M., & Wampold, B. (1981). The categorization of ethnic stereotypes by university counselors. *Hispanic Journal of Behavioral Sciences, 3*, 75–82.

Atkinson, D. R., Jennings, R. G., & Liongson, L. (1990). Minority students' reasons for not seeking counseling and suggestions for improving services. *Journal of College Student Development, 31*, 342–350.

Atkinson, D. R., & Juntunen, C. (in press). School counselors and school psychologists as school-home-community liaisons in ethnically diverse schools. In P. Pedersen & J. Carey (Eds.), *Multicultural counseling in the schools: A practical handbook.* Boston: Allyn and Bacon.

Atkinson, D. R., Maruyama, M., & Matsui, S. (1978). The effects of counselor race and counseling approach on Asian Americans' perceptions of counselor credibility and utility. *Journal of Counseling Psychology, 25*, 76–83.

Atkinson, D. R., & Matsushita, Y. J. (in press). *Journal of Counseling Psychology, 38.*

Atkinson, D. R., & Wampold, B. (1981). Affirmative action efforts of counselor education programs. *Counselor Education and Supervision, 20*, 262–272.

Bennett, S. K., & Big Foot-Sipes, D. S. (1991). American Indian and White college student preferences for counselor characteristics. *Journal of Counseling Psychology, 38*, 440–445.

Bernal, M. E., & Padilla, A. M. (1982). Status of minority curricula and training in clinical psychology. *American Psychologist, 37*, 780–787.

Boxley, R., & Wagner, N. N. (1971). Clinical psychology training programs and minority groups: A survey. *Professional Psychology, 2*, 75–81.

Canino, I. A., Earley, B. F., & Rogler, L. H. (1980). *The Puerto Rican child in New York City: Stress and mental health* (Monograph No. 4). New York: Hispanic Research Center, Fordham University.

Cannon, M. S., & Locke, B. Z. (1977). Being black is detrimental to one's mental health: Myth or reality? *Phylon, 38*, 408–428.

Carney, C. G., & Kahn, K. B. (1984). Building competencies for effective cross-cultural counseling: A developmental view. *The Counseling Psychologist, 12,* 111–119.

Casas, J. M. (1984). Policy, training, and research in counseling psychology: The racial/ethnic minority perspective. In S. D. Brown & R. W. Lent (Eds.), *Handbook of counseling psychology* (pp. 785–831). New York: John Wiley.

Casas, J. M., Ponterotto, J. G., & Gutierrez, J. M. (1986). An ethical indictment of counseling research and training: The cross-cultural perspective. *Journal of Counseling and Development, 64,* 347–349.

Cheatham, H. E., Shelton, T. O, & Ray, W. J. (1987). Race, sex, causal attribution, and help-seeking behavior. *Journal of College Student Personnel, 28,* 559–568.

Cheung, F. K., & Snowden, L. R. (1990). Community mental health and ethnic minority populations. *Community Mental Health Journal, 26,* 277–291.

Cheung, L. R. L. (1987). *Assessing Asian language performance.* Rockville, MD: Aspen Publishers.

Chin, J. L. (1983). Diagnostic considerations in working with Asian Americans. *American Journal of Orthopsychiatry, 53,* 100–109.

Corvin, S., & Wiggins, F. (1989). An antiracism training model for White professionals. *Journal of Multicultural Counseling and Development, 17,* 105–114.

Cross, W. C., & Maldonado, B. (1971). The counselor, the Mexican American, and the stereotype. *Elementary School Guidance and Counseling, 6,* 27–31.

Esquivel, G. B., & Keitel, M. A. (1990). Counseling immigrant children in the schools. *Elementary School Guidance & Counseling, 24,* 213–221.

First, J. M. (1988). Immigrant students in U.S. public schools: Challenges with solutions. *Phi Delta Kappan, 70,* 205–209.

Gim, R. H., Atkinson, D. R., & Kim, S. J. (1991). Asian-American acculturation, counselor ethnicity and cultural sensitivity, and ratings of counselors. *Journal of Counseling Psychology, 38,* 57–62.

Harper, F. D., & Stone, W. O. (1974). Toward a theory of transcendent counseling with Blacks. *Journal of Non-White Concerns in Personnel and Guidance, 2,* 191–196.

Harrison, D. K. (1975). Race as a counselor-client variable in counseling and psychotherapy: A review of the research. *The Counseling Psychologist, 5*(1), 124–133.

Haviland, M. G., Horswill, R. K., O'Conell, J. J., & Dynneson, V. V. (1983). Native American college students preference for counselor race and sex and the likelihood of their use of a counseling center. *Journal of Counseling Psychology, 30,* 267–270.

Helms, J. E. (1984). Toward a theoretical explanation of the effects of race on counseling: A Black and White model. *The Counseling Psychologist, 12,* 153–165.

Keefe, S. E. (1978). Why Mexican Americans underutilize mental health clinics: Fact and fallacy. In J. M. Casas & S. E. Keefe (Eds.). *Family and mental health in the Mexican American community* (pp. 91–108, Monograph Number Seven). Los Angeles: University of California, Spanish Speaking Mental Health Research Center.

Kennedy, D. D., & Wagner, N. N. (1979). Psychology and affirmative action: 1977. *Professional Psychology, 10,* 234–243.

King, L. M. (1978). Social and cultural influences on psychopathology. *Annual Review of Psychology, 29,* 405–433.

Korchin, S. J. (1980). Clinical psychology and minority problems. *American Psychologist, 35,* 262–269.

Kramer, M., Rosen, B., & Willis, E. (1972). Definitions and distributions of mental disorders in a racist society. In C. Willis, B. Kramer, & B. Brown (Eds.), *Racism and mental health.* Pittsburgh: University of Pennsylvania Press.

Leong, F. T. (1986). Counseling and psychotherapy with Asian Americans: Review of literature. *Journal of Counseling Psychology, 33,* 196–206.

LeVine, E. S., & Padilla, A. M. (1980). *Crossing cultures in therapy: Pluralistic counseling for the Hispanic.* Monterey, CA: Brooks/Cole.

Lopez, S. (1981). Mexican-American usage of mental health facilities: Underutilization considered. In A. Baron, Jr. (Ed.), *Exploration in Chicano psychology.* New York: Praeger.

Lopez, S. R., Grover, K. P., Holland, D., Johnson, M. J., Kain, C. D., Kanel, K., Mellins, C. A., & Rhyne, M. C. (1989). Development of culturally sensitive psychotherapists. *Professional Psychology: Research and Practice, 20,* 369–376.

Magoon, T. M. (1988). *1987/88 College and university counseling center data bank.* College Park, MD: University of Maryland Counseling Center.

Majors, R., & Nikelly, A. (1983). Serving the Black community: A new direction for psychotherapy. *Journal of Non-White Concerns in Personnel and Guidance, 11,* 142–151.

Malgady, R. G., Rogler, L. H., & Costantino, G. (1987). Ethnocultural and linguistic bias in mental health evaluation of Hispanics. *American Psychologist, 42,* 228–234.

McFadden, J., & Lipscomb, W. D. (1985). History of the Association for Non-White Concerns in Personnel and Guidance. *Journal of Counseling and Development, 63,* 444–447.

Mio, J. S., & Morris, D. R. (1990). Cross-cultural issues in psychology training programs: An invitation for discussion. *Professional Psychology: Theory and Practice, 21,* 434–441.

Moses, S. (1990, December). Sensitivity to culture may be hard to teach: APA approves practice guidelines. *APA Monitor,* p. 39.

Nguyen, L. T., & Henkin, L. B. (1983). Change among Indochinese refugees, In R. J. Sumada & S. C. Woods (Eds.), *Perspectives in immigrant and minority education.* New York: University Press of America.

Ogbu, J. U. (1987). Variability in minority school performance: A problem in search of an explanation. *Anthropology and Education Quarterly, 18,* 312–334.

Padilla, A. M., & Ruiz, R. A. (1973). *Latino mental health: A review of literature. Washington, DC: U.S. Government Printing Office.*

Padilla, A. M., Ruiz, R. A., & Alvarez, R. (1975). Community mental health services for the Spanish-speaking/surnamed population. *American Psychologist, 30,* 892–905.

Padilla, A. M., Lindholm, K. J., Chen, A., Duran, R., Hakuta, K., Lambert, W., & Tucker, G. R. (1991). The English-only movement: Myths, reality, and implications for psychology. *American Psychologist, 46,* 120–130.

Padilla, E. R., Boxley, R., & Wagner, N. N. (1973). The desegregation of clinical psychology training. *Professional Psychology, 4,* 259–264.

Parham, W., & Moreland, J. R. (1981). Nonwhite students in counseling psychology: A closer look. *Professional Psychology, 12,* 499–507.

Pomales, J., Claiborn, C. D., & LaFromboise, T. D. (1986). Effects of Black students' racial identity on perceptions of White counselors varying in cultural sensitivity. *Journal of Counseling Psychology, 33,* 57–61.

Ponce, F. Q., & Atkinson, D. R. (1989). Mexican-American acculturation, counselor ethnicity, counseling style, and perceived counselor credibility. *Journal of Counseling Psychology, 36,* 203–208.

Ridley, C. R. (1985). Imperatives for ethnic and cultural relevance in psychology training programs. *Professional Psychology: Research and Practice, 16,* 611–622.

Romero, D. (1985). Cross-cultural counseling: Brief reactions for the practitioner. *The Counseling Psychologist, 13,* 665–671.

Rosenstein, M. J., Milazzo-Sayre, L. J., Macaskill, R. L., & Manderscheid, R. W. (1987). Use of inpatient services by special populations. In R. W. Manderscheid & S. A. Barrett (Eds.), *Mental health, United States, 1987* (DHHS Publication No. ADM 87–1518. Washington, DC: U.S. Government Printing Office.

Rumbaut, R. B. (1985). Research concerns associated with the study of Southeast Asian refugees. In T. C. Owan (Ed.), *Southeast Asian mental health treatment, prevention, services, training, and research.* Washington, DC: National Institute of Mental Health.

Russo, N. R., Olmedo, E. L., Stapp, J., & Fulcher, R. (1981). Women and minorities in psychology. *American Psychologist, 36,* 1315–1363.

Sabnani, H. B., Ponterotto, J. G., & Borodovsky, L. G. (1991). White racial identity development and cross-cultural counselor training: A stage model. *The Counseling Psychologist, 19,* 76–102.

Sanchez, A. R., & King, M. (1986). Mexican Americans' use of counseling services: Cultural and institutional factors. *Journal of College Student Personnel, 27,* 344–349.

Sattler, J. M. (1977). The effects of therapist-client racial similarity. In A. S. Gurman & A. M. Razin (Eds.), *Effective psychotherapy: A handbook of research* (pp. 252–290). New York: Pergamon Press.

Scott, N. E., & Borodovsky, L. G. (1990). Effective use of cultural role taking. *Professional Psychology: Research and Practice, 21,* 167–170.

Smalley, W. A. (1984). Adoptive language strategies of the Hmong: From Asian mountains to American ghettos. *Language Science, 1,* 240–269.

Smith, E. M. J. (1985). Ethnic minorities: Life stress, social support, and mental health issues. *The Counseling Psychologist, 13,* 537–579.

Snowden, L. R., & Cheung, F. K. (1990). Use of inpatient mental health services by members of ethnic minority groups. *American Psychologist, 45,* 347–355.

Special Populations Task Force of the President's Commission on Mental Health. (1978). *Task panel reports submitted to the President's Commission on Mental Health: Vol 3.* Washington, DC: U.S. Government Printing Office.

Stikes, C. S. (1972). Culturally specific counseling: The Black client. *Journal of Non-White Concerns in Personnel and Guidance, 1,* 15–23.

Stone, G. L., & Archer, J. (1990). College and university counseling centers in the 1990s: Challenges and limits. *The Counseling Psychologist, 18,* 539–607.

Sue, D. W. (1978). Eliminating cultural oppression in counseling: Toward a general theory. *Journal of Counseling Psychology, 25,* 419–428.

Sue, D. W. (1990). Culture-specific strategies in counseling: A conceptual framework. *Professional Psychology: Research and Practice, 21,* 424–433.

Sue, D. W., & Kirk, B. A. (1975). Asian-Americans: Use of counseling and psychiatric services on a college campus. *Journal of Counseling Psychology, 22,* 84–86.

Sue, D. W., & Sue, D. (1977). Barriers to effective cross-cultural counseling. *Journal of Counseling Psychology, 24,* 420–429.

Sue, D. W. & Sue, D. (1990). *Counseling the Culturally Different: Theory and Practice.* New York: John Wiley.

Sue, D. W., & Sue, S. (1972). Counseling Chinese-Americans. *Personnel and Guidance Journal, 50,* 637–644.

Sue, S. (1977). Community mental health services to minority groups: Some optimism, some pessimism. *American Psychologist, 32,* 616–624.

Sue, S. (1988). Psychotherapeutic services for ethnic minorities: Two decades of research findings. *American Psychologist, 43,* 301–308.

Sue, S., & McKinney, H. (1975). Asian-Americans in the community mental health care system. *American Journal of Orthopsychiatry, 45,* 111–118.

Sue, S., McKinney, H., Allen, D., & Hall, J. (1974). Delivery of community mental health services to Black and White clients. *Journal of Consulting and Clinical Psychology, 42,* 794–801.

Sue, S., & Morishima, J. K. (1982). *The mental health of Asian Americans.* San Francisco: Jossey Bass.

Sue, S., & Sue, D. W. (1974). MMPI comparisons between Asian-American and non-Asian students utilizing a student health psychiatric clinic. *Journal of Counseling Psychology, 21,* 423–427.

Sue, S., Wagner, D. J., Margullis, C., & Lew, L. (1976). Conceptions of mental illness among Asian and Caucasian American students. *Psychological Reports, 38,* 703–708.

Sue, S., & Zane, N. (1987). The role of culture and cultural techniques in psychotherapy: A critique and reformulation. *American Psychologist, 42,* 37–45.

Toldson, I. L., & Pasteur, A. B. (1972). Soul Music: Techniques for therapeutic intervention. *Journal of Non-White Concerns in Personnel and Guidance, 1,* 31–39.

Torres-Matrullo, C. (1976). Acculturation and psychopathology among Puerto Rican women in mainland United States. *American Journal of Orthopsychiatry, 46,* 710–719.

Wampold, B., Casas, J. M., & Atkinson, D. R. (1982). Ethnic bias in counseling: An information-processing approach. *Journal of Counseling Psychology, 28,* 489–503.

Wu, I. H., & Windle, C. (1980). Ethic specificity in the relationship of minority use and staffing of community mental health centers. *Community Mental Health Journal, 16,* 156–168.

Young, R. L., Chamley, J. D., & Withers, C. (1990). Minority faculty representation and hiring practices in counselor education programs. *Counselor Education and Supervision, 29,* 148–154.

PART 2

The African American Client

For centuries, we have struggled to resolve a basic contradiction in our society, one which espouses the democratic principles of "liberty" and "justice," while denying these rights to African Americans. John Gardner (1968), in the book, *No Easy Victories*, writes,

> The problem of justice for the Negro has gnawed on the national consciousness ever since this nation was founded. It is, in an important sense, the American problem. If any problem is especially and peculiarly ours, with roots in our history and scars in our memory, this is it. No other modern problem touches more profoundly the values we profess to cherish. (p. 17).

Gardner concluded that history had handed his generation the task of solving it.

A quarter century later, some are claiming that we have answered the call of history, that the mistreatment of the African American has ended. They point to civil rights laws which grant African Americans the same rights as other Americans, to affirmative action programs which give "special privileges" to minorities, and to numerous gains—in education, elected offices, and general standards of living. Even Hollywood has gotten the message and expanded its line-up to African American sitcoms that portray highly affluent and well-educated African American families like "The Jeffersons," "The Cosby Show" and "Fresh Prince." African American sports giants like Michael Jordan, Bo Jackson, and Daryl Strawberry are portrayed as multimillion dollar franchises, while Bill Cosby and his wife pique the interests of talk show and tabloid audiences by their donation of 20 million dollars to an African American college.

But there is a danger in this imaging (apart from the obvious distortions) that deserves attention. In spite of enormous evidence to the contrary, African Americans historically have been viewed and, for the most part, treated in homogeneous terms—poor, lazy, violent, and more recently, rich. So, regardless of whether the label is positive or negative, some segments of the group are always left out. The danger in accepting this exaggerated view of this group—as having overcome or as being exceptionally well-off—is that the needs of other segments of the community, such as the disfranchised poor or the struggling middle class, are often ignored.

Yet, there is an even greater danger. We may also come to accept the illusion that all racial/ethnic groups have an equal chance of succeeding. To be sure, this is not a new idea. White supremacist groups obviously have argued this for centuries. But in recent years a small group of neoconservative African Americans have also been accused of holding similar views (MacNeil/Lehrer, 1991). African American conservatives like Professor Shelby Steele and Mr. William Raspberry, who fall into this group, acknowledge that discrimination still exists, but downplay the influence it has over group success. In the article, "The Myth that is Crippling Black America," Raspberry (1990) argues that African Americans have accepted, "the myth that racism is the dominant influence in our lives." He asserts that African Americans are not deprived of their rights.

> They (African Americans) can vote, live where their money permits them, eat where their appetites dictate, work at jobs for which their skills qualify them. They have their civil rights. (p. 96).

Yet, it is difficult to overlook the negative attitudes and racial violence that have lately emerged. For example, a recent survey of racial attitudes found that three out of four Whites believe Black and Hispanic people are lazier, less intelligent, less patriotic, and more prone to violence than Whites, findings that closely parallel those reported by Katz and Baraly over a half century ago (1933). Similar attitudes were also found in a survey reported in the *L.A. Times* which asked a group of Whites to identify the group they viewed least favorably: 44 percent said Blacks, 38 percent said Latinos, and 24 percent said Asians (1989).

There is also evidence to suggest that these attitudes are responsible for an increase in racial conflicts. Between 1987 and 1989, one hundred and sixty colleges reported racial incidents aimed at African Americans, Latinos, and Asians (*L.A. Times*, 1989). Numerous cases of racism within the housing industry—from mortgage lenders to realtors—have also been recorded (*U.S. News & World Report*, 1991). Even among the nation's police forces, charged with enforcing our law, incidents of race discrimination have been reported. Perhaps the most blatant (certainly the most publicized) example involved a videotaped beating of an African American motorist by members of the Los Angeles Police Department. A commission investigating the incident reported, "Racism in the department is as raw as the message sent from one White officer to another regarding the event: 'Sounds like monkey-slapping time' " (*U.S. News & World Report*, 1991, p. 18).

Much as we would like to believe that we have solved the "race problem" in our generation, examples like these leave little doubt that the problem still exists. Unfortunately, while we continue to debate the questions, millions of African American women and men struggle to stay afloat. Young, in the first article to this section, "Psychodynamics of Coping and Survival of the African American Female in a Changing World," provides insight into how African American women can better cope with the confounding problems of race and gender. A number of dysfunctional behaviors within the group are identified and addressed as well as a sociocultural context for understanding and responding to these problems. As Young suggests, the African American female represents only half of the equation. The African American male is also encumbered by a myriad of socio-racial pressures that some feel threaten the gender with extinction. Parham and McDavis in the article, "Black Men, An Endangered Species: Who's Really Pulling the Trigger?" provides a litany of statistical evidence which supports this conclusion. They examine a host of contributing factors and make a number of recommendations which can be useful to counselors and other helping professionals.

The final article to this section, "Culturally Sensitive Therapy with Black Clients," combines the African American male and female experience under the umbrella of the family. Critical issues essential to working with the African American family are outlined and discussed. Basic strategies for heightening counseling effectiveness are also presented.

References

Anderson, D. E. (1985, October 28). The struggle over the definition of our rights, *Christianity and Crisis,* pp. 417–420.

Ellis, J. E. (1990, January 22). What black families need to make the dream come true, *Business Week,* p. 29.

Gardner, John W. (1968). *No easy victories.* New York: Harper & Row.

Horton, C. P., and Smith, J. C. (1990). *Statistical Record of Black America,* Gale Research Institute, p. 484.

Katz, D., and Baraly, K. (1933). Racial stereotypes of one hundred college students, *Journal of Abnormal and Social Psychology, 28,* 280–90.

MacNeil/Lehrer NewsHour transcript, *Black perspectives,* September 6, 1991.

Painton, P. (1991, May 27). Quota quagmire, *Time,* p. 20.

Parham, T. A., and McDavis, R. J. (1987). Black men, an endangered species: who's really pulling the trigger? *Journal of Counseling and Development, 66,* 24–27.

Rainie, H., Minerbrook, S., Cooper, M., Johnson, C., Roberts, S. V., and Gest, T. (1991, July 22). Black & white in America, *U.S. News & World Report,* pp. 18–21.

Raspberry, W. (1990). The myth that is crippling black America, *Reader's Digest,* pp. 96–98.

Riechmann, D. (1989, April 30). Colleges tackle increase in racism on campuses, *Los Angeles Times,* I, p. 36.

Roberts, S. V. (1989, July 10). For the civil-rights lobby, a time to regroup, *U.S. News & World Report,* p. 30.

4

Psychodynamics of Coping and Survival of the African American Female in a Changing World

Carlene Young

Scientific breakthroughs, technological advances, and the overall, rapid pace of modern urban life are the hallmarks of the present century. The highest standard of living in the world has not been achieved without cost. African Americans, historically isolated from the mainstream, have been unable to resist the allure of this momentum that surges forth into the 21st century. African Americans can be considered more spectators than true participants in the technological renaissance. That is, the objective conditions of life confronting the majority of persons of African ancestry are still predominately those of poverty, limited employment, thwarted educational opportunities, discrimination, and overt/covert acts of racism.

Some individual African Americans have benefited from employment opportunities in professions formerly not available to their predecessors. Swinton (1988: 130) states that "in fact, there has been an increase in proportion of African Americans who can be classified as upper middle class." Yet no people have ever been judged by the condition of its exceptions. Although an African American's median income has increased in absolute dollars since 1970 (with the exception of 1982), the startling reality is one where "average median Black income for the 1990s is only $16,476 as compared to $17,765 for the 1970s" (Swinton, 1988: 132). Another view of this inequity is disclosed by the fact that the spending power of the typical African American family is considerably less than it is for the typical White family. In 1986, the median African American family had only $568 to spend for every $1,000 the median White family had to

Reprinted from *Journal of Black Studies, 20,* 208–223, 1989. © Sage Publications, Inc. Reprinted by permission of Sage Publications, Inc.

spend (Swinton, 1988: 132). Although income is not the sole indicator of a group's condition, it is a clear barometer of life chances or access to the opportunity structure.

The limited availability of employment and structural factors contribute to the maintenance of an inequitable system. There is a plethora of data that demonstrate the oppressive conditions that persist in African American communities (National Urban League, 1988; Blackwell, 1985; Pinknney, 1984). As an active and integral member of that community, the African American female has a historical legacy of experiencing these circumstances in the most exaggerated manner. How, then, does one develop effective coping and survival skills for chronic inequities which are institutionalized on a systematic basis? Socioeconomic conditions constitute significant stressors in their own right. The increased suicides among European Americans during periods of major recessions are graphic demonstrations of this point. Yet, the African American female who has the least amount of resources, lowest social status, and remains at the bottom of the socioeconomic scale assumes her role of responsibility with equanimity.

This article provides a sociopsychological analysis—within a sociohistorical framework—of contributing factors that account for increased stressors and dysfunctionality in the lives of contemporary African American females.

The stereotypic portrayal of African American women as the epitome of "strength" and as long-suffering, "motherly types" with limited individual needs is subscribed to by the majority culture. This is not to say that there are no behavior patterns that mesh with this stereotype. The difficulty lies more in the circumstances of increasing numbers of women of African ancestry, or in describing their behavior and accomplishments according to this stereotype. One insidious aspect of the stereotype is the victim's (subject's) acceptance of the stereotypic depiction as reality with subsequent internationalization of this model.

In other words, too many contemporary females are caught in the "double bind" of attempting to assume the mantle of "strength" and to function as the idealized "strong woman." The "strong woman" confronts all trials and tribulations on behalf of those she loves, perseveres with no attention to her needs as an individual or woman, and provides unlimited support and encouragement necessary for her husband/lover. The more potent the imagery of this mythical figure, the more inadequate the woman must be who believes that this is her reference point for authenticity. These qualities were idealized as heroic and evidence of the outstanding character of pioneer women (European Americans) as they stood by their men. These same attributes when applied to the African American woman are perceived by the society in general, including some African American males and females, as being negative and unfeminine. At the other end of the continuum, there is the depiction of the African American female as the seductress, the highly sexual being who is responsible for her exploitation. Somewhere in the middle of these extremes, the African American female finds herself attempting to establish an identity and to define herself.

Historical Perspective

The mystique and fascination/abhorrence with which African Americans have been regarded in the United States society is nowhere more apparent than in the depiction of the African American woman. The arrival of the African woman on the shores of the New World as slave and mother involved her in a symbolic transformation that continues to reverberate. The autonomy and independence that she enjoyed in her kinship communities were never totally expunged from her consciousness, and became part of the social heritage transmitted to each generation. As Aidoo (1981) states:

> It is too often forgotten that many Africans brought to this land, although enslaved were in varying ranges of adulthood; members of kinship communities with values, norms, expectations of behavior and had formal institutions that prescribed roles and functions obligation to kin and fellow slaves were part of the lessons taught children.

An Asante proverb reminds us that "it's a woman who gave birth to a man; it's a woman who gave birth to a chief" (Young, 1986). This proverb also speaks to the significant role of African women in terms of their status in the community and the special relationship with their children. Sudarkasa (1981b: 43) points out that:

> even though women were subordinate in their roles as wives, as mothers and sisters they wielded considerable authority, power, and influence. This distinction in the power attached to women's roles is symbolized by the fact that in the same society were wives knelt before their husbands, sons prostrated before their mothers and seniority as determined by age, rather than gender, governed relationships among siblings.

Marriage was the union of kinship groups. The extended family was the arbiter of standards and principles of behavior. "Interpersonal relationships within African families were governed by principles and values of respect, restraint, responsibility, and reciprocity" (Sudarkasa, 1981b: 44).

The African woman was independent because she worked and had complete control of her earnings. To again quote Sudarkasa (1981a):

> In most societies it was usual for females as well as males to be engaged in activities—such as farming, trading, craft production, or food-processing. . . .

The important economic roles of women in traditional West Africa were part and parcel of the overall domestic roles of wife, mother, sister, and daughter, around which the lives of most females were ordered. At the same time, through their economic roles, women played an important part in the "public sphere."

The dehumanization of African men and women required concerted efforts to obliterate culture, value, traditions, and institutions. Slave ships were crucibles where the alchemy of white superiority, religiosity, and brutality fermented the creation of the Negro—the inferior—with no life, history, or reality other than that given by the slave master. The depiction of the African male as the oversexed savage was more easily manipulated than that of the African female. The African female, while also subhuman with the vicissitudes of the male, required some minimum humane qualities in order to justify her further exploitation and usefulness as substitute caretaker, nursemaid, or "mammy." Du Bois tells us that "the crushing weight of slavery fell on Black women." In *The Damnation of Women,* Du Bois (1969: 169) avows:

> I shall forgive the white South much in its final judgment day; I shall forgive its slavery, for slavery is a world-old habit; . . . but one thing I shall never forgive, neither in this world nor the world to come: its wanton and continued and persistent insulting of the black womanhood which it sought and seeks to prostitute to its lust. I cannot forget that it is such Southern gentlemen into whose hands smug Northern hypocrites of today are seeking to place our women's eternal destiny—men who insist upon withholding from my mother and wife and daughter those signs and appellations of courtesy and respect which elsewhere he withholds only from bawds and courtesans.

Despite the historical reality of having endured some of the most brutal treatment ever perpetuated by one group on another, the African American has managed to survive to the end of the twentieth century. The extended family was instrumental in transmitting the true feelings, experiences, and effective means of developing a repertoire of survival skills. There was a forum for interpreting a hostile and dangerous environment. Young women learned role responsibilities. They also learned that they had the right to be treated with dignity and respect, and therefore felt comfortable in demanding that right as the medium for exchange and discourse.

The present day isolation in urban centers is significantly different from the isolation that accompanied segregation and Jim Crow. The latter engendered mutual support and interdependence in order to survive; group membership was essential, and group identity was frequently a badge of courage.

Sociocultural Context

The liberating aspects of the Black consciousness movement in the 1960s, a period of hard-won civil rights, and increased opportunity in some areas resulted in a unique set of circumstances for the beneficiaries of that movement. The children born to the young adults of the mid-1960s have reached adulthood. They grew up in a sociocultural environment that, for the most part, abandoned the overt, brutal manifestation of oppression, such as lynchings, public humiliation, and blatant discrimination. The rhetoric of equal opportunity, affirmative action, and full rights of citizenship served as palliatives to mask the persistent, institutionalized racism and oppression.

If one can speak of a people as an acting entity, it was as though there was a collective sigh of relief, and a generation accepted the illusion of equality and equal opportunity as real. Nonacknowledgment of the problem and either the inability or unwillingness to confront the subtle manifestations of racism by parents/mentors of cohorts born in the 1960s and 1970s had unwittingly crippled their progeny, and in effect they engaged in mass denial and repression. Denial and repression are psychological modes of adaptation or ego defenses that protect the personality. Anna Freud (1936) defined denial (motivated negation) as the "blocking of external events from entry into awareness, when perception of such stimuli is symbolically or associatively related to threatening impulses. Denial abolishes dangers 'out there' by negating them." She also stated that repression (motivated forgetting) involves an absence of ordinary drive components found in a "normal person" and constitutes "abrupt and involuntary removal from awareness of any threatening idea or memory. Most dangerous and one of the most archaic defenses, Repression or Denial is the prerequisite for any of the other defense mechanisms." These are but two of many counterproductive coping postures taken by individuals.

Sociologists present the problem as minority group response to subordinate status or dominance in intergroup relations, and identify four common patterns of reaction: acceptance, aggression, avoidance, and assimilation. Assimilation, or attempts to become socially and culturally fused with the dominant group, and Avoidance, or attempts to shun—or escape from—situations in which they are likely to experience prejudice and discrimination, are poles of one continuum (Zanden, 1983: 311).

The problems of assimilation are long-standing and have been addressed by all manner of experts. In addition to the intergroup process, assimilation occurs when minority-group individuals "undertake to lose their distinct minority-group identity and fuse themselves socially and culturally with the dominant group" (Zanden, 1983: 355). The assimilationist mode is more characteristic of children born in the 1960s and 1970s than at any other period of African American history. Some of this process can, of course, be attributed to the natural phenomena of social change and the continuity and discontinuity between generations.

The predicament lies in the fact that declamations of European Americans are assimilationist, but the institutions, socioeconomic structures, and political systems are in fact committed to exclusionary practices and continued subordination of African Americans. The significant difference from the historical integrationist mode stems from the perceived believability of being in an open society and as the beneficiaries of revolutionary changes resulting from the social upheaval of the 1960s. A more accurate depiction is one of "reform and incremental changes consistent with the nature of the system [which] make it more of what it theoretically is supposed to be" (Katz, 1983), rather than revolution. Fanon's (1967) analysis of a native people's adaptation to a colonial oppressor has universal applications:

> The Negro problem does not resolve itself into the problems of Negroes living among white men but rather of Negroes exploited, enslaved, despised by a colonialist, capitalist society that is only accidentally white.

Memmi (1967) in *The Colonizer and the Colonized,* establishes that "there are neither good nor bad colonists: there are colonists." Friere (1968: 31) described the relationship between oppressor and oppressed as one of prescription or "imposition of one man's choice upon another, transforming the consciousness of the man prescribed to into one that conforms with the prescriber's consciousness."

In this context, assimilation demands both rejection, implicit or explicit, of essential parts of oneself and internalization of the idealized other.

> The oppressed, having internalized the image of the oppressor and adopted his guidelines, are fearful of freedom. Freedom would require them to eject this image and replace it with autonomy and responsibility. It must be pursued constantly and responsibly. . . . It is the indispensable condition for the quest for human completion [Friere, 1968: 31].

Fanon (1967) provides an example from Martinique:

> It is understandable that the first action of the black man [woman] is a reaction, and since the Negro is appraised in terms of the extent of his assimilation, it is also understandable why the newcomer expresses himself only in French. It is because he wants to emphasize the rupture that has now occurred. He is incarnating a new type of man that he imposes on his associates and family.

Equivalent behavior is evidenced on a group basis by youth who overidentify with mass culture, as evidenced by the androgynous postures of the Michael Jackson and Prince phenomena.

The "bad girl" modeling of female media personalities promotes the "whorish" aspects of femininity and behavioral standards that are oppositional to traditional values in African American communities. The evolution of "Buppies" as clones of "Yuppies" is a parallel development at the adult level. Katz (1983: 36) reminds us that "the mass media in the United States have been a strong force in creating commonalty of attitudes and tastes." "Inauthentic" African Americans who assume positions of authority and proceed to act against the interests of the African American community are contemporary examples. Inauthenticity refers to posturing an African American identity of values and commitment but secretly seeking validation from Whites.

The Problem Identified

The crucial questions posed are (1) How does the individual adapt to the circumstances without losing his or her authenticity? and (2) How does one recognize the dysfunctional behavior in order to provide alternative approaches for effective coping strategies?

Contemporary urban life, characterized by alienation and diminished group identity, constitutes a perilous set of circumstances in a society that has not relinquished its need for white supremacy. Stress, adequate coping patterns, and realized potential are recurrent themes in the popular literature.

Although generally excluded from mainstream issues, African Americans are increasingly confronting these issues as separate and distinct concerns, rather than in the traditional, extended-family networks. The mutual aid system based on the African heritage of communalism, interdependence, and emotional and material support, which characterized relationships in the extended family, is being displaced by "urban values of individualism, secularism, and materialism" (Martin and Martin, 1978: 90). The problem is defined by Martin and Martin (p. 91) as one where

> human relationships among urban blacks are atomized for the most part. The attention of most extended family members is focused on their own lives, not on that of the community . . . Economic strain and constant residential and occupational mobility make it difficult to keep close contact even with family and friends. [They] have little confidence that any effort to come together with others could result in positive changes in their lives.

No one would attempt to argue that modern-day living is more stressful than the historic past of African Americans. The indicators suggest, however, that the support mechanisms, renewal systems, and opportunities for actualization that evolved and persisted throughout slavery, and the violence and intimidation periods that followed are now succumbing to the "good life." This is not to imply that African American community members have been decimated and that the extended family no longer perseveres as one of the single most important institutions in the African American experience. On the contrary, the most intact persons—those who are truly successful, in terms of self-acceptance, positive identity, actualization of their potential, and acceptance of others on their own merits—are active members of their extended-family networks. Pinderhughes (1982: 113), in *Afro-American Families and the Victim System,* summarizes the consensus of social research findings that "biculturality can cause strain and take a heavy toll in emotional stress and identity confusion, but it can also create exceptional strength, flexibility, and tolerance for diversity."

The manifestation of dysfunctional adaptations to the complexity, ambiguity, excessively competitive, and high-pressured contacts in personal and professional encounters take a variety of forms. Table 4.1 provides a listing of the more obvious ones with the affiliated psychological or ego defenses which they represent.

The majority society engages in equal or greater measures of dysfunctional or psychopathic behavior at great cost to its psychic equilibrium, institutional integrity, and individual mental health. "Confusion, conflict, moral cynicism, and disrespect for authority may arise in majority group children as a consequence of being taught the moral, religious and democratic principles of the brotherhood of man and the importance of justice and fair play by the same person and institutions who, in their support of racial segregation and relation practice, seem to be acting in a prejudiced and discriminatory manner" (Spurlock, 1973).

Alternative Approaches

The prior discussion demonstrates a signal factor in any analysis of African American women. That is, the discussion must, of necessity, deal with the African American community and the contextual interaction patterns and myriad role relationships, which include group (African American), mother, lover, daughter, sister, friend, worker, professional, and so on.

The African American female has traditionally mediated the environment and anchored her community. Studies of social change on White women have determined that

> over the course of a lifetime, the average woman experiences more role changes (acquisitions and losses, for example, of family and work roles) than does the average man (who tends to enact work and family roles simultaneously rather than alternatively). . . . Women's life changes (whether role changes or variations in role enactments) are also more likely than men's to be the result of, or at least related to, changes in the lives of their intimates [Stewart and Platt, 1983].

Table 4.1

DYSFUNCTIONAL BEHAVIOR	DEFENSE MECHANISMS*
1. UNIVERSALISTS: non-racial identity, e.g., American, human being	1. DENIAL (Motivated Negation)
2. EXCEPTIONS: not like other Blacks; intelligence, wit, attractiveness, make them special and acceptable to Whites	2. REPRESSION (Motivated forgetting) REACTION FORMATION (Believing the opposite)
3. JANUSES: militant to Blacks subservient to Whites	3. IDENTIFICATION-WITH-THE-AGGRESSOR Adopting feared traits
4. 'I AM ONLY' SYNDROME: the 1st/only Black fears losing his/her place in White setting thwarts efforts of other Blacks to achieve	4. DENIAL PROJECTION Displacement: Outward attribution to another one's own unacceptable impulses, wishes, or thoughts
5. VICTIM/MARTYR: cannot act in own best interest; accepts humiliation	5. TURNING-AGAINST-SELF (Self as object/target) Redirection of impulses inwardly against oneself instead of outwardly toward appropriate target. Results in masochistic feelings of inadequacy, guilt, depression
6. MALE DOMINANCE/FEMALE SUBMISSIVE: rigid role patterns, prescribed agendas for relationships	6. IDENTIFICATION-WITH-THE-AGGRESSOR PROJECTION REACTION-FORMATION
7. DEVALUISTS: any race, group, or culture is better/superior to Blacks	7. DENIAL DISPLACEMENT (Redirection of impulses) usually aggressive ones onto substitute target too threatening INTROJECTION Taking within; Incorporating into one's own behavior and beliefs characteristics of some external object or admired person
8. USERS/MANIPULATORS: exploit other resources, kindness, etc., for self promotion	8. IDENTIFICATION-WITH-THE-AGGRESSOR REPRESSION
9. AGGRANDIZERS: status hungry, aping middle-class behaviors, attributes, practices to extremes	9. IDENTIFICATION-WITH-THE-AGGRESSOR SUBLIMATION, Acceptable substitutes REACTION FORMATION
10. NEGATIVISTS: references to Blacks demeaning; abusive language, mannerisms, unkept appearance—view of 'relating' to Black people; self-hatred	10. IDENTIFICATION-WITH-THE-AGGRESSOR REPRESSION PROJECTION REGRESSION

*Based on S. Freud, The Ego and the Mechanisms of Defense (1936).

These circumstances are all the more true for African American women. The persistent high labor force participation rate with substandard wages, community activism, and family responsibilities are historic realities. Du Bois (1969: 183) explains one unique aspect of African American women:

> Not being expected to be merely ornamental, they have girded themselves for work, instead of adorning their bodies only for play. Their sturdier minds have concluded that if a women be clean, healthy, and educated, she is pleasing as God wills and far more useful than most of her sisters.

The development of effective coping methods becomes essential for maintenance of psychological symmetry, problem solving, goal attainment, and actualization. Lykes's (1983) definition of coping as "behavior in response to a problem" is useful, and "refers to an individual's effort to master conditions of threat, harm, or challenge that he or she perceives and that result from a problem he or she has identified." Inherent in this definition are two components: awareness/identification, and strategic action/non-action.

Consistent with this means of coping, White (1984: 71) affirms that in addition to

> predictable adult crises . . . 'passages' or critical periods, the African American adult has to cope with the social and economic obstacles created by the residual effects of racism in America throughout the life cycle. Internalizing a comprehensive understanding of the African American ethos will help the adult to develop the coping skills and internal strength necessary to continue growing and actualizing throughout the life cycle.

This point is crucial and cannot be considered peripheral to any particular problem of the moment. For without an understanding of the systemic nature of the problem—the stabilizing, and rewarding aspects of the oppression, and subordination of African Americans by White America—one is unable to liberate oneself. "Liberation is thus a childbirth, and a painful one. The man who emerges is a new man [woman], viable only as the oppressor-oppressed contradiction is superseded by the humanization of all men" (Friere, 1968: 33). According to White (1984: 71) "the comprehensive mastery and appreciation of the Black ethos is the major development task of Black adulthood."

In *Assertive Black . . . Puzzled White,* Cheek (1977: 18) provides an assertive training approach which translates the psychological theories of personality and counseling into an African American frame of reference:

> For blacks, then, one of the best definitions of assertiveness is an honest, open and direct verbal or non-verbal expression which does not have the intent of putting someone down. . . . The intention of the assertive black person should be the basis of judgment, not the response of the target person.

The importance of positive interaction patterns is fundamental. "Blacks, like everyone else, benefit from guidance in choosing more productive and satisfying ways of relating to each other—and of relating to those who are not black" (Cheek, 1977: 18) Cheek elaborates:

> And blacks, . . . need more viable alternatives as to therapies, approaches or suggested behaviors that reflect their atypical experience in a racist society. Yes, blacks need help, but it must be help fashioned from a black perspective and from a black viewpoint [p. 20].

On an individual basis, the African American woman has an equal responsibility to select a mate/partner who affirms her strengths, capabilities, and potential. The complementary nature of the support provided by each member of the relationship sustains a resilience and a positive assertion of love, respect, and trust that is enabling rather than diminishing. "The fact remains that true, authentic love—wishing for others what one postulates for oneself, when that postulation unites the permanent values of human reality—entails the mobilization of psychic drives basically freed of unconscious conflicts" (Fanon, 1967: 41). Fanon goes on to describe the "ethical orientation" in man's [woman] consciousness toward the world when he declares:

> the person I love will strengthen me by endorsing my assumption of my manhood [womanhood], while the need to earn the admiration or the love of others will erect a value-making superstructure on my whole vision of the world [p. 41].

Conclusion

The assertion, believed by many seeking partners or caught in dehumanizing relationships, that the quality of life available to one is dependent on the acceptance of unacceptable conditions imposed by another is a contradiction of fundamental values inherent in the African American experience. Further, it is a denial of one's own sense of self and responsibility to self to refuse to allow any person to abrogate integral self-esteem. This article has attempted to demonstrate that the responsibility is more than merely an individual one but is a shared group commitment in the true sense of the African American extended family life value. In *The Psychology of Blacks: An Afro-American Perspective,* White (1984: 73) encapsulates the essence of the matter in the following description:

> The ideal male-female relationship within extended family networks and in the Black community at large would be one characterized by the Afro-American values of interdependence, cooperation, and mutual respect, without a fixed classification of household, economic, and social responsibilities based on sex.

Male-female relationships that are built on a bond of sharing, nurturance, tenderness, and appreciation have the strong psychological foundation necessary to cope with the social and economic stresses that usually confront Black couples living in a country dominated by Euro-Americans.

The ability to confront the unadulterated truth with resolve and fortitude, together with spirituality, humaneness, and love of life, has been part of the unique heritage of African Americans. A denial of these attributes in the quest of modernism and desire for assimilation at all costs constitutes a form of psychosis. Generations of African Americans have not sacrificed their lives and their dreams nor withstood the most horrendous brutality in order to hand over successive generations to the mammon of self-destruction. The necessity of defining oneself and rejecting inauthentic definitions has never been more crucial.

References

Aidoo, A. A. (1981) "Asante queen mothers in government and politics in the nineteenth century," p. 65 in F. C. Steady, The Black Woman Cross-Culturally. Cambridge, MA: Schenkman.

Blackwell, J. E. (1965) The Black Community: Diversity and Unity (2nd ed.). New York: Harper & Row.

Cheek. D. K. (1977) Assertive Black . . . Puzzled White. San Luis Obispo, CA: Impact Publishers.

Du Bois, W. E. B. (1969) "The damnation of women," in Darkwater: Voices from Within the Veil. New York: Schocken.

Fanon, F. (1967) Black Skin—White Masks. New York: Grove.

Friere, P. (1968) Pedagogy of the Oppressed. New York: Seabury.

Freud, S. (1936) The Ego and the Mechanisms of Defense (Rev. ed.), Vol. 2. New York: International Universities.

Katz, D. (1983) "Factors affecting social change." J. of Social Issues 39 (4): 27.

Lykes, B. M. (1983) "Discrimination and black women." J. of Social Issues 39, (3): 8.

Martin, E. P. and J. Martin (1978) The Black Extended Family. Chicago: Univ. of Chicago Press.

Memmi, A. (1967) The Colonizer and the Colonized. Boston: Beacon.

National Urban League (1988) State of Black America 1982–1988. New York: Author.

Pinderhughes, E. (1982) "Afro-American families and the victim system," in M. McGodrick et al., Ethnicity and Family Therapy. New York: Guilford.

Pinknney, A. (1984) The Myth of Black Progress. New York: Cambridge Univ. Press.

Spurlock, J. (1973) "Some consequences of racism for children," p. 160 in C. V. Willie et. al., Racism and Mental Health. Pittsburgh: Univ. of Pittsburgh Press.

Stewart, J. A. and M. B. Platt (1983) "Studying women and change." J. of Social Issues 39 (4).

Sudarkasa, N. (1981a) "Female employment and family organization in West Africa, in F. C. Steady, The Black Woman Cross-Culturally, Cambridge, MA: Schenkman.

Sudarkasa, N. (1981b) "Interpreting the African heritage in Afro American family organization," pp. 37–53 in H. P. McAdoo, Black Families. Beverly Hills, CA: Sage.

Swinton, D. H. (1988) "Economic status of blacks 1987," p. 130 The State of Black America, 1988. New York: National Urban League.

White, J. L. (1984) The Psychology of Blacks: An Afro-American Perspective. Englewood Cliffs, NJ: Prentice-Hall.

Young, C. (1986) "Afro-American family: contemporary issues and implications for social policy," in D. Pilgrim, On Being Black: An In-Group Analysis. Bristol, IN: Wyndham Hall.

Zanden, J. V. (1983) American Minority Relations. (4th ed.). New York: Alfred A. Knopf.

5

Black Men, an Endangered Species: Who's Really Pulling the Trigger

Thomas A. Parham and Roderick J. McDavis

In recent years, articles focusing on issues faced by Black men have begun to reemerge in the popular and scientific literature. Much of the early research was directed toward trying to question or validate stereotypical personality characteristics assigned to Black men. For example, several authors described how Black men have been portrayed in much of the literature as having low self-esteem (Arnez, 1972), being sexual "super-studs" (Bernard, 1966), being female dominated (Staples, 1970), and having their greatest potential in athletics (Edwards, 1979). Conversely, other authors, who sought to paint a more positive and realistic picture of Black men, characterized them as having intact self-concepts (Banks & Grambs, 1972; Baughman, 1971) and as being strong role models and good husbands, providers, and fathers (Hill, 1972).

The theme echoed in recent studies, however, is much more alarming; that is, Black men are rapidly becoming an endangered species (Gibbs, 1984; Leavy, 1983). The notion of counseling and other human service professionals providing mental health services to Black people has also been a concern of the counseling profession for the past two decades (Gilbert, 1973; Kincaid, 1969; Smith, 1977). Despite this apparent commitment, contributors to the counseling literature have been slow to translate societal concerns into strategies for counseling Blacks more effectively. As such, the current status of Black people (particularly men) is one of the least recognized and effectively addressed issues in terms of counseling programs.

Reprinted from *Journal of Counseling and Development* 66(1) 24–27, 1987. © AACD.
Reprinted with permission. No further reproduction authorized without written permission of American Association for Counseling and Development.

In this article we address this void by describing Black men as a population at risk, examining external and internal factors that affect Black men, and offering counseling and other human service professionals recommendations for translating social concerns into programmatic interventions.

Black Men: A Population at Risk

The question "Where are all of the eligible Black men?" is usually asked by Black women seeking some sort of companionship with Black men. Or it could be Black women talking with each other about the popular opinion, not empirical documentation, that the eligible female to male ratio is approximately 7:1. The question of the disposition of Black men, eligible or not, warrants serious discussion.

Some authors have argued, with good reason, that there are social forces and environmental and institutional factors that contribute to Black men being a population at risk (Johnson, 1983; Leavy, 1983). Certainly, unemployment (28 to 30 percent among Black men, up to 48 percent among Black youth [Leavy, 1983]), poor education, inadequate health care facilities, discriminatory judicial processes (lack of adequate legal representation, racist police practices), incarceration (42 percent of the inmate population is Black [Staples, 1982]), and front line military combat duty (Butler, 1980) are factors often mentioned. As such, much of the energy generated in confronting these negative elements in American society is directed at systemic factors (i.e., creating job programs, hiring more Black police officers, appointing more Black judges, and creating educational programs).

Yet, the conservative political leaders and societal attitudes of the 1980s have signaled an end to many of these gains, which were modest at best. Evidence of the new conservatism can be found in the recent 1984 Supreme Court decision that upheld the seniority system of the Memphis Fire Department over affirmative action quotas. Clearly, more systemic approaches designed to alleviate the many social injustices are still necessary.

Restricting intervention to external factors alone, however, implies that Black men have no part in alleviating their predicament as a population at risk and that they lack the mental fortitude to deal effectively with adverse conditions in society. Such a conclusion seems questionable because Black men have survived and persevered through nearly 400 years of oppression in the United States. On the contrary, Black men must simultaneously shoulder some of the blame for their predicament and some of the responsibility for developing personal intervention strategies that will ultimately better their condition. Counseling professionals can assist Black men in developing such strategies.

External and Internal Factors

Life Expectancy

Perhaps the most disturbing factor in any discussion of Black men is that as a group they have a shorter average life expectancy, 64 years, than any other group (cf. 69, 73, and 79 years for White men, Black women, and White women, respectively) (Leavy, 1983). Although statistics should be interpreted with caution, the variables that contribute to that average are much more distressing. In his book, *Black Masculinity,* Staples (1982) helped to clarify the issue. He reported that the overall homicide rate for Black men is significantly higher than that for any other group: 42 percent of all homicide victims are Black, and the majority of the perpetrators of these crimes are also Black, predominantly male, and usually under 24 years of age.

Black youths have a 50 percent higher probability of dying before age 20 than White children (U.S. Department of Health, Education, and Welfare, 1978). But even more important, as Staples (1982) reported, the largest causes of deaths among White youths are accidents and cardiovascular disease, whereas homicide, drug abuse, suicide, and accidents are the primary causes among Black youths. There have been various attempts in the literature to explain this increase in homicides among Blacks (Poussaint, 1972; Staples, 1982), and explanations range from psychological to sociological variables. Regardless of what explanation one adopts, however, the bottom line is still the same—Black people are killing Black people.

Physical Health and Illness

Another factor affecting the average life expectancy of Black men is physical illness. That many members of the Black community, especially men, are subjected to inadequate health care (either through lack of facilities or because of underuse) has long been recognized as a contributing factor to the short life expectancy of Black men. The consequences of this dilemma, however, are becoming increasingly dramatic. Proportionately, Black men now have a higher rate of cancer than does any other group in the United States, and today the disease is killing twice as many Black men as it did 30 years ago (Johnson, 1983).

Reports also indicate that although Black men are afflicted with various forms of cancer (e.g., prostrate, colon-rectum, stomach), the most prevalent is lung cancer. Although nutritional, life-style, and other environmental factors are often implicated, the most substantial contributor seems to be cigarette smoking (Johnson, 1983). In fact, Johnson (1983) reported findings of the American Cancer Society indicating that Black men smoke more cigarettes than do those in any other age-sex group in

America. Ironically, lung cancer is one of the most difficult forms of cancer to cure and the easiest to prevent.

Alcohol Abuse

Another factor that has long been recognized for its impact on the physical and mental health of Black men is alcohol abuse. In fact, Bourne (1973) rated alcoholism as one of the leading mental health problems facing the Black community. In addition, alcohol abuse is apparently a more serious problem for Black men than for White men, White women, and Black women (Bourne, 1973). The consequences of alcohol abuse, which negatively affects both the personal and social lives of Black men, include substantial increases in the rates of homicides, arrests, accidents, assaults, and physical illnesses (Harper, 1981).

The problems of alcohol abuse among Black men are further compounded by several obstacles that make treatment of the disease difficult at best. These obstacles include scarcity of alcohol treatment facilities in the Black community, lack of education about alcohol as a drug and alcoholism as a disease, and the inability to find job placement, sources of income, and training for unemployed Black men in treatment. Harper (1981), however, suggested that the major barrier to treatment for Black men is their refusal to accept the concept of alcoholism. For many Black men, heavy drinking is the norm and is perceived as an attribute of manhood and camaraderie. As such, many Black men who drink excessively refuse to accept any alcohol treatment or other medical assistance (Harper, 1979; Williams, 1975).

Suicide

Another alarming statistic of the 1980s is that the suicide rate for Black people in general and Black men in particular is escalating. Analysis of the statistical patterns associated with suicide suggests that as urban residents of lower than average per capita income, Blacks should be least likely to commit suicide (Davis, 1981). This is not the case, however. In fact, King (1982) reported that the rate of Afro American suicide victims in a major metropolitan U.S. city was expected to exceed the overall national average for 1980 by nearly 3.5 per 100,000. After examining the 1970s data from the U.S. Bureau of the Census, King (1982) also reported that suicide among Black Americans has been primarily a youthful phenomenon. Among Black men and women, the largest percentage of suicides occurs among the age group of 20 to 34, with a 3:1 ratio of men to women.

Although the average suicide rate for Blacks, when examined over the last decade or two, is lower than the national average, the rate of increase is a serious concern. These data are striking, especially when compared with the late 19th- and early 20th-century viewpoint that suicide was a rate occurrence among Black Americans. Despite data to the contrary, Reynolds (1975) reported that, unfortunately, many Black people continue to accept this outdated notion, believing instead that suicide is still an ''Anglo'' phenomenon.

Dramatic increases in suicide rates, however, are apparent when analyzed retrospectively over the last 20 to 25 years. Data clearly indicate that the suicide rate for young Black men has been increasing steadily since the 1960s (Davis, 1981). The sharp increase in the suicide rate of young Blacks lends credibility to the notion that their lives are characterized by higher levels of stress. Ironically, much of the stress, tension, and even hostility that Black men must endure originates from sources intended as social supports for them. Nowhere is the dilemma more accurately illustrated than in the educational system.

Education

Patton (1981) argued that as the primary socializing agent, elementary and secondary education has negatively affected the achievements, self-concepts, and selected dispositional aspects of Black men. The cumulative gap between Blacks and Whites in educational achievement levels begins with kindergarten and increases through the postsecondary years (Williams, 1974). Research also indicates that Black men continue to lag in academic achievements, developing of positive self-concepts, and other key growth areas.

Additional indications of the negative consequences that the educational system has on Black men lie in the suspension rates, dropout-pushout rates, and subsequent college attendance rates for Black men. Cottle (1975) noted that Black children are suspended three times as frequently as are their White peers and for longer periods. Killalea (1980) supported this notion of differing disciplinary actions toward Black students by indicating that Black male students are not only suspended and expelled but also receive corporal punishment at rates disproportionate to their percentage of the total public school enrollment. These data, along with research suggesting that Black male students are disproportionately tracked into slower classes and lack adequate role models throughout their tenure in the educational system (Patton, 1981), help to clarify why Black male students are among the lowest groups in college eligibility and attendance rates (Thomas, 1977).

Military Service

The consequences of an inadequate education are devastating, especially when one views education as a primary prerequisite for competing in the labor market. Rather than face the harsh realities of unemployment, many Black men are focusing on what is perceived as a more constructive option, the armed forces. In fact, Binikin, Etelberg, Schexnider, and Smith (1982) reported that almost one of every five Black men born between 1957 and 1962 had entered military service.

As the nation's largest employer and trainer, the armed forces supply much needed jobs. They also prepare men to compete in the civilian labor market by providing basic training in many career fields. These factors have resulted in an unprecedented rise in the number of Black enlisted men. In fact, Biniken et al. (1982) indicated that one-third of all soldiers and nearly 20 percent of all active duty personnel were Black. Apparently, however, the armed forces have presented Black men with an uncommon blend of benefits and burdens.

The negative aspects of this overrepresentation of Blacks in the armed forces include their disproportionate cluster in combat forces and, thus, a greater likelihood of becoming a casualty of war. In addition, skills required in combat specialties are the most difficult to translate into civilian skills (Binikin et al., 1982). Black men also face discriminatory military policies and practices that inhibit their ability to receive higher occupational assignments (Moskos, 1978), retard their rate of advancement and promotion (Butler, 1976), and make it difficult to fare well in the criminal justice system of the armed forces (Shields, 1984). As such, the Black men who do not become war casualties and conclude their tenure in the service are often no more equipped to compete successfully in the job market than they were before military service.

Psychological Factors

Focusing on these harsher realities faced by Black men in America may lead one to speculate that these existing crises are class bound (i.e., restricted to lower-class, Black men); however, such is not the case. Working-, middle-, and upper-class Black men often find their futures in jeopardy as well. Although the lifestyles of economically advantaged Black men are inherently different from those of their lower-class counterparts, they are often characterized by factors that can be very stressful and detrimental.

Upwardly mobile Black men are confronted with the pressures of working in business and corporate structures dominated by Whites. If they are to survive, they must endure both the normal pressures that characterize their job functions and the pressures and anxieties that are inherent in being Black. They are confronted with proving their competence in job situations in which discrimination is practiced (i.e., denial of access to insider information) and with experiences that they do not completely understand (Campbell, 1982).

Black men must also realize that their success in the world of work is often tied to their ability to assimilate their values, behaviors, appearance, and life-styles into what the White culture deems legitimate. As a consequence, they sometimes believe that they must compromise their Blackness to survive or receive the rewards of the White corporate system (Davis & Watson, 1982). Despite marginal successes in business and corporate areas, Black men are forced, through such experiences or compromises, to pay a high emotional and physical price.

They may feel a sense of internalized anxiety, anger, frustration, and resentment because of withheld promotions, deadend jobs, lack of policy-making power, and the necessity for them to have a "dual identity" (i.e., "Got one mind for White folks to see, another for what I know is me") (Ames, 1950). These emotional reactions may be manifested through feelings of depression, decreases in energy and motivation, and even withdrawal. Also, Black men are likely to experience somatic stress reactions or ailments that include headaches, low back pain, diabetes, heart trouble, and high blood pressure.

Recommendations

From the evidence cited in this review, it is clear that Black men are facing times of extreme hardship. Furthermore, this trend is likely to continue for the foreseeable future. As such, the marshaling of societal change agents and the modification of personal behaviors is a mandate that can no longer be ignored. In this spirit, we propose the following recommendations:

1. School counselors should provide more educational seminars on parenting for Black parents. Many Black parents are unaware of the developmental stages that children experience and may not know how to respond to their male children. Parenting seminars could provide opportunities for Black parents to acquire useful skills that they can use to raise their male children. These seminars also would bring parents and counselors together in a cooperative effort to help improve the growth and development of Black men.

Because of the underrepresentation of Blacks in counseling and other helping professions, those providing services to Blacks will probably be predominantly White for some time to come. Because White counselors often lack both sufficient knowledge of dilemmas facing Black men and strategies that can be effective in working with this population, these counselors should be provided with educational training seminars to help them in supplementing their existing knowledge bases. Professional counseling associations (e.g., the American Association for Counseling and Development [AACD]) can be particularly helpful in this regard.

2. School counselors (especially those at the secondary level) should organize and lead counseling groups that help Black men develop more

positive self-concepts. Such groups could help Black men gain more confidence in their abilities and talents. Various male leaders in the Black community could be asked to participate in these group experiences and to serve as role models.

3. School counselors should help Black male children set career goals or at least explore career options early in their educational experiences. Selecting career goals can help these children understand the value of education. Career goals also can help them select the necessary work experiences to prepare them for specific careers. School counselors could structure activities and experiences that help these children become aware of various careers and motivate them to explore many career options.

4. The high rates of homicide, drug and alcohol abuse, and suicide among young Black men suggest that there may be a crisis in values among Black male children. As such, mental health counselors should develop and implement more outreach programs and services in cooperation with churches and other organizations in the Black community. These programs and services could include individual counseling, topical group discussions on relevant social issues (e.g., drugs, teenage pregnancy), and seminars on careers of the future. Using Afrocentric paradigms and constructs as a foundation, leaders of individual counseling sessions and group discussions should focus on helping young Black people promote and develop Afrocentric values based on principles of collective survival and consubstantiation (i.e., "We are of the same substance") (Nobles, 1972). The development of such a value system could prove effective in helping young Black men resist engaging in any behavior (e.g., homicide, crime, drug usage, suicide) detrimental to their peers, family, community, or themselves.

5. Mental health counselors should organize and lead discussion groups with young Black men on building strong family lives. The focus of these groups could be on confronting role definitions in which premarital sex is prescribed as a necessary prerequisite for manhood. These groups could also focus on concerns and issues that help Black men consider marriage and raising children as a very significant part of their lives. Black men could be taught how to develop healthy relationships with women and to show respect for them. Many topics and issues related to marriage and children could be discussed in such groups.

6. Counselors in colleges and universities should organize and lead discussion groups and seminars that focus on helping Black men develop effective leadership skills. The development of leadership skills could help them become future community leaders and role models for young Black men. For example, counselors might consider enlisting the help of members of Black fraternal organizations, who could develop and exercise leadership skills by working with young Black people in local communities. By conducting leadership groups and seminars, counselors in colleges and

universities could demonstrate that they are concerned about helping Black men become leaders on and off campus.

7. Black parents should provide more discipline for their Black sons. They should establish behavior limits for these children, and appropriate punishment should be used to enforce established behavior limits. For example, if a son will not obey his parents' rules, they should restrict his movements to inside the home. Discipline can be used by Black parents to create more control and structure in the lives of their sons.

8. School counseling and administrative personnel should develop formal programs, specifically designed for Black parents, to assist parents of Black male children in communicating to teachers and counselors their academic expectations for their sons. If more counselors and teachers knew Black parents' academic expectations of their sons, they could better encourage and motivate Black male students to work harder in school.

9. Black parents should spend more time raising their male children. In many Black families, sons do not receive the nurturing that daughters receive. They are allowed too much freedom to decide their life-styles, educational goals, and careers. As a consequence, many Black men never reach their full potential. Black parents, especially fathers, must invest more quality time and energy in raising their sons.

10. Our final recommendation is directed at counseling and other helping professionals who provide services to adult Black men, particularly upwardly mobile men who are experiencing moderate to heavy amounts of stress. These professionals should encourage Black men to work through issues related to stress using on-the-job support systems (e.g., colleagues, staff psychologists) or community support systems (e.g., networking in professional associations, private individual or group psychotherapy, friends). In addition, counselors may need to assist Black men in resolving the inevitable identity crises that result from conflicts between job pressures to conform and assimilate (which is often translated into giving up one's ethnic identity) and self-imposed pressures to maintain a Black identity.

References

Ames, R. (1950). Protest and irony in Negro folksong. *Social Science, 14,* 193–213.

Arnez, N. (1972). Enhancing Black self-concept through literature. In J. Banks & J. Grambs (Eds.), *Black self concept* (pp. 93–116). New York: McGraw-Hill.

Banks, J., & Grambs, J. (1972). *Black self concept.* New York: McGraw-Hill.

Bernard, J. (1966). *Marriage and family among Negroes.* Englewood Cliffs, NJ: Prentice-Hall.

Baughman, E. (1971). *Black Americans.* New York: Academic Press.

Binikin, M., Etelberg, M., Schexnider, A., & Smith, M. (1982). *Blacks and the military.* Washington, DC: Brookings Institute.

Bourne, P. (1973). Alcoholism in the urban population. In P. Bourne & R. Fox (Eds.), *Alcoholism progress in research and treatment*. New York: Academic Press.

Butler, J. (1976). Inequality in the military: An examination of promotion rates for Black and White enlisted men. *American Sociological Review, 41,* 817.

Butler, J. (1980). *Inequality in the military: The Black experience.* Saratoga, CA: Century Twenty-One.

Campbell, B. (1982, December 12). Black executives and corporate stress. *New York Times Magazine.*

Cottle, T. A. (1975). A case of suspension. *National Elementary Principal, 5,* 69–74.

Davis, G., & Watson, G. (1982). *Black life in corporate America.* New York: Anchor Press.

Davis, R. (1981). A demographic analysis of suicide. In L. E. Gary (Ed.), *Black men* (pp. 179–196). Beverly Hills, CA: Sage.

Edwards, H. (1979, April 15). The draft: No equality for Blacks. *San Francisco Examiner,* p. 3.

Gibbs, J. T. (1984). Black adolescents and youth: An endangered species. *American Journal of Orthopsychiatry, 54,* 6–21.

Gilbert, J. (1973). Counseling Black inner-city children groups. In M. M. Ohlsen (Ed.), *Counseling children in groups: A forum.* New York: Holt, Rinehart and Winston.

Harper, F. D. (1979) *Alcoholism treatment and Black Americans* (DHEW Publication No. ADM–79–853). Rockville, MD: National Institute on Alcohol Abuse and Alcoholism.

Harper, F. D. (1981). Alcohol use and abuse. In L. E. Gary (Ed.), *Black men* (pp. 169–178). Beverly Hills, CA: Sage.

Hill, R. (1972). *The strengths of Black families.* New York: Emerson Hall.

Johnson, J. (1983, March). Why Black men have the highest cancer rate. *Ebony,* pp. 69–72.

Killelea, E. (1980). *State, regional, and national summaries.* Washington, DC: Department of Health and Human Services, Office for Civil Rights.

Kincaid, M. (1968). Identity and therapy in the Black community. *Personnel and Guidance Journal, 47,* 884–890.

King, L. (1982). Suicide from a Black reality perspective. In B. Bass, G. Wyatt, & G. Powell (Eds.), *Afro-American family* (pp. 221–236). New York: Grune & Stratton.

Leavy, W. (1983, August). Is the Black male an endangered species? *Ebony.*

Moskos, C. (1978). The enlisted ranks in the all-voluntary army. In J. B. Keeky (Ed.), *The All-Volunteer Force and American society.* Charlottesville: University Press of Virginia.

Nobles, W. (1972). African philosophy: Foundations for Black psychology. In R. L. Jones (Ed.), *Black psychology* (pp. 18–32). New York: Harper & Row.

Patton, J. M. (1981). The Black male's struggle for an education. In L. E. Gary (Ed.), *Black men* (pp. 199–214). Beverly Hills, CA: Sage.

Poussaint, A. F. (1972). *Why Blacks kill Blacks.* New York: Emerson Hall.

Reynolds, A. (1975). Some clinical considerations in the prevention of suicide. *American Journal of Public Health, 48,* 333–399.

Shields, R. M. (1984). The influence of military policy on Black men. In F. Rice and W. Jones (Eds.), *Contemporary public policy perspectives and Black Americans: Issues in an era of retrenchment politics*. Westport, CT: Greenwood Press.

Smith, E. J. (1977). Counseling Black individuals: Some stereotypes. *Personnel and Guidance Journal, 55*, 390–396.

Staples, R. (1970, January). The myth of the Black matriarchy. *Black Scholar*, pp. 8–16.

Staples, R. (1982). *Black masculinity*. San Francisco: Black Scholar Press.

Thomas, G. (1977). *Access to higher education: How important are race, sex, social class, and academic credentials for college access*. Baltimore: Johns Hopkins University Press. (ERIC Document Reproduction Service No. ED 142 616)

U.S. Department of Health, Education, and Welfare. (1978). *Final mortality statistics 1977*. Washington, DC: U.S. Government Printing Office.

Williams, R. (1974). *Cognitive and social learning of the Black child: The survival of Black children and youth*. Washington, DC: Science Publications.

Williams, R. (1975). *Textbook of Black-related diseases*. New York: McGraw-Hill.

6

Culturally Sensitive Therapy with Black Clients

Laurie L. Wilson and Sandra M. Stith

A heritage of chattel slavery, segregation, and racial prejudice provides obstacles that have burdened Black Americans and affected the development of Black American families. In addition to continuous pressures of racism and oppression, Black American families face contemporary threats to family stability. Such threats include poverty, widespread drug abuse, teenage pregnancy, communicable diseases, and violent crimes. Traditional values and coping mechanisms of Black American families may not be adequate to deal with these contemporary threats to family stability. In fact, the U.S. Bureau of the Census (1983) reported that two out of three Black marriages will eventually dissolve and that in 1982 only one-half of all Black families included parents of both sexes.

More recent research, however, suggests that despite racism and its concomitant poverty, the Black family is strong. For instance, although college-educated Black men earn less than White male high school dropouts, approximately 90 percent of them are married and living with their spouses (Staples, 1985). Another example of the strength of the Black family is the fact that, contrary to popular opinion, 69 percent of Black families are not poor (Wilson, 1989).

The other 31 percent of Black families struggle for their daily survival. Ironically, they are often dependent on government and social service institutions that they "often perceive as non-supportive and exploitive" (Hayes & Mindel, 1973, p. 52). It is a serious social contradiction when a family cannot trust those who are charged to help them.

This article, focusing only on the mental health needs of Black families, describes the importance of a systemic theoretical orientation and

Reprinted from *Journal of Multicultural Counseling and Development (19,* 1) 32–43, 1991. © AACD. No further reproduction authorized without written permission of American Association for Counseling and Development.

delineates five critical issues that therapists must consider in working with Black families. Throughout this article we speak of Black families as though they are a homogeneous group, yet many variations exist. In spite of these variations, the historical and current experiences of racism and prejudice seem to be an organizing and universal experience that link Black American families and that demands our attention. Without understanding the experience of the Black family, it is not possible to meet the needs of these families.

Black Families and Therapy

Previous literature (Terrell & Terrell, 1984; Thompson & Cimbolic, 1978) has suggested that Black clients are frequently reticent to seek counseling and when they do seek therapy they frequently terminate after one session. This is not surprising given the lack of attention that has been given to understanding and treating non-White families.

There are other reasons why therapists may not be meeting the needs of their Black clients. First, White therapists and many Black therapists, who have been primarily trained in White institutions studying research based on White families, may lack a basic historical perspective on the Black family. Second, they may have stereotypical views regarding Black Americans and may not understand the unique strengths and problems faced by Black families seeking treatment. They may have basic value differences and communication difficulties with clients who are different from them. Finally, they may not recognize or understand the effect of racism on their interaction with Black families. Thus, lacking that understanding, they may interpret the Black family's reluctance to trust as resistance or noncompliance. Additionally, therapeutic theories and interventions, which primarily have been developed by White therapists and used with White clients, may not always be directly applicable to Black clients.

However, we believe that Black American families needing mental health assistance can greatly benefit from culturally sensitive family therapy. This is suggested by previous research that shows the greatest source of life satisfaction among Black Americans is their family life (Gary, Beatty, & Price, 1983). Family therapists believe that the dominant forces in personality development are located externally in current interactions in the family system. In fact, the fundamental premise of family therapy is that "people are products of their social context, and that any attempt to understand them must include an appreciation of their families" (Nichols, 1984, p. 80). In addition, family therapy may be particularly appropriate for Black families because it addresses the family in its larger social context: historical, political, institutional, and environmental factors that affect the family as a unit as well as individual family members (Minuchin, 1974).

Even though Black American families in trouble may benefit from effective family therapy, they are often reluctant to seek these services. Many Black Americans have responded to racism, oppression, and discrimination by refusing to trust persons differing from them in color, life-style, and class values (Boyd-Franklin, 1989). Hines and Boyd-Franklin (1982) pointed out that this suspiciousness is frequently a direct-learned survival response. Suspicion extends particularly to ''White institutions,'' as most clinics and mental health centers are perceived to be. Therefore, if family therapists expect to meet the needs of Black families and to encourage them to feel comfortable using family therapy, they need to develop culturally sensitive attitudes and skills. These attitudes and skills include awareness of the therapist's own cultural background, values, and biases, as well as acknowledgment of and comfort with the client's cultural differences (Pomales, Claiburn, & LaFromboise, 1986).

Five Critical Issues

Therapy with Black Americans must be consistent with their worldview, must be respectful of their history, and must be nonracist. There are at least five major issues that a culturally sensitive therapist needs to consider in working with Black families: (a) historical perspectives on the experience of Black American families, (b) the current and historical social support system of the Black American family, (c) the unique characteristics of the value systems of Black American families, (d) communication barriers that may hinder the development of trust between the Black client and a non-Black therapist, and (e) strategies for providing effective systems-based family therapy to Black clients.

Historic Perspective of Black American Families

The family is the primary source from which individuals extract a sense of self (Minuchin, 1974). All families impart values and ways of understanding life to new members. Family therapy is based on the idea that to help individuals change their behavior, the therapist must understand the context from which the individual developed and in which the individual lives. Although family therapists emphasize the importance of treating the individual in context, many focus so intensely on the here-and-now that they forget to look at the historical context from which the family developed. This blind spot may hamper the effort of the therapist (both Black and White) in working with Black families. Black families in America have a unique history. Slavery and postslavery segregation have impeded their development of a strong ethnic identity, cohesion, and direction necessary for the successful development of Black communities. During slavery Black families were separated, and extended families were discouraged. The development of Black ethnic identity, confidence, and direction was limited (Jones, 1982).

The oppression of Black Americans continued into the postslavery era, in which continuing racist actions against individuals and families only intensified remaining psychological scars. Wilson (1969) identified obstacles facing Black Americans in the postslavery era as a series of struggles: the struggles for survival, expression, participation, meaning, and fulfillment. These struggles included physical and psychological struggles; struggles to overcome negative stereotypes, struggles to develop appropriate methods for expressing anger, distress, and pain; struggles to develop a clear ethnic identity, heritage sense of self, and reason for human existence for the Black American.

Historical evidence suggests that strong family ties bound Black Americans together during the confusion that followed the Civil War. To adapt to pressures of slavery and discrimination, Black families developed the ability to persevere, organize, and succeed despite odds. Gary, Beatty, and Price (1983) reported that Black Americans continue to cite their family life as the source of most satisfaction. Hence, "traditional family life remains the one viable option for Black Americans on all socioeconomic strata because it is less subject to the vagaries of race than any other institution in American life" (Staples, 1985, p. 1011).

Without a historical perspective of the Black family, any approach to treatment of these families may fail. McAdoo (1983) emphasized that although Black families share many problems with White families, "a racist environment changes and intensifies the meaning and impact of these normative and catastrophic sources of stress" (p. 179). Although some family therapy models (e.g., Haley, 1976; Stuart, 1980) encourage therapists to avoid discussing the past with families, it seems critical that family therapists study Black history and begin to have some sense of the meaning and impact of racism on their Black clients.

In addition to difficulties that can emerge from family therapy models that encourage therapists to disregard that past, difficulties may emerge from applying family therapy models that emphasize gathering and reworking historical material (e.g., Bowen, 1978). When Black families are asked to investigate historical patterns of replication and compensation by discovering patterns in past generations, their historical experiences of slavery, separation of family members, disruption of family bonds from African ancestors, and so forth may lead them to feel incomplete or uncomfortable with their lack of historical knowledge. A historical approach, however, that focuses on more recent family patterns can be very useful in working with Black families after initial trust has been established.

Social Support Systems

Black Americans face unique psychological, environmental, and economic stresses caused by racism and oppression. Additionally, they may face problems common to many other American families, such as marital problems or parenting problems. Strong social support systems may distinguish those Black family members who are able to cope with these various problems from those who are unable to cope (Lyles & Carter, 1982). A social support system is defined as "a set of personal contacts through which the individual maintains his [or her] social identity and receives emotional supports, material aid and services, information and new social contact" (Walker, MacBride, & Vachon, as cited in Malson, 1982, p. 37).

Although the Black American family has many support systems, the two primary ones throughout history have been the church and the kin network (Comer, 1972; Malson, 1982). The importance of church and kin is consistent with the African values of sharing, affiliation, and spirituality.

The Black church is the root of social support for the Black family (Comer, 1972; Lyles & Carter, 1982; Mayes, 1938). Its members are respected and able to excel in the struggle for survival, expression; participation, meaning, and fulfillment. It helps to maintain family solidarity while also allowing for the expression of anger, distress, and pain (Lyles & Carter, 1982).

Additionally, the Black church has provided a deep sense of spirituality to Black Americans. The church and spirituality provide support plus an adaptive mechanism for coping with stress that must be recognized and incorporated into the therapeutic process (Boyd-Franklin, 1989).

Therapists should be aware that extended family relationships, including fictive or adoptive kin, provide a second important source of support for Black American families. Black co-workers may also be considered part of the extended family. These relationships may be especially important when co-workers experience prejudice on the job. Their mutual support provides a buffer to the psychological stresses of their work world. This extended support system needs to be considered in helping Black families.

Other support systems are governmental and social service agencies. Although the original intent was for these services to be auxiliary, too many families become dependent on them for day-to-day survival. A family therapist may be able to help these families renegotiate and clarify their relationship with these agencies so that they become an enhancing support, rather than a debilitating crutch.

Whether therapists choose to work with only one person in the room or with the entire family, it is important that all those considered influential in the family's lives be included in the therapist's conceptualizing and implementing treatment plans. Omitting important sub-systems may reduce the effectiveness of therapy interventions.

Contrasts in Values of Black Americans and White Americans

In addition to examining the historical influences on the Black family and their current social support network, culturally sensitive therapists must make an effort to understand similarities and dissimilarities between Black American and White American values. Whereas many similarities exist, researchers have noted that Black families emphasize values different from those of White families. For example, Pinderhughes (1982) reported that White Americans place greater emphasis on independence, achievement, material assets, planning, youth, and power; Black Americans put greater emphasis on sharing, obedience to authority, spirituality, and respect for elders and heritage.

Contemporary Black Americans ascribe to three value systems: African, American, and Victim (Pinderhughes, 1982). Within Black American families, the experience of oppression and racism (i.e., victimization) may discourage a strong sense of self-esteem and, therefore, encourage doubtful responses in communities, families, and individuals. For example, obstacles that block opportunities for education limit opportunities for advancement and employment. This in turn may lead to stress and victimization. Victim system values are a result of adaptation to racism and oppression in which individuals isolate themselves as a defense against the stresses that hinder them.

Black Americans have adapted to these systems, and although this requires great expenditure of energy and may lead to identity confusion, some Black families have been able to remain particularly clear about their identity and values. Successful adaptation varies from family to family depending on the degree of racism, poverty, and oppression and methods of social support. This accounts for the diversity in values, behaviors, and family structures in Black American families. These multiple values constitute the Black American cultural system. It is important that therapists examine these competing value systems and begin to assess the impact that each system has had on the unique stressors and coping mechanisms with which each family comes to therapy.

Class and value issues are especially important with the lower-class Black client who is primarily concerned with day-to-day survival. With these clients, long-range therapy goals must be put aside until immediate problems of daily functioning are resolved.

Allen (1978) summarized three theoretical positions that are often used to examine Black American families. The "cultural equivalent" position suggests that Black American families may be compared with White American families because their cultures are similar. The "cultural deviant'' suggests that Black American families are deviations from the norms represented by White American middle-class families. The "cultural variant" suggests that there are differences in Black American family norms due to natural adaptation to stress. With the cultural variant position, Black American family norms are seen as strengths, not weaknesses as suggest in the first two positions, which either deny differences or view the Black American family as abnormal.

To work effectively with Black families, therapists using the cultural variant model would be sensitive to the influence that racism and prejudice have on Black families. Culturally sensitive family therapists would look at Black values as strengths rather than as weaknesses. When assessing Black families, ''normal'' family functioning would be viewed from a Black rather than a White perspective. For example, a structural family therapist (Minuchin, 1974) assesses family boundaries along a continuum of extremes: enmeshment or over-involvement to extreme disengagement or emotional cutoffs. Boyd-Franklin (1989) emphasizes that "the vast majority of families fall within the normal range while the cultural norm among Black families tends to fall more within the enmeshed range. Normal, functional Black families often have very close relationships" (p. 123). Thus, therapists must be sensitive to assess Black family functioning according to Black, not White people's norms.

Overcoming Communication Barriers When Counseling Black Clients

Effective verbal and nonverbal communication for both the therapist and the client is important in successful therapy (Sue & Sue, 1977). A premature termination of therapy may result when there is miscommunication between a therapist and client due to "cultural variations in communication." This miscommunication "may lead to alienation and/or an inability to develop trust and rapport" (Sue & Sue, 1977, p. 420).

Although there is a mixture of cultures and classes in America, for verbal communication our society still recognizes "standard English" as the norm. Black Americans using Black English may be viewed negatively by White therapists. For the lower-class or ghetto Black, it may be difficult to communicate feelings, behaviors, and thoughts in standard English. Thus, "a counselee may be seen as uncooperative, sullen, negative, nonverbal, or repressed on the basis of language expression alone" (Sue & Sue, 1977, p. 422).

In discussing nonverbal communication among Blacks, Nancy Boyd-Franklin (1989) used the terms *vibes* as follows:

> Black people, because of the often extremely subtle ways in which racism manifests itself socially, are particularly attuned to very fine distinctions

among such variables in all interactions . . . Because of this, many Black People have been socialized to pay attention to all of the nuances of behavior and not just to the verbal message. The term most often applied to this multilevel perception on Black culture is "vibes." (p. 97)

Boyd-Franklin emphasized the importance of clinicians being aware that every Black client and family member is " 'checking out' him or her in terms of appearance, race, skin color, clothing, perceived social class, language, and a range of more subtle clues such as warmth, genuineness, sincerity, respect for the client, willingness to hear the client's side, patronizing attitudes, condescension, judgments, and human connectedness" (p. 96). She noted that Black families will leave treatment very quickly in the initial stage if this connection is not made with each family member.

Strategies for Providing Effective Therapy to Black Clients

Family therapy as it is traditionally practiced takes place in private practice or in community facilities. A problem-solving model of family therapy (Haley, 1976) includes several stages in the first interview: (a) social or joining stage, (b) problem stage, (c) interaction stage, and (d) goal-setting stage. Each stage is affected by the family's historical experiences, social support network, value systems, and means of communicating. In the joining stage the family is greeted by the therapist, developing trust and rapport vital to continued therapy. Without good communication, clients feel alienated and misunderstood. This, together with historical and current mistrust of White institutions, may lead to premature termination.

Both the problem stage, in which the therapist gathers information about the presenting problem, and the goal-setting stage are affected by the values of the family and the therapist. McAdoo (1988) suggested that "whether a phenomenon is viewed as a problem or solution may not be objective reality at all but may be determined by the observer's values" (p. 265). The personal values of the therapist determine both the questions asked in therapy and the way the answers are perceived (Allen, 1978).

In the interaction stage the family is asked to talk to one another while the therapist studies the family process. This stage of therapy may not be successful because (a) the therapy session usually takes place in an unfamiliar setting and (b) many Black families are affected by numerous systems such as welfare, courts, schools, public housing, extended family, and the church. The therapist who has not included the other systems in the interaction stage will not understand the influence these other systems have on the family's interaction process. Seeing Black clients in their own environment (e.g., community centers, homes, or churches) may help them participate more fully in therapy.

One early study found Black clients either passive or aggressive during the onset of therapy (Clark, 1972). This passive or aggressive behavior was seen as an expression of anger and frustration that could be easily displaced toward the therapist. The therapist should realize that the family's behavior may reflect not only their mistrust of the therapist but also their mistrust of the therapeutic process (Ho, 1987). During the onset of therapy many Blacks exhibit "healthy cultural paranoia" and refuse to develop rapport and trust with therapists from different ethnic, cultural, and value backgrounds (Grier & Cobbs, 1968; Ho, 1987). Thus, certain strategies, such as those listed as follows, may help the family therapist to provide effective culturally sensitive systematic therapy to Black clients:

1. Become aware of the historical and current experience of being Black in America.

2. Consider value and cultural differences between Black Americans and other American ethnic groups and how your own personal values influence the way you conduct therapy.

3. Consider the way your personal values influence the way you view both the presenting problem and the goals for therapy.

4. Include the value system of the client in the goal-setting process. Be sensitive to spiritual values and the value of the family and the church.

5. Be sensitive to variations in Black family norms due to normal adaptations to stress, and be flexible enough to accept these variations.

6. Be aware of how ineffective verbal and nonverbal communication due to cultural variation in communication can lead to premature termination of therapy. Become familiar with nonstandard or Black English, and accept its use by clients.

7. Consider the client's problem in the large context. Include the extended family, other significant individuals, and larger systems in your thinking, if not in the therapy session.

8. Be aware of your client's racial identification, and do not feel threatened by your client's cultural identification with his or her own race.

9. Learn to acknowledge and to be comfortable with your client's cultural differences.

10. Consider the appropriateness of specific therapeutic models or interventions to specific Black families. Do not apply interventions without considering unique aspects of each family.

11. Consider each Black family and each Black family member you treat as unique. Do not generalize the findings of any study or group of studies on Black families to all Black clients. Use the studies to help you find your way, not to categorize individuals.

Conclusion

The concept of family therapy is new to most Black families and, therefore, must be first accepted as another form of social support. "Within the Western framework, counseling is a White, middle class activity that holds many values and characteristics different from third world groups" (Sue & Sue, 1977, p. 421).

As long as racism and oppression maintain the victim system, family treatment must enable the family to cope constructively with those stresses and to counteract their pervasive influence. "Treatment must be directed toward strengthening family structure, enhancing flexibility, and reinforcing the ability of friends, community, and the larger social system to offer effective and appropriate support" (Pinderhughes, 1982, pp. 114–115). "The real challenge in therapy is to aid the Black family in rediscovering those strengths that historically have buttressed them from pervasive racism and provided them with needed support systems unavailable from other institutions" (Lyles & Carter, 1982, pp. 1122–1123).

References

Allen, W. (1978). The search for applicable theories of Black family life. *Journal of Marriage and the Family. 40,* 117–130.

Bowen, M. (1978). *Family therapy in clinical practice.* New York: Aronson.

Boyd-Franklin, N. (1989). *Black families in therapy: A multisystems approach.* New York: Guilford Press.

Clark, C. (1972). Black Studies or the study of Black people. In R. Jones (Ed.), *Black psychology.* New York: Harper & Row.

Comer, J. (1972). *Beyond Black and White.* New York: Quandrangle Books.

Gary, L., Beatty, L., & Price, M. (1983). *Stable Black families.* Final report, Institute for Urban Affairs and Research, Howard University, Washington, DC.

Grier, W., & Cobbs, P. (1968). *Black rage.* New York: Basic Books.

Haley, J. (1976). *Problem-solving therapy.* New York: Harper & Row.

Hayes, W., & Mindel, C. (1973). Extended kinship relations in Black and White families. *Journal of Marriage and the Family, 35,* 51–57.

Hines, P., & Boyd-Franklin, N. (1982). Black families. In M. McGoldrick, J. Pearce, & J. Giordano (Eds.), *Ethnicity and family therapy* (pp. 84–107). New York: Guilford.

Ho, M. K. (1987). *Family therapy with ethnic minorities.* Beverly Hills, CA: Sage.

Jones, J. (1982). "My mother was much of a woman": Black women, work, and the family under slavery. *Feminist Studies, 8(2),* 235–269.

Lyles, M., & Carter, J. (1982). Myths and strengths of the Black family: A historical and sociological contribution to family therapy. *Journal of The National Medical Association, 74(11), 1119–1123.*

Malson, M. (1982) The social support system of Black families. *Marriage and Family Review, 5(4),* 37–57.

Mayes, B. (1938). *The negro's god as reflected in his literature.* Boston: Chapman & Grimes.

McAdoo, H. (1983). Societal stress: The Black family. In H. McCubbin & C. Figley (Eds.), *Stress and the family: Coping with normative transitions* (pp. 178–187). New York: Brunner/Mazel.

McAdoo, H. (1988). The study of ethnic minority families: Implications for practitioners and policymakers. *Family Relations, 37* 265–267.

Minuchin, S. (1974). *Families and family therapy.* Cambridge, MA: Harvard University Press.

Nichols, M. (1984). *Family therapy: Concepts and methods.* New York: Gardner Press.

Pinderhughes, E. (1982). Afro-American families and the victim system. In M. McGoldrick, J. K. Pearce, & J. Giordano (Eds.), *Ethnicity and family therapy* (pp. 109–122). New York: Guilford Press.

Pomales, J., Claiburn, C., & LaFromboise, T. (1986). Effects of Black students' racial identity on perceptions of White counselors varying in cultural sensitivity. *Journal of Counseling Psychology, 33,* 57–61.

Staples, R. (1985). Changes in Black family structure: The conflict between family ideology and structural conditions. *Journal of Marriage and the Family, 47,* 1005–1013.

Stuart, R. (1980). *Helping couples change: A social learning approach to marital therapy.* New York: Guilford.

Sue, D., & Sue, D. (1977). Barriers to effective cross-cultural counseling. *Journal of Counseling Psychology, 24,* 420–429.

Terrell, F., & Terrell, S. (1984). Race of counselor, client sex, cultural mistrust level, and premature termination from counseling among Black clients. *Journal of Counseling Psychology, 31*(3), 371–375.

Thompson, R., & Cimbolic, P. (1978). Black students' counselor preference and attitudes toward counseling center use. *Journal of Counseling Psychology, 25,* 570–575.

U.S. Bureau of the Census. (1983). *America's Black population, 1970–1982: A statistical view, July 1983* (Series P10/POP83). Washington, DC: U.S. Government Printing Office.

Wilson, F. (1969). An interpretation of Afro-American history. *Social Progress, 60,* 13–23.

Wilson, N. (1989). Child development in the context of the Black extended family, *American Psychologist, 44,* 380–385.

The African American Client
Cases and Questions

1. Assume you have just been hired by a social service agency that has
    contracted to provide home-liaison services between the local schools
    and the parents of students attending these schools. Although a large
    number of the students are African American (approximately 35
    percent), your agency to date has hired only one Black home-liaison
    counselor (of a staff of twelve counselors). As a home-liaison
    counselor, your responsibilities include home visits to acquaint parents
    with community services available to them and to establish rapport
    between the parents and the schools.

    a. What expectations would you have for your first home visit with
        an African American family?
    b. What are some examples of "small talk" you might use to "break
        the ice" with the parents of a fourteen-year-old African American
        student who is consistently truant from school?
    c. Assuming none exists when you are hired, what courses and
        experiences related to African culture would you recommend that
        the school district offer to students?

2. Assume you have just accepted a counseling position in a correctional
    facility where a large number of Black inmates are incarcerated, most
    of whom come from nearby urban centers.

    a. What expectations do you have for your own performance as a
        counselor in this setting?
    b. Do you anticipate African American inmates will avail themselves
        of your services as a counselor? Why?
    c. What psychological needs can you anticipate African American
        inmates may have that you as a counselor might attempt to fulfill?
        How will you attempt to fulfill them?

3. Assume you are a counselor in a small midwestern college that is
    predominantly White but recruits Black athletes. One of the Black
    athletes (Bill) has been dating a White cheerleader (Mary) you have
    seen before for counseling. Mary, seeing you alone, has just informed
    you that Bill has moved in with her and she fears her parents will

disown her when they find out. She has also asked you if she may
bring Bill for an appointment the next day.

a. How do you feel about Mary and Bill's cross-racial living
    arrangement?
b. What are some of the issues you will want to explore with Mary
    and Bill when they come to see you together?
c. What do you suppose Mary and Bill each want to get out of
    meeting with a counselor?

The African American Client
Role Playing Exercise

Divide into groups of four or five. Assign each group member to a role and the responsibilities associated with the role as follows:

Role	Responsibility
1. Counselor	1. Assume role as a counselor or mental health worker who is assigned an African American client. Attempt to build rapport with the client.
2. Client	2. Assume role of an African American client. To play this role effectively, it will be necessary for the student to (a) identify cultural values of African Americans, (b) identify sociopolitical factors which may interfere with counseling, and (c) portray these aspects in the counseling session. It is best to select a few powerful variables in the role play. You may or may not be initially antagonistic to the counselor, but it is important for you to be sincere in your role and your reactions to the counselor.
3. Observers	3. Observe interaction and offer comments during feedback session.

This exercise is most effective in a racially and ethnically mixed group. For example, an African American student can be asked to play the client role. However, this is probably not possible in most cases. Thus, students who play the client role will need to thoroughly read the articles for the group they are portraying.

Identifying the barriers that could interfere with counseling is an important aspect of this exercise. We recommend that a list be made of the group's cultural values and sociopolitical influences prior to the role playing.

Role playing may go on for a period of five to fifteen minutes, but the time limit should be determined prior to the activity. Allow ten to fifteen minutes for a feedback session in which all participants discuss (within the group) how they felt in their respective roles, how appropriate were the counselor responses, what else they might have done in that situation, etc.

Rotate and role play the same situation with another counselor trainee *or* another African American client with different issues, concerns, and

problems. In the former case, the group may feel that a particular issue is of sufficient importance to warrant reenactment. This allows students to see the effects of other counseling responses and approaches. In the latter case, the new exposure will allow students to get a broader view of barriers to counseling.

If videotaping equipment is available, we recommend that the session be taped and processed in a replay at the end. We have found this to be a powerful means of providing feedback to participants.

PART 3

The American Indian Client

"We are not free. We do not make choices. Our choices are made for us; we are the poor. For those of us who live on reservations these choices are made by federal administrators, bureaucrats, and their 'yes men,' euphemistically called tribal governments. Those of us who live in non-reservation areas have our lives controlled by local white power elites. We have many rulers. They are called social workers, 'cops,' school teachers, churches, etc. . . . (Warrior, 1967, p. 72)

"In the old days when we were a strong and happy people, all of our power came to us from the sacred hoop of the nation, and so long as the hoop was unbroken, the people flourished. . . . Everything the power of the world does is done in a circle. The sky is round like a ball, and I heard that the earth is round like a ball, and so are all stars. The wind in its greatest power, whirls. Birds make their nests in circle, for theirs is the same religion as ours . . . Even the seasons form a great circle in their changing, and always come back again to where they were . . . Our tepees were round like the nests of birds, and these were set in a circle, the nation's hoop, a nest of many nests, where the Great Spirit meant for us to hatch our children." (Neihardt, 1972, p. 164–165)

These two quotes illustrate some very basic issues confronting American Indians and the helping professional. First, a reading of the United States' treatment of American Indians reveals a shameful and destructive past. For nearly five hundred years, American Indians have been fighting a defensive war for their right to freedom, their lands, their organization, their traditions and beliefs, their way of life, and their very lives. They have experienced massacres by the U.S. Army, have seen the Bureau of Indian Affairs systematically destroy their leadership and way of life, have known promises broken, have had their land taken from them, and have watched their children die because of inadequate health care, poverty, and suicide. By almost every measure of impoverishment and deprivation, the American Indian is the poorest of the poor. At one point, American Indians saw their population decline from over 3 million to fewer than 600,000; it now stands at about 1.5 million.

Second, while the wholesale decimation of Indians may no longer operate, cultural genocide continues to rear its ugly head in the form of institutional racism. As the second quote indicates, one of the major values among American Indians stems from their world view about the wholistic relationship between mother earth and all life. The philosophical concepts of the circle of life is viewed as continuous and reciprocal. Central to that concept is the extended family which is the primary unit of socialization emphasizing interdependency, reciprocity, and mutual obligation; it is the single most important survival mechanism. Yet, the sacred hoop of the circle has been significantly and adversely influenced by the U.S. government system. The common practice of systematically removing young children from their home environments and literally raising them in boarding schools, instituting relocation acts for the expressed purpose of assimilation, and passing numerous local, state and federal laws aimed at breaking up the experience of tribal family life struck at the heart of the American Indian world view.

These practices and laws have created disparities and inequities among American Indians and other citizens in the society. For example, the average income of American Indians is some 75 percent less than that of his/her white counterpart; the unemployment rate is ten times the national average; infant mortality after the first three months of life is three times the national average; the suicide rate of teenagers is one hundred times that of whites; and alcoholism and drug abuse, delinquency, and mental health disorders are among the highest for any ethnic group.

It is ironic that many of the whites who created these problems refer to them as "Indian problems" and have tried a variety of White-imposed methods to solve them. In essence, the attempts to solve the problems have consisted of imposing White solutions on the Indian; turn the Indian into a White and the problem will go away! The U.S. government has also imposed a legal definition of their identity: An individual must have an Indian blood quantum of 25 percent to be considered an Indian. Such an arbitrary definition has caused problems both in and out of the community. Such attempts are not only manifestations of cultural oppression, they have marked a failure on the part of Whites to understand that the twenty-five hundred years of Indian histories and cultures have little in common with European-based cultures.

In one of the best descriptive analyses of American Indian mental health policy, LaFromboise provides us with valuable demographic data concerning American Indian status and adjustment to U.S. culture. Her article reveals that American Indians are experiencing significant mental distress, that the availability of psychological services geared to American Indians is both low and inappropriate and that the understanding of the traditional healer role in Indian culture may provide a clue for future direction in providing more relevant services. She offers some valuable insights into assumptions held by American Indians about western psychology and assumptions psychologists hold about American Indians. LaFromboise concludes her article by recommending policy and action in the areas of education, training and political-organizational involvement of psychologists.

Western approaches to counseling and psychotherapy are often antagonistic to the life experiences and cultural values of American Indians. In "Counseling Intervention and American Indian Tradition: An Integrative Approach," LaFromboise, Trimble and Mohatt advocate moving away from such approaches toward the use of culturally sensitive methods more consistent with native values and beliefs. The authors discuss three types of psychological interventions—social learning, behavioral, and network therapy which may prove helpful in working with American Indians. Above all, they strongly indicate that the weakening or dissolution of the extended family system is a key element in the disruption of healthy family functioning. In view of the importance of the extended family, therapeutic approaches that are family oriented may produce more satisfactory results.

The final article in this section, ''Counseling Native Americans: An Introduction for Non-Native American Counselors,'' Thomason attempts to provide a primer on counseling Native American clients. He presents and discusses a Native American healing model based upon indigenous healing beliefs and practices. The author provides an excellent outline of how to approach a counseling session with an American Indian client. Specific examples and suggestions are provided. He warns, however, that while learning all one can about native cultures is important, the best teacher in the counseling encounter remains the live interaction with the client.

Counselors must not only recognize the historical American Indian experience of oppression and exploitation, but also be alert to how their conventional training in mental healthy practices may be inappropriate for the life-styles and values of American Indians. To impose them blinding is to perpetuate oppression of the most damaging kind.

References

Neihardt, J. (1972). *Black Elk speaks.* New York: Simon & Schuster Pocket Books.
Warrior, C. (1971). We are not free. In A. M. Josephy, Jr. (Ed.), *Red power* p. 72. New York: McGraw-Hill.

7

American Indian Mental Health Policy

Teresa D. LaFromboise

The American Indian population is culturally heterogeneous, geographically dispersed, and remarkably young. There are 200 tribal languages still spoken today. The diversity found in some 511 federally recognized native entities and an additional 365 state-recognized American Indian tribes defies distinct categorizations (Manson & Trimble, 1982). The 1980 census indicated that the American Indian population numbered approximately 1.5 million, nearly double the 1970 count (U.S. Department of Commerce, 1983). It also verified that American Indians have become increasingly urbanized, both for subsistence and for gainful employment. In 1980, 24 percent of the American Indians in this country lived on reservations. The 20.4 year median age of American Indians and 17.9 year median age of Alaska Natives is significantly younger than the median age of the U.S. population in general (30.3 years).

American Indians are generally unaffected by national economic cycles; unemployment is consistently extremely high among Indians and Alaska Natives. It hovers at about 30 percent on most reservations and ranges from a high of over 70 percent on some plains reservations to a low of 20 percent in the case of more prosperous tribes (U.S. Senate Select Committee on Indian Affairs, 1985).

Poverty and prolonged unemployment have combined with substandard housing, malnutrition, inadequate health care, shortened life expectancy, and high suicide rates to affect and limit opportunities for educational attainment. American Indians and Alaska Natives 25 years and older have an average of 9.6 years of formal education. This is below the national mean of 10.9 years and is the lowest of any major ethnic group in the United States (Brod & McQuiston, 1983). Nearly one third of all American Indian adults are classified as illiterate, and only one in five men has a

Reprinted from *American Psychologist,* 1988, *43*(5), 388–397. Copyright 1988 by the American Psychological Association. Reprinted by permission.

high school education (Price, 1981). Dropout rates between the eighth and ninth grades in some urban areas range from 48 percent to 85 percent (Jacobson, 1973) and approach 50 percent in Bureau of Indian Affairs boarding schools and day schools on reservations (Hopkins & Ready, 1978; U.S. Senate Committee on Labor and Public Welfare, 1969). Only 16 percent of the American Indian students who enter universities complete an undergraduate degree, compared to 34 percent of their White counterparts (Astin, 1982). This can undoubtedly be attributed to the stressful pressures American Indian students have experienced in the dominant White culture of higher education institutions (Edgewater, 1981).

Although it is apparent that American Indians have shown impressive reservoirs of strength and coping mechanisms in the face of these environmental realities (Special Populations Subpanel on Mental Health of American Indians and Alaska Natives, 1978), they experience high rates of mental health disorders associated with social stress. For example, overall rates of alcohol and drug abuse are high, but prevalence varies tremendously from tribe to tribe and by age within tribes (Mail & McDonald, 1980; Oetting, Edwards, Goldstein & Mason, 1980). A congressional hearing on Indian juvenile alcoholism and drug abuse reported that 52 percent of urban Indian adolescents and 80 percent of reservation Indian adolescents engaged in moderate to heavy alcohol or drug use as compared to 23 percent of their urban, non-Indian counterparts (U.S. Senate Select Committee on Indian Affairs, 1985). The hearing revealed that in some American Indian communities, children as young as four years of age can be found drinking and using inhalants.

Delinquency and arrest rates of American Indians are among the highest of any ethnic minority group in this nation (U.S. Department of Justice, 1976). American Indians in urban areas are taken into police custody for violations committed under the influence of drugs or alcohol four times as often as Blacks and ten times as often as Whites (Jepsen, Strauss, & Harris, 1977). Youth are likewise arrested more often than the norm for offenses committed while under the influence of alcohol.

American Indians have been characterized as "aliens in their own land" for the past 100 years. Cultural epidemiologists claim that forced acculturation to urban living increases individuals' vulnerability for developing psychological problems (Kemnitzer, 1973; Spindler & Spindler, 1978). Barter and Barter (1974) noted the heightened stress involved when Indians adapt to the dominant culture and at the same time are forced by their choice of residency into relinquishing their sovereign rights to health, education, and welfare on reservation land.

Psychological disturbance is often primarily a reaction to life conditions, and mental illness can be a tragic manifestation of unsatisfactory adjustment to a social-psychological environment that provides few satisfactory options for human action (DeLeon, 1977). There is a severe imbalance in favor of studies that focus on pathological disorders of American Indians to the neglect of investigations of milder transient problems and of research on familial or sociocultural antecedents of psychopathology. The most glaring gap, however, is the failure to examine the effective strategies currently employed by American Indians for coping with numerous stressors.

Only three community-wide American Indian epidemiological studies of psychopathology exist. The prevalence rates of psychological dysfunction range from a low of 1 percent per 2,000 to a high of 37 percent per 1,000; depression and adjustment reactions are the most prevalent problems (Roy, Chaudhuri, & Irvine, 1970; Sampath, 1974; Shore, Kinzie, Thompson, & Pattison, 1973). Manson, Shore, and Bloom (1985) recently reported that the prevalence of depression within select Indian communities may be four to six times higher than that in the studies noted above. Media attention to American Indian suicide recently stimulated national concern over a problem emphasized by service providers and researchers for quite some time ("Suicides of Young Indians," 1985). The suicide rate among Indian adults is over twice as high and that of school-aged children three times greater than that of the American White majority (U.S. Congress, Office of Technology Assessment, 1986). Harras (1987) reported that the annual suicide rate in some tribes has increased by about 200 percent in the past two decades to a rate of 18 per 100,000.

Given the magnitude of these social and psychological problems, what mental health services are currently available to American Indians?

Available Psychological Service Providers

In 1976 there was only one psychologist of any ethnic background for every 43,000 American Indian people (Welch, 1976). A recent survey of psychological personnel reported that 180 American Indians held master's or doctoral degrees in psychology (Stapp, Tucker, & VandenBos, 1985), boosting the personnel rate to one American Indian psychologist for every 8,333 Indian people. This rate compares most unfavorably to the current availability rate of one psychologist for every 2,213 people in the general population.[1] Of those 180 self-identified American Indian psychologists, 102 reported involvement in research activities and 36 in educational

The author appreciates the assistance of Robert F. Arnove in providing reactions to this work and assisting in the articulation of American Indian mental health policy.

Correspondence concerning this article should be addressed to Teresa D. LaFromboise, 223 School of Education, Stanford University, Stanford, CA 94305.

1. This figure was arrived at by dividing the 1980 U.S. population of 226 million people by Stapp, Tucker, and VandenBos's (1985) estimate of 102,101 available psychological personnel.

activities in addition to their involvement in mental health service delivery. These figures suggest that American Indian underrepresentation in fields of applied psychology continues to be a serious concern.

Because there are so few American Indian psychologists as role models and so few psychologists serve American Indians on Indian reservations, few Indian students seriously consider university training in psychology. For example, there are currently only five American Indian American Psychological Association (APA) minority Fellows despite extensive, continuous efforts to recruit applicants. Moreover, tribal efforts at career development have placed priority on training in the medical and legal professions since the early 1970s. Finally, the Indian Health Scholarship Program only recently began to consider counseling psychology in addition to clinical psychology applications from American Indian students for clinical scholarships.

There is only one American Indian employed by the National Institute of Mental Health (Raglin, personal communication, July 15, 1986) and one by the APA (J. Jones, personal communication, April 4, 1986). Few American Indian psychologist are involved in mental health legislative decision making beyond the provision of testimonial support (P. Zell, personal communication, May 2, 1986). The Society of Indian Psychologists (LaFromboise, 1987) and the National Indian Counselors Association, the two professional organizations that have emerged to articulate the need for more Indian psychologists in Indian communities, also try to counteract the high turnover rate of mental health services providers in the Indian Health Service and provide support for mental health workers who must often cope with undesirable working conditions. Members have found it advantageous to have a professional forum to articulate American Indian philosophical underpinnings within psychology as well as share strategies for the coordination of coexisting conventional and traditional Indian psychological service delivery. Members of both of these organizations frequently express difficulty in delivering psychological services to Indian clients, even to those who may come from their own tribe. Too often, educators assume that because a person is of American Indian descent, that person knows how to organize, support, and develop indigenous community resources.

Utilization of Psychological Services

The U.S. government initiated mental health programs for American Indians and Alaska Natives in 1965. By 1977, 40 reservation mental health programs were supported by the federal Indian Health Service. In that same year, there were 60,000 visits by American Indian and Alaska Native clients to outpatient facilities (Beiser & Attneave, 1978). Forty percent of all clients who utilize the Indian Health Service mental health programs were treated for depression, anxiety, and adjustment reactions (Rhodes, Marshal, Attneave, Echohawk, Bjork, & Beiser, 1980). An unpublished summary of a random sample of patient caseloads in three urban health clinics indicated that 30 percent of the presenting complaints were attributable to mental health problems (American Indian Health Care Association, 1978). However, 55 percent of the American Indian clients seen in Seattle mental health centers were highly unlikely to return after their initial contact as compared to a 30 percent dropout rate among other groups (Sue, 1977). The disparity between American Indians in need and those who use psychological services has been attributed to difference in values and expectations among practitioners and clients, but it is also due to neglect by representatives of the U.S. government and the profession of psychology itself in promoting adequate mental health services or health maintenance activities (Liberman & Knegge, 1979).

A number of surveys suggest that American Indians in need of help are less aware of the kinds of psychological services available to them than are most Americans (Dinges, Trimble, Manson, & Pasquale, 1981; Red Horse, Lewis, Feit, & Decker, 1978; Trimble, Manson, Dinges, & Medicine, 1984). Even those aware of available services underutilize them because of perceptions that the existing services are unresponsive to their needs (Barter & Barter, 1974). Dukepoo (1980) identified fear, mistrust, and insensitivity as major barriers to mental health service utilization in the Southwest. Manson and Trimble (1982) further suggested that underutilization is the result of negative attitudes toward non-Indian psychologists who are presumably insensitive to the cultural complexities of Indian problems. In some cases, tribal judges and school administrators have considered bussing Indian children in need of psychological assessment as far as 2,044 miles to assure that American Indian psychometricians could conduct the evaluation (R. LaFromboise, personal communication, July 10, 1980). Alternatives proposed for these situations often represent attempts to link traditional community-based practices with relevant modern approaches to mental health. Realistically, however, there are many obstacles to the implementation of more effective delivery systems.

Delivery of Services
The Indian Health Service

The largest single provider of mental health services to American Indians is the Indian Health Service (IHS). The IHS annually provides inpatient and outpatient care to more than .75 million urban and rural American Indians and their family members through direct care or contract services. The Mental Health Program administrative center in Albuquerque, New

Mexico administers social service and mental health programs in eight regional areas through 100 units composed of hospitals, clinics, and satellite centers (Schultz, 1976). Unfortunately, the IHS fails to distinguish between initial visits and repeat visits in its record keeping, which obfuscates any estimates of American Indian mental health service utilization rates (W. B. Hunter, personal communication, July 23, 1986).

Funds appropriated for mental health services within the IHS budget for the fiscal year 1985 amounted to $10,518,000, and funds for alcoholism services amounted to $24,149,800. Together, these categories accounted for only 7.3 percent of the total IHS budget allocations for direct and contract care. If the Indian Health Care Improvement Act were authorized, then previously authorized awarded funds could be allocated to decrease the backlog of mental health care services, expand services to include prevention services, and provide more rehabilitative interventions for substance abuse and other problems. The presently allocated budget covers, at best, crisis intervention and emergency care (U.S. Committee on Interior and Insular Affairs, 1985). For this reason, the IHS is now drafting a national plan for more culturally responsive mental health services to Indians (S. Nelson, personal communication, September 8, 1987).

More services are delivered by paraprofessionals and social workers in the IHS system than by psychologists, psychiatrists, or psychiatric nurses. The stark absence of psychologists in many IHS service centers is of less concern to tribal leaders than the need for 1,500 physical health professionals (e.g., physicians, registered nurses, dentists, optometrists, audiologists, and pharmacists). The standard rationale for mental health prevention efforts—that from 60 percent to 70 percent of medical office visits among the U.S. general population are for problems primarily psychological rather than physical in nature (Dörken & Associates, 1976)—falls on deaf ears. Also, reports of a wide range of problems for which Indian people seek services, including alcohol misuse, anxiety, depression, cultural conflict, and suicide attempts, often are overlooked (Rhodes, Marshal, Attneave, Echohawk, Bjork, & Beiser, 1980).

Bureau of Indian Affairs

In addition to the IHS, the Department of the Interior's Bureau of Indian Affairs (BIA) maintains 123 offices across 12 geographic areas, serving 281 tribes with a total population of approximately 649,000 people. Its community service division coordinates educational and social service branches where psychological services are also available. The educational branch is charged with consultant, advisory, and administrative responsibility for programs with American Indian youth and adults. These programs are supported by tribal and state contracts and conducted in federal boarding schools and other BIA educational and vocational guidance centers. The social service branch provides child welfare and family services, including help with problems from family disintegration and emotional instability. Unfortunately, diagnostic observations are seldom a matter of formal record keeping in the BIA, and there is little or no postreferral monitoring.

Urban Indian Health Care Programs

In the early 1970s, American Indian communities began to assume more direct control of the management and provision of health services. In 1972 the IHS began funding urban programs through its community development branch under the general authority of the Snyder Act (1921). By 1984, 37 urban health programs in 20 states were implemented on a contractual basis with the Indian Health Service. Recently, some of these programs have expanded to include as high as 20 percent of the fiscal expenditure for a wide range of programs designed to help urban Indians alleviate individual and family problems (U.S. Congress, Office of Technology Assessment, 1985). More innovative programs include the Seattle Indian Health Board's seminar series on traditional medicine, tribal beliefs and mental health, culture conflict, and self-awareness for service providers (Putnam, 1982) and the San Francisco Urban Indian Health Board's weekend drop-in mental health clinic primarily for homeless clients. It is difficult to determine whether the most innovative programs are found on or off Indian reservations because urban Indian mental health programs receive more attention than reservation programs among those interested in contract care services.

State and Local Mental Health Services

The extent to which Indians use private or public mental health services is unknown. Relatively few Indians seek private care given the availability of services provided by other institutions, but cases do exist where American Indians travel substantial distances to seek services from therapists known to be effective by the Indian community. Many urban and reservation Indians are served by city, county, or state mental health facilities. The points of entry into these facilities are diverse—state hospitals, Veterans Administration hospitals, day treatment centers, other programs such as the Job Training Partnership Act Program, and families (Manson & Trimble, 1982). Referral activities to acquaint potential clients with the mental health services in the surrounding area are conducted by Indian centers and Indian social service programs. Unfortunately, record keeping in these service delivery agencies is also uncoordinated, complicating an assessment of client satisfaction with services or utilization patterns.

University Counseling Centers

An increasing number of American Indian university students are seeking psychological services during their academic training, especially if American Indian psychologists are available. University environments typically reinforce formal methods of seeking help. The utilization rate of American Indian students for initial visits at the University of California-Berkeley clinic was 75 percent (A. Uemura, personal communication, July 10, 1986). Haskell Indian Junior College reported a direct referral rate of 50 percent and an indirect referral rate of 79 percent primarily for alcohol-related problems, personal counseling, and campus violations (B. Smith, personal communication, July 8, 1986). American Indian women in private university settings reported using formal psychological services when difficulties arose in their academic progress more frequently than their counterparts in state universities (LaFromboise, 1986). University students in their home environment indicate they would seek help from family members before seeking psychological services. Increased utilization of psychological services in academic settings by American Indians attests to the supportive functions of counseling in competitive educational arenas. This service use also provides an excellent opportunity to demonstrate the benefits of psychological interventions because the clientele will likely return to their communities upon completion of a degree.

Tribally Based Mental Health Care Programs

American Indian tribes residing on reservations were empowered with freedom to design a wide range of services, including mental health care, through the Indian Self-Determination and Education Assistance Act of 1975 (PL 93–638). To date, 61 different tribal health programs have been established under contract to the Indian Health Service, but fewer than half of these programs have a mental health component.

The use of traditional healers who both help and heal remains a priority over all other forms of clinical treatment in several tribally based communities. In recent years there appears to have been a renaissance and revitalization of traditional healing practices (Attneave, 1974; Mohatt, 1985). A research and intervention project on the Rosebud Reservation in South Dakota was designed by Sioux medicine men in collaboration with Western psychologists and was entitled ''Identity Through Traditional Lakota Methods.'' The psychological interventions employed were deemed successful by community members because they reinforced traditional ways of life (Mohatt & Blue, 1982). Attneave (1974) reported a successful two-way referral system between Indian Health Service staff and traditional healers in an Eskimo village. The first director of the IHS mental health program also reported recurring evidence of successful collaboration with

Navajo healers and the establishment of a school for traditional healers (Bergman, 1974).

Not all attempts at collaboration with traditional healers are considered successful. In fact, Dinges, Trimble, Manson, and Pasquale (1981) asserted that most attempts by psychologists to establish working relationships with healers failed due to confusion regarding credibility, fee for service, professional efficacy, technical explanations, and patient expectations. Traditional community and kinship networks of support may be the most effective delivery agencies.

American Indian communities both on and off reservations have traditionally practiced informal caregiving through the extended family. Even though diverse Indian families have transformed over time because of geographic movements and intertribal marriages, relational values have remained intact, and extended family networks provide extensive psychological support (Red Horse, Lewis, Feit, & Decker, 1978). Carolyn Attneave (1969) saw the need to make more explicit the ongoing reciprocal support of Indian extended families with urban Indians through ''network therapy.'' This support was necessary because their residence within the dominant culture constrained cultural activities that normally sustained network exchanges. In network therapy the focus of help giving is to mobilize the family, relatives, and friends into a socially interdependent force that can be attentive and responsive to emotional distress within the family in order to counteract the depersonalizing atmosphere of urban life. Red Horse (1982) applied the cultural network model in Minneapolis with Indian adolescents in a family-as-treatment model entitled the Wido-Ako-Dade-Win Program. Political organizations also represent an important source of support. Over 200 Indian political organizations exist in the United States and Canada that provide psychological and social support, as well as support for advocacy within various levels of the government to bring about changes in everything from the treatment of American Indians in history books to increased funds for the economic development of American Indian resources. The ''elders' movement'' is a social network that actively seeks older people to provide religious and personal counseling (Price, 1981). The actions of these networks and political organizations reflect general American Indian value systems and beliefs, as well as particular notions concerning health.

Assumptions American Indians Hold about Psychology

American Indian communities are distinguished by many ties among tribal members and strong group cohesion, particularly in times of crisis. Indian people have concerns about psychological concepts like ''mental health,'' "personality," and "self" because of the absence of naturalistic or holistic concepts in the design and implementation of therapeutic processes. Mental health translates in the Lakota (Sioux) language as *ta-un* (being in a state of well-being). Ta-un requires certain categories of action and introspection prior to engagement in social relations or group collective actions (Medicine, 1982). Among the Hopi, a person in a state of well-being is peaceful and exudes strength through self-control and adherence to the universal American Indian values of wisdom, intelligence, poise, tranquility, cooperation, unselfishness, responsibility, kindness, and protectiveness toward all life forms (Trimble, 1981).

Further guidance in understanding American Indian assumptions about psychology emerges from an analysis of the work of traditional healers who have challenged Western psychologists for centuries not to separate cultural ideals and practice (Dell, 1980). Primeaux (1977) stated that traditional medicine potentially embraces a broad spectrum of forces that are interwoven in all aspects of being. Carl Gorman stated that a traditional healer is actually a doctor, counselor, priest, and historian (Greenberg & Greenberg, 1984). Additionally, a healer is viewed as a safekeeper of ancient legends, which are maintained through the power of the spoken word. The healer uses the wisdom of spiritual legends for insight into human behavior and to explain emotional and behavioral problems (Power, 1982).

Many American Indians believe that mental illness is a justifiable outcome of human weakness or the result of avoiding the discipline necessary for the maintenance of cultural values and community respect. The Coyote stories, for example, contain a theme of danger associated with excessively individualistic behavior (e.g., greed, envy, trickery). Individualization of responsibility is emphasized as a means of achieving community solidarity rather than a mechanism for personal achievement. Thus, the focus on maintaining cultural values is one way of controlling individuals' preoccupation with themselves and their personal symptoms.

American Indian psychologists generally describe only a few culturally specific categories of disease causation (Trimble, Manson, Dinges, & Medicine, 1984) and tend to attach diagnostic labels to clients less frequently than non-Indian psychologists (Horowitz, 1982; Kelso & Attneave, 1981). When problems arise in Indian communities, they become not only problems of the individual but also problems of the community. The family, kin, and friends coalesce into a network to observe the individual, find reasons for the individual's behavior, and draw the person out of isolation and back into the social life of the group. The strong social and symbolic bonds among the extended family network maintain a disturbed individual within the community with minimal coercion.

In some cases the tribe has ritually adopted the individual suffering from mental disorders into a new clan group (Fox, 1964). Disturbed individuals in certain tribes are encouraged to attend peyote meetings that involve confession of a ritualized rather than personal nature and collective discussions (see Wallace, 1958, for specific examples). The cure may involve confession, atonement, restoration into the good graces of family and tribe, and intercession with the spirit world. Treatment usually involves a greater number of individuals than simply the client and healer; often the client's significant others and community members are included.

The informal resources and reciprocal exchanges of goods and services in American Indian communities diminish the impact of troubled individuals on group functioning. This system allows typically autonomous individuals sanctioned opportunities to unite in the social control of disruptive behavior. Thus, the collective treatment of psychologically troubled individuals in tribal groups not only serves to heal the individual but also to reaffirm the norms of the entire group (Kaplan & Johnson, 1964). The goal of therapy is not to strengthen the client's ego but to encourage the client to transcend the ego by experiencing the self as embedded in and expressive of community (Katz & Rolde, 1981). Inner motivations and unique experiences involving repression, self-esteem, ambivalence, or insight are ignored, and symptoms are transformed into elements of social categories rather than personal states. New solutions to problems or new ways to see old problems become possible through interconnectedness with the community.

American Indians who engage in individual therapy often express concern about how conventional Western psychology superimposes biases onto American Indian problems and shapes the behavior of the client in a direction that conflicts with Indian cultural life-style orientations and preferences. The incompatibility between conventional counseling approaches and indigenous approaches has been discussed by numerous writers (Jilek-Aall, 1976; Trimble, 1982; Trimble & LaFromboise, 1985). Many American Indians recognize the need for professional assistance only when informal community-based helping networks are unavailable.

Assumptions Psychology Holds about American Indians

Psychologists have sought to describe, measure, and understand tribal social phenomena; discover cultural patterns; and explain the practices of diverse American Indian groups for numerous decades. Unfortunately, little has been done regarding their psychological problems other than to document them (LaFromboise & Plake, 1983; Trimble, 1977). Most psychological interventions have been culturally myopic and have not accepted assumptions or procedures that could be helpful to Indian clients. Treatment reports rarely account for the functional aspects of American

Indian problems, nor do they recognize the efficacy of coping interventions that have been used for centuries.

A primary difference between Western and American Indian psychology involves a difference of values. Beginning with the work of Freud, psychologists have tried to conduct therapy within a "value-free" framework. Even though the accepted view is that many of the central targets of therapy (e.g., matters of work, marriage, and adjustment) are value laden, most psychologists choose to adopt a quasi-medical, value-free position in order to avoid the diverse social and religious values of Western society (Rappaport & Rappaport, 1981). In contrast, however, many well-intentioned psychologists believe that they could best help American Indians by helping them adjust to Western value systems or create a more personal value system of their own. As noted earlier, the American Indian approach to psychology assigns importance to healers and therapists as value keepers of the tribe. Much of the work of American Indian therapy centers around the process of deciphering traditional American Indian values that come into conflict with the values espoused by the dominant culture (Trimble, 1981).

The current U.S. mental health care system operates primarily on a scarcity paradigm regarding mental health resources, with university-trained specialists being considered the only valid healers (Katz, 1986). This paradigm still holds even though professionals have argued persuasively that communities can play a vital role in promoting mental health (e.g., Jung, 1972; Rappaport, 1981; Sarason, 1977). Unfortunately, the same psychologists trained during the progressive social era of the 1960s now appear aligned with fiscal conservatives who emphasize the cost ineffectiveness of helping grass-roots institutions involved in therapeutic efforts (Rappaport, 1981). As psychology becomes increasingly more guild oriented, its members attend to pronouncements of the zero-sum gain and restrict mental health delivery to those individuals and agencies who are properly licensed and accredited (i.e., those that are reimbursable by insurance or are supported by grants or by established social agencies).

The Euro American tradition, on which contemporary psychology (Spence, 1985) is based, espouses an Aristotelian worldview that promotes dualisms, weakens community, and diminishes a sense of rootedness in time and place. The Anglo American emphasis on personal agency has fostered material prosperity, freedom, and autonomy for the privileged classes. However, the consequences include alienation and narcissistic self-absorption (Bellah, Madsen, Sullivan, Swidler, & Tipton, 1985).

Psychology also maintains a distinction between scientific and alternative therapeutic styles (Torrey, 1972). Psychologists believe that working class clients rely on superstitious or physical explanations of personality problems rather than insight-oriented therapies. Paraprofessionals, traditional headers, and community mental health representatives who run essential programs in American Indian communities are not considered to be bona fide professionals and are often subjected to excessive scrutiny. The profession assesses techniques used by Western, licensed therapists with PhDs as scientific, whereas practices of paraprofessional and indigenous healers are considered to be "largely magical" (Hippler, 1975, p. 24).

Even the process of prevention is different between Western psychologists and American Indians (Robbins, 1982; Shore & Nicholls, 1975). Western psychologists often select high-risk clients and offer them prepackaged programs to teach them how to adjust to circumstances (Rappaport, 1981). Thus, prevention efforts maintain a self-serving, aloof flavor unlike the transforming intention of American Indian prevention ceremonies. Further evidence of the individualistic orientation of psychology involves a reluctance to combine therapies despite the fact that consumers make pragmatic decisions to do so, often blending theoretically conflicting psychological interventions (Katz & Rolde, 1981). American Indian clients experience little, if any, conflict about integrating both traditional and "modern" conventional psychological approaches (Meyer, 1974). These distinctions must be considered in light of American Indian approaches that emanate from a holistic, community-involved perspective that implies a spiritual dimension as well (Katz, 1986; Mohatt, 1985).

Even recently trained psychologists are quick to develop a "clinical mentality" that emphasizes action and a sense of responsibility to individual clients and professional colleagues over a service orientation to the larger community (Goldstein & Donaldson, 1979). Therapy as currently practiced by American Indians is often seen by Anglo professionals as having comparative insignificance within an overall system of health care delivery. These professionals view the perceptions of the community as unimportant and focus on the therapeutic process between the client and the therapist. This therapeutic enterprise is very individualistic. It emphasizes immediate experiencing, intrapsychic processes, and individual motivation rather than community-oriented social causes of illnesses and issues of cohesiveness. Psychologists help clients develop the ego or defenses to mediate between the influences of significant others and the larger society (Frank, 1973). Psychologists also tend to use the strategies common in most theoretical orientations to provide clients with new, corrective experiences and offer them direct feedback in order to somehow change their psychological and emotional lives (Schofield, 1964, p. 994).

Currently, psychologists are trained within a university model that emphasizes lecture-dominated and cognitive-centered pedagogy. Training has conceptually changed little despite the recommendations of the Vail and Dulles conferences (Boll, 1985; Dulles Conference Task Force, 1978; Korman, 1974). Trimble (1982, p. 150) has described this model as leaving students dramatically lacking in the necessary skills for work in unique cultural settings. A typical program in counseling and clinical psychology, for example, involves technical training in everything from principles of psychopathology to research methods, but it rarely includes training in community consultation and social change intervention or alternatives to individual intervention (Atkinson, 1981). Courses on culturally distinct clients are regulated ''to the periphery of the curriculum where they have been subject to the vagaries of faculty politics, budgetary constraints, and student activism or apathy'' (Gibbs, 1985, p. 426). Sandwiched in the program are clinical practicums, supervised instruction and internships, and some sort of resident practicum, which is often devoid of professional character development in areas such as empowerment, transformation, and synergy paradigms. Following the completion of course work and successful defense of a dissertation or thesis, the trainee is granted a degree (usually the doctorate). The trainee subsequently may seek a state license to practice his or her chosen profession. Such a situation, whether intentional or not, tends to inhibit the student from pursuing cross-cultural interests and subtly influences the student's socialization more solidly into the mainstream profession of psychology.

If non-Indian professionals are to be trained in American Indian cultural styles of healing, it is necessary to understand the process by which Indians become competent as healers. The process begins with the search to find a master teacher or healer willing to accept the student as an apprentice. The decision of who is trained by whom is solely decided by the two people involved. The apprenticeship process can begin as early as adolescence, and the apprenticeship can last for the full duration of training. The healer decides what tasks an apprentice is ready to perform (Bergman, 1974). The interaction of student and healer combines elements of course work, supervision, therapy, and scholarship. Although apprentices receive formal education, the main structure of their education is determined by needs apparent in the apprenticeship. Classes, laboratories, and other university trappings are regarded as adjuncts, not the essence of education.

Recommendations for Policy and Action

Recruitment, Education, and Training

1. Academic institutions should make every effort to acquaint American Indians with the benefits of pursuing careers in psychology and increase and expedite the recruitment of American Indian students to psychological training programs.

2. Psychological training programs should revise their curriculum to include the impact of cultural environment and contextual effects on American Indian behavior (Trimble, LaFromboise, Mackey, & France, 1982).

Course work should begin with a non-Western point of departure, relying on the history of past practice to remind students to analyze indigenous methods and learn from them prior to developing psychological interventions. The sociopolitical history that American Indians have undergone and the present impact of that history should be reviewed. Topics on social influence variables (LaFromboise & Dixon, 1981), appropriate problems for presentation in therapy (Blue, 1977; Dauphinais, LaFromboise, & Rowe, 1980), styles of therapeutic communication (Dauphinais, Dauphinais, & Rowe, 1981), and the personal attributes of a psychologist (Haviland, Horswill, O'Connell, & Dynneson, 1983) should be included.

3. The training of psychologists should include community-based practicum internships in order that psychologists develop a sensitivity to the effects of their own worldviews on American Indian clients.

Students must learn how American Indian communities are organized, supported, and developed, in order to use networking skills with them (Brammer, 1985). Mohatt (see LaFromboise & Trimble, in press) suggests a tribally based community internship year consisting of intense exposure to American Indian religious and transcendental values and experiences. Interns would study interactions among the therapist, the client, and the client's culture (Lenrow, 1978) and learn to use individuals and families as brokers, interpreters, and supporters for clients. American Indians would witness the potential of psychology to improve American Indian mental health as they interact with interns endeavoring to integrate cultural healing beliefs and psychotherapy practices.

4. Mental health service providers should build on clients' strengths while helping clients maintain their membership in social networks and remain in natural communities in the least restrictive environment (President's Commission on Mental Health, 1978). The empowerment of American Indians relies on diagnostic methods that evaluate the functioning of an individual's natural support system, examines the established linkages between the natural support systems and the professional caregiving systems, and maintains respect for privacy and general collaboration. In a community-empowerment model, the community functions as the locus for services, mechanism for the development of professional and lay helping networks, foundation for the development of community-relevant mental health programming, and means of client involvement (Biegel & Naparstek, 1982).

Rappaport and Rappaport (1981) recommended a two-stage process that focuses on different aspects of the disturbance process. Psychologists would treat symptoms, and traditional support systems would function to manage secondary anxiety or existential value-laden issues. The coordination of psychologists with resources in the Indian community (e.g., community volunteers, indigenous helpers, extended family resources, and other nonprofessional sources) in help-giving activities enhances organizational effectiveness. By working with already established channels of communication and power structures, psychologists could more easily increase their social influence (Kiesler, 1980). Katz (1983–1984) recommended community healing resources. He advocated a process of transformation that involves linking individuals and organizations so that disparate groups might create agreement on how to manage central issues. In order to operate within a transformational system or an empowerment system, the psychologist needs to emphasize developmental processes rather than treatment processes.

Political-Organizational Involvement

5. American Indian tribal governments must assume a more active stance in regulating the quality of psychological service provision.

McShane and Bloom (1984) have recently encouraged American Indian tribes to assume a more active role in the provision of mental health services through regulatory authority of the Indian Self-Determination and Education Assistance Act of 1975. They exhorted tribes to require tribal licensure in addition to state licensure for psychologists who practice within reservations or within American Indian programs in urban areas. This procedure has already been employed, with researchers conducting investigations on reservations in the form of "scientific ordinances" (Efrat & Mitchell, 1974).

Tribal licensure would allow Indian communities the control necessary to set their own priorities for development and their own criteria for competence in service provision. Presumably, tribal governments would try their best to recruit American Indian and non-Indian psychologists who meet the highest available standards, who are eligible for licensure in the surrounding vicinity, and who can move freely in bicultural, professional circles surrounding the reservation. It has been suggested that requirements for tribal licensure include prior course work or supervised experience in American Indian studies and in cross-cultural psychology. It is hoped that this approach to demonstrate firm guidance and concern by tribal governments would attract more psychological professionals to work in American Indian communities.

6. Those interested in improving the status of American Indians within psychology should become actively involved in all levels of professional and governmental organizations. Increased American Indian involvement in policy-making arenas will sensitize professionals to their needs and allow opportunities for American Indians to use their skills and knowledge in advocating for appropriate actions to redress their mental health needs. Professionals can add relevance to social policy matters by fostering coalitions between grass roots representatives and professional associations.

The formulation of mental health policy should begin with affected people articulating to officials what social policies and programs are necessary (Elmore, 1979). By mobilizing efforts and funding resources for improvement in these critical areas, psychologists can practice their ethical responsibility to use their clinical skills and academic knowledge to work for change in eliminating social and racial inequality.

References

American Indian Health Care Association. (1978). *Six studies concerning the assessment of mental health needs in the Minneapolis—St. Paul area: A Summary.* Unpublished manuscript, American Indian Health Care Association, Minneapolis, MN.

Astin, A. W. (1982). *Minorities in American higher education.* San Francisco, CA: Jossey-Bass.

Atkinson, D. (1981). Selections and training for human rights counseling. *Counselor Education Supervision, 21,* 101–108.

Attneave, C. L. (1969). Therapy in tribal settings and urban network intervention. *Family Process, 8,* 192–210.

Attneave, C. L. (1974). Medicine men and psychiatrists in the Indian Health Service. *Psychiatric Annals, 4,* 49, 53–55.

Barter, E. R., & Barter, J. T. (1974). Urban Indians and mental health problems. *Psychiatric Annals, 4,* 37–43.

Beiser, M., & Attneave, C. (1978). Mental health services for American Indians: Neither feast nor famine. *White Cloud Journal, 1,* 3–10.

Bellan, R. N., Madsen, R., Sullivan, W. M., Swidler, A., & Tipton, S. M. (1985). *Habits of the heart.* Berkeley, CA: University of California Press.

Bergman, R. L. (1974). The medicine men of the future—Reuniting the learned professionals. In A. B. Tulipan, C. L. Attneave, & E. Kingston (Eds.), *Beyond clinic walls* (pp. 131–143). University, AL: University of Alabama Press.

Biegel, D. E., & Naparstek, A. J. (Eds.). (1982). *Community support systems and mental health.* New York: Springer.

Blue, A. W. (1977). A study of native elders and student needs. *BIA Education Research Bulletin, 5,* 15–24.

Boll, T. J. (1985). Graduate education in psychology: Time for change? *American Psychologist, 40,* 1029–1030.

Brammer, L. M. (1985). Nonformal support in cross-cultural counseling and therapy. In P. Pedersen (Ed.), *Handbook of cross-cultural counseling and therapy* (pp. 87–92). Westport, CT: Greenwood Press.

Brod, R. L., & McQuiston, J. M. (1983). American Indian adult education and literacy: The first national survey. *Journal of American Indian Education, 1,* 1–16.

Dauphinais, P., Dauphinais, L., & Rowe, W. (1981). Effects of race and communication style on Indian perceptions of counselor effectiveness. *Counselor Education and Supervision, 21,* 72–80.

Dauphinais, P., LaFromboise, T., & Rowe, W. (1980). Perceived problems and sources of help for American Indian students. *Counselor Education and Supervision, 20,* 37–46.

DeLeon, P. H. (1977). Psychology and the Carter administration. *American Psychologist, 32,* 750–751.

Dell, P. F. (1980). The Hopi family therapist and the Aristotelian parents. *Journal of Marital and Family Therapy, 6,* 123–130.

Dinges, N., Trimble, J., Manson, S., & Pasquale, F. (1981). The social ecology of counseling and psychotherapy with American Indians and Alaska Natives. In A. Marsella & P. Pedersen (Eds.), *Cross-cultural counseling and psychotherapy* (pp. 243–276). New York: Pergamon Press.

Dörken, H. & Associates. (1976). *The professional psychologist today: New developments in law, health insurance, and health practices.* San Francisco, CA: Jossey-Bass.

Dukepoo, P. C. (1980). *The elder American Indian.* San Diego, CA: Campanile.

Dulles Conference Task Force. (1978, June). *Expanding the roles of culturally diverse peoples in the profession of psychology.* (Report submitted to the Board of Directors of the American Psychological Association). Washington, DC: American Psychological Association.

Edgewater, J. L. (1981). Stress and the Navajo university students. *Journal of American Indian Education, 20,* 25–31.

Efrat, B., & Mitchell, M. (1974). The Indian and the social scientist: Contemporary contractual arrangements on the Pacific Northwest coast. *Human Organization, 33,* 405–407.

Elmore, R. F. (1979). Backward mapping: Implementation research and policy decisions. *Political Science Quarterly, 80,* 601–612.

Fox, J. R. (1964). Witchcraft and clanship in Cochiti therapy. In A. Kiev (Ed.), *Magic, faith, and healing: Studies in primitive psychiatry today* (pp. 174–200). New York: Free Press.

Frank, J. D. (1973). *Persuasion and healing: A comparative study of psychotherapy* (2nd ed.). Baltimore, MD: Johns Hopkins University Press.

Gibbs, J. T. (1985). Can we continue to be color-blind and class-bound? *The Counseling Psychologist, 13* 426–435.

Goldstein, M.S., & Donaldson, D. J. (1979). Exporting professionalism: A case study of medical education. *Journal of Health and Social Behavior, 20,* 322–337.

Greenberg, H., & Greenberg, G. (1984). *Carl Gorman's world.* Albuquerque: University of New Mexico Press.

Harras, A. (1987). *Issues in adolescent Indian health: Suicide* (Division of Medical Systems Research and Development Monograph Series) Washington, DC: U.S. Department of Health and Human Services.

Haviland, M. G., Horswill, R. K., O'Connell, J. T., & Dynneson, V. V. (1983). Native American college students' preference for counselor race and sex and the likelihood of their use of a counseling center. *Journal of Counseling Psychology, 30,* 267–270.

Hippler, A. E. (1975). Thawing out some magic. *Mental Hygiene, 59,* 20–24.

Hopkins, T. R., & Reedy, R. L. (1978). Schooling and the American Indian high school student. *BIA Education Research Bulletin, 6,* 5–12.

Horowitz, A. V. (1982). *The social control of mental illness.* New York: Academic Press.

Indian Self-Determination and Education Assistance Act, Pub. L. No. 93–638 (1975).

Jacobson, D. (1973). *Alaskan Native high school dropouts. A report prepared for project ANNA.* (ERIC Document Reproduction Service No. ED 088651)

Jepsen, G. F., Strauss, J. H., & Harris, V. W. (1977). Crime, delinquency and the American Indian. *Human Organization, 36,* 252–257.

Jilek-Aall, L. (1976). The western psychiatrist and his non-western clientele. *Canadian Psychiatric Association Journal, 21,* 353–359.

Jung, C. (1972). *Two essays on analytical psychology.* Princeton, NJ: Princeton University Press.

Kaplan, B., & Johnson, D. (1964). The social meaning of Navajo psychopathology and psychotherapy. In A. Kiev (Ed.), *Magic, faith, and healing* (pp. 203–229). New York: Free Press.

Katz, R. (1983–1984). Employment and synergy: Expanding the community's healing resources [Special issue]. *Prevention in Human Services, 3,* 201–225.

Katz, R. (1986). Healing and transformation: Perspectives on development, education and community. In M. White & S. Pollak (Eds.), *The cultural transition: Human experience and social transformation in the Third World and Japan* (pp. 41–64). London: Routledge and Kegan Paul.

Katz, R., & Rolde, E. (1981). Community alternatives to psychotherapy. *Psychotherapy: Theory, Research and Practice, 18,* 365–374.

Kelso, D. R., & Attneave, C. L. (1981). *Bibliography of North American Indian mental health.* Westport, CT: Greenwood Press.

Kemnitzer, L. S. (1973). Adjustment and value conflict in urbanizing Dakota Indians measured by Q-sort technique. *American Anthropologist, 75,* 687–707.

Kiesler, C. A. (1980). Mental health policy as a field of inquiry for psychology. *American Psychologist, 35,* 1066–1080.

Korman, M. (1974). National conference on levels and patterns of professional training in psychology. *American Psychologist, 29,* 441–449.

LaFromboise, T. (1986, June). *Bicultural competence for American Indian self-determination.* Paper presented at the Thirteenth Annual McDaniel Conference, Stanford, CA.

LaFromboise, T. (1987). Special commentary from the Society of Indian Psychologists. *American Indian Alaska Native Mental Health Research, 1,* 51–53.

LaFromboise, T., & Dixon, D. (1981). American Indian perceptions of trustworthiness in a counseling interview. *Journal of Counseling Psychology, 28,* 135–139.

LaFromboise, T., & Plake, B. (1983). Toward meeting the educational research needs of American Indians. *Harvard Educational Review, 53,* 45–51.

LaFromboise, T., & Trimble, J. (in press. Counseling intervention and American Indian tradition: An integrative approach. *The Counseling Psychologist.*

Lenrow, P. (1978). Dilemmas of professional helping: Continuities and discontinuities with folk helping relationships. In L. Wispe (Ed.), *Altruism, sympathy, and helping* (pp. 263–290). New York: Academic Press.

Liberman, D., & Knegge, R. (1979). Health care provider-consumer communication in the Miccosukee Indian community. *White Cloud Journal, 1,* 5–13.

Mail, P., & McDonald, P. R. (1980). *Tulapai to Tokay, a bibliography of alcohol use and abuse among Native Americans of North America*. New Haven, CT: HRAF.

Manson, S., Shore, J., & Bloom, J. (1985). The depressive experience in American Indian communities. A challenge for psychiatric theory and diagnosis. In A. Kleinman & B. Good (Eds.), *Culture and depression* (pp. 331–368). Berkeley: University of California Press.

Manson, S. M., & Trimble, J. E. (1982). American Indian and Alaska Native communities: Past efforts, future inquiries. In L. R. Snowden (Ed.), *Reaching the underserved: Mental health needs of neglected populations* (pp. 143–163). Beverly Hills, CA: Sage.

McShane, D., & Bloom, J. (1984). *Transcultural training and service delivery: Training and certifying of mental health professionals*. Unpublished manuscript, Oregon Health Sciences University, Portland, OR.

Medicine, B. (1982). New roads to coping—Siouan sobriety. In S. Manson (Ed.), *New directions in prevention among American Indian and Alaska Native communities* (pp. 189–212). Portland, OR: National Center for American Indian and Alaska Native Mental Health Research.

Meyer, G. G. (1974). On helping the casualties of rapid change. *Psychiatric Annals, 4*, 44–48.

Mohatt, G. V. (1985, August). *Cross-cultural perspectives on prevention and training: The healer and prevention*. Paper presented at the meeting of the American Psychological Association, Los Angeles, CA.

Mohatt, G. V., & Blue, A. W. (1982). Primary prevention as it relates to traditionally and empirical measures of social deviance. In S. M. Manson (Ed.), *New directions in prevention among American Indian and Alaska Native communities* (pp. 91–116). Portland, OR: National Center for American Indian and Alaska Native Mental Health Research.

Oetting, E. R., Edwards, B. A., Goldstein, G. S., & Manson, V. G. (1980). Drug use among adolescents of five southwestern Native American tribes. *The International Journal of the Addictions, 15*, 439–445.

Powers, W. K. (1982). *Yuwipi, vision and experience in Oglala ritual*. Lincoln: University of Nebraska Press.

President's Commission on Mental Health. (1978). *Task panel report to the President* (Vols. 1–4). Washington, DC: U.S. Government Printing Office.

Price, J. A. (1981). North American Indian families. In C. Mendel & R. Habenstein (Eds.), *Ethnic families in America* (pp. 245–268). New York: Elsevier.

Primeaux, M. H. (1977). American Indian health care practices: A cross-cultural perspective. *Nursing Clinics of North America, 12*, 55–65.

Putnam, J. S. (1982). *Indian and Alaska Native mental health seminars: Summarized proceedings*. Seattle, WA: Seattle Indian Health Board.

Rappaport, H., & Rappaport, M. (1981). The integration of scientific and traditional healing. *American Psychologist, 36*, 774–781.

Rappaport, J. (1981). In praise of paradox: A social policy of empowerment over prevention. *American Journal of Community Psychology, 9*, 1–25.

Red Horse, J. G., Lewis, R. L., Feit, M., & Decker, J. (1978). Family behavior of urban American Indians. *Social Casework, 59*, 67–72.

Red Horse, Y. (1982). A cultural network model: Perspectives for adolescent services and paraprofessional training. In S. M. Manson (Ed.), *New directions in*

prevention among American Indian and Alaska Native communities
(pp. 173–185). Portland, OR: National Center for American Indian and Alaska
Native Mental Health Research.

Rhodes, E. R., Marshal, M., Attneave, C. L., Echohawk, M., Bjork, J., & Beiser, M.
(1980). Mental health problems of American Indians seen in outpatient facilities
of the Indian Health Service. *Public Health Reports, 96,* 329–335.

Robbins, M. (1982). Project Nak-nu-we-sha: A preventive intervention in child abuse
and neglect among a Pacific Northwest Indian community. In S. M. Manson
(Ed.), *New directions in prevention among American Indians and Alaska Native
communities* (pp. 233–248) Portland: Oregon Health Sciences University.

Roy, C., Chaudhuri, A., & Irvine, O. (1970). The prevalence of mental disorders
among Saskachewan Indians. *Journal of Cross-Cultural Psychology, 1,* 383–392.

Sampath, B. M. (1974). Prevalence of psychiatric disorders in a southern Baffin
Island Eskimo settlement. *Canadian Psychiatric Association Journal, 19,*
363–367.

Sarason, S. (1977). *The psychological sense of community: Prospects for a
community psychology.* San Francisco, CA: Jossey-Bass.

Schofield, W. (1964). *Psychotherapy: The purchase of friendship.* Englewood Cliffs,
NJ: Prentice-Hall.

Schultz, J. L. (1976). *White medicine Indian lives. . . . As long as the grass shall
grow. . . .* Fort Collins: Colorado State University.

Shore, J. H., Kinzie, J. D., Thompson, D., & Pattison, E. M. (1973). Psychiatric
epidemiology of an Indian village. *Psychiatry, 36,* 70–81.

Shore, J. H., & Nicholls, W. M. (1975). Indian children and tribal group homes:
New interpretations of the Whipper Man. *American Journal of Psychiatry, 132,*
454–456.

Snyder Act, 25 U.S.C. 13 (1921).

Special Populations Subpanel on Mental Health of American Indians and Alaska
Natives. (1978). *A good day to live for one million Indians.* Washington, DC:
U.S. Government Printing Office.

Spence, J. T. (1985). Achievement American style: The rewards and costs of
individualism. *American Psychologist, 40,* 1285–1295.

Spindler, G. D., & Spindler, L. S. (1978). Identity, militancy, and cultural
congruence: The Menomonee and Kainai. *Annals of the American Academy,
436,* 73–85.

Stapp, J., Tucker, A. M., & VandenBos, G. R. (1985). Census of psychological
personnel: 1983. *American Psychologist, 40,* 1317–1351.

Sue, S. (1977). Community mental health services to minority groups: Some
optimism, some pessimism. *American Psychologist, 32,* 616–624.

Suicides of young Indians called epidemic. (1985, October 6). *New York Times,* p. 4.

Torrey, E. F. (1972). What western psychotherapists can learn from witch doctors.
American Journal of Orthopsychiatry, 42, 69–76.

Trimble, J. E. (1977). The sojourner in the American Indian community:
Methodological issues and concerns. *Journal of Social Issues, 33,* 159–174.

Trimble, J. E. (1981). Value differentials and their importance in counseling
American Indians. In P. Pedersen, J. Draguns, W. Lonner, & J. Trimble (Eds.),
Counseling across cultures (pp. 203–226). Honolulu: University Press of Hawaii.

Trimble, J. E. (1982). American Indian mental health and the role of training for prevention. In S. M. Manson (Ed.), *New directions in prevention among American Indian and Alaska Native communities* (pp. 147–168). Portland: Oregon Health Sciences University.

Trimble, J. E., & LaFromboise, T. (1985). American Indians and the counseling process: Culture, adaptation, and style. In P. Pedersen (Ed.), *Handbook of cross-cultural mental health services* (pp. 127–134). Beverly Hills, CA: Sage.

Trimble, J., LaFromboise, T., Mackey, D., & France, G. (1982). American Indians, psychology and curriculum development: A proposal reform with reservations. In J. Chunn, P. Dunston, & F. Ross-Sheriff (Eds.), *Mental health and people of color* (pp. 43–64). Washington, DC: Howard University Press.

Trimble, J. E., Manson, S. M., Dinges, N. G., & Medicine, B. (1984). American Indian concepts of mental health: Reflections and directions. In P. Pedersen, N. Sartorius, & A. Marsella (Eds.), *Mental health services: The cross-cultural context* (pp. 199–220). Beverly Hills, CA: Sage.

U.S. Committee on Interior and Insular Affairs. (1985). *Reauthorizing and amending the Indian Health Care Improvement Act.* (House of Representatives Report No. 99–94). Washington, DC: U.S. Government Printing Office.

U.S. Congress, Office of Technology Assessment. (1985). *Survey of urban Indian health programs* (Internal document). Washington, DC: U.S. Government Printing Office.

U.S. Congress, Office of Technology Assessment. (1986). *Indian health care* (OTA–H–290). Washington, DC: U.S. Government Printing Office.

U.S. Department of Commerce, Bureau of the Census. (May, 1983). *1980 census of population: Characteristics of the population* (U.S. Summary, PC 80–1–B1). Washington, DC: Author.

U.S. Department of Justice, Federal Bureau of Investigations. (1976). *Crime in the United States 1972: Uniform crime reports.* Washington, DC: U.S. Government Printing Office.

U.S. Senate Committee on Labor and Public Welfare. (1969). *Indian education: A national tragedy—A national challenge* (Special Subcommittee on Indian Education Report No. 91–501). Washington, DC: U.S. Government Printing Office.

U.S. Senate Select Committee on Indian Affairs. (1985). *Indian juvenile alcoholism and eligibility for BIA schools* (Senate Hearing 99–286). Washington, DC: U.S. Government Printing Office.

Wallace, A. (1958). Dreams and wishes of the soul: A type of psychoanalytic theory among seventeenth century Iroquois. *American Anthropologist, 60,* 234–248.

Welch, W. (1976, April). Wanted: An American Indian psychologist. *Behavior Today,* pp. 2, 3.

8

Counseling Intervention and American Indian Tradition: An Integrative Approach

Teresa D. LaFromboise, Joseph E. Trimble, and Gerald V. Mohatt

One need not be a historian to federal Indian policy to detect movement in Indian Health Service mental health policy away from conventional psychological thought toward the recognition of culturally sensitive mental health approaches that maintain Indian community values (Nelson, 1988). Development of new service delivery approaches may have implications for the education and training of counseling psychologists and is likely to occur in the wake of this new policy.

This article outlines the process of helping from an American Indian traditional healing perspective and describes beliefs associated with efforts toward maintaining wellness and overcoming psychological disturbance. Studies addressing social influence variables that contribute to cultural clashes associated with individual and group counseling are reviewed along with research that supports the efficacy of selected counseling interventions with Indian clients. Considerations for the employment of culturally unique and conventional psychological interventions to advance the goal of Indian empowerment are enumerated. Tribal diversity and structural similarities are suggested in case material illustrating typical case presentations found in service delivery settings with American Indians. Finally, future directions in counseling and research training to prepare counseling psychologists to integrate conventional counseling interventions with American Indian tradition are provided.

Reprinted from *The Counseling Psychologist, 18*(4), 628–654. © Sage Publications, Inc.
Reprinted by permission of Sage Publications, Inc.

American Indians and the Helping Process

Traditional American Indian tribal groups have unique perspectives on both the process and theory of counseling and therapy (LaFromboise, 1988). These views differ considerably from those of the dominant society. Knowledge of and respect for an Indian worldview and value system—which varies according to the client's tribe, level of acculturation, and other personal characteristics—is fundamental not only for creating the trusting counselor-client relationship vital to the helping process but also for defining the counseling style or approach most appropriate for each client.

In general, American Indians, especially more traditional or "nativistic" ones, believe that "mental health" is much more spiritual and holistic in nature than conventional psychological definitions would suggest (Locust, 1988; Trimble, Manson, Dinges, & Medicine, 1984). The term "medicine" for many Indians refers to a practice not limited to treating bodily disorders such as disease and injury. In addition, it represents a healing system based on the belief that the "forces of good and evil are interwoven in all aspects of the physical, social, psychological and spiritual being and it is difficult to isolate one aspect for discussion (Primeaux, 1977, p. 55)." According to certain traditional Indian views, a person and his/her psychological welfare must be considered in the context of the community (ef. Trimble & Hayes, 1984).

When problems arise in Indian communities, they become not only problems of the individual but problems of the community. The family, kin, and friends coalesce into an interlocking network to observe the individual, and find comprehensible reasons for the individual's behavior, draw the individual out of isolation, and integrate the individual back into the social life of the group (LaFromboise, 1988). The strong social and symbolic bonds among the extended family network surface to maintain a disturbed member within the community with minimal coercion (Dinges, Trimble, Manson, & Pasquale, 1981).

Many American Indians attribute their psychological or physical problems to human weakness and the propensity to avoid the personal discipline necessary for the maintenance of cultural values and community respect. American Indian psychologists seemingly adhere to these spiritual attributions. They tend to attach diagnostic labels to clients less frequently than do non-Indian psychologists, and they generally describe only a few culturally specific categories of disease causation (Kelso & Attneave, 1981; Neliegh, 1988; Trimble et al., 1984). According to the few small community-based studies of American Indians and Alaska Natives that have been completed, the most prevalent psychological diagnoses associated with weaknesses and neglect within these populations involve depression, anxiety, adjustment reactions, and psychoses. Drug and alcohol abuse are often associated with these disorders (Manson, Walker, & Kivlahan, 1987; Rhoades et al., 1980; Roy, Chaudhuri, & Irvine, 1970; Sampath, 1974; Shore, Kinzie, Hampson, & Pattison, 1973; Trimble, Padilla, & Bell, 1987).

Traditional ceremonies reinforce personal adherence to cultural values and remind participants of the importance of strengthening and revitalizing family and community networks. The sweat lodge ceremony and the peyote meetings practiced through the Native American church by some tribes involve self-disclosure and confessions on the part of those seeking guidance. These and other indigenous healing practices facilitate purification and prayer.

Ceremonial rituals have been of interest to social scientists and non-Indian interveners since early contact. Depending on philosophy, non-Indians saw these practices either as anthropologically interesting or as a major hindrance to their attempts to civilize native people. This latter perspective prevailed and led to laws that outlawed religious healing practices of Indian people and put intense pressure on local people not to attend healing ceremonies. In spite of this pressure, medicine men continued their practices.

Only in the late 1960s and 1970s did the *Zeitgeist* change. In 1978, the American Indian Religious Freedom Act (PL 95–134) affirmed that traditional religious ceremonies could be practiced with the same protection offered all religions under the Constitution. Priests now attend ceremonies, physicians and nurses meet with medicine men, psychologists and medicine men meet in case conferences, and rituals such as the sun dance are held publicly (Mohatt, 1978). The numbers of indigenous people attending such ceremonies have increased dramatically and now involve not only traditional people but also more acculturated tribal members.

This Indian traditional healing process, however, unlike conventional psychological interventions, usually involves more than the client and therapist or healer. The client's significant others and community members often are asked to participate (cf. LaBarre, 1964; Wallace, 1958). The "cure" may require more than therapeutic agents and can also include confession, acts of atonement, restoration into the good graces of family and tribe, and intercession with the spirit world. Thus the collective treatment of psychologically troubled individuals in tribal groups not only serves to heal the individual, but also to reaffirm the norms of the entire group (Kaplan & Johnson, 1964).

Medicine men and women organize a complex set of rituals that serve not only to treat but to prevent illness of a psychological or physical nature. These rituals involve a type of gift exchange that commits the seeker (the client) to attending future ceremonies, thereby becoming immersed in a way of life. Finally, through participation in ceremonial life, a worldview, in which the universe is seen as a complex balance among transcendental forces, human beings, and the natural environment, is revealed (Hammerschlag, 1988). These forces are mutually compatible as long as people respect the natural laws of governing how transactions are to be organized (e.g., respect for taboos such as incest, for an animal's spirit when it is hunted and killed, for ways to speak to others).

The goal of therapy from a traditional healing perspective, then, is not to strengthen the client's ego but to encourage the client to transcend the ego by experiencing self as embedded in and expressive of community (Katz & Rolde, 1981). Inner motivations and unique experiences involving repression, self-esteem, ambivalence, or insight are downplayed, and the experience of symptoms is transformed into elements of social categories rather than being a personal state of mental health. New solutions to problems or new ways to see old problems become possible through interconnectedness, creativity, and wisdom within the ceremonial life of the community (see Powers, 1982; Sandner, 1978; and Walker, 1980 for further information on traditional ceremonies in Indian life). Therefore, prevention and intervention always have a religious and cosmological framework; the medicine man both prays and doctors. Religion and psychology intertwine.

Cultural Clash with Conventional Counseling

Traditionally oriented therapy (e.g., behavioral, person-centered, psychodynamic) clearly takes a different tack than one typically expected by many Indian clients. Psychological training as it is conducted today fosters a "clinical mentality" that emphasizes action and a sense of responsibility to individual clients and professional colleagues over a service orientation to the larger community (Goldstein & Donaldson, 1979). It views as less important the perceptions of the community and focuses instead on the therapeutic process between the client and the therapist. The incompatibility between conventional counseling approaches and indigenous approaches has been discussed by numerous writers (Jilek-Aall, 1976; Manson & Trimble, 1982; Trimble, 1981; Trimble & LaFromboise, 1985; Wax & Thomas, 1961). The self-focus of most conventional counseling emphasizes immediate experience and intrapsychic process for personal change rather than consideration of social causes of illnesses and issues of community cohesion.

There is considerable evidence to support the view that counseling services designed around a conventional individual therapy regime are indeed inappropriate for service deliveries in Indian communities. Several recent studies suggest that American Indian clients' expectations, goals, and attitudes toward therapy may differ significantly from those of the non-Indian client (see Trimble & Fleming, 1989).

The extreme mistreatment of American Indians by the U.S. government including broken treaties, unwarranted violence, and attempted genocide has clearly fostered a good deal of mistrust of the government and non-Indians on the part of Indian people (Lockhart, 1981; Trimble, 1987a). Coupled with racism invoked by non-Indians, Indian clients may perceive all non-Indian (including a non-Indian counselor) as potentially racist and interfering until they prove themselves otherwise (cf. Trimble, 1988). American Indian clients and potential referral sources often hold a number of negative expectations or perceptions regarding counselors and the counseling process that could prevent them from developing a trusting relationship with the counselor and engaging in successful therapy (LaFromboise, Dauphinais, & Lujan, 1981, Schoenfeld, Lyerly, & Miller, 1971).

Unfortunately, problems caused by even a few ignorant or malicious non-Indians can erode potential trust or rapport between "outsiders" and Indian communities. A recent tragedy on the Hopi reservation in Northern Arizona provides an extreme example of this phenomenon. It was discovered that a trusted and well-respected White schoolteacher had sexually abused 94 of his students during his nine years at the reservation school ("Molester Put Lasting Scars," 1987; "Assault on the Peaceful," 1988). Since the incident, life on the reservation has been disrupted by the effects of the teacher's crimes. Sadly, tribal leaders assert that they can no longer trust outsiders' presence within the community.

Besides the open oppression or racism practiced against many Indian people, there are other, more subtle forms of oppression leveled even by those Whites and non-Indians who are "trying to help" Indians. Patronizing attitudes and "missionary zeal" on the part of majority group members are but two kinds of insensitivity experienced by a number of Indians. Both create significant barriers to trust and communication, especially in the context of a counseling relationship. A patronizing attitude is often shown in the counselor's lowering of expectations for minority clients (Bishop & Richards, 1987). Missionary zeal is characterized by the counselor's over-interest or obsession with the minority's culture and customs (LaFromboise, 1983; Trimble & Hayes, 1984). Both maneuvers serve to undermine estimations of the counselor's empathy, trustworthiness, or respect for the client.

In addition to experiencing anxiety regarding patronizing attitudes and missionary zeal, Indian clients may also fear that the counselor—as a member of the dominant culture—will try to influence American Indian value structures rather than help Indians solve their problems, and thereby alienate them from their own people and traditions. In fact, those American Indians who do engage in individual therapy often express concern about the extent to which the majority culture and conventional western psychology superimpose their biases onto American Indian problems. They also express concern about the shaping of their behavior in a way that conflicts with Indian culture life-style orientations and preferences. Although conventional psychological approaches have attempted to avoid the problem of clients' cultural diversity by attempting to conduct therapy in a value-free counseling environment, the evidence suggests that the problems with this practice are twofold.

First, as mentioned earlier, it is clear that the role of therapy in traditional American Indian society has been to reaffirm cultural values and consider the individual in the context of the community. For at least some Indians seeking assistance from a therapist, a value-free environment is not appropriate to their expectations or needs. Instead, they may want someone to help them to assert their traditional value system and define the problem within the context of that network.

Secondly, psychological therapy programs—in both theory and practice—are derived from and serve to affirm the values of American culture. They are not value-free but are infused with the individualistic philosophy and priorities of the dominant culture. These biases must be recognized and corrected in order to create a fair and effective counseling environment for minorities who do not wish to change their values to match those of the dominant culture (Katz & Rolde, 1981).

There is also some concern that certain counseling orientations, such as those emphasizing intrapsychic adjustment, involve processes that can serve to pacify and eliminate legitimate anger and political initiative—that therapy may reinforce ignoring or smoothing over serious problems rather than creating necessary social and personal change (Bulhan, 1985). Furthermore, the perceived lack of privacy of social service agency information within close-knit communities may also be a strong deterrent to seeking and continuing treatment at local clinics (Solomon, Heisberger, & Winer, 1981). Prospective clients may fear the stigma of seeking psychological help should anyone discover their participation in therapy (A. Blue, personal communication, August 26, 1985; G. France, personal communication, November 10, 1980).

Despite these pitfalls, Indian adolescent clients hold positive expectations for the therapist and the counseling process. They hold hope that a counselor will be someone who is an expert and therefore knowledgeable enough to give them concrete, practical advice about their problems (LaFromboise, Dauphinais, & Rowe, 1980). They have indicated that counselor trustworthiness is crucial to effective counseling (Dauphinais, LaFromboise, & Row, 1980; LaFromboise & Dixon, 1981). Given historical and contemporary oppression and cultural clashes associated with the act of seeking help, trustworthiness probably is more important for Indians than it is for non-Indians seeking psychological assistance. Increased knowledge of other relevant social influence variables might facilitate badly needed reform in these areas.

Studies Support Cultural Uniqueness

Several studies in the last decade have attempted to define the role of particular counselor qualities and/or skills that promote successful therapy with American Indian adults and school children. Other studies have tried to assess the reasons for seeking counseling in these people's lives. Some of the research exploring whether conventional counseling should be modified to better accommodate Indian expectations of counseling will be outlined in this section. First, it has been found that—in addition to trustworthiness—an understanding of the client's cultural values and the willingness to engage in outreach activities in the community are qualities that American Indians expect from an effective counselor (Dauphinais et al., 1980).

Although Indian youth report that counselors need not be of Indian background in order to be helpful as long as they are trustworthy (LaFromboise & Dixon, 1981), the question of counselor-client racial/ethnic similarity has yielded conflicting results until the introduction of methodological innovations by Donald Atkinson and his colleagues. Recent findings now indicate that racial or ethnic similarity appears to be less important than counselor educational level or attitudinal similarity for African Americans (Atkinson, Furlong, & Poston, 1986), Asian Americans and Hispanic Americans (Atkinson, Poston, Furlong, & Mercado, 1989). However, Ponterotto's useful replication (Ponterotto, Alexander, & Hinkston, 1988) seems to suggest that, to the extent that minority students lack access to ethnic contacts and are isolated in the society of the dominant culture, the more important it becomes to have a counselor of similar race or ethnicity. A preliminary report (Bennett, BigFoot, & Thurman, 1989) using this investigative model with Native American clients, appears to show the importance of ethnic similarity to be generally consistent with that described above for other minorities. However, this investigation is attempting to verify unique within-group preferences related to cultural identity or commitment and is still in progress.

The success of psychological interventions for Indian clients, however, may be affected by the type of communication style a counselor elects to use. Dauphinais, Dauphinais, and Rowe (1981) found that American Indian students rated both non-Indian and Indian counselors as more credible when they used a culturally relevant counseling style than when these counselors used a nondirective counseling style.[1] In fact, the neo-Rogerian, "facilitative communication" verbal response style—the preferred means of establishing rapport and trust with clients that is taught in many counselor training programs—was found counterproductive not just for Indians, but was considered questionably effective for most American ethnic minorities as well (Atkinson, Morton, & Sue, 1989).

One help-seeking factor (type of client problem) has been found to vary among Indian and non-Indian populations. For instance, female American Indian students reported a strong preference for a female counselor if the problem was personal rather than an educational or vocational concern (Littrell & Littrell, 1982). To find significant differences regarding the type of problems reported and the type of individuals students would confide in about these problems. Dauphinais, LaFromboise, and Rowe (1980) surveyed Oklahoma American Indian and non-Indian high school students. Differences were found not only between Indians and non-Indians but also between Indians from rural areas and those from boarding and metropolitan public schools. Indian boarding school students, for example, nominated problems associated with depression more frequently than did rural or metropolitan students. Indian students differed from non-Indian students in indicating several types of problems that they would not talk to anyone about (e.g., getting along with friends or not caring). In addition, Indian students from boarding and metropolitan schools, but not those from rural areas or non-Indian students, reported a reluctance to talk with anyone about problems involving parents and family members, whether or not to stay in school, and making a decision.

Indian university students often indicate that they would typically seek help from family members before seeking psychological services if they were in their home environment (LaFromboise, 1988). Evidence suggests, however, that Indian college students who do seek counseling may do so over different concerns than those of their high school counterparts. A study of 1,100 American Indian and Alaskan Native college students from five major universities reports that the most common stressful events in this population were school related: personal pressure to get good grades, fear of failure, fear of losing financial aid, difficulties in receiving financial aid, pressure to succeed, and fear of failure to meet family expectations (U.S. Congress, 1990). Furthermore, it has been reported that an increasing number of American Indian university students are seeking counseling to cope with problems that arise during their academic training, especially when there are American Indian counselors available (B. Smith, personal communication, July 8, 1986). The findings of research on reasons that Indians seek counseling and counselor attributes they view as most salient can aid in the reform of counseling services in educational settings. However, current cultural reforms within Indian communities must not be overlooked when considering services that are either educationally or community-based.

Some Considerations for Psychological Intervention

Several conventional forms of psychological intervention have been and still are in use in American Indian communities. Before briefly discussing the basic theory and practice of these orientations and then assessing their strengths and weaknesses within the context of counseling American Indian clients, the issue of Indian empowerment through retraditionalization and biculturalism must be considered.

Empowerment "refers to the development of skills enabling the person of color to implement interpersonal influence, improve role performance, and develop an effective support system" (Leigh, 1982, p. 10). The term "empowerment" is important because it embodies a way of thinking about social issues that transcends the rights/needs paradigm and the search for simple, one-sided, uniform solutions to complex sociopolitical problems (Rappaport, 1981, 1987).

The goal of empowerment is to do whatever possible so that clients can control their own lives; the underlying assumption is that people are capable of taking control but are unable to do so because of social forces and institutions that are hindering their efforts. A needs-based perspective, on the other hand, depicts people as powerless, helpless or child-like, dependent on the government or social institutions for help and support. In therapy, the interventionist strategies used to help the client gain empowerment include raising self-esteem, educating people about the ways in which an oppressive system operates and what its effects are on the individual (e.g., use of standardized tests such as the Graduate Record Exam to determine admission to institutions of higher education), mobilizing the client's interpersonal and material resources, creating or strengthening familial and extrafamilial support systems, and informing people about their tribal as well as societal rights and entitlements (LaFromboise & LaFromboise, 1982; LaFromboise & Rowe, 1983; Leigh, 1982; Lum, 1986).

For the last 20 years, many Indians have been "consumed with the tasks of revitalizing their culture, languages, and religions which are the heart of tribalism" (Fixico, 1985, p. 33) to revive Indian community empowerment. Indian scholars have labeled this movement retraditionalization. Retraditionalization relies on the use of cultural beliefs, customs, and rituals as a means of overcoming problems and achieving Indian self-determination. Tribal customs and traditions are used as sources of strength that provide culturally consistent coping mechanisms. For example, an honoring ceremony performed for a student graduating from high school might be recalled by that student to cope with an academic setback and persevere in university training.

Maintaining some traditional customs and roles, however, does not necessitate a return to all the "old ways." Many Indian women, for example, have undertaken a retraditionalization of their former roles as caretakers and transmitters of cultural knowledge in contemporary Indian life. According to Green:

> Contrary to standard feminist calls for revolutionary change, Indian women insist on taking their traditional places as healers, legal specialists, and tribal governors. Their call is for a return to forms which, they insist, involve women and men in complementary, mutual roles. (Green, 1983, p. 14)

The structure of the cultural system remains intact, but the specific jobs have been updated and modernized in accordance with societal change. Green (1983) and Allen (1986) further suggest that a complete return to the traditional roles and customs would not be desirable to all Indian women but that awareness and discussion in regard to the retraditionalization paradigm would facilitate more balanced, culturally appropriate research on Indian women. Clearly, the issue of retraditionalization of roles should be considered and addressed in effective therapy with American Indian clients.

Indians vary according to tribal and band affiliation, residential patterns, and also to the extent to which they are committed to maintaining their tribal heritage. In their classic study among the Menomini of Wisconsin, Spindler and Spindler (1958) identified five categories of ''Indianness,'' using degree of acculturation as a reference: Native-oriented, peyote cult, transitional, lower status acculturated, and elite acculturated. Loye and Robert Ryan (1982) modified the Spindler scheme as follows:

1. *Traditional*—These individuals generally speak and think in their native language and know little English. They observe ''old-time'' traditions and values.
2. *Transitional*—These individuals generally speak both English and the Native language in the home. They question basic traditionalism and religion, yet cannot fully accept dominant culture and values.
3. *Marginal*—These people may be defensively Indian, but are unable either to live the cultural heritage of their tribal group or to identify with the dominant society. This group tends to have the most difficulty in coping with social problems due to their ethnicity.
4. *Assimilated*—Within their group are the people who, for the most part, have been accepted by the dominant society. They generally have embraced dominant culture and values.
5. *Bicultural*—(Referred to in Ryan and Ryan, 1982, as transcendental)— Within their group are those who are, for the most part, accepted by the dominant society. Yet they also know and accept their tribal traditions and culture. They can thus move in either direction, from traditional society to dominant society, with ease. (pp. 6–7)

Both the retraditionalization movement and increased Indian biculturism have facilitated Indian community empowerment. American Indians have often been portrayed as people stranded between two worlds in conflict over personal preferences and cultural expectations (Hallowell, 1950). More recently, biculturalism—the ability to function effectively and be seen as competent in both worlds—is said to lead to greater cognitive functioning, and self-actualization (Akao, 1984; McCarty, 1985; McFee, 1968; Polgar, 1960). Many Indians believe that the strength of their knowledge of tribal culture augments their bicultural success.

Moses and Wilson (1985) recently stated that it might be better to suggest that Indians live in a complex world of multiple loyalties—a world that challenges, sustains, and sometimes destroys them, but seldom removes their Indianness. Awareness of these various cultural bases will help the counselor to be better prepared to assist Indian clients in coping with various life situations and efforts toward reaching full life potential. Issues associated with retraditionalization or biculturalism can be more or less readily incorporated into various theoretical perspectives underlying counseling. In order for that to occur, counseling theories must be reviewed for their facility in empowering Indian individuals and Indian communities. Person-centered, social learning, behavioral, and network theories were selected for comment in this article. Similar analysis of other counseling theories might improve decisions concerning appropriate treatment approaches with Indians.

Person-Centered

Although Rogerian therapy's on internal values and autonomy is broadly consistent with traditional American Indian values, several process-oriented aspects of this form of intervention create barriers for effective counseling of American Indian clients. The first difficulty arises from the extreme importance and centrality of the client-therapist relationship. There is certainly doubt as to whether this sort of isolated one-on-one interaction, outside the context of family and community, is a valid and/or pragmatic means of dealing with an Indian client's problems (Dauphinais et al., 1981).

This type of process focuses on the client individually, without taking into account the role that the client may perform within the family or community system and the effect of the client's attitudes and behavior on those in his or her environment. It stresses the potential for growth without considering the social issues involved. The effectiveness of the therapy also depends on the length and quality of the client-counselor relationship. Considering the high attrition rate of Indian clients that Sue, Allen, and Conaway (1978) found and the problems involved with developing trust and rapport in Indian client-counselor relations, the type of relationship necessary for successful Rogerian therapy seems unlikely.

In addition, the actual counselor-client communication style essential to this form of therapy is poorly suited for the American Indian population in general. Counselor communication emphasizes minimal encouragers, summarization, restatement, and reflection of feeling and is thus of limited use to reticent clients and those not comfortable expressing feelings. Not only are many American Indians considered "quiet" or untalkative, but a high value is placed on the restraint of emotions and the acceptance of suffering in American Indian culture (Basso, 1970; Bryde, 1971). In fact, Indians in more traditional contexts may be considered "weak" for expressing hurt feelings.

Social Learning

One counseling orientation based on social learning theory that appears to deal with diverse cultural norms better than Rogerian therapy is the skills-training paradigm. Social skills training focuses on teaching appropriate everyday skills and behavior to clients chiefly through the use of modeling and rehearsing activities. Recently, culturally tailored skills training has been successfully applied with Indian adolescents in the reduction of drinking behavior (Bobo, Cvetkovich, Trimble, Gilchrist, & Schinke, 1987; Carpenter, Lyons, & Miller, 1985; Schinke et al., 1988) and tobacco use (Schinke, Moncher, Holden, Botvin, & Orlandi, 1989); and to improve Indian parenting skills (BigFoot, 1989), professionalizing skills (LaFromboise, 1989), and bicultural competence (LaFromboise, 1983; LaFromboise & Rowe, 1983). David (1976) describes its utility in preventing intercultural adjustment problems, and further research is underway using the social skills training approach to prevent Indian adolescent suicide (Belgarde & LaFromboise, 1988).

This type of intervention has several strengths in terms of its use in American Indian populations. First, it is less culturally biased. It allows the community to define the community-level target problems to be solved (e.g., substance abuse, child neglect) and the type of behaviors appropriate for each situation (e.g., culturally appropriate assertiveness, parenting skills). Thus there is less concern on the part of the client and the community that the standards and values of the dominant culture will be imposed on the person through therapy (Bach & Bornstein, 1981). Social skills therapy also lends itself to prevention efforts in that it can address potential problems before they develop (Schinke, Schilling, Palleja, & Zayas, 1987). In addition, a major advantage of skills training for American Indian clients is its extensive use of modeling techniques. Role modeling is a major source of learning in Indian culture, so this form of therapy is both consistent with and reinforcing of that extended family tradition.

Behavioral

A third form of psychological intervention implemented in American Indian communities involves the use of behavior therapy (Penistone & Burman, 1978). This form of therapy assumes that most social behavior is learned via direct experiences through the overt and verbal reactions of others. A strength of behavioral therapy is its action-oriented focus on the present, rather than on the past. The focus is consistent with American Indian cultural worldviews (Trimble, 1981). Another positive aspect of this type of intervention is that many behavior therapy techniques lend themselves to paraprofessional implementation (Conrad, Delk, & Williams, 1974) and prevention interventions (Schinke et al., 1987).

A problem with behavior therapy, and with social skills training, can be its potential misuse through a narrow or inappropriate focus, such as when the goals of the client are not the goals targeted for change in therapy, or when behavior change processes are controlled by professionals who do not respect the client's goals. A crucial issue in the ethics of behavior therapy concerns the locus of control over definitions of environment and reinforcers. Those Indian clients who are suspicious of manipulation and the imposition of conforming behavior by the dominant culture may be less willing to participate in such therapy. However, if the client's goals are the ones addressed in therapy, if the reinforcers employed are culturally appropriate and effective, and if the reinforcers outside of therapy (both within and beyond the Indian community) are realistically planned for, behavioral approaches can be effective and powerful in achieving desired change with Indians.

Network

A growing awareness of these cultural concerns has led to efforts to integrate traditional American Indian values and existing indigenous problem-solving mechanisms into the therapy process. Network therapy is one progressive form of counseling intervention that operates on a model similar to and consistent with the more traditional Indian community-oriented guidance system discussed earlier.

In the network approach, a clan or group of family, relatives, and friends is organized and mobilized to form a social force or network that works to combat the depersonalizing aspects of contemporary life patterns especially prevalent in urban environments. The role of the counselor is that of a "catalyst." He or she helps to conduct the process, but it is the social support system which works to deal with the crisis or bring the person out of isolation (Attneave, 1969; Reuveni, 1979).

The client and his or her problem are considered and treated within the context of a larger family and community social system. In this sense, network therapy can be seen as an application of the systems theory conceptual framework to the counseling process. A systems theory perspective on psychological problems offers a way of thinking about symptoms in terms of several characteristics including their functional roles or consequences within a given system (e.g., workplace, family, community).

Network therapy is practical in process as well as in theory. It has a decidedly informal, nonprofessional approach, is conducted in the home, and sometimes involves from 40 to 70 people at one time (Speck & Attneave, 1973). Clearly, this process seems to be a more natural and less intimidating problem-solving alternative than a one-on-one client-counselor office interaction to American Indians who have been raised in a culture that has historically relied on group consensus to prevent and deal with community and tribal problems. All things considered, network therapy does seem to be a viable, culturally consistent approach for preventing and dealing with psychiatric problems in Indian communities (Schoenfeld, Halevy-Martini, Hemley-Van der Velden, & Ruhf, 1985).

Thus far we have outlined three basic strategies for effective transcultural therapy with American Indians. First, making traditional treatments more accessible to Indian clients; second, selecting culturally appropriate therapy techniques and orientations; and third, integrating traditional healing methods with culturally appropriate therapy to develop a progressive yet culturally consistent therapeutic process (Rogler, Malgady, Constantino, & Blumenthal, 1987). Of the interventions reviewed, social learning and network therapy approaches appear to have greater potential for enhancing a client's interaction with others and involvement in empowerment issues. It is assumed that increased interpersonal support brought about through these interventions will ensure more lasting changes outside the context of the counseling relationship.

Indian Diversity and Mental Health Intervention

The geographic location of American Indian mental health centers also shapes the types of counseling and clinical interventions available to clients. Centers located in urban and metropolitan areas are likely to be more oriented to Indian clients representing diverse tribal orientations with varying degrees of acculturative status. Some clients are highly acculturated and have little or no knowledge about traditions, customs, and belief systems of their relatives on the reservation or in the native village. Others, usually mobile between reservation and various urban areas in search of employment or contact with extended family members, are less familiar with the demands and life-style orientations in urban area. Often these clients are highly traditional and nativistic and, consequently, have quite different expectations from the more urbanized Indians about the role of counselors linked to urban Indian mental health clinics.

Reservation and village mental health clinics tend to be set up to respond to tribally specific customs and practices. Mental health staff and counselors are usually well known in the community and, in many cases may be related to the client through an extended family network. But, in addition to the existence of reservation and village clinics, tribal members often have access to the traditional healing systems outlined earlier, which are often preferred over the clinics. Occasionally, clients will receive services from the two entities in the hope of balancing the effectiveness of the "treatment" orientations, thus assuring that the traditional approach will cure a part of the problem not accessible by the conventional counselor.

To assist one in understanding the complexities of urban and reservation mental health services, material was obtained from Ryan and Ryan (1982) describing the circumstances one is likely to find in certain settings. These descriptions are highly condensed and are provided with the understanding that both traditional and conventional services will vary considerably from one community to the next depending, of course, on a multitude of circumstances.

The following cases describe types of Indian mental health clients and the kinds of situations that may give counselors problems. Furthermore, the cases represent two of the acculturative styles listed above. The first case illustrates reactive depression not directly related to culture; the second illustrates existential anxiety that only cultural knowledge can illuminate.

Client one was a fifty-six-year-old Ojibwa Indian woman who first came to an urban Indian mental health clinic in 1980. She was categorized as assimilated according to acculturation criteria because she was born on an Ojibwa reservation, but moved to an urban area with her family while she was still in high school. In November 1979, her father died of cancer, and she and her son moved to the city to help care for her elderly mother. In January 1980, her daughter was permanently disabled in an automobile accident that also claimed the life of her nephew. In March 1980, her eighteen-year-old son committed suicide. At the time of her first visit, she had been a widow for six years. The client suffered so much grief that she was hospitalized for reactive depression for five days at a crisis unit and was subsequently referred to a mental health clinic.

The two-year therapeutic intervention included antidepressant medication and grief therapy to help her deal with the multiple tragedies in her family. Social cognitive therapy was used to assist her acceptance and understanding of the facts that her daughter was not going to get better and that she was not responsible for her son's suicide. The next level of therapy involved behavioral and social skills training, to assist her in reentering the social sphere and receiving available community support for self-esteem enhancement. At the time of the report she had been working full time for approximately eight months and was functioning very well in the community. Her prognosis was excellent.

Client two was a twenty-eight-year-old Lakota Sioux woman who was born and lived on a reservation until she was nine years old, when she went to an off-reservation elementary boarding school for three years. She is the oldest of seven children. Her mother is an alcoholic, and the seven siblings have different fathers. From the time the client was four years old, she had been sexually abused by her mother's boyfriends. She lived with her grandparents for brief periods with some of her other siblings. When she was thirteen years of age, her mother moved the family to the city. The client married a White man who had a stable position in county government.

When the client returned to her reservation to attend her grandfather's memorial she was ridiculed by her relatives as being ''White.'' She came to the IHS clinic and asked a physician for tranquilizers because she was afraid she was going to have a breakdown. She told the doctor that her biggest problem was not understanding why her relatives would not accept her and why they considered her White. Her newly ascribed marginal acculturation status haunted her.

The non-Indian physician could not understand how being considered White was her major concern when her other problems seemed much more overwhelming to him. The client in this instance needed to be accepted by the Indian community because she rarely felt accepted by the dominant society. Network therapy could have been employed to help her relatives realize how being called White diminished the client's dignity and ethnic identity at a particularly vulnerable time. Until she encounters a counselor willing to work through various stages of her identity confusion (preferably with the help of social systems strategies), this client's prognosis is very grim.

Both culturally appropriate and inappropriate interventions commonly used in counseling Indians have been highlighted here. In the first case a combination of cognitive and behavioral therapies were employed with concern for the client's social system noted throughout treatment. Knowledge of Ojibwa beliefs about death and the grieving process was essential for the grief therapy to be effective (Densmore, 1979). In the second case treatment did not take place because of the lack of sensitivity over the importance of Indian identity and community acceptance (Trimble, 1987b) on the part of the physician. Had rapport been established during the initial hospital contact, the need for network or family therapy might have been determined. Collaboration with an elder or community leader could have sped the process along. Certainly, talk therapy alone concerning the client's identity and community acceptance, or behavior therapy alone over her reentry into the Siouan community is contraindicated.

Factors such as these can be highlighted in case material analyzed within a cultural framework. Huang and Gibbs (1989) suggest the need to first determine cultural and familial attitudes toward the problem and toward help-seeking behavior and services. They encourage counselors to consider the adaptiveness of the presenting behavior in the ecological environment and to assess the cultural congruity among the client, the family, and the community. Possible identity conflicts in culturally dissonant contexts should be assessed. Finally, the appropriateness of differential diagnostic criteria and counseling interventions within a cultural context must be explored. Further case material on American Indians can be found in Beiser (1985), Jewell (1952), LaFromboise and Low (1989), Trimble and Fleming (1989), and Tyler and Thompson (1965).

Implications for Counseling Training

These issues, although vitally important to the education and training of effective Indian helpers, and the implementation of mental health programs within Indian communities, are only beginning to be addressed in the counseling literature. Although some widely used counseling psychology texts and training manuals (e.g., Ivey, Ivey, & Simek-Downing, 1987) do discuss cross-cultural counseling questions and themes, the overwhelming majority do not. Instead, students are directed to cross-cultural compilation texts (e.g., Atkinson, Morton, & Sue, 1989; Pedersen, 1985; Pedersen, Draguns, Lonner, & Trimble, 1989) and courses with meager coverage of American Indian mental health material. And although the current American Psychological Association (APA) accreditation manual advises that approved doctoral programs should educate students regarding cultural and racial diversity (APA, 1986), there is no mention of a procedure for assessing doctoral candidates' cross-cultural competence or requiring particular bicultural skills and knowledge for doctoral licensure.

Often, clinicians and educators point out that they have little or no contact with American Indians. Many believe that the problems we continue to point out are germane to areas of the country where there are large Indian population concentrations. Often, East Coast practitioners are quick to note that their counterparts "in the West" should be mindful of the myriad of concerns and problems facing Indian clients. "After all," they maintain, "most of the Indians tend to live 'out west'." To an extent they are correct, for most Indian people do indeed live west of the Mississippi River. However, American Indians can be found in virtually every state, although the numbers may be small in some instances (e.g., Kentucky, Indiana, Vermont, Rhode Island, and West Virginia).

Over the years, we have found that many graduates of counseling psychology programs are thrust into settings where they occasionally are faced with Indian clients. Both urban and reservation American Indians form a sociocultural group greatly in need of specially trained psychologists who have a broad understanding of cultural and social phenomena not found in most textbooks and usually beyond the scope of most training programs. Because of their lack of sensitivity and training, few psychologists are able to work effectively with the Indian client. Consequently, the would-be client, aware of the insensitivity, fails to return, and preconceived notions about trust and apathy are needlessly reinforced. Such occasions are sufficiently numerous that many Indian clients flatly refuse to enter a counseling relationship regardless of the degree of their presenting problem. This is partly due to their previous experiences and to the word-of-mouth stories that circulate in Indian enclaves.

The integration of conventional counseling and American Indian traditional interventions raises some important questions for training programs in counseling psychology. First, how does one define community work and revive communities in terms of networks and empowerment? The way that health and psychological cure is organized among certain tribes suggests that "western" professionals must seriously look at how communities and families can organize themselves synergistically. Sarason (1972) begins to delineate the importance of a sense of community for psychologists. However, much of the current research and practice in counseling psychology among minority groups is specific to certain problems such as suicide prevention, prevention of cardiovascular and other diseases, gerontology, and so forth.

A psychologist within a native community or urban Indian community must discover the indigenous definition of community. This definition will serve as a guide for how to structure intervention within the goal of building community. Courses for psychology graduate students, then, need to examine what community means, how it is organized across diverse cultural groups, and how counseling interventions can facilitate community empowerment. Additionally, practical and internships within Indian communities are critical if professionals are to learn how Indian communities are organized, supported, and developed. Merely being of Indian descent does not in itself equip a student with such knowledge. Programs must face the need for Indian, and non-Indian, students and supervisors to experience native community life. Such an interplay between local university supervisors, students, and the Indian community will enrich all involved and challenge their expertise.

Second, how does a counseling psychologist intervene yet wait for choice? If choice is most central, then many of the anglo techniques that involve manipulation and persuasion without prior individual choice are culturally flawed. Although difficult to facilitate, collaboration with elders, medicine men and women, and other community leaders would be integral in the design of prevention and treatment activities. An ongoing relationship with these leaders would provide interns with an opportunity to create their role as interveners who find or develop choice. Such a process takes much time because the initial request for participation in developing interventions usually leads to stereotypic descriptions of needs without delineation of how to proceed and knowledge of what the community wants. An internship would provide the time.

Third, what is the role of religion in the structure of a community? In any discussion of healing and prevention in a Sioux community, for example, the issues of spirits, religion, and transcendence will arise. Within a native context, helping and health always have a religious dimension. If counseling psychology is to make an impact on native communities or train students to become competent psychologists in such communities, then they must look at religious and transcendental ways of understanding the world. Practitioners must learn to accept these understandings on their own terms rather than reduce them to psychology or physiology. An internship could provide intense exposure to religious and transcendental explanations. Supervisors must recognize such explanations as another system rather than as primitive witchcraft. A corollary concern is the need for training programs to consider seriously the requirement for students to further develop their character and "transform" themselves.

Fourth, when do cultural behaviors occur that "Western" programs misinterpret? Throughout this article, the importance of balance within communities and within helping transactions between healers and helpers has been emphasized. Such a balance always involves "gift" exchange. When one completes a ceremony of any type on the Rosebud reservation, for example, one provides a gift (woheyaka) to the healer, such as money, a blanket, food, artifacts, and so forth, and thus balance is created. If supervisors don't understand this custom and prohibit students from engaging in gift exchange, things go awry. Alienation results.

Fifth, what further research is needed to advance the integration of counseling psychology and American Indian tradition? Despite statistics documenting the underuse of mental health programs by American Indians that point to serious problems with the system as it exists today, there is a dearth of controlled research regarding the effectiveness of the various intervention approaches. A starting point for counseling research with American Indians is simply more descriptive research with designs adequate to separate "reservation" from "rural" from "social-class" from "acculturation" factors. Epidemiological research is needed to ascertain use rates in private, state, local, and federal agencies other than the Indian Health Service and the Bureau of Indian Affairs. Cross-tribal studies are almost nonexistent for major Indian mental health problems.

Research typically conducted by counseling psychologists could shed light on a number of important issues. Consistent findings concerning

Indian preference for same-race counselors have yet to be found. A clearer articulation of the culturally relevant Indian counseling style operationalized by Dauphinais (1981) would be helpful. There is also a strong need for research on the process of social support (or lack of it) among urban Indians of various ages and backgrounds. Longitudinal studies would be particularly useful in beginning to identify the antecedents of social isolation and the potency of various sources of cultural and social support for Indian clients and their families. Also, attention to the coping styles and life-styles of biculturally competent Indians is necessary for a shift in focus away from deficit hypotheses to the design of interventions that build on the ''natural'' strengths of Indian people and communities.

Implications and Conclusions

Throughout this article we have provided a good deal of information concerning the counseling process and related issues that focus on the first American—the American Indian. Our main intent was to draw attention to the many problems facing would-be (Indian) clients as they might exist in a variety of settings. The problems remain and are likely to continue well into the future.

Many of the points we raise in this article are not exclusive to American Indians. Counseling related articles written about Asian-, African-, and Hispanic/Latino-Americans often raise many of the same points we do (cf. Atkinson, Morton & Sue, 1989; Pedersen, 1985). From an educational and training perspective, it makes sense to include material about Indians if for no other reason than to expand a prospective counselor's knowledge about an often overlooked and sometimes ignored segment of our overall population. Moreover, a good deal of positive transfer can occur when one compares and contrasts counseling information about one culture to another. The field of counseling psychology stands to gain a great deal when the culturally unique characteristics of a population are reflected against current wisdom and conventional forms of counseling styles.

Our recommendation to expand the knowledge of counselor educators and practitioners is a modest one. We also recognize that the status of current research addresses some important concerns, and much more empirical study is clearly necessary. It is, admittedly, a somewhat difficult task to control for all the variables and contingencies within the mental health networks of Indian people in order to come up with firm conclusions about what works and what does not. We believe, however, that we have provided a framework that can serve as a guide for those keenly interested in pursuing work in this area.

Reference Note

1. In this study a culturally relevant counseling style consisted primarily of direct guidance and approval/reassurance responses with incidental use of restatements and open questions according to the Hill Counselor Response Category System (Hill, 1978).

References

Akao, S. F. (1984). Biculturalism and barriers to learning among Michigan Indian adult students. (Doctoral dissertation. Michigan State University, 1984). *Dissertation Abstracts International, 44,* 3572A.

Allen, P. G. (1986). *The sacred hoop; Recovering the feminine in American Indian traditions.* Boston, MA: Beacon

American Psychological Association (1986). *Accreditation handbook.* Washington, DC: American Psychological Association Committee on Accreditation and Accreditation Office.

Assault on the peaceful: Indian child abuse. (1988, December 26). *Newsweek,* p. 31.

Atkinson, D. R., Furlong, M. J., & Poston, W. C. (1986). Afro American preferences for counselor characteristics. *Journal of Counseling Psychology, 33,* 326–330.

Atkinson, D. R., Morton, G., & Sue, D. W. (1989). *Counseling American minorities* (3rd ed.). Dubuque, IA: William C. Brown.

Atkinson, D. R., Poston, W. C., Furlong, M. J., & Mercado, P. (1989). Ethnic group preferences for counselor characteristics. *Journal of Counseling Psychology, 36,* 68–72.

Attneave, C. L. (1969). Therapy in tribal settings and urban network intervention. *Family Process, 8,* 192–210.

Bach, P. J., & Bornstein, P. H. (1981). A social learning rationale and suggestions for behavioral treatment with American Indian alcohol abusers. *Addictive Behaviors, 6,* 75–81.

Basso, K. (1970). ''To give up on words'': Silence in western Apache culture. *Southwestern Journal of Anthropology, 26,* 213–30.

Beiser, M. (1985). The grieving witch: A framework for applying principles of cultural psychiatry to clinical practice. *Canadian Journal of Psychiatry, 30,* 130–141.

Belgarde, M., & LaFromboise, P. (1988, April). Zuni adolescent suicide prevention project. In K. Swisher (Chair). *Sociocultural parameters affecting program development in American Indian/Alaskan Native schools.* Symposium conducted at the meeting of the American Educational Research Association, New Orleans, LA.

Bennett, S. K., BigFoot, D. S., & Thurman, P. J. (1989, August). *American Indian client preference for counselor attributes.* Paper presented at the meeting of the American Psychological Association, New Orleans, LA.

BigFoot, D. S. (1989). *Parent training for American Indian families.* Unpublished doctoral dissertation, University of Oklahoma, Norman, OK.

Bishop, J. B., & Richards, T. F. (1987). Counselor intake judgments about White and Black clients in a university counseling center. *Journal of Counseling Psychology, 34,* 96–98.

Bobo, J. K., Cvetkovich, G., Trimble, J. E., Gilchrist, L. D., & Schinke, S. (1987). Cross-cultural service delivery to minority communities. *Journal of Community Psychology, 15,* 501–514.

Bryde, J. (1971). *Indian students and guidance.* Boston, MA: Houghton Mifflin.

Bulhan, H. A. (1985). *Frantz Fanon and the psychology of oppression.* New York: Plenum.

Carpenter, A., Lyons, C., & Miller, W. (1985). Peer-managed self-control program for prevention of alcohol abuse in American Indian high school students: A pilot evaluation study. *International Journal of the Addictions, 20,* 299–310.

Conrad, R. D., Delk, J. I., & Williams, C. (1974). Use of stimulus fading procedures in the treatment of situation specific mutism: A case study. *Journal of Behavior Therapy and Experimental Psychiatry, 5,* 99–100.

Dauphinais, P. (1981). *Effects of counselor race and counselor response style of American Indian youths' perception of counselor effectiveness.* Unpublished doctoral dissertation, University of Oklahoma, Norman, OK.

Dauphinais, P., Dauphinais, I., & Rowe, W. (1981). Effects of race and communication style of Indian perceptions of counselor effectiveness. *Counselor Education and Supervision, 20,* 37–46.

Dauphinais, P., LaFromboise, T., & Rowe, W. (1980) Perceived problems and sources of help for American Indian students. *Counselor Education and Supervision, 21,* 31–46.

David, K. (1976). The use of social learning theory in preventing intercultural adjustment problems. In P. Pedersen, W. Lonner, & J. Draguns (Eds.), *Counseling across cultures* (pp. 123–138). Honolulu: University Press of Hawaii.

Densmore, F. (1979). *Chippewa customs.* Minneapolis: Minnesota Historical Society.

Dinges, N., Trimble, J., Manson, S., & Pasquale, F. (1981). Counseling and psychotherapy with American Indians and Alaskan Natives. In A. Marsella & P. Pedersen (eds.), *Cross-cultural counseling and psychotherapy* (pp. 243–276). New York: Pergamon.

Fixico, M. (1985). The road to middle class Indian America. In C. E. Trafzer (Ed.), *American Indian identity: Today's changing perspectives* (pp. 29–37). Sacramento, CA: Sierra Oaks Publishing Company.

Goldstein, M. S., & Donaldson, D. J. (1979). Exporting professionalism: A case study of medical education. *Journal of Health and Social Behavior, 20,* 322–337.

Green, R. (1983). *Native American women: A contextual bibliography.* Bloomington: Indiana University Press.

Hallowell, A. I. (1950). Values, acculturation and mental health. *American Journal of Orthopsychiatry, 20,* 732–743.

Hammerschlag, C. A. (1988). *The dancing healers: A doctor's journey of healing with Native Americans.* San Francisco: Harper & Row.

Hill, C. E. (1978). Development of a counselor verbal response category system. *Journal of Counseling Psychology, 25,* 461–468.

Huang, L. N., & Gibbs, J. T. (1989). Multicultural perspectives on two clinical cases. In J. T. Gibbs & L. N. Huang (Eds.) *Children of color: Psychological intervention with minority youth* (pp. 351–274). San Francisco: Jossey-Bass.

Ivey, A., Ivey, M. B., & Simek-Downing, L. (1987). *Counseling and psychotherapy: Integrating skills, theory, and practice* (2nd ed.) Englewood Cliffs, NJ: Prentice-Hall.

Jewell, D. P. (1952). A case of a "psychotic" Navaho Indian male. *Human Organization, 11,* 32–36.

Jilek-Aall, L. (1976). The western psychiatrist and his non-western clientele. *Canadian Psychiatric Association Journal, 21,* 353–359.

Kaplan, B., & Johnson, D. (1964). The social meaning of Navajo psychopathology and psychotherapy. In A. Kiev (Ed.), *Magic, Faith, and healing* (pp. 203–229). New York: Free Press.

Katz, R., & Rolde, E. (1981). Community alternatives to psychotherapy. *Psychotherapy, Theory, Research and Practice, 18,* 365–374.

Kelso, D. R., & Attneave, C.L. (1981). *Bibliography of North American Indian mental health.* Westport, CT: Greenwood.

LaBarre, W. (1964). Confessions as cathartic therapy in American Indian tribes. In A. Kiev (Ed.) *Magic, faith, and healing* (pp. 36–49). New York: Free Press.

LaFromboise, T. D. (1983). *Assertion training with American Indians.* Las Cruces, NM: ERIC Clearinghouse on Rural Education and Small Schools.

LaFromboise, T. D. (1988). American Indian mental health policy. *American Psychologist, 43,* 388–397.

LaFromboise, T. D. (1989). *Circle of women: Professional skills training with American Indian women.* Newton, MA: Women's Educational Equity Act Publishing Center.

LaFromboise, T., Dauphinais, P., & Lujan, P. (1981). Verbal indicators of insincerity as perceived by American Indians *Journal of Non-White Concerns, 9,* 97–94.

LaFromboise, T., Dauphinais, P., & Rowe, W. (1980). Indian students' perceptions of positive helper attributes. *Journal of American Indian Education, 19,* 11–16.

LaFromboise, T., & Dixon, D. (1981). American Indian perceptions of trustworthiness in a counseling interview. *Journal of Counseling Psychology, 28,* 135–139.

LaFromboise, T., & LaFromboise, R. (1982). Critical legal and social responsibilities facing Native Americans. In I. French (Ed.). *Indians and criminal justice* (pp 21–38). Totowa, NJ: Allanheld, Osmun & Company.

LaFromboise, T. D., & Low, K. G. (1989). American Indian children and adolescents. In J. T. Gibbs, & L. N. Huang (Eds.) *Children of color: Psychological interventions with minority youth* (pp. 114–147). San Francisco: Jossey-Bass.

LaFromboise, T., & Rowe, W. (1983). Skills training for bicultural competence: Rationale and application. *Journal of Counseling Psychology, 30,* 589–595.

Leigh, J. W. (1982). *Empowerment as a process.* Unpublished manuscript, University of Washington School of Social Work. Seattle.

Littrell, J., & Lettrell, M. (1982). American Indian and Caucasian students preferences for counselors: Effects of counselor dress and sex. *Journal of Counseling Psychology, 29,* 48–57.

Lockhart, B. (1981). Historic distrust and the counseling of American Indian and Alaska Natives. *White Cloud Journal, 2,* 31–34.

Locust, C. (1988). Wounding the spirit: Discrimination and traditional American Indian belief systems. *Harvard Educational Review, 58,* 315–330.

Lum, D. (1986). *Social work practice and people of color: A process-stage approach.* Monterey, CA: Brooks/Cole.

Manson, S., Dinges, N., Lujan, C., Piño, M., Wright, B., Pepion, K., & Montoya, V. (1989). *Stress and coping among American Indian and Alaska Native college students.* Unpublished manuscript. University of Colorado, National center for American Indian and Alaska Native Mental Health Research. Denver.

Manson, S. M., & Trimble, J. E. (1982). American Indian and Alaska Native communities: Past efforts, future inquiries. In L. Snowden (Ed.), *Reaching the underserved: Mental health needs of neglected populations* (pp. 143–164). Beverly Hills, CA: Sage.

Manson, S. M., Walker, R. D., & Kivlahan, D. R. (1987). Psychiatric assessment and treatment of American Indian and Alaska Native youth. *Hospital and Community Psychology, 38,* 165–173.

McCarty, T. L. (1985). Bilingual-bicultural education in a Navajo community. (Doctoral dissertation, Arizona State University). *Dissertation Abstracts International, 45,* 3534A.

McFee, M. (1968). The 150% man, a product of Blackfeet acculturation. *American Anthropologist, 70,* 1096–1107.

Mohatt, G. V. (1978, Spring). Rosebud medicine men and associates. *Wassaja.*

Molester put lasting scars on Hopi tribe. (1987, June 1). *Arizona Republic,* p. 1.

Moses, L. G, & Wilson, R. (1985). *Indian lives: Essays on nineteenth- and twentieth-century Native American leaders.* Albuquerque, NM: University of New Mexico Press.

Neliegh, G. (1988). Major mental disorders and behavior among American Indians and Alaska Natives. *Behavioral Health Issues among American Indians and Alaska Natives: Explorations of the Frontiers of the Biobehavioral Sciences, 1* (1), 116–150.

Nelson, S. (1988). *A national plan for Native American mental health services.* Rockville, MD: Indian Health Service. Office of Health Promotion. Mental Health Planning Branch.

Pedersen, P. (Ed.) (1985). *Handbook of cross-cultural counseling and psychotherapy.* Westport, CT: Greenwood.

Pedersen, P. B., Draguns, J. G., Lonner, W. J., & Trimble, J. E. (Eds.) (1989). *Counseling across cultures* (3rd ed.). Honolulu: University Press of Hawaii.

Penistone, E., & Burman, W. (1978). Relaxation and assertive training as treatment for a psychosomatic American Indian patient. *White Cloud Journal, 1*(1), 7–10.

Polgar, S. (1960). Biculturation of Mesquakie teenage boys. *American Anthropologist, 62,* 217–235.

Ponterotto, J. G., Alexander, C., & Hinkston, J. (1988). Afro American preferences for counselor characteristics: A replication and extension. *Journal of Counseling Psychology, 35,* 175–182.

Powers, W. K. (1982). *Yuwipi, vision and experience in Oglala ritual.* Lincoln: University of Nebraska Press.

Primeaux, M. H. (1977). American Indian health care practices: A cross-cultural perspective. *Nursing Clinics of North America, 12,* 55–65.

Rapport, J. (1981). In praise of paradox: A social policy of empowerment over prevention. *American Journal of Community Psychology, 9,* 1–25.

Rappaport, J. (1987). Terms of empowerment/examples of prevention: Towards a theory of community psychology. *American Journal of Community Psychology, 15,* 121–147.

Rhoades, E. R., Marshall, M., Attneave, C., Fchohawk, M., Bjork, J., & Beiser, M. (1980). Mental health problems of American Indians seen in outpatient facilities of the Indian Health Services, 1975. *Public Health Reports, 95*(4), 329–335.

Rogler, L., Malgady, R., Constantino, G., & Blumenthal, R. (1987). What do culturally sensitive mental health services mean? The case of Hispanics. *American Psychologist, 42,* 565–570.

Roy, C., Chaudhuri, A., & Irvine, O. (1970). The prevalence of mental disorders among Saskatchewan Indians. *Journal of Cross-Cultural Psychology, 1,* 383–392.

Reuveni, U. (1979). *Networking families in crisis.* New York: Human Sciences Press.

Ryan, L., & Ryan, R. (1982). *Mental health and the urban Indian.* Unpublished manuscript.

Sampath, B. M. (1974). Prevalence of psychiatric disorders in a southern Baffin Island Eskimo settlement. *Canadian Psychiatric Association Journal, 19,* 363–367.

Sandner, D. F. (1978). Navajo medicine. *Human Nature, 1,* 54–62.

Sarason, S. (1972). *The creation of settings and future societies.* San Francisco: Jossey-Bass.

Schinke, S. P., Moncher, M. S., Holden, G. W., Botvin, G. J., & Orlandi, M. A. (1989). American Indian youth and substance abuse: Tobacco use problems, risk factors and preventive interventions. *Health Education Research, Theory and Practice, 4,* 137–144.

Schinke, S. P., Orlandi, M. A., Botvin, G. J., Gilchrist, L. D., Trimble, J. E., & Locklear, V. S. (1988). Preventing substance abuse among American Indian adolescents: A bicultural competence skills approach. *Journal of Counseling Psychology, 35,* 87–90.

Schinke, S. P., Schilling, R. F., Palleja, J., & Zayas, L. H. (1987). Prevention research among ethnic-racial minority group adolescents. *Behavior Therapist, 10,* 151–155.

Schoenfel, P., Halevy-Martini, J., Helmey-Van der Velden, E., Ruhf, L. (1985). Network therapy: An outcome study of twelve social networks. *Journal of Community Psychology, 13,* 281–287.

Schoenfeld, L. S., Lyerly, R. J., & Miller, S. I. (1971). We like us. *Mental Hygiene, 55,* 171–173.

Shore, J. H., Kinzie, J. D., Hampson, D., & Pattison, E. M. (1973). Psychiatric epidemiology of an Indian village. *Psychiatry, 36,* 70–81.

Solomon, G., Heisberger, J., & Winer, J. L. (1981). Confidentiality issues in rural community mental health. *Journal of Rural Community Psychology, 2*(1), 17–31.

Speck, R., & Attneave. C. (1973). *Family networks: Retribalization and healing.* New York: Random House.

Spindler, L., & Spindler, G. (1958). Male and female adaptations in culture change. *American Anthropologist, 60,* 217–233.

Sue, S., Allen, D. B., & Conaway, L. (1978). The responsiveness and equality of mental health care to Chicanos and Native Americans. *American Journal of Community Psychiatry, 6,* 137–146.

Trimble, J. E. (1981). Value differentials and their importance in counseling American Indians. In P. Pedersen, J. Draguns, W. Lonner, & J. Trimble (Eds.) *Counseling across cultures* (2nd ed., pp. 203–226). Honolulu: University Press of Hawaii.

Trimble, J. E. (1987a). American Indians and interethnic conflict. In J. Boucher, D. Landis, & K. Clark (Eds.) *Ethnic conflict: International perspectives* (pp. 208–230). Newbury Park, CA: Sage.

Trimble, J. E. (1987b). Self-perception and perceived alienation among American Indians. *Journal of Community Psychology, 15,* 316–333.

Trimble, J. E. (1988). Stereotypic images. American Indians and prejudice. In P. Katz & D. Taylor (Eds.), *Eliminating racism and prejudice* (pp. 210–236). New York: Pergamon.

Trimble, J. E., & Fleming, C. (1989). Providing counseling services for Native American Indians: Client, counselor and community characteristics. In P. Pedersen, J. Draguns, W. Lonner, & J. Trimble (Eds.). *Counseling across cultures* (3rd ed., pp. 145–168). Honolulu: University Press of Hawaii.

Trimble, J. E., & Hayes, S. (1984). Mental health intervention in the psychosocial contexts of American Indian communities. In W. O'Conner & B. Lubin (Eds.), *Ecological approaches to clinical and community psychology* (pp. 293–321). New York: Wiley.

Trimble, J. E., & LaFromboise, T. D. (1985). American Indians and the counseling process: Culture, adaptation, and style. In P. Pedersen (Ed.), *Handbook of cross-cultural mental health services* (pp. 127–134). Beverly Hills, CA: Sage.

Trimble, J. E., Manson, S. M., Dinges, N. G., & Medicine, B. (1984). American Indian conceptions of mental health: Reflections and directions. In P. Pedersen, N. Sartorius, & A. Marsella (Eds.), *Mental health services: The cross cultural context* (pp. 199–220). Beverly Hills, CA: Sage.

Trimble, J. E., Padilla, A., & Bell, C. (Eds.). (1987). *Drug abuse among ethnic minorities* (DHHS Publication No. ADM 87-1474). Rockville, MD: National Institute on Drug Abuse.

Tyler, I. M., & Thompson, S. D. (1965). Cultural factors in casework treatment of a Navajo mental patient. *Social Casework, 46,* 215–220.

U.S. Congress. Office of Technology Assessment. (1990). *Indian adolescent mental health* (OTA-H-446). Washington, DC: U.S. Government Printing Office.

Walker, J. R. (1980) *Lakota belief and ritual.* Lincoln: University of Nebraska Press.

Wallace, A. (1958). Dreams and wishes of the soul: A type of psychoanalytic theory among seventeenth century Iroquois. *American Anthropologist, 60,* 234–248.

Wax, R. H., & Thomas, R. K. (1961). American Indians and White people. *Phylon, 22,* 305–317.

9

Counseling Native Americans: An Introduction for Non-Native American Counselors

Timothy C. Thomason

This article provides a primer on counseling Native American clients for non-Native American counselors and psychotherapists. The diversity of this population is described and a general model of healing from a traditional Native American perspective is presented, with implications for counseling practice. Relevant research is reviewed and practical suggestions are offered for providing counseling services to Native Americans.

It is estimated that there are now over 1.8 million Native Americans, and the population is growing steadily (Attneave, 1985). There are 505 federally recognized tribal entities and an additional 365 state-recognized tribes and bands. There are 304 federal Native American reservations, and over 150 tribal languages are still spoken today (Bureau of Indian Affairs, 1988). More than half of Native Americans live in urban areas, and most large cities have at least 10,000 Native American residents (Stock, 1987). Most school and mental health counselors will, at some time, have the opportunity to provide counseling services to Native Americans, and counselors who live near reservations may see many Native American clients.

The purpose of this article is to describe some aspects of Native American culture relevant to counseling and to provide some guidelines for non-Native American counselors who may have Native American clients. The diversity of Native American culture is discussed and a model of healing from a Native American point of view is presented. Implications of the model for counseling practice are described, focusing on preparing to see a Native American client, conducting the first interview, and including theoretical considerations. Finally, suggestions for going beyond the limitations of individual counseling are offered. Findings from the very limited research base on the cross-cultural counseling of Native Americans are incorporated throughout the article.

Native Americans as a Group

Any description of Native Americans as a group is subject to some ambiguity, since not everyone agrees on how to decide who is a Native American. According to the federal government's Bureau of Indian Affairs (BIA, 1988), a *Native American* is legally defined as a person who is an enrolled or registered member of a tribe or whose blood quantum is one-fourth or more, genealogically derived. Some tribes, however, have set a lower blood quantum so more people could receive tribal benefits (Trimble, 1976). The United States Bureau of the Census does not use the BIA criteria; instead, it relies on self-identification (Manson & Trimble, 1982). A person who claims to be a Native American is usually accepted as such, regardless of blood quantum or tribal registration status, unless the person applies for tribal benefits, in which case the person must provide evidence.

The Native American population is extremely varied, and it is impossible to make general recommendations regarding counseling that apply to all Native Americans. Not only do various tribes differ from each other, but any one individual may differ greatly from other members of the same tribe (Attneave, 1982). A major variable is the degree of traditionalism of an individual versus the degree of acculturation to mainstream U.S. society. The continuum stretches from the very traditional individual born and reared on a reservation, who speaks the tribal language, to the Native American reared in a city who speaks only English and may feel little identification with a tribe (Dillard, 1983).

Even among residents of reservations, there can be significant variability. Riner (1979) examined 174 households on the Blackfeet, Sioux, and Navajo reservations and was able to distinguish among four types of households. In the "Isolated" Native American family, the home was located in a remote area of a reservation and there was a strong preference for use of the native language. Families in the "Traditional" category had bilingual homes and actively participated in tribal ceremonies. Families in the "Bicultural" category lived on a reservation and engaged in traditional ceremonies but preferred speaking English. In the "Acculturated" Native American home, English was the primary language and family activities approximated White norms. Some Native Americans who live and work in cities or nonreservation rural areas return to the reservation for ceremonies or to visit relatives. Many Native Americans have never lived on a reservation and have life-styles similar to those of their neighbors in either nonreservation rural areas or urban areas. These Native Americans may never have used a traditional healer and may not receive any tribal benefits.

Given the diversity of the Native American population, one must be careful to avoid stereotyping Native Americans based on general assumptions. Lloyd (1987) pointed out that differences within cultural groups can be greater than differences between such groups and cautioned that studying generalities about a particular culture can blind a counselor to the uniqueness of the client. Parker (1987) suggested that counselors can benefit from studying the client's culture but must keep in mind that individual clients will vary in the degree to which they reflect their culture. It is generally recognized that ignoring cultural background does the client a disservice (Larson, 1982). In an article such as this, which discusses Native Americans as a group, readers should bear in mind that general information can only be helpful in a general way, and that each client is unique and must be approached as an individual.

A Native American Model of Healing

Attitudes and beliefs about health vary somewhat among the many tribes of Native Americans in this country. It is possible, however, to describe a general model of healing that is common to many tribes as a way of illustrating how Native American ways of thinking may differ from those of non-Native Americans. Some aspects of the model can provide clues to non-Native American counselors regarding how to adapt their thinking and methods to understand and serve Native American clients more effectively. The model should be seen as an example of how some Native Americans think rather than as a description of how all Native Americans think.

One ancient Native American idea about health is that health results from having a harmonious relationship with nature. All creation is seen as a living, seamless whole. Nature is structured and follows rules of cause and effect, but not necessarily in a manner understandable to human beings (Trimble, 1981). Living in harmony with nature is accomplished by following the traditions of the tribe. Breaking a taboo or ignoring a tradition can result in a state of disharmony, which can be manifested in an individual as disability, disease, or distress (Dinges, Trimble, Manson, & Pasquale, 1981; Spector, 1985).

Nature, being whole, cannot be separated artificially into physical, mental, or social parts. Rather, all of life is seen as a spiritual process. Individuals are considered relatively insignificant compared to the tribe, and an individual's problems are considered a problem of the group

(Attneave, 1982). Time is considered to have a circular character, like the seasons. Time is not rigidly structured and there is never a lack of time; events simply begins when everyone is present (Everett, Proctor, & Cartmell, 1983; Spang, 1965). Traditionally Native American healers do not specialize in physical as opposed to mental or emotional problems, since there is no such thing as a problem in any one of these areas (Medicine, 1982).

From a traditional perspective, the term *mental health* is a misnomer, since it implies that a mental aspect of a person can be separated from the rest of the person. Except for family therapists non-Native American service providers tend to focus on individual mental health and locate psychological problems within the individual. From a traditional point of view, the individual simply exhibits a problem that is assumed to be rooted in the community (LaFromboise, 1988; Spector, 1985). It would be very rare for a traditional healer to treat an individual in isolation; the extended family, friends, and neighbors are mobilized to support the individual and get them integrated into the social life of the group (Lewis & Ho, 1989). Typically, the healing ceremonies occur in the client's usual surrounding rather than in an unfamiliar place.

When seeing a traditional healer, the patient simply presents a problem and it is up to the healer to diagnose the cause of the problem. For example, among the Navajo, the client is relatively passive throughout both the diagnostic and treatment ceremonies. The client is expectant and hopeful, but insight into the problem and all curative powers are assumed to lie with the healer, not the patient (Dinges et al., 1981). In addition, the healer makes a diagnosis without asking the patient personal questions or expecting intimate self-disclosure. In some tribes there might be collective discussion in meetings of everyone involved where the individual is encouraged to make a ritualized confession of being out of harmony with nature (Spector, 1985). Then an atonement ritual might be performed whereby the individual is restored into the good graces of family and community (LaFromboise, 1988; Wallace, 1958). Although healing rituals may be lengthy, improvement in the patient is usually expected to occur rather quickly.

Preparing to Counsel an Indian Client

The expectations of both client and the counselor can have a large impact on the success of cross-cultural counseling. The potential mismatch between the expectations of Native American clients and non-Native American counselors may explain why Native Americans often drop out of counseling. In one study, over 50 percent of Native American clients who went to mental health centers failed to return after the first interview, compared to a 30 percent drop-out rate among other groups (Sue, 1977, 1981a). Therefore counselors must strive to make the first interview with a Native American client therapeutic rather than use it simply to collect information from the client and make a diagnosis of the client's problem. Youngman and Sadongei (1974) noted that "many Indian clients simply do not know what is expected of them; the notion of what constitutes good client behavior may never have occurred to them" (p. 131). The client who is not given a good orientation to counseling and made to feel hopeful in the first session will likely not return for a second session.

The counselor can improve the odds of having a good first session with a Native American client by preparing for it in advance. The general Native American model of healing can be used to get some clues concerning how Native American clients might think about counseling. Obviously, traditionally minded clients are more likely to accept the tenets of the model than highly acculturated clients; nevertheless, many Native American clients in general would accept many of the assumptions inherent in the model. For example, following from the model we could assume that Native American clients might expect the counselor to diagnose their problem without prying too deeply into their personal life or asking many intimate questions (Edwards & Edwards, 1989). It would be reasonable for the client to expect that family members would be involved in the counseling and that improvement would occur rather quickly. Even a less traditional Native American client might have a tendency to expect a counselor to "take over" and solve the problem for the client. This tendency is understandable, considering the patronizing fashion in which most services for Native Americans have been provided in the past. A system that prevents self-determination can lead to an attitude of resignation and passivity in Native Americans (Richardson, 1981). The counselor should consider the possible expectations of Native American clients in advance of the first session and be prepared to discuss the mutual responsibilities of the counselor and the client.

Non-native American counselors should realize that their trustworthiness may be in question when seeing a Native American client. Many Native Americans feel that historically, White Americans have not been trustworthy in their dealings with Native Americans (David, 1982). The White counselor has no right to expect that Native American clients will automatically trust the counselor to have the client's interests at heart. Little empirical research has been conducted on this topic, but LaFromboise and Dixon (1981) did conduct one videotape analogue study with forty-eight Native American high school students. The students rated the effectiveness of two counselors (one Native American and one non-Native American) in two role-played counseling interactions. In the "trustworthy" role plays the counselors were attentive and responsive to the client, gave structure and direction to the interview, and displayed respect for the client's cultural identity. They used eye contact similar to that of the client, sat erect in their chair, and avoided references to time until the end of the session. In the "non-trustworthy" role play the counselors displayed opposite behaviors. The Native American students who watched the tapes considered the sessions in which the counselors enacted the trustworthy role as positive, regardless of whether the counselor was Native American or non-Native Americans. The authors of the study concluded that the perceived trustworthiness of the counselor was more important than ethnic similarity between client and counselor.

A study published the same year by Dauphinais, Dauphinais, and Rowe (1981), however, found that Native American students perceived Native American counselors as more effective than non-native American counselors. The study participants were 102 Native American eleventh- and twelfth-grade students who rated counselors on seven dimensions of perceived credibility and effectiveness. The students preferred counselors who were ethnically similar to themselves over non-Native American counselors. In a separate study conducted with sixty-two Native American college students, Haviland, Horswith, O'Connel, and Dynneson (1983) reported that all of the Native American students demonstrated a strong preference for Native American counselors.

It is understandable that, if all other factors are equal, Native American clients prefer to see Native American counselors. But according to Dinges et al. (1981), "there is precious little empirical basis for claims of superior therapeutic effectiveness of the Indian versus the non-Indian" (p. 271). Sue (1988) agreed that ethnic matching has not been shown to improve outcomes consistently, although he pointed out that ethnicity may be a distal variable and therefore only weakly related to outcome. Given the small number of trained Native American counselors, the simple fact is that most Native American clients have little choice about whom to see; most Native American clients will see non-Native American counselors (Everett et al., 1983; LaFromboise, 1988; Manson, 1982). The positive news for non-Native American counselors is that Native American clients are likely to consider them effective if they behave in a trustworthy manner. Building trust can take time, and it may help for counselors to explain to clients that they do not expect to be trusted before they have earned it (Richardson, 1981).

In preparing to see a Native American client, it can also help for the counselor to recognize that many Native Americans feel pulled between traditional tribal culture and the mainstream culture of the United States. This conflict can, in itself, constitute a problem that motivates clients to seek counseling (Larson, 1982). For example, opportunities for higher education and employment are very limited on most reservations, forcing people to leave their homes and families to move to distant urban areas. Relocating for school or work disconnects the individual from psychosocial support systems and often imposes new financial burdens. Being away from home and loved ones is stressful in itself, and the stress of coping with a new environment can increase the likelihood of anxiety, depression, and substance abuse. Many Native Americans seek a balance between honoring their traditions and surviving in the modern world. Counselors who are sensitive to these issues are better prepared to help clients explore and resolve them (Trimble & Fleming, 1989).

The counselor who often sees clients from a particular nearby tribe would benefit from learning about the history of the tribe, traditional beliefs and values, and current tribal organization. Studying both the problems and resources of the tribe could provide important information as background for seeing clients from the tribe. The counselor should also investigate the tribe's family structure, age and gender roles, and characteristics of typical nonverbal and paralinguistic behavior. Factors particularly relevant to counseling include beliefs about how problems should be resolved, the meaning attributed to illness or disability, and traditional healing practices. Information on the natural support systems, developmental stress points, and coping strategies can also be important when serving clients who live on reservations or have traditional values (Trimble, & LaFromboise, 1985). Much can be learned by making friends with Native Americans from a nearby reservation and visiting them or attending ceremonies (when invited by a member of the tribe). Many large cities have a Native American center that provides support for Native Americans who live in the area and sponsors events where non-Native Americans can meet Native Americans.

The Initial Interview

Few, if any, assumptions can be made about a Native American client who makes an appointment for counseling. Therefore, the purpose of the first interview is to allow the client and counselor to get to know each other and possibly to decide whether their working together will be fruitful. The counselor should take the lead in structuring the session and explain to the client that they will have plenty of time to get to know each other before discussing any concerns that client may have (Attneave, 1982). The atmosphere should be relaxed, casual, and nonthreatening, and the counselor should use an informal, conversational verbal style. Compared to counseling White clients, much more time may be used in social conversation as a way to build rapport. Rather than asking a series of personal questions, the counselor can use self-disclosure as a way to prompt self-disclosure on the part of the client (Everett et al., 1983). The client should be allowed plenty of time to talk in response to the counselor's statements. Questions should be avoided as much as possible so that the client does not feel pressured to talk on an intimate level before feeling comfortable to do so (Orlansky & Trap, 1987).

It helps to remember that in traditional Native American society there is no one person in a role similar to that of a counselor (Trimble, 1976). Traditionally minded Native Americans may feel quite awkward about going to see a non-Native American stranger in an office far from home to talk about personal problems. Thus, it is up to the counselor to put the client at ease and communicate to the client that there are no demands to behave a certain way or talk a certain amount. Barriers to building a relationship, such as requiring the client to complete lengthy intake forms or questionnaires, should be avoided (Everett et al., 1983). If a Native American client brings a friend or family member along to an interview, this should be accepted (Edwards & Edwards, 1989). Some clients may be reluctant to talk about their strengths and resources, since it could be interpreted as boasting (Everett et al., 1983). Others will be comfortable talking about practical issues of daily life but uncomfortable if pressed for intimate self-disclosures (Sue, 1981b). The counselor should monitor the comfort level of the client and be careful not to increase the client's anxiety.

As in any initial counseling session, the counselor should communicate warmth, caring, genuineness, and respect. As the session proceeds, the counselor can develop a picture of the client's world. How traditional are the client's values, family, and living situation? How close is the tribal identification? Is the client feeling torn between tribal culture and mainstream culture, or has the client worked out a balance between the two? How extensive is the client's support system? What are the client's expectations for counseling, and does the client have a clear sense of how counseling may help resolve the problem? By the end of the initial interview it may be possible to define the client's problem in specific terms and set some goals for counseling. Attneave (1982) cautioned that Native American clients often present a concrete problem first to see how the counselor handles it, with more serious concerns presented only after the client feels confident about the counselor's ability. The initial interview can be considered a success even if the client just gets a clear sense that counseling may be helpful and agrees to return for another session.

Counseling Theory and Process

Most of the psychological information available of Native Americans focuses on deviant patterns of adjustment such as suicide and alcoholism, and little is available that addresses cognitive, emotional, and personality processes (Trimble, Mackey, LaFromboise, & France, 1983). According to Manson and Trimble (1982), "little or no data are available on the therapist variables most closely linked to positive outcomes in psychotherapy among Indian patients'' (p. 150). In addition, virtually no research has been conducted on the relative effectiveness of various theoretical approaches to counseling Native Americans. ''Although the literature on Indian mental health is extensive, the same cannot be said for the field of counseling and Indians'' (Manson, 1982, p. 129). Nevertheless, a review of the limited literature on counseling Native Americans does reveal some consistency in recommendations for conducting counseling with Native American clients.

Miller (1982) suggested that counselors who make the effort to understand the social ecology of the Native American client's community can be effective using ''general counseling skills'' (p. 132) applied in an empathic and caring context. Most counselors and psychotherapists who have written about seeing Native American clients recommend neither psychodynamic nor nondirective approaches, and instead suggest taking a fairly active, directive approach (Dillard, 1983). This is not necessarily a behavioral approach, but one that focuses on the present more than the past or the future and emphasizes practical problem solving (Trimble, 1976). One study of Native American high school students did find that the students rated a directive verbal response style as more effective than a ''facilitative'' response style (Dauphinais et al., 1981). Spand (1965) maintained that directive counseling is more effective than client-centered counseling with reservation-based Native American clients, who may be relatively nonverbal in encounters with non-Native Americans.

Many authors report that effective counseling with clients from ethnically diverse backgrounds is short term, a historical, directive, relational, authoritative, problem focuses, and action orientated (Lefley & Bestman, 1984). According to Trimble (1976), ''the Indian is not accustomed to self-analysis nor is there a familiarity with the process of discussing with a non-Indian one's emotional conflicts'' (p. 79). Dinges et al. (1981) pointed out that a counseling approach that demands self-expression, introspective analysis, and self-conscious change of dispositions and behavior runs counter to the attitudes and values of many Native Americans. Analytic-style interpretations may seem bizarre to Native American clients, and a purely reflective or nondirective style may be regarded as a waste of time (Schacht, Tafoya, & Mirabla, 1989).

Although most writers recommend an active, practical approach to counseling Native Americans, one exception is Boyer (1964), who reported (anecdotally) great success using traditional psychoanalytic techniques with members of the Mescalero Apache tribe in New Mexico:

> As time went on, they saw that I gave no advice, no instructions, and no opinions. Instead, they discovered that simply by my using the techniques of a psychoanalytic therapist and making certain interpretations, they were not only

relieved of anxieties but also enabled to have better marital relationships, to stop drinking, and even to get rid of chronic nightmares and phobias. (p. 523)

Dillard (1983), on the other hand, contended that psychodynamic interpretations and the encouragement of emotional catharsis are rarely useful in counseling Native Americans. Trimble (1976) agreed: "Traditional counseling methods such as nondirective therapy, psychoanalysis, group therapy, etc. are not conducive to a trusting relationship with Indian clients" (p. 66).

Obviously, the theoretical approach taken depends to a large extent on the client's problem and on the counselor's assessment of the client's abilities and personality. When a client's problem is a simple lack of specific information, a quite directive approach can easily be justified. This occurs frequently in the areas of vocational counseling and vocational rehabilitation. Even here, however, care should be taken not to speak down to the client. Rather than tell the client what to do, the counselor should describe alternatives and choices and let the client decide on a course of action. This approach also works well when the client's concern is a decision to be made or a specific conflict that has to be resolved. Making decisions for the client would only reinforce paternalism (Lewis & Ho, 1989). After the client makes a decision, the counselor's role becomes one of supporting the client while the decision is implemented and being available to explore the ramifications of the decision with the client.

More important than the counselor's theoretical orientation is the client's set of beliefs about how change occurs. The counselor who can understand and get inside the client's belief system has real leverage for promoting change in a therapeutic direction. To do this, the counselor must be sensitive to the client's frame of reference and speak the client's language (in terms of how change can occur) (Trimble, 1976). Manson and Trimble (1982) pointed out that

> The clients of cross-cultural therapy do not always find themselves motivated to change in ways that are congruent with the therapist's goals and value system. Moreover, Native American clients may hold quite different beliefs about the etiology of their problems and the manner in which change can be accomplished. (p. 150)

Frank (1973) analyzed the common features of healing practices across cultures and concluded that the rationale used to explain the problem must be compatible with the belief system of the client. Both Native American and non-Native American healing systems have strengths and weaknesses and may or may not be functional in specific cultural contexts (Dinges et al., 1981). The counselor who expects a Native American client to think like a White American in the counseling situation demonstrates an ethnocentrism that can sabotage the counseling process (Matheson, 1986). Accepting and working within the client's belief system is likely to be much more effective than trying to teach the client a new belief system. Therefore, to the extent possible, counselors should try to understand the Native American client's beliefs about change and work within them.

Nonverbal Behavior in Counseling

No description of variables that affect the relationship between a Native American client and a non-Native American counselor would be complete without mention of nonverbal behavior. Many writers have touched on this issue, and sometimes the advice conflicts, which is understandable given the large number of distinct Native American cultures and the variability within each tribe. No empirical research on this topic appears in the literature, so once again we must rely on anecdote and impression and remember that individual clients may not behave in ways consistent with our expectations.

There is no universal Native American language; each tribe may have its own language, and dialects add to the variability. In remote areas language differences can be a problem, but most Native American clients likely to be seen by non-Native American counselors are fluent enough in English to communicate (Everett et al., 1983). The interpretations of nonverbal behavior is more problematic. Many authors advise non-Native American counselors to avoid intense direct eye contact, since it can be considered disrespectful, and not to expect it from clients (Attneave, 1985; Lewis & Ho, 1989; Matheson, 1986; Orlansky & Trap, 1987; Youngman & Sadongei, 1974). Non-Native Americans are advised to use a low tone of voice with Native American clients, to refrain from touching a client beyond a handshake (such as a pat on the back or a hug), and to use a soft handshake rather than a firm, aggressive one (Attneave, 1982; Everett et al., 1983; Orlansky & Trap, 1987).

Some Native Americans are offended by the suggestion that all Native Americans avoid eye contact, speak only in a low tone of voice, and have limp handshakes. It is true that such recommendations might mislead counselors and potentially do more harm than good. An alternative approach is to approach each client as an individual and take the lead from the client regarding nonverbal behavior. The counselor should note the client's behaviors, such as tone of voice, pace of speech, and degree of eye contact, and match them subtly. This can facilitate the development of rapport and is unlikely to offend the client (O'Hanlon, 1987).

Beyond Individual Counseling

While serving Native American clients, many counselors find it helpful to go beyond the traditional office setting and go into the client's community

(Schacht, Tafoya, & Mirabla, 1989). Native American reservations are open to the public, but an invitation is necessary to visit individual homes or attend most ceremonies. Visiting a client's home on a reservation or in a rural area educates the counselor on the client's living situation and shows the client the counselor's level of interest and commitment. Going to the client's home also makes it much easier to involve the client's family. Even if the family is not directly involved in the client's problem they can provide crucial support and understanding for the client (Attneave, 1969; Rappaport, 1981).

Schacht et al. (1989) developed a model of home-based therapy with Native American families that seems effective. They advised the counselor to build credibility with the Native American family by sharing meals of offering to provide practical help (such as transportation). "Flexibility regarding appointment times and greater availability to respond to crisis can also demonstrate the therapist's helpfulness and desire to be of help" (p. 28). In the informal context of the home setting clients are sometimes more receptive to advice, analogies, and appropriate self-disclosure on the part of the counselor. Attneave pioneered another field-based approach called "tribal network therapy," which enables large groups of friends and relatives to come together to pool their resources and share their strengths in coping with problems (LaFromboise & Fleming, 1990). La Fromboise (1988) pointed out that

> The collective treatment of psychologically troubled individuals in tribal groups not only serves to heal the individual but also to reaffirm the norms of the entire group. The goal of therapy is not to strengthen the client's ego but to encourage the client to transcend the ego by experiencing the self as embedded in and expressive of community. (p. 392)

In some cases it can be very helpful to collaborate with indigenous healers when seeing a reservation-based client. Some counselors get advice from traditional healers in the client's tribe or refer clients for a consultation with a traditional healer. Sometimes traditional healing practices can be combined with individual or family counseling (Lowrey, 1983; Meyer, 1974). The counselor would obviously need the client's permission to seek help from traditional healers and the issue of confidentiality would have to be clarified. The client might be able to suggest to the counselor the proper protocol to follow in locating and talking with a traditional healer from the client's tribe. Otherwise, the counselor can contact the administration offices of the tribe or the local Indian Health Service office for advice on how to collaborate with indigenous healers. On some reservations policies have been established that allow traditional healers to serve clients and be reimbursed by the Indian Health Service as consultants on a contract basis (Dinges et al., 1981). A client who has traditional values is likely to appreciate a non-Native American counselor's efforts to involve traditional healers. Heinrich, Corbine, and Thomas (1990) have described how traditional Native American healing practices such as the vision quest and the sweat lodge ceremony can be incorporated into individual or group treatment programs.

Self-help and mutual support groups have been reported to be successful among groups of Native Americans both on and off reservations (Pedigo, 1983). Many tribes offer 12-step programs for substance abuse treatment, and can usually be located by contacting the local Indian Health Service office. In urban areas the local Native American center (e.g., Denver Indian Center, Phoenix Indian Center) may provide similar services and can at least offer ideas for referral of clients to self-help and other treatment groups. Counselors who feel unqualified to serve Native American clients directly should at least be able to refer such clients to other counselors or agencies in the community.

Conclusion

Native Americans constitute a significant population that is growing and has great need for mental health and counseling services. All counselors should have a basic understanding of the history and present status of Native Americans and should be able to serve members of this group. Although the population of Native Americans is diverse and no one can be knowledgeable about all the tribes, there are some similarities in the basic values and beliefs of many Native Americans. A familiarity with general Native American ideas about healing can provide a counselor with an understanding of what traditional Native Americans may expect from a counselor. While establishing a trusting relationship with the client the counselor can learn specifics about the client's tribe and beliefs so that counseling interventions can mesh with the client's belief system and therefore be more likely to make sense to the client and lead to change (Trimble & Fleming, 1989).

Generally speaking, any skilled counselor who is sincere and meets the client as a person rather than as a case should be able to conduct therapeutic counseling with Native Americans. Following the client's lead in regard to nonverbal behavior will help to prevent misunderstandings and increase rapport. Then, a patient and informal exploration of the client's concerns will reveal whether counseling is the proper course of action. A fairly active and directive problem-solving approach can be effective with many clients, and other strategies can be used as they seem appropriate with specific clients. When individual counseling seems too limiting or ineffective, the counselor has the option of including the client's family, visiting the client's home, and possibly involving a traditional healer from the client's tribe.

Much remains to be learned about the diagnosis and treatment of psychological problems among Native Americans. Research should be conducted to determine which interpersonal strategies best facilitate rapport between Native Americans and non-Native Americans and which counseling approaches work best with various types of Native American clients on various problems. Some models for training counselors in cross-cultural awareness have been developed, and they should be compared systematically (Christensen, 1989; Pedersen, 1977). In addition, more effort should be put into recruiting Native American students into counselor education programs.

Counseling Native Americans provides an opportunity for the non-Native American counselor to develop new awareness of an important minority ethnic group and new skills in cross-cultural counseling. In the process the counselor's world is enlarged and enriched and the client receives the kind of sensitive understanding and practical help that can lead to more effective living. Although learning about Native Americans in general can help, the reader is reminded that individuals vary in the extent to which they reflect their cultural heritage. A good counselor is, in a sense, like an artist who studies light and color and design and then deliberately forgets all rules in the act of creating a painting. In a similar way, the counselor interested in serving Native Americans should learn as much as possible about Native Americans in general and specific local tribes and then forget it in the live encounter with the client, who is the best teacher.

References

Attneave, C. L. (1969). Therapy in tribal settings and urban network intervention. *Family Process, 8,* 192–210.

Attneave, C. L. (1982). American Indians and Alaska Native families: Emigrants in their own homeland. In M. McGoldrick, J. Pearce, & J. Giorando (Eds.), *Ethnicity and family therapy* (pp. 55–83). New York: Guiford.

Attneave, C. L. (1985). Practical counseling with American Indian and Alaska Native clients. In P. Pedersen (Ed.), *Handbook of cross-cultural counseling and therapy* (pp. 135–140). Westport, CT: Greenwood Press.

Boyer, L. B. (1964). Psychoanalytic insights in working with ethnic minorities. *Social Casework, 45,* 519–526.

Bureau of Indian Affairs (1988) *American Indians today.* Washington, DC: Author.

Christensen, C. P. (1989). Cross-cultural awareness development: A conceptual model. *Counselor Education and Supervision, 28,* 270–289.

Dauphinais, P., Dauphinais, L., & Rowe, W. (1981). Effects of race and communication style on Indian perceptions of counselor effectiveness. *Counselor Education and Supervision, 21,* 72–80.

Davis, W. T. (1982). The hidden minority. *Professional Psychology, 13,* 778–781.

Dillard, J. M. (1983). *Multicultural counseling.* Chicago: Nelson Hall.

Dinges, N. G., Trimble, J. E., Manson, S. E., & Pasquale, F. L. (1981). Counseling and psychotherapy with American Indians and Alaskan-Natives. In A. J. Marsella & P. B. Pedersen (Eds.), *Cross-cultural counseling and psychotherapy* (pp. 243–276). New York: Pergamon.

Edwards, E. D., & Edwards, M. E. (1989). American Indians: Working with individuals and groups. In D. R. Atkinson, G. Morten, & D. W. Sue (Eds.), *Counseling American minorities* (pp. 72–84). Dubuque, IA: William C. Brown Publishers.

Everett, F., Proctor, N., & Cartmell, B. (1983). Providing psychological services to American Indian children and families. *Professional-Psychology, 14,* 588–603.

Frank, J. D. (1973). *Persuasion and healing: A comparative study of psychotherapy.* Baltimore, MD: Johns Hopkins University Press.

Haviland, M. G., Horswith, R. K., O'Connel, J. J., & Dynneson, V. V. (1983). Native American college students' preference for counselor race and sex and the likelihood of their use of a counseling center. *Journal of Counseling Psychology, 30,* 267–70.

Heinrich, R. K., Corbine, J. L., Thomas, K. R. (1990). Counseling Native Americans. *Journal of Counseling & Development, 69,* 128–133.

LaFromboise, T. D. (1988). American Indian mental health policy. *American Psychology, 43,* 388–397.

LaFromboise, T. D., & Dixon, D. N. (1981). American Indian perception of trustworthiness in a counseling interview. *Journal of Counseling Psychology, 28,* 135–39.

LaFromboise, T. D., & Fleming, C. (1990). Keeper of the fire: A profile of Carolyn Attneave. *Journal of Counseling & Development, 68,* 537–547.

Larson, P. C. (1982). Counseling special populations. *Professional Psychology, 13,* 843–858.

Lefley, H. P., & Bestman, E. W. (1984). Community mental health and minorities: A multi-ethnic approach. In S. Sue & T. Moore (Eds.), *Community mental health in a pluralistic society.* New York: Human Sciences Press.

Lewis, R., & Ho, M. (1984). Social work with Native Americans. In D. Atkinson, G. Morten, & D. Sue (Eds), *Counseling American minorities* (pp. 51–58). Dubuque, IA: William C. Brown.

Lloyd, A. P. (1987). Multicultural counseling: Does it belong in a counselor education program? *Counselor Education and Supervision, 26,* 164–167.

Lowrey, L. (1983). Bridging a culture in counseling. *Journal of Applied Rehabilitation Counseling, 14,* 69–73.

Manson, S. M. (Ed.). (1982). *Topics in American Indian mental health prevention.* Portland, OR: Oregon Health Sciences University Press.

Manson, S. M., & Trimble, J. E. (1982). American Indian and Alaska Native communities. In L. R.Snowden (Ed.) *Reaching the underserved* (pp. 143–163). Beverly Hills, CA: Sage.

Matheson, L. (1986). If you are not an Indian, how do you treat an Indian? In H. Lefley (Ed.), *Cross-cultural training for mental health professionals* (pp. 115–130). Springfield, IL: Charles C. Thomas.

Medicine, B. (1982). New roads to coping—Siouan sobriety. In S. Manson (Ed.), *New directions in prevention among American Indian and Alaska Native communities* (pp. 189–212). Portland, OR: National Center for American Indian and Alaska Native Mental Health Research.

Meyer, G. (1974). On helping the casualties of rapid change. *Psychiatric Annals, 4,* 44–48.

Miller, N. B. (1982). Social work services to urban Indians. In J. W. Green (Ed.), *Cultural awareness in the human services.* Englewood Cliffs, NJ: Prentice-Hall.

O'Hanlon, W. H. (1987). *Taproots: Underlying principles of Milton Erickson's therapy and hypnosis.* New York: Norton.

Orlansky, M. D., & Trap, J. J. (1987). Working with Native American persons: Issues in facilitating communication and providing relevant services. *Journal of Visual Impairment and Blindness, 81,* 152.

Parker, W. M. (1987). Flexibility: A primer for multicultural counseling. *Counselor Education and Supervision, 26,* 176–180.

Pederson, P. B. (1977). The triad model of cross-cultural counselor training. *The Personnel and Guidance Journal, 55,* 94–100.

Pedigo, J. (1983). Finding the "meaning" of Native American substance abuse: Implications for community prevention. *The Personnel and Guidance Journal, 61,* 273–277.

Rappaport, J. (1981). In praise of paradox: A social policy of empowerment over prevention. *American Journal of Community Psychology, 9, 1–25.*

Richardson, E. H. (1981). Cultural and historical perspectives in counseling American Indians. In D. W. Sue (Ed.), *Counseling the culturally different* (pp. 216–255). New York: Wiley.

Riner, R. D. (1979). American Indian education: A rite that fails. *Anthropology and Education Quarterly, 10,* 236–253.

Schacht, A. J., Tafoya, N., & Mirabla, D. (1989). Home-based therapy with American Indian families. *American Indian and Alaska Native Mental Health Research, 3*(2), 27–42.

Spang, A. (1965). Counseling the Indian. *Journal of American Indian Education, 5,* 10–15.

Spector, R. (1985). *Cultural diversity in health and illness.* Norwalk, CT: Appleton Century Crofts.

Stock, L. (1987). Native Americans: A brief profile. *Journal of Visual Impairment and Blindness, 81,* 152.

Sue, D. W. (1977). Community mental health services to minority groups: Some optimism, some pessimism. *American Psychologist, 32,* 616–624.

Sue, D. W. (Ed.). (1981a). *Counseling the culturally different.* New York: Wiley.

Sue, D. W. (1981b). Evaluating process variables in cross-cultural counseling and psychotherapy. In A. Marsella & P. Pedersen (Eds.), *Cross-cultural counseling and psychotherapy: Foundations, evaluation, cultural considerations* (pp. 102–125). Elmsford, NJ: Pergamon Press.

Sue, S. (1988). Psychotherapeutic services for ethnic minorities. *American Psychologist, 43,* 301–308.

Trimble, J. E. (1976). Value differences among American Indians: Concerns for the concerned counselor. In. P. Pederson, W. J. Lonner, & J. G. Draguns (Eds.), *Counseling across cultures* (pp. 65–81). Honolulu: University Press of Hawaii.

Trimble, J. E. (1981). Value differentials and their importance in counseling American Indians. In P. Pedersen, J. Draguns, W. Lonner, & J. Trimble (Eds.), *Counseling across cultures (rev. ed.), (pp. 203–226). Honolulu: University Press of Hawaii.*

Trimble, J. E., & Fleming, C. M. (1989). Providing counseling services for Native American Indians: Client, counselor, and community characteristics. In P. B. Pedersen, J. G. Draguns, W. J. Lonner, & J. E. Trimble (Eds.), *Counseling across cultures* (3rd ed.), (pp. 177–204). Honolulu: University Press of Hawaii.

Trimble, J. E., & LaFromboise, T. D., (1985). American Indians and the counseling process: Culture, adaption, and style. In P. Pedersen (Ed.), *Handbook of cross-cultural counseling and therapy* (pp. 127–134). Westport, CT: Greenwood Press.

Trimble, J. E., Mackey, D. W., LaFromboise, T. D., & France, G. A. (1983). American Indians, psychology, and curriculum development. In J. C. Chunn, D. J. Dunston, & F. Ross-Sheriff (Eds.), *Mental health and people of color* (pp. 43–55). Washington, DC: Howard University Press.

Wallace, W. (1958). Dreams and wishes of the soul: A type of psychoanalytic theory among seventeenth century Iroqois. *American Anthropologist, 60,* 234–248.

Youngman, G., & Sadongei, M. (1974). Counseling the American Indian child. *Elementary School Guidance and Counseling, 8,* 273–277.

The American Indian Client
Cases and Questions

1. Assume you are an elementary school counselor for several rural elementary schools that enroll about twelve American Indian students each year (approximately 5 percent of the total enrollment). Although the American Indian children perform as well as the Anglo children in kindergarten, by fourth grade it is clear they are less advanced to reading, writing, and computational skills. The district in which these schools are located is quite poor, and you are one of the few specialists available to supplement the resources of the classroom teacher.

    a. Upon entering a teacher's lounge in one school, you hear the English teacher, in conversation with several other teachers, relate the American Indian students' poor performance to their family/cultural background in rather uncomplimentary terms. How would you react?

    b. What responsibility, if any, would you accept for attempting to offset the deficiencies in academic skills these Native American students have?

    c. What response would you expect to receive from American Indian students and their parents to your attempts to improve the students' academic performance (assuming you accept responsibility for doing this)?

2. Assume you are a community social worker employed by the BIA to work with reservation Indian families in which one or both of the parents have a history of chronic alcoholism.

    a. What are some of the factors you believe may contribute to alcoholism among American Indians, and how would your assumptions about the etiology of alcoholism affect your role as a social worker?

    b. What personal and professional qualities that you possess would be helpful in your work with American Indians? What qualities might be detrimental?

    c. Would you attempt to work with several families at once through group counseling? If so, how would you structure the group experience?

3. Assume you are a counselor in an urban high school that enrolls a small number of Native American students whose parents have left reservation life for the employment opportunities of a big city. Johnny Lonetree, an artistically gifted junior who regularly makes the honor roll, has just informed you that he is contemplating returning to the reservation to live with his grandparents. Johnny knows that for all practical purposes this will mean an end to his scholastic education, but he is intensely interested in being immersed in the tribal culture, specifically tribal art work.

    a. How can you best assist Johnny in his decision-making process?
    b. How might some of your own values affect how you proceed with Johnny?
    c. What are some of the social pressures (from administrators, colleagues, Johnny's parents) that are likely to be exerted upon both you and Johnny if he decides to return to the reservation?

The American Indian Client
Role Playing Exercise

Divide into groups of four or five. Assign each group member to a role and the responsibilities associated with the role as follows:

Role	Responsibility
1. Counselor	1. Assume role as a counselor or mental health worker who is assigned an American Indian client. Attempt to build rapport with the client.
2. Client	2. Assume role of an American Indian client. To play this role effectively, it will be necessary for the student client to (a) identify cultural values of American Indians, (b) identify sociopolitical factors which may interfere with counseling, and (c) portray these aspects in the counseling session. It is best to select a few powerful variables in the role play. You may or may not be initially antagonistic to the counselor, but it is important for you to be sincere in your role and your reactions to the counselor.
3. Observers	3. Observe interaction and offer comments during feedback session.

This exercise is most effective in a racially and ethnically mixed group. For example, an American Indian student can be asked to play the client role. However, this is probably not possible in most cases. Thus, students who play the client role will need to thoroughly read the articles for the groups they are portraying.

Identifying the barriers that could interfere with counseling is an important aspect of this exercise. We recommend that the list be made of the group's cultural values and sociopolitical influences prior to the role playing.

Role playing may go on for a period of five to fifteen minutes, but the time limit should be determined prior to the activity. Allow ten to fifteen minutes for a feedback session in which all participants discuss (within the group) how they felt in their respective roles, how appropriate were the counselor responses, what else they might have done in that situation, etc.

Rotate and role play the same situation with another counselor trainee *or* another American Indian client with different issues, concerns, and

problems. In the former case, the group may feel that a particular issue is of sufficient importance to warrant reenactment. This allows students to see the effects of other counseling responses and approaches. In the latter case, the new exposure will allow students to get a broader view of barriers to counseling.

If videotaping equipment is available, we recommend that the session be taped and processed in a replay at the end. We have found this to be a powerful means of providing feedback to participants.

PART 4

The Asian American Client

The Asian American population stood at seven million in 1990 and is expected to double by the year 2010. It is the fastest growing racial/ethnic group in the United States with an increase of nearly 80 percent during the 1980s. The large increase is due to the 1965 changes in immigration laws and the entry of over 700,000 Indochinese refugees since 1975. In 1984 alone, over 282,000 Asians entered the United States. As a result of the large immigration, the characteristics of the Asian American population has undergone a radical change. Japanese Americans, who previously constituted the largest group in the United States (approximately 800,000) have dropped to third place behind the Filipinos (1.4 million) and Chinese (1.2 million). Demographers predict that Filipinos will be the largest group followed by Chinese, Koreans, Vietnamese, Asian Indians, and Japanese.

Over 60 percent of the Chinese population are now recent immigrants, and with the exception of the Japanese, the other Asian populations are now principally comprised of foreign-born individuals. It is important to note that the term Asian American masks the great between-group differences among the Asian population. Some twenty-nine distinct subgroups that differ in language, religion, and values have been officially identified in the United States. Yet, despite this fact Asians continue to be perceived by many as possessing similar characteristics.

One of the most prevalent and contemporary images of Asian Americans is that of a highly successful minority that has "made it" in society. For example, the popular press has often portrayed Asian Americans as a "model" minority, using such headlines as "Success Story: Outwhiting the Whites", "The Oriental Express," and "Are they making the grade" (Newsweek, 1971; Psychology Today, 1986; U.S. News & World Report, 1984). The view that Asian Americans are a successful minority is based upon studies consistently revealing that they have low official rates of delinquency, psychiatric contact, and divorce; upon apparently high levels of educational attainment; and upon apparently high levels of family income. The conclusion one can draw from all these statistics is that Asian Americans and Southeast Asian immigrants and refugees have never been victims of prejudice and discrimination.

A closer analysis of the status and treatment of Asian Americans does not support their success story. Assaulted, murdered, denied ownership of land, denied rights of citizenship, and placed in concentration camps during World War II, Asian Americans have been subjected to some of the most flagrant forms of discrimination ever perpetrated against an immigrant group. Reference to higher median income does not take into account (a) a higher percentage of more than one wage earner in the family; (b) an equal incidence of poverty despite the higher median income; (c) lower poverty assistance and welfare than the general population; and (d) the fact that salaries are not commensurate with education levels of Asian American workers (lower salaries despite higher educational level). Statistics on education attainment are also misleading. Asian Americans present a picture of extraordinarily high educational levels for some, while a large number remain uneducated. The impression that Asian refugees are a homogeneous, privileged group is also not supported by data. For example, those who evacuated Vietnam were probably the most heterogeneous group ever to immigrate to the United States.

There is also recognition that, apart from being tourist attractions, Chinatowns, Little Saigons, Manilatowns, and Japantowns represent ghetto areas. Unemployment, poverty, health problems, and juvenile delinquency are major facts of life. Juvenile gangland warfare has also caught the public eye and, recently, the FBI stated that Asian criminal activity is fast becoming the number one crime concern in the United States. In addition, it is becoming clear that underutilization of mental health services may not be due to "better mental health," but cultural factors inhibiting self-referral (shame and disgrace associated with admitting to emotional problems, reliance on the family to prevent it from becoming public, etc.), and/or institutional policies and practices.

In a completely revised lead article, "Ethnic Identity: Cultural Factors in the Psychological Development of Asians in America," D. Sue and D. W. Sue describe the psychological development of several Asian groups in America with respect to stereotypes, unique cultural values, and experiences of racism. Personality characteristics, academic abilities, and vocational interests are described. These descriptions provide important information for counselors who work with Asian Americans and who need to look behind the "success myth" and understand the Asian experience in America.

It is increasingly recognized that traditional counseling approaches must be modified to fit the life experiences of minority clients. M. Root suggests how such modification in counseling can be made by taking into account such factors as cultural values and the experience of racism. Specific, concrete strategies are presented and discussed. Although this article deals only with certain Asian clients, it presents an example of how different approaches might be used for other Asian Americans as well.

In the last article, "Psychotherapy with Southeast Asian American Clients," Nishio and Bilmes provide specific information that counselors need to have if they are to be successful when working with one of America's newest immigrant groups. Especially relevant for counselors is to understand the dislocation and immigration experience as a tremendous source of stress. They aid us in understanding how Indochinese refugees perceive therapy differently from our culture, how the manner of symptom formation may be culturally determined, and how major cultural clashes may result from the process of counseling. In addition to providing case studies to illustrate their points, the authors provide some practical suggestions in counselor work and therapy which they believe to be more culturally sensitive.

References

McBee, S. Are they making the grade? (1984 April 2). *U.S. News & World Report.* 41–43.

Success story: Outwhiting the whites. (1971, June 21). *Newsweek,* 24–25.

McLeod, B. The oriental express. (1986, July). *Psychology Today,* 48–52.

10

Ethnic Identity: Cultural Factors in the Psychological Development of Asians in America

David Sue and Derald W. Sue

As the number of Asian Americans increase, greater attention is being placed on the impact of culture conflicts between Asian and European values. Asian and Pacific Island Americans increased in population to about six million in 1985 (Human Resources Division, 1990) and is estimated to reach ten million by the year 2000. In large part, this increase is due to the relaxation of immigration laws. Over 2,300,000 Asian and Pacific Islander refugees and immigrants arrived in the United States between 1981 and 1988 (U.S. Department of Justice, 1990). The recent influx of Asians has changed the character of the Asian population in the United States. With the exception of the Japanese, most Asian groups are now comprised of international-born individuals. Because of this large increase in the Asian population, greater attention is being placed on the impact of culture clash and racism on the development of Asian American identity.

Most studies which focus on the effects of culture on Asian Americans tend to be highly compartmentalized. For example, one can find research investigating the relationship of culture to: (a) personality characteristics (Abbot, 1970; Cook and Chi, 1984; Fong and Peskin, 1969; Meredith, 1966; D. Sue, S. Ino, and D. M. Sue, 1983; D. Sue, D. M. Sue and S. Ino, 1990; Zane, S. Sue, Hu, and Kwon, 1991); (b) child-rearing practices (DeVos & Abbot, 1966; Dornsbusch, Ritter, Leiderman, Roberts, and Fraleigh, 1987; Kitano, 1964), (c) the manifestation of behavior disorders (Bromley, 1987; Nishio and Bilmes, 1987; Westermeyer, 1988), (d) the ineffectiveness of traditional therapy (Kinzie, 1985; S. Sue and Morishima, 1982; D. W. Sue and D. Sue, 1990), and (e) acculturation (Kitano, 1989;

Matsumoto, Meredith and Masuda, 1970; Nidorf, 1985). Few attempts integrate these findings into a global description of how cultures influence the socio-psychological functioning of the ''whole'' person.

Cultural impact is clearly demonstrated in the study of Asian and Pacific Island Americans, where Asian cultural values collide with European American values. The historical meeting of these two cultures and their consequent interaction in a racist society have fundamental importance in understanding the personality characteristics, academic abilities, and vocational interests of Asians in America.

Asian Cultural Values

A discussion of Asian cultural values is difficult since Asian and Pacific Islanders are made up of over twenty-five distinct groups, each with differences in language, religion, and customs. In addition, it must be remembered that large within-group differences occur in terms of generation in the United States and acculturation levels. However, there appears to be a number of areas of similarity in Asian cultural values (Kinzie, 1985; Shon and Ja, 1982; D. W. Sue and D. Sue, 1990).

Allegiance to the parents or filial piety is a strong value. The sense of obligation to the parents is strong, especially among the male children. They are to maintain this obligation even when married. Parents are to come first. Conflicts often arise when Asian and Pacific Island Americans are exposed to the emphasis of the nuclear family with the primary allegiance to the spouse.

The role of family members are highly interdependent. The focus is on the importance of familial and not independent needs. Independent behavior which might upset the orderly functioning of the family is discouraged. The family structure is so arranged that conflicts within the family are minimized; each member has his or her own role to play which does not interfere with that of another. If a person has feelings which might disrupt family peace and harmony, he/she is expected to hide them. Restraint of potentially disruptive emotions is strongly emphasized in the development of the Asian character. The lack of outward signs of emotions have given rise to the prevalent opinion among many Westerners that Asians are ''inscrutable.''

Asian and Pacific Island families are traditionally patriarchal with communication and authority flowing vertically from top to bottom. The father's behavior in relationship to other family members is generally dignified, authoritative, remote, and aloof. Sons are generally highly valued. Asian women are expected to carry on the domestic duties, to marry, to become obedient helpers of their mothers-in-law, and to bear children, especially males.

The inculcation of guilt and shame are the principle techniques used to control the behavior of family members. Parents emphasize their children's obligation to the family. If a child acts independently (contrary to the wishes of his parents), he is told that he is selfish and inconsiderate and that he is not showing gratitude for all his parents have done for him. The behavior of individual members of an Asian family is expected to reflect credit on the whole family. Problems that arise among Asian Americans such as failure in school, disobedience, juvenile delinquency, mental illness, etc., are sources of great shame. Such problems are generally kept hidden from public view and handled within the family. On the other hand, outstanding achievement in some aspect of life (especially educational and occupational success) is a source of great pride for the entire family. Thus, each family member has much at stake in the behavior of others.

In summary, traditional Asian values emphasize reserve and formality in social relationships, restraint and inhibition of strong feelings, obedience to authority, obligations to the family, high academic and occupational achievement, and the use of shame and guilt to control behavior. These cultural values have a significant impact on the psychological characteristics of Asians in America.

Historical Experience: Cultural Racism

In defining cultural racism, Jones (1972) states that it is "... the individual and institutional expression of the superiority of ones race's cultural heritage over that of another race. Racism is appropriate to the extent that racial and cultural factors are highly correlated and are a systematic basis for inferior treatment." (p. 6). Any discussion concerning the effects of racism on the psychological characteristics of minorities is fraught with hazards. It is difficult to distinguish the relevant variables which affect the individual and to impute cause-effect relations. However, a historical analysis of Asians in America suggests that cultural racism has done great harm to this ethnic group.

Unknown to the general public, Asian Americans have been the object of much prejudice and discrimination. Ironically, the American public is unaware that no higher walls of prejudice have been raised, historically, around any other ethnic minorities than those around Asians. Asians have generally attempted to function in the existing society without loud, strong, public protests.

The first Chinese immigrants came to the United States during the 1840s. Their immigration from China was encouraged by the social and economic unrest in China at that time and by overpopulation in certain provinces (DeVos & Abbot, 1966). During this period, there was a great demand for the Chinese to help build the transcontinental railroad. Because of the need for cheap labor, they were welcomed into the labor force (Daniels, 1971). However, a diminishing labor market and fear of the "yellow peril" made the Chinese immigrants no longer welcome. Their pronounced racial and cultural differences from the White majority made them conspicuous, and they served as scapegoats for the resentment of White workers. Although Daniels (1971) mainly discusses the economic aspect for the hostility expressed against the Chinese, he points out that the anti-Chinese movement soon developed into an ideology of White supremacy which was compatible with the mainstream of American racism. Chinese were seen as "subhuman" or "heathens" and their mode of living was seen as undesirable and detrimental to the well-being of America. Laws were passed to harass the Chinese; they were denied the rights of citizenship, ownership of land, the right of marriage, etc. At the height of the anti-Chinese movement, when prejudice and discrimination against the Chinese flourished, many Chinese were assaulted and killed by mobs of Whites. This anti-Chinese sentiment culminated in the passing of the Federal Chinese Exclusion Act of 1882 which was the first exclusion act against any ethnic group. This racist immigration law, justified by the alleged need to excluded masses of "cheap Chinese labor" from the United States, was not repealed until 1943 as a gesture of friendship toward China, an ally of the United States during World War II.

Likewise, the Japanese in America faced severe hostility and discrimination from White citizens. Japanese began immigrating to the United States during the 1890s when anti-Chinese sentiment was great. As a result, they shared in the pervasive anti-Asian feeling. Originally brought in to fill the demand for cheap agricultural labor and coming from an agrarian background, many Japanese became engaged in these fields (Kitano, 1969). Their fantastic success in the agricultural occupations, coupled with a racist climate, enraged many White citizens. Legislation similar to the anti-Chinese acts was passed against the Japanese, and individual-mob violence repeated itself. Such cries as "The Japs must go" were frequently echoed by the mass media, labor and political leaders. In response to hostility toward members of their race, both Chinese and Japanese formed their own communities to isolate and protect themselves from a threatening racist society.

Within this background of White racism, it became relatively easy for White society to accept the relocation of 110,000 Japanese Americans into camps during World War II. Their pronounced racial and cultural characteristics were enough justification for the atrocious actions taken against the Japanese. The dangerous precedent created by American reaction to the Japanese is an ever-present threat that racial strains can again result in a repeat of history.

There can be no doubt that cultural racism has been practiced against the Chinese and Japanese. Many people would argue that, today, Asian

Americans face no such obstacles. The myth that Asians represent a "model minority" and are successful and functioning well in society is a popular belief often played up by the press: "Asians: To America with skills;" "Now the fastest-growing minority, many are excelling in school, achieving on the job and otherwise making it in America (*Time*, July 8, 1985, p. 1); "Asian Americans: Are they making the grade?" (*U.S. News & World Report*, April 2, 1984); and "A formula for success" (*Newsweek*, April 23, 1984). Such articles downplay the problems faced by Asians in the United States. Studies of Indochinese refugees indicate that they suffer from more psychological problems than found in the general population (Westermeyer, Vang & Neider, 1983). Over one third of the Vietnamese, and two-thirds of the Hmong and Laotians living in the United States have family incomes below the poverty level as compared to approximately 10 percent of the U.S. population (Census Bureau, 1988). In addition, Asian refugees have run across prejudice and discrimination. Some feel that the racism faced by Asians is subtle and indirect, although most remember the case of a Chinese American who was killed by two White Detroit auto workers because they thought he was Japanese and therefore responsible for the layoffs in the automotive industry. A report by the Commission on Civil Rights in 1986 concluded that anti-Asian activities such as violence, vandalism, harassment and intimidation continue to occur. In addition, Asians believe that job discrimination occurs in the United States. They are underrepresented in the managerial positions (*Newsweek*, May 11, 1987). Although advances have been made, it is still apparent that social and economic discrimination is being practiced against Asian Americans. Attention will now be focused on the psychological costs of culture conflict.

Culture Conflict

Jones (1972) believes that many forms of culture conflict are really manifestations of cultural racism. Although there is nothing inherently wrong in acculturation and assimilation, he believes that ". . . when it is forced by a powerful group on a less powerful one, it constitutes a restriction of choice; hence, it is no longer subject to the values of natural order." (p. 166). This occurs when the values of ethnic minorities are evaluated through that of the dominant culture. For example, values of filial piety, modesty, and restraint of emotions are important to Asian groups. However, the dominant culture which values independence and assertiveness often views Asian values negatively and as deficits (Chin, 1983).

When an ethnic minority becomes increasingly exposed to the values and standards of the dominant host culture, there is progressive inculcation of these norms. The conflict between one's cultural values and the desire to become Westernized is illustrated in the following case:

> Quy is a 13-year-old Vietnamese presenting with headaches and loss of appetite. She has been in the United States for 2 years, resides with a distant relative, is fluent in English, and receives excellent grades. Quy relates that she is tense and nervous inside because she does not feel comfortable with American friends yet. More importantly, she is fearful that she will be rejected by her Vietnamese peer group if they find out she has been here only 2 years. She has worked hard to get rid of her accented English, and does not let on that she can read and write perfectly in Vietnamese, as most of her Vietnamese group cannot. . . . The girls in her group seem also to her to be "too free," and she is in conflict as to whether to emulate them. She is aware that her desire to create an identity or selfhood through affiliation with a high status group, and therefore bolster her social standing and self-esteem, has let instead to a sense of self-loathing because of her own hypocrisy, secrecy, and false identity (Nidorf, 1985, p. 410–411).

Quy sees the Westernized Vietnamese group as sophisticated and acquainted with the new culture. She is afraid to be different but ashamed of her need to maintain a false front. As Asians become Westernized, many begin to view the majority culture values as more admirable. Unfortunately, hostility to a person's minority cultural background may cause Asians to turn their hostility inward. Such is the case when Japanese American females express greater dissatisfaction with their body image than Caucasian females (Arkoff & Weaver, 1966). Fourth and fifth generation Asian American children have more negative feelings about their physical appearance than do Caucasians (Pang, Mizokawa, Morishima & Olstad, 1985). Kitano (1989) believes that Asian Americans can be classified along four dimensions of acculturation: (1) High Assimilation and Low Ethnic Identity. Individuals in this group identify primarily with Western values and have little identification with their ethnic culture; (2) Low Assimilation, Low Ethnic Identity. These individuals are truly marginal. They do not have a sense of identity with either culture and tend to be dysfunctional; (3) High Assimilation, High Ethnic Identity. Biculturalism or the ability to accept both cultural systems is characteristic of individuals in this group; and (4) Low Assimilation, High Ethnic Identity. Many recent immigrants and refugees are in this category. They want to stick with traditional values and keep contact with outsiders at a minimum.

Psychological Characteristics of Asian American Students

The cultural background of Asian Americans and the historical and continuing forces of White racism have left their mark on the current life-styles of Asian Americans. Although it is difficult to impute a direct cause-effect relationship between these forces and the psychological characteristics of Asian Americans, the following descriptions certainly seem consistent with their past background. The remaining sections will focus upon the personality traits, academic abilities, and vocational interests of Asian Americans.

Personality Characteristics

The large majority of studies done examining personality characteristics have involved Chinese and Japanese American populations and we must be careful in generalizing the findings to other Asian American populations. In a study conducted at Berkeley, D. W. Sue and Kirk (1973) found that Chinese and Japanese American students responded similarly on several personality measures and demonstrated a tendency to evaluate ideas on the basis of their immediate practical application and to avoid an abstract, reflexive, and theoretical orientation. Because of their practical and applied approach to life problems, they tend to be more intolerant of ambiguities and to feel much more comfortable in well-structured situations. Asian Americans also appear less autonomous and less independent from parental controls and authority figures. They are more obedient, conservative, conforming, and inhibited. In interpersonal relationships, they tend to be cautious in directly expressing their impulses and feelings. In comparison to Caucasian norms, the Asian American students appear more socially introverted and will more often withdraw from social contacts and responsibilities. Other researchers report that Asians have more difficulty with assertion (Fukuyama & Greenfield, 1983; D. Sue, Ino, & D. M. Sue, 1983), score lower on dominance and aggression (Fenz & Arkoff, 1962; Johnson & Marsella, 1978) and higher in introversion, passivity, and self-restraint (Bourne, 1975; Meredith & Meredith, 1966; Conner, 1975).

Asian cultural values, emphasizing restraint of strong feelings, obedience, dependence upon the family, and formality in interpersonal relations, are being exhibited by these students. These values are in sharp contrast to the Western emphasis on spontaneity, assertiveness, and informality. Because of socialization in well-defined roles, there is a tendency for Asian students to feel more comfortable in structured situations and to feel uncomfortable in ambiguous ones. As a result, they may tend to withdraw from social contacts with those outside their ethnic group or family. As discussed later, their minority status and sensitivity may make them suspicious of people. It is possible, also, that their concrete and pragmatic approach was reinforced because it possessed social and economic survival value.

Although the results of personality measures on Asian Americans appear to be consistent and fit Asian cultural values, several cautions must be made. First, most of the studies were done on college samples, involve relatively small numbers, and involve primarily Japanese and Chinese subjects. Questions remain about how generalizable the findings are. Second, the paper and pencil measures may not have cross-cultural validity. For example, several studies (D. Sue, Ino, & D. M. Sue, 1983; D. Sue, D. M. Sue & Ino, 1990) have found discrepancies between self reports of anxiety and the ability to perform assertively in role-play situations. We need to determine if responses on personality measures mean the same for Asian populations. Third, as Chin (1983) points out, differences in personality are nearly always seen from the Western perspective and receives a negative interpretation. The response on personality measures is probably a function of both cultural values and a reaction to a society dominated by the Western perspective.

Academic Abilities

The major Asian American groups have done very well academically in the United States. A greater number of Asian and Pacific Islanders complete high school than that found in the total U.S. population (74.8 percent versus 66.5 percent) and twice as many complete four years of college (32.9 percent versus 16.2 percent) (U.S. Census Bureau, 1988). In the Westinghouse Science Talent Search for 1986, all the top five winners were of Asian descent. Nearly one third of Asian students taking the California Achievement test scored at or over the 90th percentile in math (McLeod, 1986). However, Asian Americans do show consistently lower verbal scores on aptitude tests than do Whites of all non-Asian students (S. Sue, 1990). Asian Americans are overrepresented in the most prestigious universities (over 10 percent at Harvard, nearly 20 percent at Berkeley, and nearly 10 percent at Princeton) (Hassan, 1987). However, as Leung (1990) notes, ". . . as the numbers of Asian Americans rise and their achievements in education continue, education for many qualified Asian Americans, especially in select institutions, may become less and less a reality" (p. 6). It would appear that many of the universities are beginning to place barriers to the admission of Asian American students.

Although attention is placed on Asian American achievement, many groups are undereducated. There are four times as many Chinese and Filipinos with fewer than four years education when compared to Caucasians in the United States (Nishi, 1982). Certain groups of Asian and Pacific Islanders show a less than 50 percent completion of high school

(Hmong, 22.3 percent, Laotians 31.4 percent, and Cambodians 42.6 percent) (U.S. Census Bureau, 1988). Research should be directed toward determining the factors involved in the low achievement of certain Asian groups.

The reason for academic success for most Asian Americans in the United States is unclear. Some feel that the promotion of academic achievement within the Asian culture is an important factor. Others believe that education is a perceived avenue of advancement when other areas are closed. It is also possible that a combination of cultural value and societal access are involved in the academic success of Asian Americans. (Sue, & Okazaki, 1990).

Vocational Interests

Most educators, pupil personnel workers, and counselors throughout the West and East Coasts have frequently remarked on the abundance of Asian students entering the physical sciences. Surveys undertaken at the University of California, Berkeley (Chu, 1971; Takayama, 1971) reveal that approximately 75 percent of Chinese and 68 percent of Japanese males enter the physical sciences. Using the Strong Vocational Interest Blank, the Berkeley studies compared the interests of Chinese Americans, Japanese Americans, and all other students. Chinese American men expressed more interest in the physical sciences (mathematician, physicist, engineer, chemist, etc.) than all other students. Although not statistically significant, Japanese American men also tended to express more interest in these occupations requiring more verbal interactions (salesperson, advertising executive, lawyer, and journalist). Similar results were obtained in a sample of Chinese males attending the University of Michigan. Approximately 80 percent were majoring in the physical sciences in comparison with only 35 percent of male Caucasians (D. Sue, Ino, & D. M. Sue, 1983).

The Asian American females has a profile similar to their male counterparts. They exhibited more interest in business occupations, applied-technical fields, biological and physical sciences, and less interest in verbal-linguistic fields, social science and aesthetic-cultural occupations. Among a groups of Chinese American female students, 54 percent were majoring in the physical sciences versus 22 percent of their Caucasian counterparts (D. Sue, D. M. Sue, & Ino, 1990)

Reasons for the greater interest in the physical sciences involve both cultural and societal factors. Personality tests have indicated that Asians prefer structured rather than ambiguous tasks. Occupations that require verbal assertion may conflict with the value of restraint in expression. There is greater acceptance and understanding of science. Among Southeast Asian refugees and immigrants, career plans that are acceptable to parents involve medicine, dentistry, teaching and pharmacy. Ones that have less acceptance are art, music, and writing (Carlin & Sokoloff, 1985). In addition, discrimination and prejudice might play a part. Occupations requiring people-contact are more likely to put individuals at risk for exposure to racism. Career plans need to be carefully explored with Asian Americans so as not to limit their choices.

Conclusions

The psychological characteristics exhibited by Asian Americans are related to their culture and the interaction with Western society. Any study of ethnic minorities in America must necessarily deal with the forces of racism inherent in American culture. Since there are no Asian Americans untouched by racism in the United States to use as a control group, the relationship of racism to psychological development becomes a complex issue that cannot easily be resolved. If an attempt is made to use control groups in Taiwan, Hong Kong, or China, the problem becomes clouded by the whole complex of other social and cultural differences. For these reasons, the analysis presented in this article must be seen as somewhat tentative and speculative. Hopefully, further research will help clarify this issue.

References

Abbott, K. A. (1970). *Harmony and Individualism.* Taipei: Orient Cultural Press.

Abbott, K. A. & Weaver, H. (1966). Body image and body dissatisfaction in Japanese-Americans. *Journal of Social Psychology, 68,* 323–330.

Bourne, P. G. (1975). The Chinese student: Acculturation and mental illness. *Psychiatry, 38,* 269–277.

Carlin, J. E. & Sokoloff, B. Z. (1985). Mental health treatment issues for Southeast Asian refugee children. In T. C. Owan (Ed.), *Southeast Asian Mental Health.* (pp. 91–112). Rockville, MD: National Institute of Mental Health.

Chin, J. L. (1983). Diagnostic considerations in working with Asian-Americans. *American Journal of Orthopsychiatry, 53,* 100–108.

Chu, R. (1971, Winter) *Majors of Chinese and Japanese students at the University of California, Berkeley, for the past 20 years* (Project Report, AS 150, Asian Studies Division) Berkeley: University of California.

Conner, J. W. (1975). Value changes in third generation Japanese Americans. *Journal of Personality Assessment, 39,* 597–600.

Cook, H. & Chi, C. (1984). Cooperative behavior and locus of control among American and Chinese American boys. *Journal of Psychology, 118,* 169–177.

Daniels, R. (1971). *Concentration camps USA: Japanese Americans and World War II.* New York: Holt, Rinehart, & Winston.

DeVos, G. & Abbot, K. (1966). *The Chinese family in San Francisco.* Unpublished master's thesis, University of California, Berkeley, CA.

Fenz, W. & Arkoff, A. (1962). Comparative need patterns of five ancestry groups in Hawaii. *Journal of Social Psychology, 58,* 67–89.

Fong, S. L. M. & Peskin, H. (1969). Sex-role strain and personality adjustment of China-born students in American: A pilot study. *Journal of Abnormal Psychology, 74,* 563–567.

Fukuyama, M. A. & Greenfield, T. K. (1983). Dimensions of assertiveness in an Asian-American population. *Journal of Counseling Psychology, 30,* 429–432.

Hassan, T. E. (1987). Asian-American admissions: Debating discrimination. *The College Board Review,* No. 142, 19–46.

Human Resources Division (1990). *Asian Americans: A status report.* Washington, DC: U.S. General Accounting Office.

Johnson, R. A. & Marsella, A. (1978). Differential attitudes toward verbal behavior in students of Japanese and European ancestry. *Genetic Psychology Monographs, 97,* 43–76.

Jones, J. M. (1972) *Prejudice and racism.* City, MA: Addison-Wesley.

Kinzie, J. D. (1985). Overview of clinical issues in the treatment of Southeast Asian refugees. In T. C. Owan (Ed.), *Southeast Asian Mental Health* (pp. 91–112.). Rockville, MD: National Institute of Mental Health.

Kitano, H. H. L. (1964). Inter- and intra-generational differences in maternal attitude toward child rearing. *Journal of Social Psychology, 63,* 215–220.

Kitano, H. H. L. (1969). *Japanese-Americans: The evolution of a subculture.* Englewood Cliffs, NJ: Prentice-Hall.

Kitano, H. H. L. (1989). A model for counseling Asian Americans. In P. B. Pedersen, J. G. Draguns, W. J. Lonner, J. E. Trimble (Eds.), *Counseling across cultures* (pp. 139–152). Honolulu: University of Hawaii Press.

Leung, P. (1990). Asian Americans and psychology: Unresolved issues. *Journal of Training and Practice, 4,* 3–13.

McLeod, B. (1986). The Oriental express. *Psychology Today,* pp. 48–52.

Meredith, G. M. (1966). Amae and acculturation among Japanese-American college students in Hawaii. *Journal of Social Psychology, 70,* 171–180.

Meredith, G. M. & Meredith, C. W. (1966). Acculturation and personality among Japanese-American college students in Hawaii. *Journal of Social Psychology, 68,* 175–182.

Nishi, S. M. (1982). The educational disadvantage of Asian Pacific Americans. *P/AAMHRC Research Review, 1,* 4–6.

Nisdorf, J. F. (1985). Mental health and refugee youths: A model for diagnostic training. In T. C. Owan (Ed.), *Southeast Asian Mental Health* (pp. 391–430). Rockville, MD: National Institute of Mental Health.

Pang, V. O., Mizokawa, D. T., Morishima, J. K. & Olstad, R. G. (1985). Self-concept of Japanese-American children. *Journal of Crosscultural Psychology, 16,* 99–109.

Sue, D., Ino, S. & Sue, D. M. (1983). Nonassertiveness of Asian Americans: An inaccurate assumption? *Journal of Counseling Psychology, 30,* 581–583.

Sue, D., Sue, D. M. & Ino, S. (1990). Assertiveness and social anxiety in Chinese American women. *Journal of Psychology, 123,* 155–163.

Sue, D. W. & Kirk, B. A. (1972). Psychological characteristics of Chinese American students. *Journal of Counseling Psychology, 19,* 471–478.

Sue, D. W. & Kirk, B. A. (1973). Differential characteristics of Japanese-American and Chinese-American college students. *Journal of Counseling Psychology, 20,* 142–148.

Sue, D. W. & Sue, D. (1990) *Counseling the culturally different.* New York: John Wiley.

Sue, S. & Morishima, J. K. (1982). *The mental health of Asian Americans.* Washington, DC: Jossey-Bass

Takayama, G. (1971). *Analysis of data on Asian students at UC Berkeley, 1971.* (Project Report, AS 150, Asian Studies Division) Berkeley: University of California.

U.S. Commission on Civil Rights (1986). *Recent activities against citizens and residents of Asian descent.* Washington, DC: U.S. Commission on Civil Rights.

U.S. Department of Justice (1990). *Statistical yearbooks of the immigration and naturalization service (1981–1988).* Washington, DC: U.S. Government Printing Office.

Westermeyer, J. (1988). DSM III psychiatric disorders among Hmong refugees in the United States: A point prevalence study. *American Journal of Psychiatry, 145,* 197–202.

Westermeyer, J. Vang, T. F. & Neider, J. (1984). Symptom change over time among Hmong refugees: Psychiatric patients versus nonpatients. *Psychopathology, 17,* 168–177.

Zane, W. S., Sue, S., Hu, L-T., & K, J-H. (1991). Asian-American Assertion: A social learning analysis of cultural differences. *Journal of Counseling Psychology, 38, 63–70.*

11

Guidelines for Facilitating Therapy with Asian American Clients

Maria P. P. Root

Ethnicity is a powerful yet sometimes subtle determinant of an individual's pattern of thinking, feeling, and acting regardless of color or level of acculturation. Cultural patterns associated with one's ethnic heritage guide the individual to determine how to express distress, when to seek help, and from whom to seek help. For Asian Americans, the family can be an extremely important point of reference as a microcosm of cultural heritage and identity. Presenting problems need to be understood, diagnosed, and treated with knowledge of the cultural context of the person presenting for help.

Recognizing the importance of the culture and family as a context for understanding presenting problems, however, does not remove all the barriers which are currently present for Asian Americans seeking therapy. Other factors must be understood to structure therapy as a more beneficial form of treatment for Asian America. Both guidelines and suggestions are offered to remove some of the obstacles to help-seeking and to prevent premature termination—both of which have contributed to the underutilization of mental health services by Asian Americans.

Explanations for Underutilization of Services

Compared with other ethnic groups such as Blacks, Asian Americans have underutilized mental health resources (President's Commission on Mental Health, 1978; Sue & McKinney, 1975). The pattern of underutilization is striking given that Asian Americans face the same stressors any minority,

Root, M. P. P. (1985). Guidelines for facilitating therapy with Asian American clients. *Psychotherapy, 22,* 349–356. Copyright 1985 by *Psychotherapy*. Reprinted with permission of the editor.

immigrant group faces, including racism, immigration, and economic disadvantages. But unlike many other minority populations, the diverse Asian American populations have been viewed as an upwardly mobile population that poses few problems or demands on the mental health systems of this country (Sue & Morishima, 1982).

It is striking, given the expected need of mental health services for the various Asian American populations, that services are underutilized. Sue & McKinney (1975), in a survey of 17 Seattle mental health centers, found that only 100 clients of 13,198 clients seeking mental health services were Asian Americans, which is a rate significantly lower and disproportionate with the proportion of Asian Americans making up the greater Seattle area. The significantly lower rate of utilization of mental health services of Asian Americans compared with Whites is of concern given additional studies which suggest that by the time Asian Americans seek treatment they are experiencing a greater level of distress (Sue & McKinney, 1975; Sue & Sue, 1974) and would be expected to need more service or receive service for a longer period of time.

Recent research suggests that the Asian American's pattern of mental health utilization does not necessarily reflect a lack of need. Several explanations are emerging. Morishima (1975) suggests that because of the tendency of many Asian Americans to experience stress psychosomatically, help-seeking may occur from medical professionals rather than mental health professionals. Organic explanations of distress may initially be sought for symptoms such as headaches, loss of appetite, difficulty sleeping, allergies, digestive problems also associated with stress, depression, and anxiety. Tsai *et al.* (1980) offer several reasons why Asian Americans may underutilize mental health services in a study of Chinese Americans. First, the individual's view of the cause of mental distress and/or emotional problems may encourage him or her to problem solve on their own without letting family members know the true extent of their distress. Sue (1976) surveyed Asian (Chinese, Japanese, and Filipino Americans) and White students' conceptions of mental illness. The results of their survey generally supported the notion that the Asian American students tended to believe that mental health was maintained by the avoidance of morbid thoughts. In 1974, Lum (cf. Sue & Morishima, 1982) presented similar results in a survey of Chinese American residents of San Francisco's Chinatown. Residents commonly believed that mental health was maintained through the avoidance of bad thoughts and exercise of willpower. Such explanations logically guide individuals to attribute their distress to personal weakness. Behaviorally and cognitively, the individual may try to shut down any distressing thoughts or feelings, which may further exacerbate distress. A case illustration is provided.

Ms. H is a 26-year-old Chinese American woman. It was suggested to her that she seek some counseling because she was crying at work and complaining of feeling as though she was "coming apart at the seams." However, it was noted that although she was feeling extremely distressed and desperate, considering suicide, she had not allowed her family to see that she was so distressed. Around the family she was able to carry out her responsibilities and act as though everything were normal. However, away from the family she was crying, missing days of work, and starting to experience symptoms of panic at work.

At the first interview, Ms. H revealed that in the last six months her life had changed considerably. Her paternal grandmother, who has lived with the family since Ms. H was very young, had a stroke which partially paralyzed her. Of the five daughters in the family, it was determined that Ms. H should sleep on the floor of her grandmother's room at night because she was the lightest sleeper. Every night she attends to her grandmother's needs at least once. Three weeks prior to the interview, Ms. H reports that her White American boyfriend of three years to whom she was planning to be married announced that they were incompatible. They had been unable in the last six months to spend much time together because of her responsibilities to her grandmother. Finally, she reports being unhappy with the amount of time she was spending in activities related to her music. Ms. H was unable to articulate some of her dilemma as one of feeling conflict over what she wanted to do and feeling that she had obligations to the family which were in direct conflict.

Service providers may not be responsive and sensitive enough to clients' fears and beliefs about the causes of their distress and expectations about recovery. As a result, a client's presentation may appear to be more disturbed than it actually would be in the context of the client's background, or vice versa. Service providers need to have an understanding of cultural proscriptions for the types of symptoms one is likely to manifest given their cultural background. The diagnosis may be difficult, as in the case of Mr. T.

Mr. T is a 33-year-old, married, Korean man who has lived in the United States for seven years. He grew up in a farming village in Korea and moved to the city where he met his future wife. She was studying nursing while he went to college on a scholarship. After the marriage, Mr. T. realized that he was not in love with his wife. He felt that she was attracted to him because of his achievements at school. They came to the United States so that he could pursue a graduate degree in engineering. However, six years later he had not finished his degree and had significant requirements left to complete. His wife, on the other hand, had been able to obtain some training to receive her nursing diploma and was working to support their family.

Mr. T has had contact with the mental health system at least four times in the last three years. At the time that he sought the current consultation his wife had announced two months earlier that she wanted a divorce. Since then they had lived separately and Mr. T's daughter had lived with his wife. Mr. T was without a job and his wife refused to support him. Two months earlier he had reported to a local emergency room because of headaches and nausea but was told that there was no reason to admit him. He was referred to outpatient therapy because it was determined that his distress was psychosomatic. At the time of this consultation Mr. T felt that his distress was the result of psychological weakness in his ability to use his willpower to overcome his distress. He was hesitant to explain why he was leaving his current counseling relationship. He suggested that his current psychiatrist was too young, and that another counselor was unable to be sympathetic to his needs.

Mr. T described a pattern of isolation since he had left his farming community for college. Currently he was isolated from the Korean community, believing that many of the people sided with his wife and were therefore unavailable to him. In college he had felt that class and world experience kept him apart from his peers. Mr. T prided himself on his education and insight into his problems, claiming that he was sophisticated unlike his wife who still retained many ''primitive'' ideas of Korea.

Stigma and shame may arise over experiencing mental distress. Experiencing psychological distress and changes in the ability to function may lead individuals to feel that they have failed to achieve what their family expects of them. Further disgrace would be called for if the individual were to seek help outside of the family. Prizzia & Villanueva King (1977) surveyed Chinese, Hawaiian, Japanese, Filipino, and Samoan ethnic groups in Hawaii and found that people sought help from family first. Help-seeking outside the family was still kept close to the cultural community; outside the family, priests were approached first, then public sources, and psychiatrists, last. The case of Ms. C illustrates some of these issues.

Ms. C, a 36-year-old Filipino, came to the mental health center after discharge from a psychiatric hospital for a suicide attempt by overdose on medication. She was nervous, made little eye contact, and repeatedly asked if she was crazy. Upon taking her history, she revealed (and it was later confirmed) that in the past 14 months she had been mugged three times, in all cases by black males. Two of these occasions had occurred as she left different jobs where she worked as an RN. Ms. C had become increasingly suspicious of black males, afraid to walk by herself, and unable to work. She was experiencing dizzy spells and severe lapses of concentration which she felt made it impossible for her to return to work. She had been given medication by a physician to address some of the post-trauma symptoms she was experiencing. During a time of isolation, feeling hopeless that she would ever feel better, and unable to perform her duties as a nurse or daughter, she overdosed on her medication.

Ms. C had immigrated to this country eight years prior, leaving her husband and three children in the Philippines. While studying for her RN license, she worked and supported not only herself, but also sent money back to her parents to support some of her youngest brothers and to provide for her own children. She had recently been successful in helping her parents to immigrate to the United States.

She had recently moved from her aunt's house because she could not pay her rent since she had quit working. She was currently living in the basement of a house she had found for her parents. She was distressed that her savings were running out and that her parents were old (recently immigrated) and she was unable to support them. After the first interview, her parents, aunt, and family friend who Ms. C felt had supplanted her as a daughter and niece in the family were asked to come in.

Similarly, a family may not seek services for the anticipated disgrace or reflection on their parenting skills that the need to go outside the family reflects. This is the case in the family described.

The F family was referred for counseling by the school counselor and vice-principal. They sought counseling for their daughter, Angie, a twin, because of her failing grades, difficulty participating in class, social isolation, and tearfulness. The older twin, Mary Lou, in contrast to Angie, did well in school and had many friends.

Upon providing the consultation for the F family, it became clear that the parents were extremely frustrated. Both Mr. and Ms. F were well educated and held good jobs. Mr. F was Filipino and Ms. F was Chinese. Both families of origin valued education and Mr. and Ms. F had made every effort to provide their daughters with the best educational experiences possible. They discussed all the different ways in which they had tried to motivate Angie to improve her grades, and while counseling had been suggested four years ago because similar behavior was already apparent, it was only at this time that they felt they had exhausted all their personal resources and were following the recommendations of the school counselor whom they had come to trust.

The cost of mental health services may prohibit clients from obtaining treatment. Most private practitioners set fees for service that create barriers to seeking mental health for individuals with lower incomes (Owan, 1975; cf. Sue & Morishima, 1982). Additionally, needing to use the family resources for distress which does not appear to be rational or is a sign of personal weakness may make it even more difficult to seek services as in the case of Ms. M.

Ms. M, a 17-year-old Eurasian (Japanese Caucasian) was referred by her older, married sister when she revealed her suicidal feelings. Her sister referred her to seek help at their family's health-care agency. Ms. M is the youngest daughter of a Japanese mother and Caucasian father who had been divorced for two years. At the time of the consultation, she was unhappy in her current living situation with her mother and an older brother who was now acting as a father. In addition, she had recently terminated a relationship with her boyfriend of two years. She had not told her mother about her depression so that she would not distress her. Ms. M was aware of her mother's suicide attempt prior to the divorce.

Ms. M's mother was contacted by telephone. She expressed wanting to come in with her daughter but that her daughter had not asked her. She worried that Ms. M might feel uncomfortable with her present and might not be able to talk about what was necessary for her to feel better. In talking with the mother, it was apparent that she sensed her daughter's distress, but did not know how to respond to her. Additionally, she revealed that her daughter needed to be strong and come to terms with things within herself and by herself. Ms. M's mother was concerned about the cost of consultation because her income was derived from full-time babysitting that provided barely enough income to meet bills. Ms. M worked as a waitress after school and on weekends.

Services may not be conveniently available due to hours or distance. Language barriers may cut off many individuals or recently immigrated families from being able to obtain services. Language barriers and insufficient income provide a double barrier to the accessibility of services and the availability of problem-solving strategies.

Once the Asian American reaches treatment, additional barriers may contribute to premature termination from therapy. Sue & McKinney (1975) demonstrated that of 100 cases of Asian Americans who had sought psychotherapy services from Seattle area mental health clinics, the majority dropped out of treatment after one session, a rate of 60 percent higher than that of White clients seeking services. In contrast to White clients who averaged almost eight sessions for treatment, Asian Americans averaged slightly more than two sessions for treatment. Shon & Ja (1982) suggest that premature termination from treatment may occur because of communication problems, confusion over how psychotherapy works, conflict over the direction of psychotherapy, or unacceptable values that mental health practitioners may use to determine healthy functioning for the Asian American which do not consider cultural rules.

The Family's Role at Presentation

Shon & Ja (1982) Sue & Morishima (1982) and Sue (1981) provide discussions of Asian American families with attention to cultural diversity among and within ethnic groups. What is valued in the Asian American family varies among the populations which are summarily referred to as Asian Americans and reflects the cultural diversity among the Asian Americans and Pacific Island populations. Understanding Chinese families will not automatically mean that one will understand Filipino families or Japanese families. In fact, as literature has emerged on the mental health of Asian Americans, clinicians, sociologists, educators, and researchers are taking the time to elaborate on the important differences between the ethnic groups subsumed under the label Asian American (Le, 1983; Munoz, 1983; Santos, 1983; Sue et al., 1983; Yamamoto & Iga, 1983; Yamamoto & Kubota, 1983; Yu & Kim, 1983).

Kleinman *et al.* (1978) emphasize that the service provider needs to have knowledge of the individual's culture and level of acculturation to be able to make an assessment of normal versus abnormal functioning. It can be assumed that as one's level of acculturation increases, the influences of cultural heritage may be more indirect and less obvious, but nevertheless are present. When an individual seeks help, the guidelines for facilitating healthy adaptation and functioning must attend both to the larger American culture and the culture of his or her specific ethnic group. As mentioned before, the individual's problems and plans for treatment need to be evaluated in context, specifically, culture and family.

An individual's involvement with the family of origin is not necessarily an accurate indication of how much influence the family or culture has over the beliefs and perceptions an individual has about the world and his or her relationship to it. This observation is important in that many Asian Americans have attempted to deny their cultural and ethnic background in an attempt to come to terms with their own individual identities. (Sue, 1981). The author assumes that the influences of ethnicity are powerful and cross-generational.

The Family's Role in the Referral

The family often seeks intervention or refers the identified patient for treatment when they are at a loss as to how to help. Obviously, the family is expressing their concern and at this point of referral, the person who is symptomatic is likely to be extremely distressed. Most Asian American families will be outwardly willing to come in with the distressed family member and be outwardly supportive in the treatment process. At other times, the individual, an adult, will come in alone self-referred or referred by an agency. The client does not want family members to come in because he or she feels ashamed and does not want to burden them. The belief that recovery rests in the exercise of willpower may explain the tenacity of a distressed individual who needs support, but does not want the family to be involved.

By the case illustrations provided above, it becomes apparent that the presenting problems are not unique to Asian or Pacific American clients. However, ethnicity does play a role in the etiology of the problem, the symptoms, help-seeking behavior, and acceptance of the treatment plan. In the cases of Ms. C and Ms. M it is observed that the families are not functioning normatively given the cultural context and level of acculturation. It would be expected that these families would be more supportive and in Ms. M's case more protective. In order for Ms. C and Ms. M to function more adaptively, their families need to become more available to them to reduce some of their feelings of isolation and to restore family functioning to a more normative system.

Many times the referrals described above are at risk for dropping out of treatment prematurely. The F family was embarrassed to seek help. While they were the most educated siblings in both of their families, none of their brothers or sisters had encountered such difficulties with their children. They came to treatment reluctantly feeling that as parents they were failing. It is important for the therapist to be sensitive to the pressures of the extended families as well as the personal sense of failure the parents were feeling, particularly Ms. F who had major responsibility for their daughters' performance in school as Mr. F made it clear. Ms. C is at risk for dropping out of treatment once she starts to feel the least bit better. To be in treatment may confirm her family's perception that she is weak and crazy. Ms. M is at risk for dropping out so that she does not disappoint or worry her family, particularly her mother. Her family's detachment and her mother's sense of failure as a parent (her mother repeatedly tells her that she must be strong and solve things within herself) are powerful deterrents to continue treatment. Ms. H is at risk for premature termination so that she does not let her family down. Mr. T is at risk for termination as a result of a pattern of isolation and lack of ability to develop trust and comfort in a relationship besides the cultural factors present.

Two conditions must exist to engage the client or family in the therapy process so that the likelihood of premature termination with Asian American individuals and families can be decreased. First, the family must feel that the therapist understands and accepts their reasons for distress. Second, the therapeutic context must make sense so that there will be positive expectations of the therapy. These two conditions are important for any form of therapy. However, with Asian American clients, the therapist must consider that because of cultural rules for illness and treatment, the "curative factor" associated with the therapy process may differ from those assumed in traditional therapies developed for application to the majority culture. If these two conditions are facilitated, there is a much greater chance that the family will continue treatment.

Facilitating the Therapeutic Process

In this section the two conditions mentioned in the previous section (accepting the clients' view of distress and communicating this understanding, and helping therapy to make sense) are discussed as they are relevant to facilitating the therapeutic process. Therapy with the Asian American family as with the individual client does not require that a therapist necessarily develop new skills. The skills central to being an effective therapist remain the same, such as, being able to hear what the client is trying to communicate, respecting the client, and formulating treatment goals which take into account clients' levels of functioning, their resources, and their environment. Neither the problem situations nor the types of family dysfunction that occur are new. What may be new to the therapist is consideration of the context within which the problems exist. It is necessary that the service provider be willing to acknowledge that his or her prejudices, biases, and definitions of healthy psychological functioning may not be as adaptive for clients within their cultural context. Therefore, the therapist also needs to know what is normative functioning in the different groups of Asian and Pacific American families for which they provide consultation and therapy.

Successful therapy also requires that the therapist be sensitive to the factors which contribute to a client's or family's willingness to cooperate and adhere to a treatment plan. Additionally, the therapist needs to be cognizant of the potential administrative and practical barriers to families' continuing treatment. Each of these contributions to therapy is discussed below.

Understanding and Accepting the Presenting Problem

The first session is extremely important, as it is the point at which the individual or family will determine if therapy can help them. Thus, it is important that the client or family feel that they are understood, that their views of the problems are respected, and that their difficulties in seeking treatment are understood. The therapist's tasks are to join with each person involved in the consultation as he or she attempts to respect each person's reasons for seeking a consultation and goals sought.

Joining with the clients will be central to developing the trust and confidence of clients who may be skeptical about therapy as a means of helping them to feel better. It can be helpful to give the individual or family permission to acknowledge how difficult it may have been to decide to seek therapy or a consultation. Find out how many individuals or agencies the client or family has contacted before they reached the current consultation. Furthermore, the therapist can acknowledge and anticipate what clients may experience during the first appointment, including: looking for a solution, affirmation that they are not crazy, embarrassment over having to seek help from a mental health professional, confusion or puzzlement over how therapy can be helpful.

Oftentimes when an individual or family is referred for treatment, the symptoms are indicative of the trouble that he or she is having in solving problems in a different way. This type of dysfunction usually occurs as the family life cycle reflects required changes in roles and relationships with immigration, births, separation, marriage, retirement, and death. These aspects of the changing family cycle are experienced by all families, who must also accommodate to the stress.

The role of ethnicity in therapy becomes salient in assessing the understanding the presenting problem. The therapist needs to determine what is healthy for this family compared with other families of similar background and generation in the United States, and how the family has responded to this change in the family life cycle in previous generations. For example, how did the parents of a twenty-three-year-old Japanese female (first generation born in the United States) leave their respective families of origin? Is their daughter attempting to leave their home in a very different way, which may be misinterpreted by the parents? The clinician can help the family to understand their differences in interpretation of behavior. By acknowledging each individual's view of the problem, the therapist joins with each member involved and then can offer an alternative view of the problem which may be more readily accepted.

Several questions may be relevant in the therapist's attempt to understand the individual's or family's distress. For example, when families present, the following questions may be relevant:

How has the acceptable and implicit family structure and hierarchy been threatened or changed?

Who has become the symptom bearer?

What are the possible purposes of the symptom?

How do family members understand the symptom?

Who else has been a symptom bearer?

How were their symptoms relieved?

How does the symptom attempt to restore balance in the individual or family system?

How can the therapist aid the family in achieving a change in structure which does not feel so threatening yet respects normative cultural rules?

For the client seeking help individually, several questions are also relevant in understanding the presenting problem. Such questions include:

Why does the client feel therapy will be helpful?

Who has the recommended therapy?

Who knows that they have sought help?

What would significant others think about counseling?

What are the client's reasons for not wanting to include significant others in the therapy process or awareness of their distress?

What has the client tried to do to relieve their distress?

Obviously, the questions that are relevant to understanding the purposes of the client's or family's help-seeking behavior are not unique to Asian American clients. However, if the answers to these questions are assumed, the therapist may be operating under inaccurate assumptions, which will be reflected in their understanding of the problem.

Subsequently, the therapist may have difficulty in getting the client or family to return for follow up.

Helping Therapy to Make Sense

Many Asian American clients and families will not have previously had contact with the mental health system. They have had contact with the medical system. This is a model of authority which is congruent with some of the structure inherent in Asian American family functioning. It is extremely important to educate the client as to how therapy works differently from medicine, and how your role as a therapist is similar but different from the relationships they are accustomed to with a medical doctor.

Sue (1981) outlines some discrepancies between traditional psychotherapy practice and Asian or Pacific Americans' cultural patterns which may make therapy confusing. First, mainstream Western models of psychotherapy distinguish between physical and mental health. With Asian Americans, physical and mental health may be viewed more synonymously. Second, communication of satisfaction and dissatisfaction may be more indirect by the standards than the therapist is used to. For example, if the client disagrees with the therapist, this may not be expressed openly or strongly; expression of feelings may be restrained, clients may self-disclose minimally, and family members may be protected. Many of the values of families and clients will be observed as a client or family seek advice, expect the therapist to tell them what to do, and look for concreteness and structure. Third, clients may bring in the expectation that they must exercise willpower and discipline in order to change. Fourth, language difficulties make a demand on therapists to make sure they understand clients and how they may use words differently from those of the therapist. Fifth, traditional psychotherapy assumes an individual-centered focus expecting ambiguity as part of the therapeutic process. Such an orientation may confuse the client who may be expecting direction. Sixth, while silence may be a sign of resistance for some clients, in this culture silence may be a sign of respect.

Because of the differences in cultural patterns, traditional assumptions upon which mainstream American psychotherapies are based will be challenged. Furthermore, the standard goals of therapy may be incongruent with cultural values. Guidelines for facilitating the initial therapeutic contact are offered.

1. Find out what clients' beliefs are about mental and emotional problems. Determine how other similar problems in the family have been addressed. This provides information on the implicit rules of the family as well as their level of acculturation.

2. Most clients, because of their cultural context and relationships with other helping systems, will expect the therapist to be an authority and to tell them what they have to do in order to feel better. It is suggested that to facilitate the likelihood of a family's coming back, they need therapy to make sense. They need to have sense of what they will have to do. Providing an overview of the therapeutic plan, types of changes that may need to occur, and who needs to be involved may enhance the family's trust in the therapist and their view of his or her competence.

3. Many clients will come into therapy hoping to be able to leave with an answer and will look to some concrete methods of approaching problem solving. A brief therapy model is a positive model with Asian Americans as it can be a model of health. It is a model that helps persons and families become unstuck.

4. As in any therapy, it is important to determine the limits in helping the family and how to become a part of the system. As a positive part of the system, the therapist can transfer to appropriate members in the family.

5. Try to anticipate reasons for which the client or family would not come back for a second appointment. Attempt to check these possibilities out in the first session as well as address them with the clients. For example, the therapist may share their concern that if the individual feels better after the consultation he or she may not return to follow-up. Such a pattern would increase the likelihood of a relapse in symptoms in the near future without the individual understanding why or having developed the tools to prevent or remedy such a relapse.

Reducing Barriers to Obtaining and Continuing Treatment

Additional factors are briefly discussed which will familitate the individual's or family's ability to seek treatment as well as continue in treatment.

1. Clinic or private practice hours may determine whether or not a family can come in even if they are very distressed. It will be difficult for many family members to ask for time off from work and further for them to explain why they need the time off. Evening hours and weekend hours increase the likelihood that a family will be able to obtain help.

2. The cost of private practice fees can be prohibitive to seeking help. Sliding scale fees or barter systems may allow the client to pay for service, since they will often be unwilling to accept free services or have exceptions made for them.

3. If the therapist is not very experienced working with Asian Americans, families, or has difficulty with the language of the family, a cotherapist may provide a solution. A cotherapist can complement the therapist's lack of experience or skills.
4. Many families may need help with other social service systems or legal systems. Many therapists will not see it a fit use of their time to help someone maneuver through the social system. This is a legitimate request for a family or individual, and by helping with this request, stressors may be relieved for the client.

References

Kleinman, A. M., Eisenber, L. & Good, B. (1978). Culture, illness, and care: Clinical lessons from anthropologic and cross-cultural research. *Annals of Internal Medicine,* 88, 251–258.

Le, D. D. (1983). Mental health and Vietnamese children. *In* G. J. Powell, J. Yamamoto, A. Romero and A. Morales (Eds.), *The Psychosocial Development of Minority Group Children.* New York: Brunner/Mazel.

Morishima, J. K. (1975). Early History, 1950–1965: The meeting of the twain. *In* J. K. Morishima (Ed.), *Report on the Asian American Assessment Colloquy.* Washington, DC: Child Development Associate Consortium.

Munoz, F. U. (1983). Family life patterns of Pacific-Islanders: The insidious displacement of culture. *In* G. J. Powell, J. Yamamoto, A. Romero and A. Morales (Eds.), *The Psychosocial Development of Minority Group Children.* New York: Brunner/Mazel.

President's Commission on Mental Health (1978). *Report to the President,* 4 vols. Washington, DC: U.S. Government Printing Office.

Prizzia, R. & Villaneuva-King, O. (1977). *Central Oahu Community Mental Health Needs Assessment Survey. Part III: A Survey of the General Population.* Honolulu: Management Planning and Administration Consultants.

Root, M. P. P., Ho, C. & Sue, S. (19XX). Training counselors for Asian Americans. *In* Harriet Lefley (Ed.), *Cross-Cultural Training for Mental Health Professionals.* Springfield, Ill.: Charles C. Thomas.

Santos, R. A. (1983). The social and emotional development of Filipino-American children. *In* G. J. Powell, J. Yamamoto, A. Romero and A. Morales (Eds.), *The Psychosocial Development of Minority Group Children.* New York: Brunner/Mazel.

Shon, S. P. & Ja. D. Y. (1982). Asian families *In* M. McGoldrick, J. K. Pearce and J. Giordana (Eds.), *Ethnicity and Family Therapy,* New York: Guilford Press.

Sue, D., Sue, D. W. & Sue, D. M. (1983). Psychological development of Chinese-American children. *In* G. J. Powell, J. Yamamoto, A. Romero and A. Morales (Eds.), *The Psychosocial Development of Minority Group Children.* New York: Brunner/Mazel.

Sue, D. W. (1981), *Counseling the Culturally Different: Theory and Practice.* New York: John Wiley.

Sue, S. (1976). Conceptions of mental illness among Asian and Caucasian-American students. *Psychological Reports,* 38, 703–708.

Sue, S. & McKinney, H. (1975). Asian Americans in the community mental health care system. *American Journal of Orthopsychiatry,* 45, 111–118.

Sue, S. & Morishima, J. K. (1982). *The Mental Health of Asian Americans.* San Francisco: Jossey-Bass.

Sue, S. & Sue, D. W. (1974). MMPI comparisons between Asian American and non-Asian students utilizing a student health psychiatric clinic. *Journal of Counseling Psychology,* 21, 423–427.

Tsai, M., Teng, L. N., & Sue, S. (1980). Mental status of Chinese in the United States. *In* A. Kleinman and T. Y. Lin (Eds.), *Normal and Deviant Behavior in Chinese Culture,* Hingman, Mass.: Reidel.

Yamamoto, J. & Iga, M. (1983). Emotional growth of Japanese American children. *In* G. J. Powell, J. Yamamoto, A. Romero and A. Morales (Eds.), *The Psychosocial Development of Minority Group Children.* New York: Brunner/Mazel.

Yamamoto, J. & Kubota, M. (1983). The Japanese-American family. *In* G. J. Powell, J. Yamamoto, A. Romero and A. Morales (Eds.), *The Psychosocial Development of Minority Group Children.* New York: Brunner/Mazel.

Yu, K. H. & Kim, L. I. C. (1983). The growth and development of Korean-American children. *In* G. J. Powell, J. Yamamoto, A. Romero and A. Morales (Eds.), *The Psychosocial Development of Minority Group Children. New York: Brunner/Mazel.*

12

Psychotherapy with Southeast Asian American Clients

Kazumi Nishio and Murray Bilmes

Since the fall of Saigon in 1975, the influx of Southeast Asian refugees to the United States has been enormous, especially in the western and southern states. Approximately 250,000 Southeast Asian refugees were admitted to the United States from the spring of 1975 through the fall of 1979 (U.S. Department of Health, and Welfare, 1979). Between 1980 and 1984 more than 450,000 additional refugees arrived in the United States from the same area (Bureau of Census, 1985, 1986). Immigration of these refugees has slowed considerably since then, but they are still trickling into the country as part of the family reunification (U.S. Committee for Refugees, 1987). At present, few mental health agencies exclusively and effectively serve Asian American clients. Those that do are mainly located in big cities.

Not all of these visible new Americans, however, live in cities where Asian American mental health services are available and in which Southeast Asians are on the staff. In such places where special services do not exist, traditional mental health service workers are called on to work with these new clients.

In the Santa Rosa area (Sonoma County, California), for example, about 2,500 Asian refugees are currently struggling to adjust to life in a new, culturally unfamiliar country (Indochinese American Council, 1986). Mental health problems, such as depression, violence (within and outside the family), alcoholism, drug abuse, gambling, schizophrenia, suicidal attempts, and psychosomatic symptoms are prevalent (Nishio, 1982). However, there are no mental health services designed specifically to meet the special needs of these people. The clients are generally unfamiliar with Western mental health approaches, and the counselors who treat them have

Nishio, K., & Bilmes, M. (1987). Psychotherapy with Southeast Asian American clients. *Professional Psychology: Research and Practice, 18,* 342–346. Copyright 1987 by the American Psychological Association. Reprinted by permission.

little training to help them understand such culturally different clients. Thus the Asian refugee, in spite of urgent and critical needs, is largely neglected.

This article attempts to provide pertinent background information on Southeast Asian culture and practical suggestions for counselors who work with these clients.

The term *Southeast Asian American* includes people of various ancestry—Vietnamese, Lao, Cambodian, Hmong, Mien, and other ethnic groups. Each of these peoples has a distinct language, group identity, history, and tradition. However, Southeast Asian Americans share common cultural values such as family orientation, interdependency, and religious and philosophical teachings.

The following brief explanation of demographic features and discussion of attitudes and cultural values should not be regarded either as definitive or as applicable to all cases. The life experiences of individual Southeast Asian Americans may, of course, differ greatly.

Demographic Features of Southeast Asian Refugees

The first wave of refugees came to the United States during the evacuation of Saigon in 1975. Many of these newcomers were fairly well-educated Vietnamese, employees of the U.S. government or of American-sponsored industry, Vietnamese government officials, and professionals (Chan, 1981). Among the Vietnamese were ethnic Chinese. Initially, the smaller numbers of refugees from Cambodia and Lao were also mainly U.S. government employees or Royal Lao government figures. Many spoke some English.

Subsequent waves of refugees, who came from rural, farming areas, were less sophisticated, often belonging to lower socioeconomic groups, unable to speak English and without knowledge of the Western way of life. Many had passed through extreme ordeals, escaping under life-threatening conditions and subsequently enduring long stays in refugee camps in Thailand and Malaysia with uncertainty about their future (Nicassio, 1985). These were involuntary immigrants who had virtually no choice but to come to the United States, and even now, many are still separated from their families, who remain in refugee camps.

The number of Cambodian refugees increased dramatically when the second wave arrived. During the period 1971 to 1980, 7,739 Cambodian immigrants were counted by the Census Bureau, whereas in the shorter period of 1981 to 1984, 66,542 new Cambodian immigrants reached the United States (Bureau of Census, 1985, 1986). This population had suffered the massacres of the Pol Pot regime, many experiencing extreme atrocities with hellish physical and emotional traumas.

In the treatment of Southeast Asian refugees, knowledge of certain characteristics of these ethnic members is important. Necessary knowledge includes recognition of the differences among refugee groups, of the social and economic status of the patients, awareness of the degree of knowledge they may have of Western culture, their English-speaking ability, individualized experiences of trauma, and their membership in the family support system and in the ethnic community.

Attitude Toward Therapy

Psychotherapy is foreign to most Indochinese refugees. Life difficulties such as marital problems, children's behavioral problems, and problems of interpersonal relationships are often met stoically. This attitude toward life problems tests many Western therapists, who tend to try to "fix" the problem of "change" the client. However, if these ethnic Asians cannot simply endure misfortune, they are likely to find solace or seek help from family members, friends, or relatives. Sometimes they will go to the shaman, priest, or leader of their ethnic community for advice, or they may engage in rituals to eliminate evil spirits thought to be causing their problems (Egawa & Tashima, 1982; Moon & Tashima, 1982). Psychotherapists providing intangible services for a fee are unknown in most of the Asian nations from which these refugees come. Because many do not perceive mental health treatment as relevant to their problems or discomfort, such services in the United States remain outside their repertory of choice.

When Moon and Tashima (1982) asked 396 Asian refugees (Cambodians, Vietnamese, Hmong, Lao, Mien, and ethnic Chinese from Vietnam) from whom they would seek help for depression and other problems related to family, marriage, finance, isolation, work, and so forth, the refugees did not select providers from the outside (psychiatrists, counselors, teachers, and social workers). Lao and Mien refugees, for example, would in case of need turn to members of their communities for aid. Ethnic Chinese and Vietnamese respondents would rely on themselves, family, or friends. When marital problems were the issue, many Hmong would look to other family members to help them resolve their difficulties, but they would not seek such help in the case of depression, isolation, and financial problems. Among Cambodians, friends were the primary source of help for depression and isolation, and the ethnic community was the main source for assistance in marital problems. For problems diagnosed here as psychological problems, very little consideration was given to professional help by all examined ethnic groups.

In most cases, when Asian refugees come to a traditional mental health agency—typically a hospital or a county mental health service—they perceive the referral as a choice initiated by physicians, social service workers, the court, or other public health personnel, not as their own choice. They will seek mental health help only as a last resort, and they tend to have little faith in the process.

Case Example 1: A Vietnamese family was referred to therapy with a Western-trained American psychotherapist after an adolescent daughter's hospitalization following "bizarre behavior." In one session, because the therapy was supposed to focus only on the daughter, the fact that the patient's grandfather had died just four hr previously was not brought out. Also, following a later session when the therapist focused on the dynamic of wife and husband as a possible affecting factor on the daughter's behavior, the couple failed to keep the subsequent appointment. The couple told the therapist over the telephone that they would come to see him only as long as the marital issue was not addressed.

In this case the family treated the therapy session as if it were a transaction between themselves and a governmental agency, going through the required motions with suspicion. Disclosed feelings of sadness over the father's death or discussing private marital problems with a stranger was unthinkable. As far the family was concerned, these issues, as well as other private emotions, were irrelevant in the context of curing the child's mental illness.

Somatization of Symptoms

Among Asians, many psychological problems are expressed as somatic complaints (Tung, 1978). Many Southeast Asian refugees believe that the health of the body and mind are inseparable. Illness of the mind, then, is treated by attending to the body (Moon & Tashima, 1982). Chien and Yamamoto (1982) stated, for example, that patients often attribute anxiety to kidney malfunction, hormonal imbalance, or malnutrition. Some refugees attribute mental illness to a metaphysical cause—within *yin-yan,* an imbalance of male and female light and darkness, or hot and cold in bodily functions (Tung, 1978). The spirit world and supernatural forces such as "bad wind" are also believed to affect physical and mental health (Indochinese Cultural & Service Center, 1982). Each cultural subgroup has its own malevolent spirits that, as with Cambodians' ancestral spirits, cause mental illnesses.

In addition to the concept of the inseparability of body and mind, shame and the stigma of mental illness also affect the reporting and treatment of mental illnesses among Southeast Asian refugees. In this group a disproportionately large number of physical complaints in which emotional difficulties are suspected have been reported (Kinzie & Manson, 1983). Mental illness brings social disgrace to the family because each individual member is a reflection of the entire family (Indochinese Cultural & Services Center, 1982; Sato, 1975). Thus aside from supernatural forces, the only culturally acceptable expression of mental illness is through recognizable physical complaints such as headaches, stomach pains, seizures, and paralysis.

More than 60 percent of the Southeast Asian clients who brought physical complaints to a community health center in San Diego, California were diagnosed as having psychogenic problems (Egawa & Tashima, 1981). The most commonly presented problem (39 percent) at the Indochinese Psychiatric Clinic in Oregon was multiple somatic symptoms (Kinzie & Manson, 1983). Under extreme stress, it is true, any person may manifest conversion disorder (American Psychiatric Association, 1980). However, the prevalence of conversion disorder as well as the overpresence of psychosomatic illness among Southeast Asian refugee populations is significant (Nishio, 1982).

Case Example 2: A fifty-four-year-old Cambodian man became paralyzed. Extensive medical examinations revealed no organic cause, and he was diagnosed as having a psychogenic conversion disorder. The man had been depressed since he came to the United States two years before the episode. He could not find a job and could not support his family. As he was ashamed of his inability to take care of his family and continue in his role of the household, the secondary gain of paralysis was great. He was able to receive welfare assistance, and his wife stayed by his bedside for twenty-four hr a day as a required helper. He did not seem to possess the desire to get well. Because he and his family members did not recognize and acknowledge the psychological side of his physical condition, they insisted that Western medicine should be able to cure what they perceived as a purely physical illness. By the time the patient was referred to a psychotherapist, his condition was severely aggravated. When the therapist suggested an indigenous healer to perform a ritual to get rid of the demon, the patient insisted his condition was too advanced for such a remedy. The patient's refusal to help and his failure to follow the prescribed muscle exercises eventually led to serious physical atrophy.

Independence Versus Interdependence

Western culture almost invariably values independence. Dependence, on the other hand, is a key concept applicable to human relations in many Asian countries. A person asks another person's benevolence and receives indulgent support from other people (Doi, 1962). In return, the recipient is obligated to be dutiful and to repay the favor. This interdependency is the basis of a strong sense of family and community.

Many Asians live in an extended family situation. In the case of refugees, not only the grandparents, uncles, and aunts but also acquaintances often live together in this country. Limited housing, of course, sometimes forces this closeness upon them, but a wish to maintain interdependent relationships is a strong factor in maintaining such close living arrangements. The welfare of the family or community often has priority over individual needs (Sue & Sue, 1972). If independence is encouraged too sharply by a Western therapist, it may weaken or even destroy important sources of support and belongingness.

Case Example 3: A Laotian couple was referred to psychotherapy by a minister of their church. The husband was alcoholic and beat his wife. When the couple first went to a Western psychotherapist, the therapist encouraged the wife to leave her husband and lead an independent life. The couple immediately quit therapy and went to an Asian therapist. That therapist first acknowledged the dependency of the wife and the supremacy of the man over the wife. Gradually, after the trust relationship was built, the merit of a more independent wife was pointed out; for example, if the wife took more responsibility, she would be less of a burden on her husband, and he would have more time for himself.

Practical Suggestions

As seen in Case Example 1, the Asian American patient often regards therapy as a businesslike transaction that should be devoid of emotion and revelation of private matters. If the therapist pushes for more open feelings and seeks inner thought too early in the session, the patient quickly threatens to drop out. It is necessary to accept the patient's polite front as part of the self and not regard it as resistance. The patients may regard therapists as teachers, and Asian refugees are more likely, especially in the beginning, to expect wise and concrete guidance and advice rather than to seek insight into their own behavior.

One has to be aware, however, that acceptance of advice in the session does not necessarily mean the patient will follow the advice, especially if it requires open communication of feelings. Education concerning how to benefit from psychotherapy becomes essential. Let them experience a small success and some relief. Encourage them, if they are ready, to talk about the tragic and horrifying experience of escaping from the enemies in their own country. Many refugees report lighter feelings after venting these living memories, and they appreciate the interest and concern that Western therapists show to them. Many of these new Americans are learning English and want to communicate their histories and their needs to the best of their ability. The extensive use of an interpreter during the intake interview and the history-taking and information-gathering sessions, although often necessary, especially in the case of older clients who have no English-speaking ability, may hinder the establishment of an alliance between client and therapist. The patient usually does not come to the institution per se; the patient comes to see the counselor or therapist as somebody he or she knows and has come to trust. To help build that trust and to establish a personal relationship, with or without an interpreter, the therapist may show his or her interest and concern for the patient by making visits to the ethnic community, which plays a vital role in the patient's life, as well as to the patient's home.

The patient in Case Example 2 did not seek help until his condition became extreme. He also presented his mental problems in the form of physical illness—a culturally sanctioned expression of mental illness. As showing one's weakness is shameful, the therapist must not too eagerly suggest that the client is being treated for emotional illness and minimize the physical complaints. Medication and injection are important to Southeast Asian peoples. Educating medical doctors about the prevalence of psychosomatic disorders among Asian refugees may prompt earlier referral to psychotherapy. The use of indigenous healers in early stages should also be considered, as it is a common belief that bad spirits cause mental disturbances. Ethnic community leaders are often able to help the therapist find those who can perform rituals in conjunction with psychotherapy. Sometimes therapists can create their own rituals, which may have a salutary effect if they are performed with sincerity. Hollow rituals, on the other hand, will soon be recognized as false by the patients. Relaxation techniques, breathing exercises, hypnosis, meditation, and biofeedback can be used. Phrases like ''too much stress'' and ''too much worry'' are readily accepted to describe the connection between physical and psychological conditions.

The Western value of independence often is not useful to the Asian refugee, as indicated in Case Example 3. Traditional interdependency among family and community has to be respected in the right circumstances.

As Asian refugee women observe American women's freedom and independence, a desire to emulate the American woman may lead to conflicts with their own cultural values. Sometimes such women, in imitating the behavior of Western women, become demanding or promiscuous. Thus it is important to point out the responsibilities that come with independence and freedom. In Case Example 3 the strength of the wife ''behind the scenes'' was discussed so as to enable her to bring out this strength appropriately while developing an understanding of how inadequate her husband was feeling in this new country. In time the couple achieved a new balance, and the husband stopped beating his wife. His drinking problem also stopped when his wife and the therapist took a strong stance indicating that drinking was not acceptable.

It is not easy for Western therapists to side with chauvinistic husbands who regard their wives as part of the property. It may require considerable patience and understanding on the part of the therapist to tolerate Confucius's teaching and centuries-old traditions.

Sometimes it may be advisable to match male therapists with male patients and female therapists with female patients because in Asian cultures the gap between male and female roles is great. Male patients may not feel that female therapists are important enough or powerful enough to be of use to them. Female patients may be shy and become easily intimidated by male therapists, especially the bearded ones. However, it would be a disservice to perpetuate this female-inferior attitude among Southeast Asian refugees. It is well to learn in time that one great virtue of living in this country is to be able to acknowledge the equality and the importance of men and women.

Conclusions

In this article, only a few of the many cultural values and culturally based attitudes toward therapy are discussed. Yet even these present a complex picture for the Western therapist. It is not easy to work with patients who do not believe in Western modes of therapy. It may be wise to incorporate indigenous modes of healing, when appropriate, into the treatment process. Education as well as letting them experience a little success may gradually build patients' confidence in the therapeutic process. Making a personal connection and initially occupying the role of teacher may be the best means through which the therapist can help the Asian refugee accept and use mental health services. Therapists need to be aware of culturally accepted ways of expressing mental problems, such as through psycho-somatic disorders, because mental illness carries a strong stigma and produces a deep sense of shame. It is well to remember that many of these clients believe that the body and mind are inseparable. The importance of the ethnic community to the Asian refugees must not be neglected because it plays a significant part in their mental health.

It may sometimes be trying for the Western therapist to have to understand and accept cultural values that he or she personally opposes. But once the Western therapist realizes that the Asian refugee values the concept of dependency or interdependency more than that of independence, the more easily he or she can understand the social principles inherent in that concept. However, when the concept manifests itself in the subjugation of wife to husband, the therapist may experience difficulty in accepting it. A constructive attitude may be achieved if the therapist does not totally accept the refugee's concept or demand absolute adherence to Western values. Sensitivity and awareness of differences can possibly bring about a new state of balance.

It may take more than the usual therapeutic skill and facility with language to reach the Asian refugee's heart. If the therapist shows concern, learns the different characteristics of each group along with the patient's unique cultural values, and understands his or her history and plight, the therapist will be able to touch and aid many refugees who are in desperate need of help.

References

American Psychiatric Association (1980). *Diagnostic and statistical manual of mental disorders* (3rd. ed.). Washington DC: Author.

Bureau of Census (1985). *Statistical abstract of the United States.* Washington, DC: U.S. Department of Commerce.

Bureau of Census (1986). *Statistical abstract of the United States.* Washington, DC: U.S. Department of Commerce.

Chan, K (1981). Education for Chinese and Indochinese. *Theory Into Practice, 20*(1), 35–44.

Chien, C., & Yamamoto, J. (1982). Asian-American and Pacific-Islander patients. In F. Acosta, J. Yamamoto, & L. Evans (Eds.), *Effective psychotherapy for low-income and minority patients.* New York: Plenum.

Doi, L. T. (1962). *Amae*—A key concept for understanding Japanese personality structure. *Psychologia, 5,* 1–7.

Egawa, J. E., & Tashima, N. (1981). *Alternative service delivery models in Pacific/Asian American communities.* San Francisco: Pacific Asian Mental Health Research Project.

Egawa, J. E., & Tashima, N. (1982). *Indigenous healers in Southeast Asian refugee communities.* San Francisco: Pacific Asian Mental Health Research Project.

Indochinese American Council (1986). *Refugee statistics in Sonoma County.* Santa Rosa, CA: Indochinese American Council.

Indochinese Cultural & Service Center (1982). *Southeast Asian health care.* Portland, OR: Indochinese Culture & Service Center.

Kinzie, D. J., & Manson, S. (1983). Five-year's experience with Indochinese refugee psychiatric patients. *Journal of Operational Psychiatry, 14* (2), 105–111.

Moon, A., & Tashima, N. (1982). *Help seeking behavior and attitudes of Southeast Asian refugees.* San Francisco: Pacific Asian Mental Health Research Project.

Nicassio, P.M. (1985). The psychological adjustment of the Southeast Asian refugee. *Journal of Cross-Cultural Psychology, 16* (2), 153–173.

Nishio, K. (1982). *Southeast Asian refugee mental health project* Unpublished manuscript.

Sato, M. (1975). The shame factor: Counseling Asian Americans. *Journal of the Asian American Psychological Association, 5* (1), 20–24.

Sue, D., & Sue, S. (1972). Counseling Chinese-Americans. *Personnel and Guidance Journal, 50,* 637–644.

Tung, T. M. (1978). *Health and disease: The Indochinese perspective.* Paper presented at the annual Health, Education, and Welfare Mental Health Projects Grantee Conference, San Francisco.

U.S. Committee for Refugees (1987). *World refugee survey; 1986 in reviews.* Washington, DC: American Council for Nationalities Service.

U.S. Department of Health, and Welfare (1979). *The Congress Indochinese refugee assistance program.* Washington, DC: Social Security Administration, Office of Refugee Affairs.

The Asian American Client
Cases and Questions

1. Assume you are a high school counselor in a large suburban high school. A Japanese American student whom you have seen for academic advising on several occasions has just shared with you his involvement as a marijuana dealer. Although attempting to hide his emotions, the student is clearly distraught. He is particularly concerned that a recent arrest of a marijuana supplier will eventually lead authorities to him.

   a. How *might* the student's cultural background affect his feelings as he shares this problem?
   b. What kind of input from you as a counselor do you think this student wants/needs most?
   c. Can you anticipate any prejudicial reaction on the part of the school administration (if the student's behavior is uncovered) as a result of the student's racial/ethnic background?

2. Assume you are a community psychologist employed by a community agency which provides psychological services to a population of middle-class Japanese American families, among others. A Young Buddhist Association (YBA) has asked you to speak on "resolving intergenerational conflict" at its next meeting. (Your agency is aware that generational conflict has become a major problem in this community in recent years.)

   a. What do you think are some of the causes of the intergenerational conflict being experienced by these young people and their parents?
   b. Other than your talk, what services do you feel qualified to render these young Japanese Americans and their families?
   c. How do you think these services will be received by the YBA members and their families?

3. Assume you are a high school counselor who has been asked by the dean of Guidance to organize and moderate a number of value clarification groups. You plan to set up six groups of eight students each from a list of volunteers, although seven students were referred by teachers because they are nonparticipators in class. Six of the seven students referred by teachers are Asian Americans.

a. Will the composition of your six groups be determined by the fact that six of seven teacher referrals are Asian American?
b. What goals do you have for your six groups and for the individual members of these groups?
c. How will our own cultural/educational background affect the way in which you relate to the six Asian American students?

The Asian American Client
Role Playing Exercise

Divide into groups of four or five. Assign each group member to a role and the responsibilities associated with the role as follows:

Role	Responsibility
1. Counselor	1. Assume role as a counselor or mental health worker who is assigned an Asian American client. Attempt to build rapport with the client.
2. Client	2. Assume role of an Asian American client (Chinese, Japanese, or Indo-Chinese refugee). To play this role effectively, it will be necessary for the student client to (a) identify cultural values of Asian Americans, (b) identify sociopolitical factors which may interfere with counseling, and (c) portray these aspects in the counseling session. It is best to select a few powerful variables in the role play. You may or may not be initially antagonistic to the counselor, but it is important for you to be sincere in your role and your reactions to the counselor.
3. Observers	3. Observe interaction and offer comments during feedback session.

This exercise is most effective in a racially and ethnically mixed group. For example, an Asian American student can be asked to play the Asian American client role. However, this is probably not possible in most cases. Thus, students who play the client role will need to thoroughly read the articles for the group they are portraying.

Identifying the barriers that could interfere with counseling is an important aspect of this exercise. We recommend that a list be made of the group's cultural values and sociopolitical influences prior to the role playing. For example, how might restraint of strong feelings, preference for structure and activity, and trust/mistrust be manifested in the client?

Role playing may go on for a period of ten to fifteen minutes, but the time limit should be determined prior to the activity. Allow ten to fifteen minutes for a feedback session in which all participants discuss (within the group) how they felt in their respective roles, how appropriate were the counselor responses, what else they might have done in that situation, etc.

Rotate and role play the same situation with another counselor trainee *or* another Asian American client with different issues, concerns, and problems. In the former case, the group may feel that a particular issue is of sufficient importance to warrant reenactment. This allows students to see the effects of other counseling responses and approaches. In the latter case, the new exposure will allow students to get a broader view of barriers to counseling.

If videotaping equipment is available, we recommend that the session be taped and processed in a replay at the end. We have found this to be a powerful means of providing feedback to participants.

PART 5

The Latino Client

There is no single label that adequately describes the ethnically diverse groups that make up the Latino population. It includes Mexican Americans, Puerto Ricans, Cubans, and Central and South Americans, each representing a distinct land of origin and yet linked by common language and cultural heritage. When viewed as a combined population, they are the fastest growing ethnic minority in America. During the decade of the 1980s, the group increased five times as fast as the rest of the nation, reaching 22.3 million by 1988 (U.S. Bureau of the Census, 1990 C.P.H-1-6). At its present rate of growth, some are predicting that the group will surpass African Americans in the near future as America's largest ethnic minority.

But Latinos are not only unique in their size and growth rate. As a rule, they have also tended to cluster in fewer parts of the country than other ethnic groups. For instance, nearly 90 percent of the population is found in nine states: California, Texas, New York, Florida, Illinois, New Jersey, Arizona, New Mexico, and Colorado. Moreover, the vast majority of the population is congregated in major urban centers. Yet it is precisely these phenomena—close clustering and rapid growth—that have produced a combination of strengths and challenges for the Latino community.

From a cultural point of view, the densely populated Latino community has proven to be a mecca for preserving and enhancing the culture. As is true in the case of all human groupings, culture plays an essential role in the life of the Latino; it allows the distinct traits— knowledge, beliefs, values, religion, customs—of the group to be passed on from one generation to the next. It is in part because of this unique population pattern that the Latino culture has persisted and evolved in America, providing its members with a sense of strength and security.

Their size and demography have also proven to be a source of strength in the political arena. For example, 40 percent of all congressional seats and 71 percent of the 270 electoral votes needed to elect our president are found in the nine states that are heavily populated by Latinos. According to a report in *The Hispanic Almanac* (1984), these phenomena have already produced significant results. ''The growth in numbers and the increased political sophistication of Hispanics has meant an increase in the number of Hispanic elected officials on almost all levels of government'' (p. 151.)

High growth rate has also produced its share of problems. Latinos suffer many of the same problems that confront other ethnic minorities in inner cities. Poor schools, overcrowded classrooms, and campus violence have become a fact of life in many Latino communities, according to *U.S. News & World Report* (1987). Low-paying jobs and high unemployment help to lower the overall standard of living for many Latinos. The U.S. Bureau of Census recently reported that 28.1 percent of Latino families live in poverty compared to 9.2 percent of non-Latino families (Current

Population Report, Series P-60 No. 175). Further, it places the median income for all Latino families at $23,400, while that of non-Latino families stands at $35,200 (Schick & Schick, 1991). As Schick and Schick (1991) indicate, members of this group are far more likely to be victims of crime than their White counterparts.

To a large degree, this situation can be explained by a cycle of poverty set in motion with the early immigration of Latinos to this country. Ancestral immigrants of many present-day Latinos came to the United States from non-industrial, agrarian-based countries that for the most part were unskilled and Spanish speaking. (A major exception was the first wave of the Cuban population, many of whom were middle-class and skilled when they migrated). Their life-style, customs, and language set them apart from the dominant society, making them the object of stereotyping, prejudice, and discrimination. Thus, Latinos were forced to join the millions of other American ethnic minorities in competition for scarce jobs and low pay. The pattern was set, and each new generation has been condemned to the perpetual cycle of poverty and group discrimination.

In the first article to this section, "Hispanic/Latino Communities: Psychological Implications," Comas-Díaz thoroughly discusses the socio-cultural, health, emotional, and environmental pressures which impact Latino communities and their implications for counseling. Special attention is also given to the role of psychologists in working with this population as well as a number of implications for training and practice.

In the second article, "What Do Culturally Sensitive Mental Health Services Mean?" the authors discuss a number of salient conditions necessary for conducting culturally sensitive therapy with Latinos. Each condition is thoroughly discussed in terms of its relevance to the Latino experience. Current approaches to counseling are critiqued and recommendations made for enhancing therapist effectiveness.

In the final chapter to this section, Espin sensitizes the reader to a myriad of obstacles confronting the Latino migrant. Three psychological stages of migration are discussed as well as the unique challenges they pose for the Latino immigrant. Issues of gender, separation, acculturation, and language are also addressed as having special implications for counseling.

When taken together, the articles in this section provide the counseling professional with a wealth of comprehensive information and insight that is vital to working effectively with the Latino.

References

U.S. Bureau of the Census, Census of Population and Housing—Summary Population and Housing Characteristics, P. H. 1–6, 1990.

U.S. Bureau of the Census, Current Population Report, Series P-60, #175, 1990.

The Hispanic Almanac. (1984). New York: Hispanic Policy Development Project, Inc.

Schick, F. L., & Schick, R. (1991). *Statistical handbook on U.S. Hispanics.* Phoenix, AZ: The Oryz Press.

For Latinos, a growing divide (1987, August 10). *U.S. News & World Report,* p. 47–49.

13
Hispanic Latino Communities: Psychological Implications

Lillian Comas-Díaz

ABSTRACT: Hispanic/Latino communities are diverse and heterogeneous. Many of these communities continue to be plagued by sociocultural, health, emotional and environmental problems. These conditions are discussed along with their psychological implications. The role of psychologists in addressing these issues is delineated. Implications for the training and practice of professional psychologists working with these communities are also presented.

The Hispanic/Latino population in the United States constitutes a diverse and heterogeneous community comprising groups with distinct historical, economical, political and racial differences. The Hispanic population consists of 63 percent Mexican Americans, 12 percent Puerto Rican, 6 percent Cuban, 10 percent Central and South American, and 8 percent Other Hispanic (Bureau of the Census, 1985). Some Hispanics have recently immigrated, while the families of others have been in the United States since long before the arrival of the Pilgrims. The term Hispanics, as used by the U.S. Bureau of the Census, encompasses both persons of Spanish origin or decent, and those who designate themselves as Mexican, Mexican American, Chicano, Puerto Rican, Boricua, Cuban or Other Spanish/Hispanic (Hispanics, 1984). However, some Hispanics refer to themselves as Latinos, thereby stressing their Latin American background.

The diversity among Hispanics is further evidenced in demographic variables such as geographical distribution, urban-rural dwelling, level of acculturation, national origin (Mexican, Puerto Rican, Cuban, etc.) socioeconomic class, gender, and age. Moreover, diversity among Hispanics is mediated by their generational status, language preference, and

Comas-Díaz, L. (1990). Hispanic/Latino communities: Psychological implications. *The Journal of Training & Practice in Professional Psychology, 4*(1), 14–35. Reprinted with permission of the editor.

political status (immigrant or native). Immigrants can be further divided into those who are documented and those who are not.

This article discusses psychosocial needs of Hispanic communities and their psychological implications in addition to the psychologist's role in addressing them.

Demographic Overview

The Hispanic population in the United States is estimated to be approximately 16.9 million, representing 7.2 percent of the total population (Bureau of the Census, 1985) and is a rapidly growing population. Between 1980 and 1985 it grew from 14.6 million to 16.9 million, increasing 16 percent. This growth is partly attributable to a high fertility rate. The National Coalition of the Hispanic Health and Human Services Organization (COSSMHO) (1988) reported that the 1981 Hispanic fertility rate was the highest of any group, with 97.5 births per 1,000 women aged 14–44 years. This figure represents 50 percent higher than the rate of 65 for non-Hispanic women. There were differences in fertility rate among Hispanic subgroups: Mexican American, 112.3; Puerto Rican, 73.5; and Cuban, 47.2 (Ventura, 1987).

Another reason for the Hispanic growth is the substantial immigration to the United States from Spanish-speaking countries. The census figures do not account for the number of legal and undocumented Latin American individuals who are continuously entering the United States. Though the figures are unreliable, the total annual undocumented immigration is generally estimated to be around a half million, coming from Mexico, Central America, and the Caribbean (Hispanics, 1984).

Hispanics tend to be a young population. Their median age is 25 years as compared to 31.4 years in the total population (Bureau of the Census, 1985). However, there is diversity on this variable among Hispanic groups, with Mexican Americans being the youngest and Cubans being the oldest. Because many Hispanic females are now entering their childbearing years, and because they tend to bear more children and at younger ages than other ethnic groups, the Hispanic population on average will continue to be relatively younger than the rest of the population for some time (Hispanics, 1984).

There are approximately 3.9 million Hispanic families in the United States with 72 percent being married couples. Moreover, a significant proportion (23 percent) of the total families are female headed (Bureau of the Census, 1985). Contrary to popular belief, 71 percent of the Hispanic population was born in the United States, as opposed to 29 percent which was foreign born.

According to the 1985 census, the proportion of Hispanic families below the poverty level was more than double that of non-Hispanic families. Hispanic groups' intradiversity is also found here, with Puerto Rican families having the highest poverty rate, and Cubans the lowest.

Another factor related to Hispanics' income level is their employment status. In general, Hispanic unemployment is significantly higher than that of Anglos, though not as high as the Black population (COSSMHO, 1988). The high Hispanic unemployment rate tends to limit this population's access to health care. For example, Villareal (1986) reports that one fifth of Hispanic adults are medically disadvantaged, in that they lack health insurance and do not have a regular source of medical care, partly due to financial problems and/or because they did not know where to seek care. In addition, Hispanics' low educational level adversely affects their health status. The lower the education of the head of the household, the poorer are the family's health and its access to care (Villareal, 1986).

Education represents the most serious gap in achievement between Hispanics and other groups, ranging from preschool through graduate training levels (Hispanics, 1984). Although Hispanic school achievement is improving, it is still a serious problem for Mexican Americans and Puerto Ricans. Educational differences exist among the diverse Hispanic subgroups. For example, the 1985 Census reported that only 42 percent of Mexican Americans had completed high school, while 63 percent of the Central/South Americans had achieved this educational level. The Hispanic drop-out rate remains very high, contributing to a vicious cycle. For instance, the educational disadvantage of Hispanics at the elementary and secondary level, in addition to the small proportion of Hispanics who graduate from high school, result in significantly lower representation in higher education institutions (Hispanics, 1984).

The ability to speak English has been linked to Hispanic school achievement. Most of the Hispanic population in the United States speaks English, as opposed to 24 percent that is Spanish monolingual (COSSMHO, 1988). Contrary to stereotype, some Hispanics do not speak Spanish or do so with English accents (Villaescusa, 1985).

In sum, Hispanics in the United States tend to be young, poor, with high fertility rates, and less than a high school education. Although they reside in every state, Hispanics tend to be urban and to be concentrated in the Southwestern, Southeastern, and Northeastern areas of the United States. They are diverse in ethnicity, socioeconomic class, color, geographic distribution, generational status, degree of acculturation, and language preference.

Refugee Populations

The Latin American refugee population deserves special attention. Increasing numbers of immigrants are arriving from Central American countries, particularly El Salvador and Nicaragua. Their profile tends to be quite different from that of other Hispanic/Latino groups in the United States. Partly due to ongoing civil wars, Salvadorans and Nicaraguans are becoming the fastest growing subset of Hispanic immigrants (Leslie & Leitch, 1989). Many of them are considered political refugees and displaced individuals (Vargas, 1984) who clearly require specialized mental health services. For instance, Central American immigrants are more likely to suffer from post traumatic stress disorder than are Mexican immigrants (Cervantes, Salgado de Snyder & Padilla, 1989).

The experiences of Central American immigrants differ from those of other Hispanics. For instance, Vargas (1984) distinguishes between the political exile and the displaced person. The political exile tends to be more educated, resourceful; who made a choice, being aware of its consequences; and usually has made some arrangements and established some support in the United States. For example, Cubans and most Chileans in the United States can be considered political exiles. On the other hand, many Central Americans fit more into the category of displaced persons, who tend to come from lower socioeconomic backgrounds, with a history of oppression and exploitation; who leave their country without preparation or support abroad; and are suddenly displaced due to a forced emigration (Leslie & Leitch, 1989). These circumstances increase their vulnerability to health-related and emotional dysfunctions.

As an illustration, Salvadorans bring to the United States severe problems resulting from the civil war trauma. In her study of Salvadorans residing in California, Vargas (1984) enumerates problems such as depression, explosive and antisocial behavior, domestic violence (wife battering and child abuse), and substance abuse.

In discussing Salvadorans' situation in the Washington D.C. area, Comas-Díaz (1987) found many Salvadorans to be suspicious of the system, partly due to the fear of being discovered and deported. They are also afraid of other Hispanics and Salvadorans as well, fearing that they may be spies of the Salvadoran government, which has the power to retaliate against relatives back in El Salvador. Consequently, those seeking help may not reveal personal information such as address and birthdate that could easily identify them. Many Salvadorans also have ''survivor's paranoia'' (Comas-Díaz, 1987). Severity of exposure to war is related to paranoiac ideation, anxiety, and depression in Salvadorans (Petuchowski, 1988). More specifically, psychologists should be careful about confronting Salvadorans who resist offering personal information. Similarly, the survivor's guilt, prevalent among individuals with traumatic war experiences, can be translated into an attitude toward life in which hopelessness and helplessness prevail.

Salvadoran children and adolescents face special problems. Many of these youngsters encounter Blacks for the first time in their life and racial tensions between Salvadoran and Black adolescents have occurred. For example, the financial constraints and the lack of resources that characterize Black and Salvadoran inner city populations of Washington, D.C., help to broaden the gap between these two ethnic groups (Comas-Díaz, 1987). Salvadoran parents tend to overprotect their offspring, transplanting the behaviors used in El Salvador to the United States. Within this context, the "other" is the enemy, and parents emphasize survival, regardless of means, as a priority. Anecdotal information reveals that these tensions have escalated to the emergence of racial/ethnic gangs, where violence has been reported between the two groups (Comas-Díaz, 1987).

The racial tension between Salvadoran and Black youngsters emerges partly due to their competition for limited resources. Linguistic and cultural differences, including Salvadoran youngsters' "paranoia," also impede the development of satisfactory racial relations. Consequently, interventions designed to improve racial relations among these groups need to be instituted.

In a study surveying Central Americans' demographic profile, Leslie & Leitch (1989) found that their utilization of community services was low, with the loss of job as the only event that would lead them to seek help. The researchers found that when help was sought, it was for concrete services (job, shelter, food). Although the investigators report that these issues are important, they also recommend that attention be focused on emotional, psychological and interpersonal needs.

Cultural Values

For Hispanics/Latinos, as with any ethnic group, cultural context is crucial for effective delivery of psychological services. Thus, understanding Hispanic cultural values, family dynamics, health beliefs and practices, as well as the process of acculturation, increases psychologists' effectiveness.

In the traditional extended Hispanic family, members beyond the nuclear unit are considered integral (Bernal & Gutierrez, 1988; Falicov, 1982; Garcia-Preto, 1982). The value of *familismo* (familism), extends kinship relationships beyond nuclear family boundaries. Familism emphasizes interdependence over independence, affiliation over confrontation, and cooperation over competition (Falicov, 1982).

Traditionally, the Hispanic family is patriarchal, with an authoritarian father and a submissive mother (Falicov, 1982). Males and females are taught two very different codes of sexual behavior. Whereas Hispanic women are traditionally expected to be sentimental, gentle, intuitive, impulsive, docile, submissive, and dependent, the men are expected to be rational, profound, strong, authoritarian, independent, and brave (Senour, 1977).

The superficial appearance of the power distribution between Hispanic males and females can be deceiving. In a study of sex roles among Hispanics in the United States, Canino (1982) found that on the surface, both husband and wife espoused traditional attitudes. However, when Puerto Rican couples were interviewed more extensively and were observed during actual decision making, most of them shared the decision-making process. Similarly, among Mexican American couples, sex role stereotyping as it affects the decision-making process is also deceiving. Falicov (1982) reports that while in some Mexican American families the husbands are domineering and patriarchal, others are submissive and depend upon their wives to make major decisions, while still other families have a more egalitarian power structure.

Traditional Hispanic sex roles are also undergoing change among Hispanics in the United States, where they are not reinforced by the mainstream American culture. Furthermore, cultural transition itself often encourages a sexual role reversal for many Hispanic men and women. Role reversal has occurred among many low-income Hispanic immigrants since it is often easier for the women to obtain employment in the United States by selling their sewing and domestic skills than it is for the men (Comas-Díaz, 1989).

Such role reversals potentially create marital and family problems. However, cultural transition tends to give individuals a certain plasticity, particularly within their gender roles. Despite the superficial rigidity of Hispanic sex roles, there is flexibility which allows for change. For example, Comas-Díaz (1989) reports that challenging traditional dysfunctional sex roles is easier to accomplish with couples who are coping with cultural differences than those who remain in a culturally homogeneous environment.

Another cultural value ingrained in the traditional Hispanic family is *respeto* (respect). This concept governs all positive reciprocal interpersonal relationships, dictating the appropriate deferential behavior toward others on the basis of age, socioeconomic position, sex, and authority status. By virtue of their therapeutic and healing functions, psychologists are perceived as authority figures and, as such, are awarded *respeto*.

Cultural fatalism, or the belief that some things are meant to happen regardless of the individual's intervention, is common among some Hispanics. Cultural fatalism reflects an external locus of control in which people perceive the events that happen to them to be the result of luck, fate, or powers beyond their control (rather than dependent on their own behavior) (Rotter, 1966). Some Hispanics with an external locus of control believe that mental illness is God's way of testing the individual. Cultural fatalism also relates to socioeconomic class and ethnic identity. Ross, Mirowsky, and Cockerham (1983) found that while persons of Mexican identity tended to have a fatalistic outlook on life, this fatalism was more pronounced among those individuals from a lower socioeconomic class.

Analogously, religion, like culture, can be a pervasive force influencing the behavior of Hispanics. Hispanics' adherence to traditional Catholic values, particularly the religious value placed on enduring human suffering and on self-denial, may prevent some Hispanics from seeking psychological treatment (Acosta, Yamomoto, & Evans, 1982). Within this context, churches tend to provide support and, at times, substitute for the extended family the immigrants left behind.

Despite their religious beliefs, some Hispanics believe in folk healing. These beliefs are consistent with the premise that they can make contact with God and the supernatural without the intervention of the traditional church (García-Preto, 1982). Similarly, Hispanics typically place a high value on spiritual matters.

Psychologists need to recognize that at times, (particularly during crisis), many Hispanics, regardless of their acculturation, may adhere to folk beliefs. Along these lines, Castro, Furth, and Karlow (1984) investigated whether less-acculturated Mexican women has a significantly different conceptual system of beliefs concerning health and illness than more acculturated Mexican and Anglo women. Their findings revealed that Mexican American women expressed mild acceptance of Mexican folk beliefs, a moderate acceptance of hot-cold folk beliefs and a strong acceptance of biomedical beliefs (e.g. that cardiovascular stress causes illness). The less-acculturated women reported a somewhat lower sense of responsibility and control over their own health, and a strong belief in hot-cold theory. According to the researchers, the findings suggest that Mexican-origin women have a dual system of belief which tends to weaken but not disappear with increasing acculturation. Likewise, some Hispanics will seek the services of folk healers while simultaneously receiving mainstream professional health and psychological care.

Acculturation

Acculturation is a central variable in the delivery of psychological services to Hispanics (Padilla, 1980). Acculturation encompasses a wide continuum, including assimilation, or the adjustment that Hispanics make to become more mainstream oriented (Padilla, 1980). Biculturalism postulates that mainstream culture is incorporated without losing Hispanic culture traits (Szapocznik & Kurtines, 1980). Acculturation is a fluid quality; thus bicultural individuals can be more Hispanic oriented in one context and more mainstream oriented in another context. Still, another acculturation model suggests that a new hybrid culture develops out of both the original and the host cultures (Moore & Pachon, 1985).

Some of the factors related to acculturation among Hispanics include: (a) Generational status (including years of residence in the United States, age at immigration); (b) language preference; (c) occupational and educational status; and (d) frequency of mobility to the original country. In an inpatient mental health program for Mexican Americans, Dolgin (1985) developed a simple and pragmatic way of assessing the patient's degree of acculturation. He suggested that clinicians ask the following questions: 1. What is your language preference? 2. What generation descent are you? 3. Would you rate yourself as being more Hispanic/Latino oriented or Anglo/Black (or other) oriented?

Mental Health and Health Status

The Hispanic culture does not differentiate between physical and emotional concerns (Padilla & Ruiz, 1973) the same way the majority culture does. For example, Hispanics generally believe that strong emotions may cause physical illness (Maduro, 1983). Therefore, they see mental state affecting physical condition and vice versa. Many Hispanic patients are steered to mental health services through the medical system. It has been stated that Mexican Americans seek out professional mental health services as a last resort, usually seeking out other health service providers initially (Keefe, Padilla, & Carlos, 1978).

Hispanics have been identified as a high risk group for mental health problems. Bernal and Gutierrez (1988), Martinez (1988) and Ramos-McKay, Comas-Díaz & Rivera (1988) report a high need for mental health services for the main three Hispanic groups in the United States, namely Cubans, Mexican Americans, and Puerto Ricans. The authors identify depression, anxiety, and substance abuse as major mental health problems.

The fact that many Hispanics are of low socioeconomic status seem to increase their vulnerability to mental health problems. Moreover, membership in an ethnic minority group may be considered a stressor in itself, thus, increasing Hispanics' vulnerability to mental health problems (Comas-Díaz, 1989). For instance, Ruiz (1975) identifies a sense of powerlessness and a loss of self esteem among members of minority groups in relation to their oppressive conditions, as well as with their reactions to culture shock. Moreover, (im)migration and the subsequent culture shock may engender anxiety and depression (Garza-Guerrero, 1974). This transitional experience usually is accompanied by feelings of irritability, anxiety, helplessness, and despair. It is believed that culture shock is accompanied by a process of mourning brought about by the individual's loss of family, friends, language, and culturally determined values and attitudes, leading to depression (Garza-Guerrero, 1974).

In a similar vein, depression has been identified as a major problem among Hispanics (Normand, Iglesias, & Payn, 1974). Partly due to their gender roles, Hispanic women, in particular, are vulnerable and hence, have been diagnosed as suffering from depression more than their male counterparts (Amaro, Pares-Avila & Campa, 1987; Moscicki, et al, 1989).

Alcoholism

Although no national data are available, alcoholism has been recognized as a major problem among the Hispanic population (Gomez, 1982). Similarly, the Report of the Secretary's Task Force on Black and Minority Health (1986) stated that there was an indication that Hispanics, particularly young males, suffer disproportionate health consequences as a result of their alcohol intake.

Studies quoted by the Task Force suggest that death rates from cirrhosis among Mexican Americans and Puerto Ricans may be higher than among the general population. The 1979 National Institute on Alcohol Abuse and Alcoholism National Survey indicated that based on self-reported data, Hispanic males ages 18 and older had higher levels of heavy drinking and higher rates of alcohol-related problems than non-minorities. Hispanic females reported being either abstainers or light drinkers.

A self-report study conducted in northern California found that drinking among Hispanics was positively associated with being young, single, separated or divorced (Caetano, 1984). For females, drinking was associated with higher income and education. For males, it was associated with being Catholic. When compared with the rest of the population in the sample, Hispanic males were found to be prone to drink more often and drink more on each occasion than the general population. Conversely, females tended to drink less than the general population and reported higher rates of abstention and lower rates of use when drinking.

As previously indicated, alcohol intake has been identified as a major health problem among Hispanics. Most of the findings are based on self-reported data, which have the disadvantage of not being validated by objective criteria. Moreover, cultural expectations may inhibit the acknowledgement of drinking. This may particularly be operative for some Hispanic females (Comas-Díaz, 1986), who may be prone to deny their actual alcohol intake. It is suggested that more research on drinking behavior among Hispanics be conducted, using methodology other than self-report measures.

Drug Abuse

There are no national data on drug abuse among Hispanics, except that inhalant abuse is a major problem (Delgado & Treviño, 1985). Inhalant abuse is a common problem among Hispanic youths. Padilla, Padilla & Morales (1979) found that the prevalence of inhalants among Mexican American children and adolescents in Los Angeles barrios was 14 times higher than that of the general population. The Hispanic population that resides in inner cities is at greater risk of drug abuse and its consequences. A study's finding suggests that Hispanics have higher rates of drug use than White non-Hispanics for marijuana, cocaine, heroin, and illicit methadone (Frank, 1983).

The Report of the Secretary's Task Force (1986) found that data from hospital emergency room cases and from drug abuse rehabilitation programs indicated that Hispanics were more likely than White non-Hispanics to report problems with heroin, cocaine, or PCP. During the period of 1982–84, the cocaine-related deaths among Hispanics tripled, while they doubled among White non-Hispanics. New York City medical examiner case reports (1976–1980) indicated an overrepresentation of Hispanics among narcotic addiction deaths (COSSMHO, 1988).

AIDS

Drug abuse among Hispanics leads to an even more serious problem. The AIDS epidemic in Hispanic communities is alarming. The number of Hispanics who have developed AIDS is disproportionate when compared with their numbers in the general population (Amaro, 1988). Although Hispanics constitute only 7.9 percent of the United States population, they account for 14 percent of all reported AIDS cases, nearly 20 percent of all cases among women, and 23 percent of all pediatric AIDS cases (COSSMHO, 1988). Intravenous (IV) drug use and unsafe sexual practices account for the disproportionate occurrence of AIDS in the Hispanic population (Nyamathi & Vasquez, 1989). Forty two percent of the male cases and over 80 percent of the female cases are IV related (Centers for Disease Control, 1989). Additionally, drug-related transmission is associated in 77 percent of Hispanic pediatric cases compared with 32 percent of cases among White children (Centers for Disease Control, 1989).

In California the number of AIDS cases among Hispanic/Latino women has been increasing more rapidly than among non-Hispanic females (California AIDS Update, 1988). Some subgroups of Hispanic women may be at higher risk than others. Amaro (1988) reports that the highest proportion of women with AIDS reside in New York, California, Florida, Puerto Rico, New Jersey, and Texas (Racial/ethnic breakdowns of AIDS cases, 1988). Given that the major Hispanic groups residing in these areas are Puerto Ricans, Dominicans, and Cubans, Amaro (1988) suggests that these Hispanic women may be at most risk.

In sum, Hispanics face a wide range of barriers to health care. The lack of medical insurance among Hispanics is a serious impediment (COSSMHO, 1988). A correlate of this problem is the pattern of seeking health care for acute conditions, or emergency situations, and not for preventive reasons. This behavior has implications for Hispanics' ability to follow up treatment and socioeconomic barriers may prevent clients from keeping health and mental health appointments, due to child care costs and the lack of transportation.

Psychological Interventions with Hispanics/Latinos

Many Hispanic communities experience socioeconomic, health and psychosocial problems. Consequently, Hispanics' psychological needs require a comprehensive approach. Issues such as health status, culturally relevant treatment, and the incorporation of reality and environmental issues require integration into the delivery of psychological services. Likewise, Cervantes and Castro (1985) have argued for the conceptualization of a stress-mediation-outcome framework while working with Hispanic patients. They see psychological disturbances as the result of an interaction between the person, the environment, and his or her resources (both internal and external) in confronting stressful life circumstances.

Prevention and Education

As suggested by the sociodemographic profile of many Hispanic individuals, prevention and education emerge as integral components in the delivery of psychological services to these communities. Problems such as AIDS, alcoholism and drug use need to be targeted for prevention and education. In order to be effective, however, preventive programs need to be both culturally and linguistically appropriate.

The model of community psychology can prove useful in working with Hispanic/Latino populations. For example, community psychology values of cultural pluralism or the right to be different, and the belief that many human problems are those of person-environment fit, rather than those of personal incompetence or inferior psychocultural contexts (Rappaport, 1977), are highly relevant for Hispanic communities. Within this perspective, a psychologist working with Hispanic populations collaborates with health providers, is familiar with Hispanic/Latino cultural values, and actively interacts with the formal and informal support networks. Support networks include, but are not limited to, extended family members, community, indigenous and religious leaders, neighborhood organizations, tenant groups, churches, and schools. Within this framework, it is important to use the *servidor* system within Hispanic communities. This social support network is composed of individuals residing in and/or delivering services to the Hispanic community (Escobar & Randolph, 1982).

Prevention activities require community-oriented efforts and should incorporate strategies for the development of appropriate educational materials for targeted groups. Analogously, in working with Central American immigrants, Leigh and Leitch (1989) recommend an active community outreach in order to inform this population of the availability of mental health and social services. Additionally, these authors recommend preventive education for emotional problems. Similarly, psychological interventions designed to improve racial relations between Hispanic adolescents (particularly Central Americans) and Black adolescents need to be instituted.

Mental health professionals need to be conversant with a physical health perspective because Hispanics do not tend to separate physical from emotional well being. Given that many Hispanics tend to somaticize emotional problems (García-Petro, 1982; Ramos McKay, et al., 1988), an integrated approach to physical and mental health can prove comprehensive and effective.

Similarly, Hispanics' complex treatment expectations are congruent with this approach. Hispanic patients presenting at a community mental health clinic expressed psychological complaints including depression, anxiety, concentration problems, obsessions and compulsions, fears, and sleep problems, in addition to physical and financial problems, (Comas-Díaz, Geller, Melgoaz, & Baker, 1982). These patients also show grounding in psychological precepts in that they accept unconscious feelings, ambivalence towards others, and desire a therapeutic relationship in which they can talk freely about themselves and their problems, thoughts and feelings.

Hispanic/Latino populations at high risk need to be specially targeted. Psychological interventions for Hispanic/Latino women at risk for depression and AIDS require familiarity with Hispanic gender roles and family values, in addition to an awareness of environmental and living conditions. Similarly, children and adolescents can be targeted for school desertion and drug abuse. Hispanic/Latino males need to be targeted for alcoholism and drug abuse. Central American refugees, particularly those exposed to war-related violence, need to be targeted for post traumatic stress disorder treatment.

The AIDS epidemic among Hispanic communities requires immediate attention. Because prevention and education programs appear to be one of the most effective strategies for saving lives, it is imperative that culturally-sensitive AIDS education programs incorporate a realistic approach to the survival needs of Hispanics. Education and prevention messages need to take into account cultural and family values that may have an impact on sexuality and drug use (Worth & Rodriquez, 1987). Nyamathi & Vasquez (1989) assert that educational sessions should emphasize the male role of protecting the family and the female role of taking care of the children. When condom use is culturally interpreted as protecting the family Hispanics may better accept the practice. High-risk Hispanic women, children, adolescents and men need to be targeted. Individual, couple, and family counseling can also be useful in coping with the emotional sequelae of AIDS. In studying Hispanic women at risk for AIDS, Nyamathi and Vasquez (1989) found that these women identified loss of control, low self-esteem, and helplessness as major emotional needs. These needs can be partly addressed in counseling and psychotherapeutic situations.

Psychotherapy

Regardless of patients' socioeconomic status, psychotherapy can ameliorate psychic pain and empower the individual. However, traditional psychotherapy needs to be embedded in a cultural context in order to be effective for many Hispanics. The sense of family is so central, that Canino and Canino (1982) have argued that mental illness among Hispanics is a family, rather than individual, affair and they recommend family involvement in mental health treatment.

A variety of treatment modalities has been used with Hispanics. Some clinicians use cultural values such as familism in family therapy (Canino & Canino, 1982) and gender roles in all-female (Hynes & Werbin, 1977) and in all-male (De La Cancela, 1986) group psychotherapy. Several treatment orientations have been successfully utilized including behavioral (Stumphauzer & Davis, 1983), cognitive and behavioral (Comas-Díaz, 1981), dynamically oriented (Olarte & Lenz, 1985), and feminist (Comas-Díaz, 1988) psychotherapies. There is no single method or approach that can be considered the best for treating Hispanics; some patients respond better to one approach/modality of treatment and some to another, depending on their presenting complaints (Comas-Díaz, 1989).

Regardless of the treatment approach/modality used with Hispanic patients, clinicians need to address the complex set of treatment expectations Hispanics have involving a multiplicity of psychological, physical, and environmental dimensions. For instance, Comas-Díaz (1989) recommends the application of behavioral approaches such as relaxation techniques and assertiveness training during the beginning phase of treatment, while maintaining a dynamic conceptualization of the therapeutic process.

Linguistic issues in psychotherapy are pivotal in the diagnosis and treatment of Hispanics (Marcos, Urcuyo, Kesselman, & Alpert, 1973). Language variables can also affect the process of psychotherapy (Rozensky & Gomez, 1983). Ideally, a bilingual psychologist can better address psycholinguistic issues such as language switching and the usage of words that do not have a literal translation in English or Spanish. However, given the limited number of bilingual mental health professionals, many psychologists have no other choice but to use trained interpreters with monolingual or English-limited patients.

Along these lines, Acosta and Cristo (1981) describe the development and successful implementation of a bilingual interpreter program in which interpreters are specially trained in advanced development of bilingual proficiency, interpreting style, and in the usage of mental health terminology. The interpreters participate in ongoing training involving supervisory and peer feedback, role playing, and viewing of audio and video tapes of actual therapist/patient interactions. They also work as community aides. Bilingual/bicultural professional staff coordinate the program and act as supervisors. The authors contend that their model has significantly increased the utilization of clinics by Hispanic patients.

Ethnic identity constitutes a major issue among Hispanic psychotherapy patients (Gomez et. al, 1982). In their work with ethnoculturally translocated individuals, members of ethnic minority groups, and patients in cross-cultural psychotherapy, Comas-Díaz and Jacobson (1987) introduce the ethnocultural identification process. They argue that these patients frequently experience disturbances of their ethnocultural identities, resulting in their attributing ethnocultural qualities to their therapists during therapy. Ethnocultural identification may be used to foster a therapeutic identification in which the therapist reflects pieces of the patient's conflicted ethnocultural identity. The authors state that ethnocultural identification can be utilized as an auxiliary therapeutic tool to facilitate coping with changing cultural values and transitional experiences, and to promote the integration of the ethnocultural self into a consolidated sense of identity.

Training and Practice Implications

The professional psychologist working in Hispanic/Latino communities needs to adhere to a comprehensive perspective encompassing health, mental health and socioeconomic issues. Both health psychology and community psychology orientations seem to suit the special needs of these populations, with special attention to education and prevention activities.

The professional psychologist also needs to be sensitive to Hispanic/Latino cultural values and familiar with cross-cultural psychotherapy skills. Traditional psychotherapeutic skills are extremely useful, particularly if psychologists are empathic with their patients' diverse realities. Along these lines, self knowledge with respect to feelings and countertransferential reactions that Hispanic patients tend to conjure in psychologists is extremely important. In order to achieve this, psychologists may need to use clinical consultation as needed when working with these patients.

Summary and Conclusions

The Hispanic/Latino communities constitute diverse groups with distinct historical, economical, political and racial backgrounds. Many Hispanics are plagued by sociocultural, physical and mental health problems. Some of the physical and mental health problems include AIDS, alcoholism, drug abuse, depression and anxiety. A health psychology orientation in addition to a community psychology paradigm seem to best fit the Hispanic/Latino communities' multiple needs. Special emphasis should be given to prevention and education efforts that are culturally and linguistically relevant for the populations at risk.

Psychotherapy can be effective in addressing emotional and psychological needs, in addition to decreasing psychic pain and empowering individuals, couples, families and groups. Many treatment orientations and modalities have been successfully used. These include behavior, cognitive, psychodynamic, and feminist approaches within individual, family, group, and couple treatment formats. However, in order to be effective, psychologists need to understand traditional and changing Hispanic cultural values including sex roles, religious and folk beliefs, as well as the process of acculturation. Linguistic considerations and issues relating to ethnic identity also require special emphasis while working with this population. In sum, a comprehensive perspective encompassing physical, emotional, sociocultural, environmental and contextual variables is highly recommended in the delivery of psychological services to Hispanic/Latino communities.

References

Acosta, F. X., & Cristo, M. H. (1981). Development of a bilingual interpreter program: An alternative model for Spanish-speaking services. *Professional Psychology, 12* (4), 474–481.

Acosta, F. X., Yamamoto, J., & Evans, L. A. (1982). *Effective psychotherapy for low income and minority patients.* New York: Plenum Press.

Amaro, H. (1988). Considerations for prevention of HIV infection among Hispanic women. *Psychology of Women Quarterly, 12,* 429–443.

Amaro, H., Pares-Avila, J. & Campa, R. (1987, October). *Risk factors with depression: Preliminary findings on Mexican and Puerto Ricans from the Hispanic HANES.* Presentation made at the 115th Annual Meeting of the American Public Health Association. New Orleans, Louisiana.

Bernal, G. & Gutierrez, M. (1988). Cubans. In L. Comas-Díaz & E. E. H. Griffin (Eds.). *Clinical guidelines in cross-cultural mental health.* New York: John Wiley and Sons.

Bureau of the Census, U.S. Department of Commerce (1985). *Persons of Spanish origin in the United States: March 1985 Current Population Reports* (Series P-20, No. 403). Washington, DC: U.S. Government Printing Office.

Caetano, R. (1984). Hispanic drinking practices in northern California. *Hispanic Journal of Behavioral Sciences, 6* (4), 345–364.

California AIDS Update (1988). *AIDS among Hispanics in California*, pp. 9–10.

Canino, G. (1982). Transactional family patterns: A preliminary exploration of Puerto Rican female adolescents. In R. E. Zambrana (Ed.) *Work, family, and health: Latina women in transition* (pp. 27–36). New York: Hispanic Research Center. Fordham University.

Canino, G., & Canino, I. A. (1982). Culturally syntonic family therapy for migrant Puerto Ricans. *Hospital and Community Psychiatry, 33* (4), 299–303.

Castro, F. G., Furth, P., & Karlow, H. (1984). The health beliefs of Mexican, Mexican American and Anglo American Women. *Hispanic Journal of Behavioral Sciences, 6* (4), 365–383.

Centers for Disease Control (1989, March). *HIV/AIDS Surveillance,* Atlanta.

Cervantes, R. C. & Castro, F. G. (1985). Stress, coping and Mexican American health: A systematic review. *Hispanic Journal of Behavioral Sciences, 7,* 1–73.

Cervantes, R. C., Salgado de Snyder, V. N. & Padilla, A. M. (1989). Post traumatic stress disorder among immigrants from Central America and Mexico. *Hospital and Community Psychiatry, 40,* 615–619.

Comas-Díaz, L. (1981). Effects of cognitive and behavioral group treatment in the depressive symptomatology of Puerto Rican women. *Journal of Consulting and Clinical Psychology, 49* (5), 627–632.

Comas-Díaz, L. (1986). Puerto Rican alcoholic women: Treatment considerations. *Alcoholism Treatment Quarterly, 3* (1), 47–57.

Comas-Díaz, L. (1987, March). Salvadoran adolescents' adjustment to the United States: Implications for race relations. *Race relations and adolescents: Coping with new realities. Hearing before the Select Committee on Children, Youth, and Families, House of Representatives. (pp. 75–81). Washington, DC: U.S. Government Printing Office. (Obtained from the Superintendent of Documents, Congressional Sales Office, U.S. Government Printing Office, Washington, DC 20402).*

Comas-Díaz, L. (1988). Feminist therapy with Hispanic/Latino women: Myth or reality? *Women and Therapy, 6* (4), 39–61.

Comas-Díaz, L. (1989). Culturally relevant issues and treatment implications for Hispanics. In Diane R. Koslow and E. Salett, (Eds.) *Crossing cultures in mental health.* Washington, DC: Society for International Education Training and Research (SIETAR).

Comas-Díaz, L., Geller, J. D., Melgoza, B., & Baker, R. (1982, August). *Attitudes and expectations about mental health services among Hispanics and Afro-Americans.* Paper presented at the 90th Annual American Psychological Association, Washington, DC.

Comas-Díaz, L., & Jacobsen, F. M. (1987). Ethnocultural identification in psychotherapy. *Psychiatry, 50* (3), 232–241.

COSSMHO. (1988). *Delivering preventive health care to Hispanics: A manual for providers.* Washington, DC: National Coalition of Hispanic Health and Human Services Organizations (COSSMHO).

De La Cancela, V. (1986). A critical analysis of Puerto Rican machismo: Implications for clinical practice. *Psychotherapy, 2* (2), 291–296.

Delgado, J. L. & Treviño, F. M. (1985). The state of Hispanic health in the United States. In M. G. Obledo (Ed.), *The state of Hispanic America:* Vol, V, (pp. 35–47). Oakland, California. The National Hispanic Center for Advanced Studies and Policy Analysis and the National Hispanic University.

Dolgin, D. (1982). *The Hispanic treatment manual.* Unpublished manuscript. Boulder, Colorado: Colorado State Hospital.

Escobar, J. & Randolph, E. (1982). The Hispanic and social networks. In R. Becerra, M. Karno, & J. Escobar (Eds.). *Mental health and Hispanic Americans* (pp. 41–51). New York: Grune & Stratton.

Falicov, C. J. (1982). Mexican families. In M. McGoldrick, J. K. Pearce, & J. Giordano (Eds.). *Ethnicity and family therapy* (pp. 134–163). New York: The Guilford Press.

Frank, B. (1983, June). *Drug use among tenants of single room occupancy (SRO) hotels in New York.* NY: New York State Division of Substance Abuse.

García-Preto, N. (1982). Puerto Rican families. In M. McGoldrick, J. K. Pearce, & J. Giordano (Eds.). *Ethnicity and family therapy (pp. 164–186). New York: The Guilford Press.*

Garza-Guerrero, A. C. (1974). Culture shock: Its mourning and vicissitudes of identity. *Journal of the American Psychoanalytic Association, 22,* 408–429.

Gomez, A. G. (1982). Puerto Rican Americans. In A. Gaw (Ed.). *Cross cultural psychiatry.* Boston: John Wright.

Gomez, E. A., Ruiz, P., & Laval, R. (1982). Psychotherapy and bilingualism: Is acculturation important? *Journal of Operational Psychiatry 13* (1), 13–16.

Hispanics: Challenges and opportunities (1984, June). New York: Ford Foundation. (available from the Ford Foundation, Office of Reports, 320 East 43rd St., New York, N.Y. 10017).

Hynes, K., & Werbin, J. (1977). Group psychotherapy for Spanish-speaking women. *Psychiatric Annals, 7* (12), 52–63.

Keefe, S. W., Padilla, A. M., & Carlos, M. L. (1978). *Emotional support system in two cultures: A comparison of Mexican Americans and Anglo Americans* (Occasional Paper No. 7). Los Angeles: University of California, Spanish Speaking Mental Health Research Center.

Leslie, L. A. & Leitch, M. L. (1989). A demographic profile of recent Central American immigrants: Clinical and service implications. *Hispanic Journal of Behavioral Science, 11* (4), 315–329.

Maduro, R. (1983). Curanderismo and Latino views of disease and curing. *The Western Journal of Medicine, 139* (6), 868–874.

Marcos, L. R., Urcuyo, L., Kesselman, M. & Alpert, M. (1973). The language barrier in evaluating Spanish American patients. *Archives of General Psychiatry, 29,* 655–659.

Martinez, C. (1988). Mexican Americans. In L. Comas-Díaz & E. H. Griffith (Eds.). *Clinical guidelines in cross cultural mental health.* New York: John Wiley & Sons.

Moore, J. & Pachon, H. (1985). *Hispanics in the United States.* Englewood Cliffs, N.J.: Prentice-Hall.

Moscicki, E. K., Locke, B. Z., Rae, D. S., & Boyd, J. H. (1989). Depressive symptoms among Mexicans: The Hispanic Health and Nutrition Examination Survey. *American Journal of Epidemiology, 130* (2), 348–360.

Normand, W., Iglesias, J. & Payn, S. (1974). Brief group therapy to facilitate utilization of mental health services by Spanish-speaking patients. *American Journal of Orthopsychiatry, 44* (1), 37–49.

Nyamathi, A. & Vasquez, R. (1989). Impact of poverty, homelessness and drugs on Hispanic women at risk for HIV infection. *Hispanic Journal of Behavioral Sciences, 11* (4), 299–314.

Olarte, S. W., & Lenz, R. (1984). Learning to do psychoanalytic therapy with inner city population. *Journal of the American Academy of Psychoanalysis, 12* (1), 89–99.

Padilla, A. M. (Ed.). (1980). *Acculturation: Theory, models and some new findings.* Boulder, CO.: Westview Press.

Padilla, E. R., Padilla, A. M. & Morales, A. (1979). Inhalant, marijuana, and alcohol abuse among barrio children and adolescents. *International Journal of Addictions, 14, 945–964.*

Padilla, A. M. & Ruiz, R. (1973). *Latino mental health: A review of literature.* Rockville, MD: National Institute of Mental Health.

Petuchowski, S. R. (1988). *Psychosocial adjustment problems of war refugees from El Salvador.* Unpublished doctoral dissertation. University of Maryland. College Park, MD.

Racial/ethnic breakdowns of AIDS cases by state (1988). *COSSMHO AIDS Update. 2,* (p. 3). Washington, DC: National Coalition of Hispanic Health and Human Services Organizations (COSSMHO).

Ramos-McKay, J., Comas-Díaz, L, & Rivera, L. (1988). Puerto Ricans. In L. Comas-Díaz & E. H. Griffith (Eds.) *Clinical guidelines in cross cultural mental health.* New York: John Wiley & Sons.

Rappaport, J. (1977). Community psychology: Values, research and action. New York: Holt, Rinehart & Winston.

Report of the Secretary's Task Force on Black and Minority Health (1986). *Hispanic health issues. Volume VIII.* Washington, DC: U.S. Government Printing Office.

Ross, C. E., Mirowsky, J. & Cockerham, W. C. (1983). Social class, Mexican culture, and fatalism: Their effects on psychological distress. *American Journal of Community Psychology, 11,* 383–399.

Rotter, J. B. (1966). Generalized expectancies for internal versus external control of reinforcement. *Psychological Monographs, 80* (1, Whole No. 609).

Rozensky, R. H. & Gomez, M. Y. (1983). Language switching in psychotherapy with bilinguals: Two problems, two models, and case examples. *Psychotherapy: Theory, Research and Practice, 2* (2), 152–160.

Ruiz, P. (1975). Symposium: Group therapy with minority group patients. *International Journal of Group Psychotherapy, 24* (4), 392–398.

Senour, M. N. (1977). Psychology of the Chicana. In J. L. Martinez (Ed.) *Chicano psychology* (pp. 329–342) New York: Academic Press.

Stumphauzer, J. S., & Davis, L. C. (1983). Training Mexican American mental health personnel in behavior therapy. *Journal of Behavior Therapy and Experimental Psychiatry, 14* (3), 215–217.

Szapocznik, J. & Kurtines, W. (1980). Acculturation, biculturalism and adjustment among Cuban Americans. In A. Padilla (Ed.). *Acculturation.* Boulder, CO: Westview Press.

Vargas, G. (1984, Autumn). Recently arrived Central American immigrants: Mental health needs. *Research Bulletin* (pp. 1–3). Los Angeles: Spanish-Speaking Mental Health Research Center.

Ventura, S. J. (1987). Births of Hispanic parentage, 1983 and 1984. *Monthly Vital Statistics Report, 36* (4), (Supplement, PHS 87 1120). Hyattsville, MD: Public Health Service. National Center for Health Statistics.

Villaescusa, H. (1984). *Hispanic history and demographics: Dialogue of health concerns for Hispanics,* 1–6. Bethesda, MD: U.S. Department of Health and Human Services, National Institutes of Health.

Villareal, S. F. (1986). Current issues in Hispanic health. In *Report of the Secretary's Task Force on Black and Minority Health, Vol. VII: Hispanic Health Issues,* 11–42. Bethesda, MD: U.S. Department of Health and Human Services, National Institutes of Health.

Worth, D. & Rodriguez, R. (1987, January-February). *Latino Women and AIDS.* SIECUS Report, 5–7.

14

What Do Culturally Sensitive Mental Health Services Mean? The Case of Hispanics

Lloyd H. Rogler, Robert G. Malgady,
Guiseppe Costantino, and Rena Blumenthal

Two events converged in the decade of the 1960s to focus attention on the need for culturally sensitive mental health services for economically disadvantaged minority populations. First was the rise of the civil rights movement, when Blacks and other minority groups insisted that the institutional structure of American society be more responsive to their needs and less exclusionary of their participation as citizens in a pluralistic democracy. Second was the nationwide development of community mental health programs. As these programs expanded to cover new, economically disadvantaged catchment areas with populations that had never before received professional mental health care, many of the deficiencies of traditional service systems and therapies became evident. Traditional therapies, based largely on the therapeutic needs of middle-class clients, often proved to be of questionable effectiveness with minority persons living in inner-city neighborhoods, thus prompting pleas for culturally sensitive modalities.

Culturally sensitive mental health services are especially important for Hispanics, because they are the most rapidly growing minority population in the United States; according to census figures, the Hispanic population was 14.6 million in 1980, and it has had a 6.1 percent annual growth rate since 1970. Moreover, demographic studies of the Hispanic population indicate that Hispanics are younger, less educated, poorer, and more likely to live in inner-city neighborhoods than the general population and that they confront language problems. This constellation of characteristics

Rogler, L. H., Malgady, R. G., Costantino, G., & Blumenthal, R. (1987). What do culturally sensitive mental health services mean? *American Psychologist, 24,* 565–570. Copyright 1987 by the American Psychological Association. Reprinted by permission.

makes Hispanics vulnerable to mental health problems requiring psychotherapeutic services.

The past two decades have witnessed an explosive growth in the literature focusing on Hispanic mental health. This literature is pervasively critical, documenting the multiple barriers that, in the face of massive need, keep Hispanics from receiving adequate mental health care (Rogler et al., 1983). At the core of the literature's criticism is the charge, once again, that mental health services targeted for Hispanics are not culturally sensitive. Thus, the question arises: What do culturally sensitive mental health services mean? To answer this question, we examined the use of the concept by mental health practitioners and researches in their work with Hispanics. In doing so, we uncover three broad approaches to cultural sensitivity: first, rendering traditional treatments more accessible to Hispanics; second, selecting an available therapeutic modality according to the perceived features of Hispanic culture; and third, extracting elements from Hispanic culture and using them to modify traditional treatments or as an innovative treatment tool. The first purpose of this article is to describe the components of cultural sensitivity within each of the three approaches mentioned above. The second purpose is to examine the relationship between culture and therapy in the literature on Hispanics by posing a fundamental question: Must the content of all culturally sensitive therapies stand in an isomorphic, mirror-like relationship to the client's culture? Inferences drawn from the literature and our own research justify raising this question.

Increased Accessibility of Treatment

The first and most basic approach to culturally sensitive mental health care involves increasing the accessibility of traditional treatments of Hispanic clients. This issue can be understood in the context of Freidson's (1970) argument that two characteristics of a cultural subpopulation are likely to influence the utilization of the professional medical system. The first involves the level of congruence between the client's and the professional's understanding of illness and treatment—the greater the level of accord, the more likely it is that the client will seek out and retain professional services. The second characteristic involves the ethnic group's lay referral system, which ranges from a loose/truncated system, allowing the individual great leeway in personal health decisions, to a cohesive/extended system, pressing the individual to act according to the values of the cultural milieu. The least utilization of health services occurs in communities that have a marked incongruence between cultural and professional values combined with a cohesive/extended lay referral structure. Such a lay referral system is likely to inhibit the use of professional services and to provide alternative routes to coping with health needs in a culturally congruent way.

Research suggests that many Hispanics fit into this categorization (Rogler et al., 1983). Thus, an accessible treatment program for Hispanics should increase the congruence between professional mental health values and indigenous Hispanic values and also incorporate elements of the lay referral system to forward its own purpose.

A variety of attempts have been made in recent years to develop more accessible treatment programs for Hispanics in diverse mental health settings. Karno and Morales (1971), for example, described the creation of a mental health clinic specially modified to the perceived needs of Hispanics. Preventive services, consultation with other community agencies, and crisis intervention were incorporated into the program along with traditional services. Although they did not provide evidence, Karno and Morales (1971) stated that "in a context of cultural and linguistic familiarity and acceptance" Mexican Americans respond just as well to traditional treatment as Anglos. Scott and Delgado (1979) discussed the issues arising during the development of a mental health program for Hispanics within a community clinic. They believed that the program became effective after the recruitment of a bilingual/bicultural staff, integration of the program into the structure of the host facility, and coordination of the program's effort with the needs of the Hispanic community. Abad, Ramos, and Boyce (1974), describing their experience in establishing a mental health clinic in a community mental health center in New Haven, emphasized the need to gain the support of local religious and political leaders prior to commencing the effort. To succeed, the clinic had to maintain a credible presence in the institutional structures affecting the Puerto Ricans' lives. Similar programs were described by Cuellar, Harris, and Naron (1981) within an inpatient institutional setting and by Normand, Iglesias, and Payn (1974) and Rodriguez (1971) on a small-group basis within large hospital settings.

The lowest common denominator of cultural sensitivity with Hispanics is generally that of linguistic accessibility. Indeed, for many treatment innovators, the primary efforts have been focused on the hiring of bilingual/bicultural staff, thus overcoming the most blatant communication barriers that exist between clients and staff. The importance of even such

This research was supported by Grant 2R01 MH30569-06A from the Center for Minority Group Mental Health Programs (National Institute of Mental Health) to L. H. Rogler, Director of the Hispanic Research Center, Fordham University, and also by Grant 1R01 MH33711 from the Center for Minority Group Mental Health Programs to G. Costantino. Research Associate of the Hispanic Research Center. We wish to thank Janet Cohen and Stasia Madrigal for their editorial assistance.

Correspondence concerning this article should be addressed to Lloyd H. Rogler, Hispanic Research Center, Thebaud Hall, Fordham University, Bronx, NY 10458.

minimal outreach efforts is dramatized by the innovative use of paraprofessionals by Acosta and Cristo (1981). Assuming that Hispanics' needs for mental health services would likely continue to exceed the availability of Hispanic therapists, they developed a bilingual interpreter program in a psychiatric clinic. The interpreters were recruited from the same neighborhoods as the clients and were trained in key concepts of psychotherapy and the nomenclature used in clinical settings. They also acted as cultural consultants, explaining to English-speaking therapists the meanings conveyed by patients during therapy. In spite of the awkwardness inherent in introducing a third party into a therapeutic relationship, the success of this program in increasing accessibility of services seems to justify the approach: The percentage of Spanish-speaking patients admitted to the clinic doubled with such efforts. Indeed, there is additional evidence, both longitudinal and cross-sectional, that such innovations do increase utilization rates in Hispanic communities (Bloom, 1975; Trevino, Bruhn & Bunce, 1979).

By reaching out to the ethnic network in the community, the professional system has found that it can attract Hispanics to use and retain its services, advance professional conceptions of mental health, and partially bypass alternative coping patterns indigenous to Hispanic culture. At the same time, by incorporating members of the ethnic network into the professional system, key elements of the lay culture are assimilated. All such forms of increasing accessibility therefore represent the first approach to providing culturally sensitive mental health services.

Selection of Treatments to Fit Hispanic Culture

In addition to treatment accessibility, another area of concern calling for cultural sensitivity has been the treatment Hispanics receive once they enter the mental health system. Without such a concern, the incongruous, but nevertheless conceivable, situation could occur of Hispanics having greater access to culturally inappropriate therapeutic modalities. The possibility of this occurring was noted in the development of a mental health clinic for Puerto Ricans in New Haven (Abad et al., 1974, p. 590). Thus the second approach to cultural sensitivity is the selection of a therapy modality to coincide with perceived Hispanic cultural characteristics.

Some researchers and therapists have argued that treatment decisions ought not to preclude the use of psychoanalytic concepts and techniques with ethnic minority clients. Maduro and Martinez (1974) claimed that "more self-aware individuals are needed to confront insidious social realities in the outer world, as well as unconscious themes in the inner world" (p. 461). They believed that Jungian dream work is congruent with Mexican culture, in that folk healers often specialize in the interpretation of dreams, and that such traditional analytic treatments are accessible and appropriate to their Hispanic clientele. Nonetheless, the attitudes of Maduro and Martinez represent a minority opinion. Frontline mental health practitioners working in inner-city, economically depressed, Hispanic neighborhoods were among the first to level criticism at insight-oriented psychoanalytic therapy as both uneconomical and irrelevant to the context of Hispanic life (Ruiz, 1981; Sue & Sue, 1977). Their widely shared image of the psychologically distressed Hispanic was of a person pressured and harassed by problems of poverty, slum life, and lack of acculturation into American society. The image of such a client taking his or her place on the proverbial psychoanalytic couch for a long-term therapy designed to nurture insight into repressed impulses caricatured psychoanalysis as an absurdly inconsequential modality. For this reason, few psychoanalytic therapists sought to address Hispanic's emotional problems, and a pervasive view developed that insight-oriented techniques were too esoteric to respond to the massive stresses impinging on the majority of Hispanic clients.

Bluestone and Vela's (1982) work stands as an exception to this pattern of neglect, for they proposed that a series of culturally informed adjustments can be made in the use of insight-oriented therapy with Puerto Ricans living at the bottom of the socioeconomic heap. Notwithstanding such adjustments, they recognized that suitable candidates for insight-oriented intervention must be relatively free from external chaos, display a persistent motivation to remain in therapy, have a long-term outlook on life, and possess a capacity for insight. The issue remains, however, that even with a liberal interpretation of these qualifications, traditional insight therapy would be an inappropriate modality for most members of economically disadvantaged, inner-city Hispanic communities. Ruiz (1981) made this point rather bluntly, speaking in reference to treatment of inner-city Hispanic clients: "Do they need brilliant insights into the etiology of . . . paranoia? Do they need to become more introspective or psychodynamically oriented? The answers to these questions are negative" (p. 202).

As an alternative to insight-oriented therapies, others have suggested individualized treatment selection: Culturally sensitive therapy must accord with the needs of the individual client. However, in broadly discussing cultural traits, one can easily fall into the trap of disregarding the substantial differences between Hispanic subcultures (Gurak & Rogler, 1980) and individual differences within specific groups. In this context the work of Ruiz (1981) is a valuable contribution to clarification of the concept of cultural sensitivity. Ruiz acknowledged the diversity of subcultures that fall under the catch-all phrase "Hispanic" and the difficulty of identifying as a Hispanic a person who is bicultural or sufficiently assimilated to be considered Anglo. Clearly, treatment decisions cannot be based on a simplistic criterion such as a Spanish surname. Ruiz believed that culturally sensitive treatment plans should be based on the objective assessment of the degree of biculturalism that the individual client manifests, and he provided rich examples of integrated treatment plans that may span the continuum from the "most Hispanic" to the "most Anglo" client. Prior to selection of a therapy modality for a given client, the therapist conducts an assessment of the client's linguistic skills in English and Spanish (both dominance and preference) and of the client's general level of acculturation.

Ruiz illustrated his point by describing the disposition of a case classified at the "most Hispanic" extreme—a non-English-speaking, unacculturated Mexican living in an impoverished, inner-city, Hispanic community. The initial assessment included a detailed medical history in Spanish (involving family members) and a physical examination to rule out organic etiology. Next, Ruiz focused of the hierarchy of the client's need, first stressing the immediacy of counseling aimed at the basic problems—such as health, housing, immigration status, and economic survival—that confronted the client on a daily basis. Based on the client's social immersion within a complex extended-family network (as is common within Mexican American communities), a family-oriented therapy with the goal of stress reduction was administered by a Spanish-speaking and bicultural therapist. Ruiz insightfully argued that disposition to treatment by psychodynamic or even behavior modification techniques was premature.

Acculturation refers to the complex process whereby the behaviors and attitudes of the migrant change toward the dominant group as a result of exposure to a cultural system that is significantly different. A variety of acculturation measures have been published recently for diverse Hispanic subcultures, including Mexican Americans (Cuellar, Harris, & Jasso, 1980), Cubans (Szapocznik, Scopetta, & King, 1978), and Puerto Ricans (Inclan, 1979). Following such assessments, the therapist is able to make a more judicious decision about the particular treatment to be given.

However, acculturation signifies a process of change with multiple components. Some components change more rapidly than others, as shown by the Rogler and Cooney (1984, pp. 71–98) study of intergenerationally linked Puerto Rican families. This means that treatment decisions based on the client's level of acculturation still confront some ambiguity. From one moment to the next, the therapist with a transcultural orientation may need to address issues pertaining to the client's traditional culture, the culture of the host society, or some emergent product of both cultures. Nevertheless, the point to be stressed is that individualizing the treatment process is the primary and preferred mode of dealing with the problem.

Thus, the second approach to the delivery of culturally sensitive mental health services involves distinguishing between those acculturated Hispanics who can be treated as if they were Anglos and those who require some sort of special treatment modality reflecting their adherence to

Hispanic culture. It is the treatment of this latter population that leads to the third approach to culturally sensitive treatment.

Modifying Treatments to Fit Hispanic Culture

If the therapy is selected to fit the client, aspects of the therapy can also be adapted to fit the client's culture. A clear example of using an element from the client's ethnic culture to complement and modify the provision of conventional therapy is given in Kreisman's (1975) account of treating two Mexican American female schizophrenics who thought of themselves as *embrujadas* (bewitched). The essence of Kreisman's treatment modification was merely to concur that they were indeed bewitched. The therapist's acknowledgment of bewitchment and of the need for folk remedies broke through the plateau that had been reached in conventional therapy, thus enabling further therapeutic progress. In this context, elements of the client's culture were incorporated into the treatment without abandoning or compromising the therapist's chosen modality.

A somewhat different example of using an element of the client's culture is provided by the language-switching techniques employed by Pitta, Marcos, and Alpert (1978), who postulated that emotional expression is freer and more spontaneous in one's native tongue, whereas the use of a second language fosters intellectual defenses and control. The language in which therapy is conducted is chosen according to both patient characteristics and phase of treatment, and language-switching is used as a therapeutic technique. The medium into which this technique is incorporated is a traditional, insight-oriented psychotherapy that is in no other way modified for the needs of the ethnic client. Again, neither the conception of therapy nor the therapeutic role is altered, but an ethnic characteristic of the client is introduced to buttress the treatment modality.

One of the most ambitious programmatic efforts made to adapt treatment modalities to the perceived traits of a Hispanic population is that of Szapocznik and his collaborators (Szapocznik et al., 1979). They developed objective measures of Cuban value orientations and acculturation that are used to guide therapeutic intervention. According to their theory of intrafamily tension and stress, the greater the disparity in acculturation between family members, the greater the family tensions and stresses. Szapocznik et al. (1978) maintained that the treatment of the acculturation problems of Cuban families should stand in an isomorphic, mirror-like relationship to the clients' cultural background: ''Cubans' value structure must be matched by a similar set of therapeutic assumptions'' (p. 116). The selection of family therapy as the treament was predicated on the notion that Cubans are family oriented. Having determined through their research that the Cuban value system prizes lineality, Szapocznik et al. had the family therapist assume a position of authority to restore or reinforce parental authority over the children. Szapocznik and his colleagues outlined a detailed sequence of therapeutic interventions deduced from their findings on the cultural characteristics of Cuban clients and implemented in compliance with the assumption that therapeutic content should mirror the culture.

More recently, Szapocznik, Kurtines, and Fernandez (1980) recognized that other treatment modifications with Hispanic clients need not follow a rigid isomorphic pattern with respect to the culture. Sometimes the objective of treatment is to change culturally prescribed behavior. For example, Boulette (1976) observed the ubiquity of the "subassertiveness" pattern common among Mexican American women. This pattern, judged to be psychologically dysfunctional, became the target for a therapeutic program to train Mexican American women to be more assertive. The ultimate purpose was for the women to overcome the somatic complaints and symptoms of depression and anxiety thought to result from culturally prescribed submissiveness. Other Hispanic groups have similar cultural patterns (Rogler & Hollingshead, 1985). Boulette's therapeutic approach raises important issues when placed in the context of the lives of persons who are rooted in first-generation, traditional ethnic culture and who are at the bottom rung of the socioeconomic ladder. In such a context, Hispanics pervasively experience gender-based role segregation (Rogler & Cooney, 1984), pp. 99–124). Among spouses, there is a sharp distinction between *trabajo de hombre* (men's work) and *trabajo de mujer* (women's work) as well as sex-based differences in leisure patterns and inequities in power tending to favor the husbands. How does the development of assertiveness interact with such role segregation? Will the women's assertiveness clash with the culturally prescribed submissiveness imbedded in role segregation? The questions can be raised, but the research required to answer them is not available.

Nonetheless, contrasted with earlier accounts prescribing that therapeutic activities and structure should mirror Hispanic culture, Boulette's antithetical view raises intriguing questions. Once the cultural characteristics of a minority ethnic group have been adequately documented, how should the characteristics be taken into account during treatment? Is effective therapy necessarily that which attempts the preservation of traditional cultural elements, or should acculturation, assimilation, or adaptation to the host society sometimes take priority? Perhaps advocacy on behalf of preserving traditional cultural elements, no matter how well intentioned, ought not always or exclusively shape the nature of therapeutic interventions. On the other hand, the values of the host society similarly should not be idealized as reflecting universal standards of mental health.

It is our contention that when therapy modalities are modified to address the needs of Hispanic clients, the adapted therapy need not isomorphically reflect the client's cultural characteristics. We suggest that therapeutic gains can be made when traditional cultural patterns are bent or redirected according to predetermined therapeutic goals. Thus, the first step in the process of treatment modification is to determine the ethnic group's traits of likely therapeutic relevance and then employ them directly or transform them as needed. Isomorphic reinforcement of cultural traits implies that they are necessarily adaptive, whereas, on the other hand, departures from this assumption imply that some cultural traits serve as an obstacle to therapy and that acculturation to the values of the host society is an additional and valid standard of adjustment. It also assumes that cultural elements can be modified within the treatment according to the implicit goals of the therapy without impugning their value and purpose as functional cultural traits in the immigrant's society of origin. The modifications imply the development of hypotheses reflecting the intricacies of the many possible connections between various cultural traits and the therapies administered. The ultimate aim should be relief from psychological distress and the adaptation of the Hispanic client to the new host society in such a way that ethnic identity and pride are not negated or belied.

Developing a Culturally Sensitive Modality With Children

A third approach to cultural sensitivity, modification of treatment, also is in evidence when specific elements from the client's culture are used as the vehicle for therapeutic intervention. *Cuento* or folktale therapy, a recent innovation (Costantino, Malgady, & Rogler, 1986), provides an illustration. Cuento therapy is a modeling technique based on the principles of social learning theory, but it takes as its medium the folktales of Puerto Rican culture and focuses them on psychologically distressed Puerto Rican children.

Although much of the aforementioned literature has dealt with the mental health of Hispanic adults, little attention has been directed to second-generation Hispanic children who, trapped between two cultures, are at high risk of mental disorder. For this reason, we attempted the development of cuento therapy. The therapy was administered by bilingual/bicultural therapists in a mental health clinic with a catchment area that is predominantly Puerto Rican. The objective in telling folktales to the children was to transmit cultural values, foster pride in the Puerto Rican cultural heritage, and reinforce adaptive behavior.

To conduct the therapy, the therapist read the folktales in both English and Spanish to the children and led a group discussion on the meaning or moral of the story, highlighting the "good" and "bad" behaviors of the characters. The stories quickly captured the attention of the children, who identified readily with the characters portrayed. In the next step of the intervention, the group participants role played the various characters in the story. This activity was videotaped, and afterward the children viewed themselves on tape and discussed the role-playing activities with the therapist in relation to their own personal problems. The therapist then proposed new scenarios for role playing, and the children acted out solutions to problems presented in the scenarios. The therapist verbally reinforced adaptive behavior and corrected behavior that was maladaptive.

To examine the question of whether therapy should isomorphically reflect the culture, some of the children were told folktales as they appeared in original folklore, thus replicating cultural elements without changing them. Departing from the isomorphic assumption, other children were told folktales that had been changed in order to convey the knowledge, values, and skills useful in coping with the demands of the sociocultural environment of the host society's inner-city neighborhoods. In the adaptation of stories, moral issues were retained from the original story, but other changes were made: Cultural objects comprising the setting changed from a rural tropical scene to an urban, Hispanic neighborhood; culturally based interpersonal patterns also were changed—for example, authoritarian control of a younger sibling by an older one was transformed into the problem of maladaptive influences from peers in an urban setting and the overcoming of fear in resisting such influences.

The interested reader is invited to turn elsewhere for a full statement of the experimental design and procedures used to evaluate cuento therapy and the study's findings (Costantino, Malgady, & Rogler, 1985). Here, it is important to note that cuento therapy, compared to traditional group therapy and nonintervention, significantly reduced trait anxiety. Moreover, the therapy group with cuentos adapted to American society evidenced a greater reduction in trait anxiety, and this effect remained stable one year after the intervention. Thus, there is empirical justification for the development of both therapies that take elements unchanged from the clients' culture and those that adapt such elements to the host society.

Conclusions

The three approaches to cultural sensitivity presented here can be viewed metaphorically as a pyramidal structure. At the base lie the numerous programs that have made efforts to improve the accessibility of mental health services to Hispanic populations. Moving up the pyramid, we find programs that have gone several steps further in this process and that choose treatments according to the cultural characteristics of Hispanics. At the top are those programs modifying traditional therapy modalities according to an understanding and evaluation of ethnic characteristics or creatively deriving the therapeutic vehicle from the cultural milieu. Although our analysis of culturally sensitive treatment was prompted by Hispanic concerns, in principle we believe that this pyramidal structure can be extended to other migrant and culturally different groups.

The development of new therapeutic modalities out of specifically relevant cultural traits is always an ambitious and difficult task. Efforts to render therapeutic modalities culturally sensitive, no matter how persuasive or attractive they are, must ultimately attend to the final objective of relieving the client of psychological distress and of improving his or her level of effective functioning in the society. It should no longer be sufficient for a clinician merely to assert cultural sensitivity on the basis of good intentions alone: As an alternative, we invite our colleagues to situate their clinical innovations in the pyramidal framework developed here. From our attempt to order conceptually the many uses and meanings of cultural sensitivity, it is the concept of therapeutic isomorphism that emerges as a major contribution to the field. Thus, we invite our colleagues also to attend to the distinction we have drawn between isomorphic reinforcement and departures from isomorphism in the interest of the clients' well-being, not only in working with Hispanic clients but with any culturally different clientele.

To attend to such issues, research must be conducted. As Padilla, Ruiz, and Alvarez (1975) stated, "An innovative treatment program is self-defeating unless validating research is conducted . . . to guide the development of programs with the greatest probability of success" (p. 900). It is particularly important that innovative modalities, such as cuento therapy, not become part of the vast pool of untested therapies, but the task of validation should not deter us from creating new, culturally sensitive therapeutic programs.

References

Abad, V., Ramos, J., & Boyce, E. (1974). A model for delivery of mental health services to Spanish-speaking minorities. *American Journal of Orthopsychiatry, 44* (4), 584–595.

Acosta, F., & Cristo, M. (1981). Development of a bilingual interpreter program. An alternative model for Spanish-speaking services. *Professional Psychology, 12* (4), 474–482.

Bloom, B. (1975). *Changing patterns of psychiatric care.* New York: Human Sciences Press.

Bluestone, H., & Vela, R. (1982). Transcultural aspects in the psychotherapy of the Puerto Rican poor in New York City. *Journal of the American Academy of Psychoanalysis, 10* (2), 269–283.

Boulette, T. (1976). Assertive training with low income Mexican American women. In M. R. Miranda (Ed.), *Psychotherapy with the Spanish-speaking: Issues in research and service delivery* (pp. 67–72). Los Angeles: University of California, Spanish Speaking Mental Health Research Center.

Costantino, G., Malgady, R., & Rogler, L. (1985). *Cuento therapy: Folktales as a culturally sensitive psychotherapy for Puerto Rican children* (Hispanic Research Center Monograph No. 12). Maplewood, NJ: Waterfront Press.

Costantino, G., Malgady, R., & Rogler, L. (1986). Cuento therapy: A culturally sensitive modality for Puerto Rican children. *Journal of Consulting and Clinical Psychology, 54,* 639–645.

Cuellar, I., Harris, L, & Jasso, R. (1980). An acculturation scale for Mexican American normal and clinical populations. *Hispanic Journal of Behavioral Sciences, 2,* 199–217.

Cuellar, I., Harris, L., & Naron, N. (1981). Evaluation of a bilingual bicultural treatment program for Mexican American psychiatric inpatients. In A. Baron (Ed.), *Explorations in Chicano psychology* (pp. 165–186). New York: Praeger.

Freidson, E. (1970). *Profession of medicine.* New York: Dodd, Mead.

Gurak, D., & Rogler, L. (1980). New York's new immigrants: Who and where they are. The Hispanics. *New York University Education Quarterly, 11* (4), 20–24.

Inclan, J. (1979). *Family organization, acculturation and psychological symptomatology in second generation Puerto Rican women of three socioeconomic classes.* Unpublished doctoral dissertation, New York University.

Karno, M., & Morales, A. (1971). A community mental health service for Mexican Americans in a metropolis. *Comprehensive Psychiatry, 12* (2), 116–121.

Kreisman, J. (1975). The curandero's apprentice: A therapeutic integration of folk and medicinal healing. *American Journal of Psychiatry, 132* (1), 81–83.

Maduro, R., & Martinez, C. (1974). Latino dream analysis: Opportunity for confrontation. *Social Casework, 55,* 461–469.

Normand, W., Iglesias, J., & Payn, S. (1974). Brief group therapy to facilitate utilization of mental health services by Spanish-speaking patients. *American Journal of Orthopsychiatry, 44* (1), 37–42.

Padilla, A., Ruiz, R., & Alvarez, R. (1975). Community mental health services for the Spanish-speaking/surnamed populations. *American Psychologist, 30,* 892–905.

Pitta, P., Marcos, L., & Alpert, M. (1978). Language switching as a treatment strategy with bilingual patients. *American Journal of Psychoanalysis, 38,* 255–258.

Rodriguez, I. (1971). Group work with hospitalized Puerto Rican patients. *Hospital and Community Psychiatry, 22* (7), 219–220.

Rogler, L., & Cooney, R. (1984). *Puerto Rican families in New York City: Intergenerational processes* (Hispanic Research Center Monograph No. 11). Maplewood, NJ: Waterfront Press.

Rogler, L., & Hollingshead, A. (1985). *Trapped: Puerto Rican families and schizophrenia.* Maplewood, NJ: Waterfront Press.

Rogler, L., Santana-Cooney, R., Costantino, G., Earley, B., Grossman, B., Gurak, D., Malgady, R., & Rodriguez, O. (1983). *A conceptual framework for mental health research on Hispanic populations* (Hispanic Research Center Monograph No. 10). New York: Fordham University.

Ruiz, R. (1981). Cultural and historical perspectives in counseling Hispanics. In D. Sue (Ed.), *Counseling the culturally different* (pp. 186–215). New York: Wiley.

Scott, J., & Delgado, M. (1979). Planning mental health programs for Hispanic communities. *Social Casework, 60,* 451–455.

Sue, D. W., & Sue, D. (1977). Barriers to effective cross-cultural counseling. *Journal of Counseling Psychology, 24,* 420–429.

Szapocznik, J., Kurtines, W., & Fernandez, T. (1980). Bicultural involvement and adjustment in Hispanic American youths. *International Journal of Intercultural Relations, 4,* 353–365.

Szapocznik, J., Scopetta, M., Hervis, O., Ladner, R., Alegre, C., Truss, C., Santisteban, D., & Rodriguez, A. (1979). The Spanish Family Guidance Center of Miami. *Research Bulletin, 4,* (Available from Fordham University, Hispanic Research Center, Thebaud Hall, Bronx, NY 10458).

Szapocznik, J., Scopetta, M., & King, O. (1978). Theory and practice in matching treatment to the special characteristics and problems of Cuban immigrants. *Journal of Community Psychology, 6,* 112–122.

Trevino, F., Bruhn, J., & Bunce, H. (1979). Utilization of community mental health services in a Texas-Mexican border city. *Social Science and Medicine, 13* (3a), 331–334.

15

Psychological Impact of Migration on Latinas: Implications for Psychotherapeutic Practice

Oliva M. Espin

The unique stresses created by the process of immigration into another country and the need for grieving the loss of the home country and loved ones are important psychological processes confronted by all immigrants and refugees. Frequently, the psychological effects of migration and its specific impact on women will manifest themselves in issues brought to the attention of psychotherapists working with Latinas. There is evidence that the impact of migration on women and their roles is different from the impact of the same process for men (Andizian et al., 1983), and more research is needed in this area.

For both immigrants and refugees, the process of migration implies a certain degree of culture-shock that entails mourning the loss of the old country and of love objects, coupled with the need to confront new situations and interpersonal encounters (Garza-Guerrero, 1973; Grinberg & Grinberg, 1984). Factors such as perceived or real freedom to migrate, relative ease or difficulty of this process, sense of responsibility for those left behind, and conditions in both the home and host countries, interact in specific ways with culture-shock for each individual migrant. For example, leaving the home country through illegal means that can be life threatening has a different psychological impact than does arrival in a new country via legal entry.

Espin, O. M. (1987). Psychological impact of migration of Latinas: Implications for psychotherapeutic practice. *Psychology of Women Quarterly, 11,* 489–503. Copyright 1987 Division 35, American Psychological Association. Reprinted with the permission of Cambridge University Press.

Some intrapsychic factors such as ego strength, decision making skills, resolution of feelings of loss, and the ability to tolerate ambiguities, including gender-role ambiguities also influence migrants' adaptation processes. Shirley (1981) found that these factors actively interact with the joy and hope created by the opening of new doors and opportunities and, in some cases, with the escape from real or perceived life-threatening conditions. Other factors pertaining to the new country such as language proficiency, ability to find a job, losses or gains in status or social class, educational level, degree of similarity between the two cultures, and reception by citizens of the host country also determine and influence the experience of migration and subsequent adaptation (Stade, Doran, & Satterfield, in press; Taft, 1977).

These factors vary substantially for males and females. Thus, the unique interplay of issues pertaining to the psychological make-up of the individual Latina, specifics of the home subculture and social class, and the characteristics of North American culture can facilitate or interfere with the adaptation process.

The purpose of this article is to review and analyze clinical material relating to the psychological correlates of the process of migration in Latina women and girls and to suggest implications for the psychotherapeutic process. Most of the clinical evidence and examples presented in the paper are garnered from my own practice.

The Psychology of Migration and Acculturation

An understanding of the psychological processes involved in adaptation to another culture is essential for the understanding of the psychological implications of migration. Acculturation can be distinguished from assimilation in that acculturation does not imply the disappearance of all values, customs, and behaviors originating in the home culture as implied in the "melting pot" ideology of assimilation. While acculturation is inevitable to some degree for all migrants, it does not need to be disruptive in a negative sense. Healthy acculturation may resolve itself into healthy biculturalism (Szapocznik & Kurtines, 1980).

Regardless of gender and cultural background, the process of immigration involves important psychological changes that take place before and after arrival in the new country. These changes continue to take place throughout the life of the immigrant and include the development of a new identity (Garza-Guerrero, 1973).

Psychological Stages of the Migratory Process

Clinical observations have led me to think of the process of migration as having three stages: (a) the initial decision concerning relocation, (b) the actual geographical move into another country, and (c) the adaptation to a new society and way of life. At each step of the way, men and women will experience the process differently. For instance, at the decision making stage, women may not be consulted about their preference to leave or stay, whereas most men participate in the family decision to leave or make the decision themselves. At the relocation stage, particularly in situations of escaping dangerous political conditions, women's physical endurance may be questioned and they might not be provided the same opportunities to escape. At the third stage, when acculturation and adaptation are taking place, modifications of women's gender roles may be more dramatic than those experienced by men.

Acculturation and adaptation to a new culture may also follow several stages (Arredondo-Dowd, 1981). These include initial joy and relief, followed by disillusionment with the new country. Finally, if the process is successfully completed, the migrant moves into acceptance of the good and the bad in the host country, and thus into adjustment and reorganization coupled with adaptation to a new situation (Garza-Guerrero, 1973; Grinberg & Grinberg, 1984).

The process of adaptation, however, is not linear. The multiple intrapsychic and behavioral changes required for successful acculturation occur at many levels and may proceed at a different pace at each one of them.

If rejection and distance of the host culture becomes the preferred mode of coping with the new society and way of life, the adaptation process may never by successfully completed. The traditional expectations for the role of women in Latin culture may even foster the isolation of some women from the mainstream culture. These Latinas will seldom seek psychotherapy on their own either because they may be reluctant to do so, unable to afford it, or likely to encounter opposition from family, friends, or husbands who may view psychotherapy as an invasion of family privacy. When traditional Latinas consult a psychotherapist, they may have come into therapy following referral by a medical doctor, as a result of repeated somatic complaints. The high incidence of somatic complaints presented by Latinas with a traditional cultural orientation might be an expression of actual frequency of somatization of conflicts that is prevalent in traditional cultures (Kleinman, 1980).

On the other hand, somatic complaints might be the symptoms of a masked depression or of one of the many types of emotional disorders that frequently are presented with a cluster of somatic complaints. It is possible that traditional Latinas have few other ways to seek help, or that generally they are only aware of ''feeling bad'' without being able to pinpoint the source of those feelings. Perhaps some of the women simply do not know what else to talk about with a ''doctor,'' or do not want to talk with a stranger about their more intimate feelings about themselves and their families, and find it easier to continue to discuss physical symptoms instead. The fact that mental health professionals and physicians frequently prescribe tranquilizers and other medication for these patients rather than psychotherapy may also serve to reinforce the belief that they have some kind of physical illness.

Whatever the reason for the high incidence of somatic complaints, the fact is that those complaints are constantly presented by Latino clients (Abad, Ramos, & Boyce, 1974), especially by women. If the therapist does not show in some way that these somatic complaints are being addressed, the woman client who comes from a traditional cultural orientation is likely to see the treatment as irrelevant and may terminate the therapy.

Although some Latinas may choose the traditional role expectations, most Latina immigrants find that these are neither functional nor satisfying. Culturally-based conflicts may develop when newly encountered patterns of gender roles combined with greater access to paid employment for women open new economic, social, and emotional options which create an imbalance in the traditional power structure of the family (Torres-Matrullo, 1980). These women may consult a therapist at their own initiative and they may or may not be very explicit about the interrelationship between the migratory process and their feelings of distress.

Gender Role Conflicts

Women and girls from a Latin background are presently acculturating into North American society at a time when the role of women in this culture is in flux. Sometimes they may come from countries where official government policies or other forces are also fostering a transformation of the role of women, or from urban professional environments which have also been affected by the global feminist movement. But in other instances, they may come from very traditional rural environments where adherence to traditional gender roles is considered of primary importance. These factors combine to create some confusion as to what is appropriate behavior for women in the newly-found North American culture. Frequently, the contradictions between home and host cultures are stronger for women than for men in terms of what constitutes appropriate gender-role behavior.

Role conflicts in migrant families tend to occur mostly along lines that coincide with age and gender differences (Szapocznik & Kurtines, 1980). It is a common clinical observation that parents tend to be distressed by their children's more rapid pace of acculturation and that husbands tend to become resentful of their wives' apparent new independence and challenge of their patriarchal authority. Research shows that even though the pace of acculturation tends to be slower for females in all other aspects, they tend to acculturate faster than males when it comes to gender roles (Ginorio,

1979). Immigrant families may become entrenched in traditional social and sex-role norms as a defense against the strong pressures to acculturate. The home culture may become idealized and its values, characteristics, and customs may become a symbol of the stable parts of personal identity and probably the strongest defense against any sense of identity loss that might be engendered by acculturation. This attempt to preserve "old ways" tends to increase intergenerational and gender-role conflicts in the family.

In addition to gender, other factors such as age, class, and race affect the process of acculturation and adaptation for migrants. Light-skinned, young, and educated migrants usually encounter a more favorable reception in the United States than dark-skinned, older, and uneducated newcomers. These differences in reception may or may not parallel the migrant's experiences in the home culture. For example, when a migrant comes from a country where she belongs to the racial majority or where, as in Latin countries, racial mixtures are the norm, the experience of turning into a minority in the United States and encountering overt racial discrimination becomes a disorienting experience. In addition, economic need combined with lack of fluency in the new language frequently add to the experience of downward mobility in employment, particularly for refugees. This loss of status creates frustration and tensions in the family. Because of the increased employability of women and the loss of status and authority of the father in the family, further conflict related to gender norms often develops.

Psychotherapy with Migrant Latina Women

Seldom will a Latina woman present herself for therapy stating that she has "acculturation problems" or "psychological problems due to immigration." Most typically, an immigrant Latina seeks therapy because of personal problems similar to those presented in therapy by other women: Because she is depressed, has trouble in developing relationships, feels disoriented, or has a specific situational problem such as conflicts with her husband, partner, children, parents, or co-workers. However, as does every individual who comes to therapy, she has a unique history that modulates and defines the parameters of her specific problem or problems. In the case of immigrant women, their individual histories are influenced by the experience of migration and by the circumstances surrounding that experience as well as by the vicissitudes of their own personal and family histories.

The specific socio-political, economic, and historical circumstances that motivated the migration affect the individual psychological development and the process of therapy. The impact of these circumstances may appear more clearly in Latina women who are refugees than in those women who are voluntary migrants because of the danger surrounding the departure of most refugees and the impossibility of returning regularly to the country of origin. In addition, the problems presented in therapy by women who migrate alone may have different characteristics than those presented by women who migrate with their families.

Latina women who migrate alone have to struggle not only with loneliness, but also with feelings of shame and guilt and with the sociocultural expectations about the role of women that present themselves both externally and intrapsychically. On the one hand they feel freer of family control and have more flexibility in looking for new patterns of behavior in response to acculturation than those who migrate with other family members. On the other hand, they may continue to have traditional expectations for their own roles and behaviors that may not be realistic in the new context. In addition, they may have to contend with criticism from other immigrants from the same country for not conforming to traditional roles. Because they are alone, they may in fact need to acculturate faster.

These women, even if they constitute a numerical minority among immigrants, present unique challenges for therapeutic work. For example, an adolescent girl or a young woman who left her country without her family may find herself affected by a premature and traumatic separation from her parents that can stall or delay the process of healthy psychological separation in adulthood (Rodriguez-Nogues, 1983). Paris (1978) likens the forced individuation from the parent caused by leaving their country to the effect of the impossibility of completing the rapprochement period in the life of a child. In order for a child to successfully complete their individuation and reconciliation with the parents in adulthood, periodic, return to parents is essential for refueling, and yet is impossible for young refugee women. When the rapprochement is interrupted as it is in the case of these refugee women, guilt, frustration, restlessness, and lowered self-esteem could develop.

The impossibility of contacting parents during the course of therapy may prevent the woman from working out conflicts that may have originated before the separation took place. Although some similarities may be encountered when parents are deceased, major differences are present in the case of migrant women: Dead parents cannot be affected by the woman's present anger or resentment. Living and geographically inaccessible parents, on the other hand, can be affected by anger. The migrant woman, particularly if she does not have regular contact with them, frequently feels guilty about her anger toward parents who are geographically distant and perceived to be in a situation of more or less danger in the country of origin. A monthly long-distance phone call to an absent mother does not provide the time to address any problematic issues.

Another example of women strongly affected by the inability to work out problematic feelings may be a mother who, at migration time, was forced by her relatives, ex-husband or situational factors to leave her children behind. This woman's feeling of guilt and loss were exacerbated by the lack of contact with her growing children.

The feelings of guilt and loss usually associated with migration become heightened by this inaccessibility. Even when, the refugee may be allowed to return to her country of origin for brief visits, the time needed for working through issues will not be available in a week or two of family re-encounter after many years. And, even if they can have extended visits home, the family does not witness the change experienced by the woman in the new country, so they can dismiss or deny the importance of those changes in her life.

Thus, therapy proceeds in a void for migrant women. They have to learn to understand, express, and experience feelings concerning distant family members without ever fully testing those feelings in their interpersonal context where they originated.

When the migration has been preceded by situations of political persecution that may include experiences of torture or the disappearance of family members, other unique factors may be part of the therapy. Moreover, some of the traumatic events experienced by women refugees are directly associated with their gender. For example, repeated rape or other forms of sexual abuse or harassment may have been used as a means of torture. Or they may have been subjected to rape and harassment at the hands of their ''protectors'' or ''saviors'' during their escape from their country of origin.

Persons who have been subjected to these experiences may suffer from post-traumatic stress reactions that may vary in intensity for each individual (Figley, 1985; Molesky, 1986). Post-traumatic stress reactions may manifest themselves through nightmares, numbing of feelings, and overwhelming feelings of guilt. Empirical evidence seems to indicate that sadness, depression, and more serious pathology may recur or develop many years after the actual migration took place. This phenomenon seems to be particularly true of immigrant and refugee women who have suffered traumatic experiences in the process of migration, have lost their networks of female relatives and childhood friends through migration, or did not participate in the decision to migrate (Rumbaut, 1977; Telles, 1980). For the woman suffering from post-traumatic stress, therapy can provide a needed outlet. Because some of the experiences of torture and abuse suffered by refugees are so inconceivable to people who have lived in the United States all their lives, the woman refugee from a Latin American country sometimes has difficulty expressing what she has undergone without feeling she is seen as a liar. Mental health professionals have observed that just the telling of the experiences, the opportunity to speak about what was sometimes felt as unspeakable may in itself be therapeutic for these women (Cienfuegos & Monelli, 1983; Figley, 1985). To be able to talk about these experiences and be believed provides an enormous relief for the woman who has experienced torture and political persecution before migration.

Young women or adolescent girls who migrate with their families although accompanied and protected, confront the question of how to "become American" without losing completely their own cultural heritage. Role models of successful bicultural Latinas are scarce. A bicultural Latina therapist can thus provide an invaluable service just by being available to the young woman as a role model.

Girls frequently express their adolescent rebellion against the parental culture by refusing to speak Spanish at home, rejecting cultural customs, and generally reacting negatively toward their parents and native culture. Since American society at large encourages immigrants to deny their cultural heritage, the adolescent Latina finds plenty of support from adults in positions of authority to challenge her parents' values. Often conflicts over authority are played out around issues of appropriate sexual behavior such that dating and other behavior related to sexuality become the focus of conflict between parents and daughters (Espin, 1984). One of the most prevalent myths encountered by Latina immigrants is that all American women are "free" with sex. For the parents and the young woman alike, "to be Americanized" may be equated with becoming sexually promiscuous.

The question of loyalties to the home culture may manifest itself in other ways. For example, the parents of an adolescent Cuban girl became outraged and reacted with apparent unjustified violence to her interest in the new Cuban music, a popular form of song that developed in Cuba after the Revolution. Since she had come to this country when she was 2 years old, her interest in the music was simply an innocent way of familiarizing herself with something Cuban or simply just listening to music, while for her parents her interest was a political statement that had negative connotations.

Affective and Cognitive Implications of Language Use

Language is an important variable in psychodynamic psychotherapy with Latinas. Extensive discussion of the affective and cognitive implications of bilingualism and language use in therapy is beyond the scope of the paper. However, it is important to address this issue because even for those Latinas who are fluent in English, or who have lost fluency in the use of their first language, Spanish remains the language of emotions because it was in Spanish that affective meanings were originally encoded (Espin, 1982). To try to decode those affective meanings through the use of another language may be problematic at best. Psychotherapy relies too heavily on language to ignore its psychological implications for the therapeutic process, especially for persons who may constantly be changing between two languages or who are participating in a therapeutic process that is carried on in their second language.

Several authors have commented on the importance of language choice in therapy with bilinguals (Espin, 1982; Krapf, 1955; Marcos, 1976a, 1976b; Rosensky & Gomez, 1983). According to Marcos (1976a), bilinguals may appear to be withdrawn in their second language when they are not fully proficient in it. In this case, the attention paid to how things are said in therapy may distract attention from what is being said, thus impairing the therapeutic process. Conversely, proficient bilinguals may use independence between their two languages as a mechanism for the compartmentalizing feelings (Marcos & Alpert, 1976). These mechanisms may render unavailable certain areas of the bilingual's intrapsychic world. Marcos and Urcuyo (1979) also describe the subjective experience of some language-independent bilinguals who experience a dual sense of self as a consequence of using different languages. According to De la Cancela,

> The implications for psychotherapy of these difficulties may be that affects are blocked, hence, the client has difficulty in benefiting from catharsis and abreaction. As such, verbalization of feelings may turn out to be an arduous intellectual task which brings little relief to the client. Additionally both positive and negative transferences may be unsatisfactorily expressed leading to displacement or acting-out in the therapeutic relationship (1985, p. 430).

In my own clinical practice I have encountered instances in which the importance of language is expressed directly and those in which it is expressed indirectly. Manifestations of the impact of language in therapy with Latina clients are not clearly understood because the use of language in therapy has always been studied and described from a monolingual point of view (e.g., Havens, 1986). An example of an intuitive sense of the importance of the first language in therapy was provided by a college-age Puerto Rican woman who sought me out for therapy specifically because I could speak Spanish. She was fluently bilingual and did not need Spanish to communicate her feelings with a relative degree of sophistication. However, it was important to be in therapy with a Spanish-speaking therapist because, in her own words, "My problems are with my family and my family speaks Spanish, so my problems are in Spanish." Other clients have approached me as a therapist presenting variations of the same idea.

An indirect example suggesting the importance of the first language in therapy was provided by a professional woman who, having immigrated to the United States at a very young age, preferred to use English for her therapy even though she wanted a therapist who was "culturally sensitive." After two years in therapy conducted in English with minimal interspersed use of some common Spanish words, she came to a session in which she spoke only Spanish. At the end of the session, I pointed out that I had noticed we had used Spanish uninterruptedly during the hour. She stated that there was nothing special in her language change in that particular session, that she just wanted to practice her Spanish more frequently: The content of the session, in fact, had not been particularly deep or cathartic, so I went along with her expressed perception that there was nothing to her change in language. She never came back after that session. I must confess that her abrupt and unanticipated departure from therapy baffles me. But what is clear is that her change to Spanish on that particular day was not innocuous. Perhaps she was developing a negative maternal transference that became suddenly intensified by speaking to me in the only language her mother spoke or perhaps the use of Spanish brought up some other intense feelings that remained unacknowledged while she used English. Needless to say, I have never again treated lightly any shifts in language during therapy with bilingual women.

On the other hand, bilinguals conversing with each other habitually switch from one language to another without any significant psychological pattern being apparent. Speakers may choose expressions in the native or second language depending on the relative applicability of the expression to the context. As a bilingual therapist working with bilingual women, I try to remain alert to their language choice and switches as any therapist would remain alert to a client's choice of words. But, very specifically, I try to remain alert to possible areas of conflict that are being avoided or expressed by sudden shifts in language.

But while the use of English in therapy may act as a barrier and a resistance in dealing with certain components of the psyche, the second language can act as a facilitator for the emergence and discussion of certain topics. Some of these may be taboo topics or words in Spanish while others may refer to the new components of the self acquired through the process of acculturation after English became the primary or most used language. Gonzalez-Reigosa (1976), has demonstrated that taboo words in the language of origin elicit more anxiety than either taboo words in the second language or indifferent words in the first language.

The facilitative features of the second language become most evident when the topic discussed is sexuality. Latino culture has fairly traditional views of female sexuality (Espin, 1984, 1985a). For Latinas, English provides a vehicle for discussing sexual issues in therapy that may be too embarrassing to initiate with the use of forbidden Spanish words. In my practice I find this is particularly significant for Latina lesbians, who will describe their life situation and choices most frequently using terminology in English and will tend to avoid equivalent words in Spanish.

In addition to the emotional value associated with either the first or second language, an important aspect of language usage for bilinguals is its connection with self-esteem. In the United States, Spanish bilingualism is frequently associated with an inferior social status. Bilingual skills in Latinos are frequently devalued and rejection of bilingual parents as "ignorant" people who are contrasted with "educated" monolingual teachers may be encouraged in schools. The use of Spanish in therapy may be difficult because of these negative connotations, but may become an important instrument for reclaiming parts of the self that may have been rejected as negative through the process of acculturation.

Issues of Loss and Grief in Therapy with Immigrant Women

Loss, grief, and mourning are issues of primary importance when working in therapy with immigrants and refugees. Attempts to understand the psychological distress experienced by immigrants and refugees have generally focused on factors in the new environment and the need to cope with them or acculturative stress (Berry & Annis, 1974). However, the loss of home country and loved ones plays a significant role in the immigrant's adjustment. These feelings of loss must be resolved through a grieving process that can be facilitated by the therapy. In its normal form the grieving process involves a moderate level of emotional disorganization which may be manifested by apathy, insomnia, loss of appetite, irritability, angry outbursts, psychosomatic symptoms, and other signs of distress. When grief is delayed or inhibited because the loss is denied or otherwise defended against, the normal signs can take pathological forms by becoming prolonged or exaggerated (Lindemann, 1944). Parkes (1975) suggested several features by which to identify unresolved grief: a gradual process of realization from denial of the grief to recognition and acceptance of it: alarm reactions such as anxiety and other related physiological symptoms: an urge to search and find the lost object: anger and guilt; feelings of internal loss of self; identification with the lost object; and, pathological variants of grief. Telles (1980) has observed the effects of delayed grief on Cuban women who experienced a reactivation of this grieving process at the time of retirement from their jobs after many years of residing in the United States. The depression and emotional distress manifested by these women could be traced directly to the lack of successful mourning for the losses created by the migration in earlier years.

While the grief of the bereaved can be traced to the nature of the relationship to a specific person, in migration the lost object is vague and the loss pervasive. Migrants have lost country, culture and loved ones; in other words, what Ticho (1971) refers to as the "average expectable environment," which includes everyday patterns of relationships, obligations, networks, familiar food, places and people, and the behaviors that are considered "normal" in the home culture. When all those habitual patterns are disrupted at the same time and new patterns have to be learned, the amount of distress experienced by the migrant can be considerable. The magnitude of this loss is seldom understood by the immigrant or by others. Sometimes it may require returning to the homeland for the immigrant to realize what his loss had entailed (Espin, 1985b). Even supportive friends and social service agencies are more interested in the woman's adaptation to her new life than in her feelings about who or what was left behind in the home country.

Latina immigrants struggle to maintain contact with the home country, either through physical proximity or through food, music, and other immigrants from the home country. In therapy, the effort to recover the lost objects (e.g., mother, country) may be expressed through strong transferential reactions, particularly when the therapist comes from the same country or culture.

Preoccupation with "what could have been" if the woman had not left her country is a central theme in therapy with migrants. This preoccupation is expressed both through concern with what could have happened in her life had she stayed in her country of origin and concern with what has been gained by the migration. Not infrequently, the immigrant experiences feelings of guilt in relation to people and relationships left behind. New loyalties to individuals and relationships developed in the host country, including the therapeutic relationship, are frequently experienced as betrayal of the parents or the home country. In other words, "invisible loyalties" may interfere with the course of the therapy and with the process of adaptation to the new country. Boszormenyi-Nagy and Spark (1973) have discussed extensively the impact of "invisible loyalties" in personality development and relationships. "Invisible loyalties" can create powerful paralyzing and compulsive behavioral and emotional effects in individuals and, families. They constitute an important aspect of the conflicts presented by immigrant Latinas in psychotherapy.

Conclusions

Because this article is about the stressors created by migration and their implications for psychotherapy with immigrant Latinas, emphasis has been placed on conflictual situations. However, it is important to understand that many of the reactions discussed in this paper are not pathological. It is important that the therapist interpret these reactions as natural consequences of a disturbing process and not as signs of individual pathology. This is not to deny that some Latinas will in fact present pathological manifestations whose sources existed prior to migration.

The therapist working with immigrant Latinas should acquire knowledge and information about each woman's reasons for migration, including the political and economic conditions in her country of origin and the specific circumstances in the woman's life that motivated her migration (Espin, 1985a, 1985b). Because some of the events described by Latinas in therapy are so extreme, it is important for the therapist to be aware of her own countertransferential reactions to the client (Ticho, 1971).

Therapy should provide assistance in the grieving process and with the resolution of "invisible loyalties" they may be hindering adjustment. At the same time, therapy should assist the client in maintaining loyalties and emotional proximity to those people and places that constitute the sources of her identity. Therapy can provide support in managing conflicts in the woman's relationships that might occur as a consequence of changes in her traditional roles and in newly acquired behaviors.

Bilingual/bicultural therapists can be especially helpful in assisting Latinas to resolve some of those concerns and to adapt successfully to their new lives. But the fact that there is a dearth of Latina psychotherapists poses additional problems in the treatment of this population. Anglo therapists who are sensitive and competent in integrating cultural variables in their treatment plan may provide the necessary support and skills needed to assist immigrant Latinas in their process of adaptation. However, the question remains of how cultural sensitivity can be identified or achieved. Lack of research data and information do not allow for clear identification of what requisite experience, background, and communication skills are necessary for competence in the conduct of psychotherapy with immigrant Latinas or with any other ethnic minority population, for that matter.

Until further information from research and clinical practice is available, some of the ideas discussed in this paper can serve to identify stressors present in the lives of immigrant Latinas, as well as issues to be addressed in therapy with this population and initial questions for further exploration.

References

Abad, V., Ramos, J., & Boyce, E. (1974). A model for delivery of mental health services to Spanish-speaking minorities. *American Journal of Orthopsychiatry, 44,* 584–595.

Andizian, S., Catani, M., Cicourel, A., Dittmar, N., Harper, D., Kudat, A., Morokvasic, M., Oriol, M., Parris, R. G., Streiff, J., & Swetland, C. (1983). *Vivir entre dos culturas.* Paris: Serbal/UNESCO.

Arrendondo-Dowd, P. (1981). Personal loss and grief as a result of immigration. *Personnel and Guidance Journal, 59,* 376–378.

Berry, J. W., & Annis, R. C., (1974). Acculturative stress: The role of ecology culture and differentiation. *Journal of Cross-Cultural Psychology, 5,* 382–405.

Boszormenyi-Nagy, I., & Spark, G. M. (1973). *Invisible loyalties: Reciprocity in intergenerational family therapy.* New York: Harper & Row.

Cienfuegos, A. J., & Monelli, C. (1983). The testimony of political repression as a therapeutic instrument. *American Journal of Orthopsychiatry, 53,* 43–51.

De La Cancela, V. (1985). Toward a sociocultural psychotherapy for low-income ethnic minorities. *Psychotherapy: Theory, Research and Practice, 22,* 427–435.

Espin, O. M., (1982, October). Language issues in psychotherapy with fluent bilinguals. Paper presented at a clinical seminar at Wellesley College Stone Center, Wellesley, MA.

Espin, O. M. (1984). Cultural and historical influences on sexuality in Hispanic/Latin women: Implications for psychotherapy. In C. Vance (Ed.), *Pleasure and danger: Exploring female sexuality* (pp. 149–164). London: Rutledge & Kegan Paul.

Espin, O. M., (1985a). Psychotherapy with Hispanic Women: Some considerations. In P. Pedersen (Ed.), *Handbook of cross-cultural counseling and psychotherapy,* (pp. 165–171). Westport, CT: Greenwood Press.

Espin, O. M. (1985b, November). Roots uprooted: Dealing with historical dislocation. Paper presented at the Women's Theological Center, Boston, MA. (Abridged version published in *Sojourner,* 1986 February, pp. 22–23.)

Figley, C. R. (Ed.). (1985). *Trauma and its wake: The study and treatment of Post-Traumatic Stress Disorder.* New York: Brunner/Mazel.

Garza-Guerrero, C. (1973). Culture shock: Its mourning and the vicissitudes identity. *Journal of the American Psychoanalytic Association, 22,* 408–429.

Ginorio, A. (1979). A comparison of Puerto Ricans in New York with native Puerto Ricans and Caucasian- and Black-Americans on two measures of acculturation: Gender role and racial identification. (Doctoral dissertation, Fordham University) *Dissertation Abstracts International, 40,* 983B–984B.

Gonzalez-Reigosa, F. (1976). The anxiety-arousing effect of taboo words in bilinguals. In C. D. Spielberger & R. Diaz-Gurrero (Eds.). *Cross-cultural anxiety (pp. 89–105). Washington, DC: Hemisphere.*

Grinberg, L., & Grinberg, R. (1984). *Psicoanalisis de la migracion y del exilio.* Madrid; Alianza Editorial.

Havens, L. (1986). *Making contact: Uses of language in psychotherapy.* Cambridge, MA: Harvard University Press.

Kleinman, A. (1980). *Patients and healers in the context of culture.* Berkeley: University of California Press.

Krapf, E. E. (1955). The choice of language in polyglot psychoanalysis. *Psychoanalytic Quarterly, 24,* 343–357.

Lindemann, E. (1944). Symptomatology and management of acute grief. *American Journal of Psychiatry, 101,* 141–148.

Marcos, L. (1976a). Bilinguals in psychotherapy: Language as an emotional barrier. *American Journal of Psychotherapy, 30,* 522–560.

Marcos, L. (1976b). Bilingualism and sense of self. *American Journal of Psychoanalysis, 37,* 285–290.

Marcos, L. R., & Alpert, M. (1976). Strategies and risks in psychotherapy with bilingual patients: The phenomena of language independence. *American Journal of Psychiatry, 133,* 1275–1278.

Marcos, L. R., & Urcuyo, L. (1979). Dynamic psychotherapy with the bilingual patient, *American Journal of Psychotherapy, 33,* 331–338.

Molesky, J. (1986). The exiled: Pathology of Central American refugees. *Migration World, 14* (4), 19–23.

Paris, J. (1978). The symbolic return: Psychodynamic aspects of immigration and exile. *Journal of the American Academy of Psychoanalysis, 6,* 51–57.

Parkes, L. M. (1975). *Bereavement: Studies in grief in adult life.* New York: International Universities Press.

Rodriguez-Nogues, L. (1983). Psychological effects of premature separation from parents in Cuban refugee girls: A retrospective study. (Doctoral dissertation, Boston University) *Dissertation Abstracts International, 44,* 1619B.

Rosensky, R., & Gomez, M. (1983). Language switch in psychotherapy with bilinguals: Two problems, two models and case examples. *Psychotherapy: Theory, Research and Practice, 20,* 152–160.

Rumbaut, R. D. (1977). Life events, change, migration and depression. In W. E. Fann, I. Karocan, A. D. Pokorny, & R. L. Williams (Eds.), *Phenomenology and treatment of depression* (pp. 115–126). New York: Spectrum.

Shirley, B. (1981). A study of ego strength: The case of the Latina immigrant woman in the United States. (Doctoral dissertation, Boston University). *Dissertations Abstract International, 42,* 2583A–2584A.

Stade, C., Doran, T., & Satterfield, J. (in press). *A road well traveled: three generations of Cuban American women.* Newton, MA: EDC.

Szapocznik, J., & Kurtines, W. (1980). Acculturation, biculturalism and adjustment among Cuban Americans. In A. Padilla (Ed.), *Acculturation: Theory models and some new findings* (pp. 139–159). Boulder, CO: Westview Press.

Taft, R. (1977). Coping with unfamiliar cultures. In N. Warren (Ed.), *Studies in cross-cultural psychology* (pp. 121–153). New York: Academic.

Telles, P. (1980, March). The psychosocial effects of immigration upon aging Cuban women. Paper presented at the National Hispanic Feminist Conference, San Jose, CA.

Ticho, G. (1971). Cultural aspects of transference & countertransference. *Bulletin of the Menninger Clinic, 35,* 313–334.

Torres-Matrullo, C. (1980). Acculturation, sex-role values and mental health among mainland Puerto Ricans. In A. Padilla (Ed.), *Acculturation: Theory, models and some new findings* (pp. 111–137). Boulder, CO: Westview Press.

The Latino Client
Cases and Questions

1. Assume you are a counselor at a large state university that has publicly stated support for all its federally mandated affirmative action programs. Recently, however, the Sociology Department's graduate admission procedure has been under fire by the campus newspaper for its practice of reserving 20 percent of its new admissions for Chicano students (the state in which the school is located is composed of 20 percent Chicanos).

   a. How do you feel about the selection procedure described?
   b. What action would you take in view of your feelings?
   c. What impact would you expect this to have on your ability to relate to Chicano students?

2. Assume you are a counselor in a state-run rehabilitation agency. A Puerto Rican paraplegic enters your office looking very sullen and begins to question your ability to help her. She points out that you cannot possibly understand her problems since you are not encumbered, as she is, by the forces of multiple oppression.

   a. How will you respond to her charges?
   b. What doubts do you have about your ability to work with this client?
   c. What are come of the cultural factors in which you need to be sensitive in working with this client?

3. Assume you are a counselor in an urban elementary school with a student enrollment that is 60 percent Anglo, 40 percent Chicano. Several physical confrontations have occurred in the school cafeteria recently, apparently the result of insult trading between Anglos and Chicanos over "Mex" and "Gringo" food. The school principal has asked you to work with some of the students involved.

   a. How do you plan to work (what is your role) with these students?
   b. Do you anticipate any difficulty in establishing a relationship with either the Anglo or Chicano students? How will you deal with the difficulty?
   c. What community resources might you want to tap in dealing with this problem?

The Latino Client
Role Playing Exercise

Divide into groups of four or five. Assign each group member to a role and the responsibilities associated with the role as follows:

Role	Responsibility
1. Counselor	1. Assume role as a counselor or mental health worker who is assigned a Latino or Latina client. Attempt to build rapport with the client.
2. Client	2. Assume role of a Latino or Latina client. To play this role effectively, it will be necessary for the student to (a) identify cultural values of Latinos, (b) identify sociopolitical factors which may interfere with counseling, and (c) portray these aspects in the counseling session. It is best to select a few powerful variables in the role play. You may or may not be initially antagonistic to the counselor, but it is important for you to be sincere in your role and your reactions to the counselor.
3. Observers	3. Observe interaction and offer comments during feedback session.

This exercise is most effective in a racially and ethnically mixed group. For example, a Latino or Latina student can be asked to play the Latino or Latina client role. However, this is probably not possible in most cases. Thus, students who play the client role will need to thoroughly read the articles for the group they are portraying.

Identifying the barriers that could interfere with counseling is an important aspect of this exercise. We recommend that a list be made of the group's cultural values and sociopolitical influences prior to the role playing.

Role playing may go on for a period of five to fifteen minutes, but the time limit should be determined prior to the activity. Allow ten to fifteen minutes for a feedback session in which all participants discuss (within the group) how they felt in their respective roles, how appropriate were the counselor responses, what else they might have done in that situation, etc.

Rotate and role play the same situation with another counselor trainee *or* another Latino or Latina client with different issues, concerns, and

problems. In the former case, the group may feel that a particular issue is of sufficient importance to warrant reenactment. This allows students to see the effects of other counseling responses and approaches. In the latter case, the new exposure will allow students to get a broader view of barriers to counseling.

If videotaping equipment is available, we recommend that the session be taped and processed in a replay at the end. We have found this to be a powerful means of providing feedback to participants.

PART 6

Implications for Minority Group/Cross-Cultural Counseling

16
Future Directions in Minority Group/Cross-Cultural Counseling

In the first three chapters we defined some of the terms used in cross-cultural counseling, discussed the need to recognize within-group differences among racial/ethnic minority groups, and examined how the counseling profession has responded to the needs of racial/ethnic minority people. Chapters 4 through 15 provided information about the counseling needs and experiences of the four major racial/ethnic minority groups in the United States. In this chapter we will examine the current models for practice, training, and research that have implications for cross-cultural counseling in the future.

Counseling Practice

In Chapter 3 it was noted that a great deal of criticism has been directed at the conventional counseling role of psychotherapy. Time-bound, space-bound, cathartic psychotherapy is seen as largely irrelevant to ethnic minority life experiences and needs. Rather than demanding that the client adapt to the counselor's culture, critics argue that the counselor should adjust to and work within the client's culture. Furthermore, ethnic minority individuals are by definition oppressed, and it is highly unlikely that any minority client problem is ever totally free of this oppression. Providing an empathic ear so that the client can reassess past experiences, or even changing the client's behavior so that he or she can cope better with the environment, does not eliminate the oppression.

The counselor, critics argue, needs to get out of the office and meet the client in the client's environment. While some racial/ethnic minority clients may come to the attention of counselors in schools and social service agencies, others will go unserved unless counselors reach out to them, perhaps by providing pro bono services through community agencies. Racial/ethnic minority clients in educational settings are often hesitant to contact counselors (Calia, 1966), and Haettenschwiller (1971) urges counselors to make the initial contact with minority students on the students' home ground, thus establishing the counselor as a person, ". . . to whom the student can turn when confronted by the uncertainty and ambiguity of institutional demands" (p. 31). Grevous (1985) advises that a home visit will help the counselor better understand a Black client. Woods (1977) describes a counseling services program that relies heavily on group counseling and group activities rather than on traditional one-to-one counseling and, in keeping with an outreach philosophy, the group sessions are often, ". . . conducted at students' apartments for potluck dinners, and at local beaches and parks for picnics and games" (p. 417).

By making him/herself available in the client's environment, the counselor is in a better position to respond to client needs at the time they are experienced. Exposure to the client's world may also help the counselor understand the cultural experience of the client and may enhance the counselor-client relationship. Furthermore, the counselor as an outreach worker may be in a position to directly observe the environmental factors that are contributing to the client's problems, and the counselor is thus less likely to attribute deviations from majority norms to pathology. In addition to direct exposure to the environment of minority clients, counselors should become actively involved in community and social programs and activities in the racial/ethnic minority communities (Wilson & Calhoun, 1974).

In addition to getting out into the client's environment, we believe the counselor needs to provide additional professional roles as alternatives to the conventional psychotherapy role. For the most part, these roles are not really new, since they have been proposed and to some degree implemented in the past (Pine, in a 1972 article, refers to them as "old wine in new bottles"). They are "new," however in that they have not gained widespread acceptance by the counseling profession, and the conventional psychotherapy role remains solidly entrenched as the counselor's primary modus operandi.

In general it can be said these alternative roles involve the counselor more actively in the client's life experiences than does the conventional role; some of them also share a preventative thrust rather than the more traditional remedial focus. Because of this there is considerable overlapping of the role functions, but each includes some aspects that are unique to the role. The alternative roles to be discussed are: (a) advocate, (b) change agent, (c) consultant, (d) adviser, (e) facilitator of indigenous support systems, and (f) facilitator of indigenous healing methods. We also offer a brief discussion of how conventional psychotherapy and conventional counseling can be applied more effectively with ethnically diverse clients than they have in the past.

Advocate

All ethnic minority individuals, by definition, are oppressed to some degree by the dominant society. Some of these ethnic minority individuals and groups have developed skills that help them deal with discrimination. Others, particularly recent immigrants, may lack the English-speaking skills and economic power to confront and/or deflect oppressive environments. In these situations the client or clients may need an advocate rather than a psychotherapist.

As an advocate, the counselor speaks on behalf of the client, often confronting the institutional sources of oppression that are contributing to the client's problems. The counselor need not represent a particular client or group of clients; rather, the entire minority culture experiencing an injustice may function as the client. In this role the counselor represents a client or group of clients who have brought a particular form of discrimination to the counselor's attention. Being an empathic counselor who suggests alternative ways of coping with a particular problem is not enough; the counselor must be willing to pursue actively alternative courses with or for the client, including making a personal contact for the client who is overwhelmed by the bureaucracy (Mitchell, 1971b). Not infrequently, the injustice involves the institution employing the counselor. If the client's goals are in conflict with those of the institution, the counselor must decide to represent the client and not the institution or the system (Williams & Kirkland, 1971), presumably within ethical restrictions imposed by the profession. Since an ethnic minority client is involved, the advocate has the added responsibility for making certain that the minority person can benefit fully from the social and economic resources of the majority culture without losing what is unique and valued in his/her own culture (Maes & Rinaldi, 1974).

The advocate role is extremely important for counselors in ethnically diverse schools (Esquivel & Keitel, 1990), particulary those with recent immigrants. The National Coalition of Advocates for Students (1988) has developed a number of recommendations for advocacy on behalf of immigrant students. School counselors (and other school personnel) are urged to advocate that their school: (a) ensure that all school personnel understand that immigrant children have a legal right to free, appropriate public education; (b) restructure those policies and practices that sort immigrant students into programs which prepare them for inferior futures; (c) ensure that immigrant students (and all students) experience a school environment free of victimization, harassment, and intergroup conflict; and (d) ensure a more equitable allocation of resources to those (typically inner city) schools that serve immigrant students.

Change Agent

According to Egan (1985), "change agent refers to anyone who plays an important part in designing, redesigning, running, renewing, or improving any system, subsystem, or program" (p. 12). As a change agent, the counselor attempts to change the social environment that oppresses racial/ethnic minorities. As suggested in Chapter 3, a major criticism of the traditional counseling model is the focus on intrapsychic sources of the client's problem and on psychotherapy as the primary intervention for resolving the problem. As a change agent, the counselor helps the client identify the external sources of his or her problem as well as methods of resolving the problem. Rather than encouraging the client to "own the problem," the counselor helps the client become aware of the oppressive forces creating the problem. Then together the counselor and client develop a strategy for eliminating or reducing the effect of the oppression on the client's life. This is often done by facilitating the formation of racial/ethnic minority political groups. Through political power, racial/ethnic minorities and other disenfranchised groups are able to bring about change in their social and physical environment. The counselor serving as a change agent frequently assumes a low-visibility profile, often finding it useful to mobilize other influential persons in the offending institution so as to bring about change (Waltz & Benjamin, 1977).

In the mid-1960s, the Division 17 Professional Affairs Committee of the American Psychological Association suggested that college counselors need to accept responsibility for changing university environments to benefit all ethnic minority students.

> Problems of institutional racism are paramount on a university campus. Counseling alone on discrimination issues will be ineffective. Counseling psychologists must involve themselves in affirmative action programs, sponsor symposia and workshops on racism in society, and actively involve themselves in programs of cultural awareness. (Ivey, 1976, p. 10–11).

Lewis and Lewis (1977) identified four ways the counselor can serve as a change agent: the counselor can assess community needs, coordinate activities and resources, provide training in skill building, and advocate change. Ponterotto (1987) has described a multi-modal approach to counseling Mexican Americans that includes a change agent component and that appears equally applicable to other ethnic groups. The change agent component of the approach involves identifying the social, environmental, and institutional factors that are oppressing the client but that are external to his/her control. The counselor first acknowledges the oppressive environment and then helps the client organize a plan for confronting the situation directly and/or helps the client identify agencies that could facilitate elimination of the problem.

As a change agent, however, the counselor need not necessarily spend his/her time confronting institutional bureaucracy. The counselor can work directly with majority clients in an attempt to move them toward the goal of reducing racist attitudes. Katz and Ivey (1977) describe a racism-awareness training program that involves a reeducation process designed, ". . . to raise consciousness of White people, help them identify racism in their life experience from which their racist attitudes and behaviors have developed, and move them to take action against institutional and individual racism" (p. 487). The six phases of the program are designed to help participants to:

1. Increase their understanding of racism in society and themselves.
2. Confront discrepancies existing between the myths and reality of American ideology and behavior.
3. Sort through some of their feelings and reactions that were triggered by phases 1 and 2.
4. Confront the racism in the White culture that their own actions support.
5. Understand and accept their Whiteness.
6. Develop specific action strategies to combat personal and institutional racism (p. 487).

Katz and Ivey's suggestion that racism is a White problem and White counselors should assume a major role in dealing with it makes sense. European American counselors are, in some respects, in the best position to confront the majority population with their own stereotypic attitudes and behaviors.

Consultant

According to Hansen, Himes, and Meier (1990), consultation involves a collegial relationship between the consultant and the consultee (or client), who work together to affect the behavior of a third party. A distinction between the change agent role and the consultant role is that a primary goal of the former is to alleviate existing problems while a primary goal of the latter is to prevent the problems from developing. The consultant role differs from the adviser role in that, in the former role, the client (often high in acculturation) initiates contact with the counselor to seek help in preventing a problem; as an adviser, the counselor initiates contact with the client (often low in acculturation) to advise the client of unanticipated problems.

In the consultant role, counselors can help ethnic minority clients learn skills needed to interact successfully with the dominant society. For example, some minority clients lack assertiveness skills. According to Wood and Mallinckrodt (1990):

members of many ethnic minority groups have values about assertive responding that differ markedly from those of the dominant culture. The resulting inability to perform skills valued by the dominant culture may place ethnic minority persons at a significant disadvantage for coping in the majority society'' (p. 5).

LaFromboise and Rowe (1983) propose social skills training as a strategy for helping American Indians learn to relate to non-Indians. They suggest that a skills training approach is particularly applicable to American Indian clients because: (a) ''it is less culturally biased than alternative approaches stemming from the academic tradition,'' (b) it can be used to prevent as well as remediate problems, (c) it involves the use of modeling in small group settings, a procedure compatible with American Indian methods of transmitting knowledge, (d) it has been found to be more effective than alternative treatments, and (e) it is applicable to the kinds of problems American Indians are currently experiencing.

Adviser

Some ethnic minority individuals, particularly recent immigrants, simply are not aware of the kind of discrimination they may face or the kinds of problems they may encounter as a result of overt or covert racism. In this case the counselor may be of most assistance by advising these individuals about the problems they or their families may encounter; the goal is to prevent problems. The adviser role is similar to the consultant role except that the counselor initiates discussion of the potential problem with the client.

The role of adviser has been eschewed historically by the counseling profession. For the past four decades the counseling literature has criticized advise giving while promoting such alternative counselor behaviors as listening, facilitating, and supporting. In reality, however, advise may be exactly what recent immigrants need in order to prevent problems before they have a chance to develop. An example of advise giving would be to advise recent immigrants of the discrimination they will face in the job market and that their children may face in school. Further, the counselor should advise recent immigrants what they and their children might do to reduce the impact of such discrimination.

Facilitator of Indigenous Support System

It is probably correct to state that every culture in the world has developed some form of social support to help prevent and remediate psychological and relationship problems. In fact, counseling can be thought of as a social support system that evolved as our economic base shifted from agriculture to industry to technology and people became more mobile and removed from their family support systems (Tyler, 1961). Like counseling, social support systems often provide a medium for advice-giving, consultation, modeling, catharsis, reinforcement, and advocacy. Thus, social support systems serve many of the same functions as do counselors, but support systems are more socially acceptable within many cultures than is professional counseling.

When people first begin immigrating in large numbers from a particular country, as from Vietnam in 1975, to the United States, their indigenous social support systems are often in disarray and nonfunctional. However, these pre-existing social support systems frequently can be adapted to fit the new situation, or new support systems can emerge in the context of the new cultural milieu. Examples of indigenous social support systems that play an important role in many ethnic minority communities include extended ethnic community centers, family networks, neighborhood social networks, ethnic churches, and ethnic advocacy groups.

Counselors can facilitate the development of indigenous support systems by publicly acknowledging the important role they play, by supporting government and private funds to build community centers, and by encouraging ethnic organizations (e.g., ethnic churches, ethnic service organizations) to provide such services. Counselors can also facilitate the use of indigenous support systems by referring clients to them.

Facilitator of Indigenous Healing Methods

Just as all cultures have developed support systems to help prevent psychological and relationship problems, all cultures have developed methods of intervening with these problems once they develop. While the psychological healing methods of various cultures may have common elements (Torrey, 1972, Tseng & McDermott, 1975), each has evolved within a cultural context and is effective because members of that culture believe in its efficacy. Individuals who believe in a healing regimen are likely to follow it and invest themselves in making it successful.

Pedersen (1976) has discussed the need for counselors who are engaged in international cross-cultural counseling to be aware of the culture's indigenous mental health care systems. Focusing specifically on the Native American population, Torrey (1970) has suggested that mental health workers should structure their activities to supplement, not supplant, the existing system of mental health services among American Indians and Eskimos. Conventional counseling may be totally ineffective for someone who believes that their psychological problems are the result of an ''evil eye'' or an inappropriate diet. For this reason, Cayleff (1986) suggests that:

> . . . when counseling ethnic and racial minorities, certain belief systems of the client must be considered if quality care is to be given. This entails understanding and honoring folk belief systems such as (a) the humoral hot-cold theory of physical and mental disease . . . , (b) *curanderismo* . . . and belief in folk disease . . . , and (c) religious healing rituals and practices (p. 345).

Understanding and honoring folk belief systems does not mean that the counselor must begin incorporating these healing methods in his/her own practice. But it does mean that the counselor must accept that healing methods from the client's culture are more likely to be effective with the client than are conventional psychotherapeutic strategies from the dominant culture (Berthold, 1989).

Within most other U.S. minority groups, culturally relevant procedures have evolved to assist the individual who is experiencing a psychological problem. Frequently, counselors are unaware of or are disdainful of these procedures, preferring to engage the client in the very counseling process so heavily criticized by minority representatives. The inevitable result is a mismatch of treatment and need, loss of credibility in the counselor, and the client's disengagement from counseling. We would like to suggest that counselors may be able best to serve their minority clientele by attempting to facilitate rather than discourage use of indigenous support systems. According to Cayleff (1986), counselors violate the ethical principle of beneficence (doing good by preventing harm) if they fail to honor the client's belief system (p. 345).

The counselor working with a minority client might begin the facilitative process by exploring with the client how he/she has dealt with similar problems in the past. Familiarity with the client's culture will help the counselor understand culturally relevant healing methods that may assist the client. Not all cultural adaptations to psychological problems engender growth, and in some instances the client may be too acculturated to benefit from procedures developed by the minority culture. In these instances, the facilitative process begins with an exploration of processes with which the client feels comfortable. A key distinction in these cases, however, is that the exploration serves to discover a process for resolving the client's difficulty, not as a process for resolving a problem in and of itself.

Basically, the counselor can facilitate indigenous healing methods by (1) referring the client to an indigenous healer, and (2) incorporating the healing methods of the indigenous culture in his/her counseling practice. Referring the client to an indigenous healer requires that the counselor be familiar with healers from various cultures and their credibility within the racial/ethnic community. Incorporating the healing methods of various cultures into a counseling practice is more problematic. First of all, it is doubtful if individual counselors can become skilled in the healing method of multiple cultures. In fact, we caution against such activity without proper training and indoctrination by indigenous healers. Second, and most important, healing methods from various cultures can involve contradictory beliefs, creating concern about the integrity of the counselor's own belief system.

Conventional Counseling

The Education and Training Committee of Division 17 (1984) of the American Psychological Association has defined counseling psychology as:

> a psychological specialty in which practitioners help others improve their well-being, alleviate their distress, resolve their crises, and increase their ability to solve problems and make decisions. Counseling psychologists enable and facilitate psychological growth and development by helping others better use existing resources and skills, or by guiding them in developing new ways to help themselves. (p. 1)

This definition of counseling psychology suggests that counselors help clients remediate existing problems, prevent problems, and make decisions. The remediation of existing problems is a healing function that we will discuss under the next heading, conventional psychotherapy. In this section, which we entitle conventional counseling, we focus on the role of helping clients make decisions and prevent problems.

We believe that helping clients to make decisions is a universal process that applies across the various cultures within the United States. Basically, this process involves listing alternatives, considering the possible consequences of each alternative, weighing the probability of each alternative, and choosing an alternative. In helping racial/ethnic minority clients to make decisions, however, it is extremely important that the counselor is sensitive to cultural values and to oppressive forces that may impinge on decision-making. It is also extremely important that the counselor be aware of his/her own cultural biases that may be influencing the client's decision-making and to acknowledge these biases to the client.

Smith (1985) describes a preventative, self-help model of counseling ethnically diverse clients labeled the "Stress, Resistant, Delivery Model" or SRD model. According to Smith (1985), the SRD model "puts emphasis on sources of stress rather than on the symptoms of stress," and the counselor "not only helps the client to become aware of the forces in his or her life but also how to marshal resources to relieve stressful forces" (p. 568). The SRD model involves three steps, the first of which is to identify the sources of stress impinging on the client. The second step is to analyze the internal and external factors that mediate the stress as well as the stress-resistant forces within the individual and his/her culture. The third step is to identify a method of delivering services to the client that emphasizes a self-help approach.

Conventional Psychotherapy

While the exclusive use of psychotherapy as the intervention of choice with racially/ethnically diverse clients is inappropriate, the elimination of psychotherapy as a counseling tool with special populations would be equally ill-advised. Obviously, ethnically diverse clients can experience the same mental disorders that afflict nonminority clients. Further, many ethnically diverse clients are bicultural and feel very comfortable with traditional forms of psychotherapy. Thus, when the goal of counseling is to remediate an existing psychological problem, the counselor may want to provide psychotherapy if the client is bicultural and if the problem is no longer being maintained by external sources of oppression.

When providing psychotherapy for racial/ethnic minority clients, counselor credibility may be more important than knowledge of the client's indigenous culture per se, particularly for highly acculturated clients. S. Sue and Zane (1987) have suggested that although knowledge of a client's culture and techniques generated by this knowledge are important when working with ethnically diverse clients, their primary importance in psychotherapy may be to establish therapist credibility. These authors argue that both knowledge of a client's culture and culturally specific forms of intervention may be distal to therapeutic outcome. More directly related to therapeutic outcome, they argue, are therapist credibility and giving, two processes particularly relevant when working with ethnically diverse clients. Credibility is a function of ascribed status and achieved status. Ascribed status is assigned by others; achieved status is primarily a function of the therapist's skills. Sue and Zane (1987) suggest that three factors are significantly linked to achieved status:

> 1. *Conceptualization of the problem.* If the client's problems are conceptualized in a manner that is incongruent with the client's belief systems, the credibility of the therapist is diminished.
>
> 2. *Means for problem resolution.* If the therapist requires from the client responses that are culturally incompatible or unacceptable, the achieved credibility of the therapist is diminished.
>
> 3. *Goals for treatment.* If the definitions of goals are discrepant between therapist and client, credibility of the therapist will be diminished. (p. 41).

By giving, S. Sue and Zane (1987) are referring to the need to offer clients a benefit from therapy as soon as possible. Giving does not mean a short-term treatment for the client's problem but rather a meaningful gain early in therapy. The authors suggest that anxiety reduction, depression relief, cognitive clarity, normalization of experiences, reassurance, hope and faith, skills acquisition, a coping perspective, and goal setting are examples of therapeutic giving.

Selecting an Appropriate Role

Selecting from among these various roles the most appropriate one for a particular racial/ethnic minority client and a particular problem can be a difficult and confusing task. Atkinson, Thompson, and Grant (in press) have addressed this problem by suggesting that at least three factors need to be taken into account when selecting an appropriate role. These three factors are: (a) locus of problem etiology; (b) client's level of acculturation; and (c) goal of counseling. Locus of problem etiology refers to problem causes that range from external to internal. Externally caused problems are those imposed on the client by the environment; in the case of racial/ethnic minority clients these externally imposed problems are often a function of oppression. Job discrimination based on racial/ethnic bias is an example of an externally imposed problem. Mood swings, irrational fear, and weak impulse control are examples of problems assumed to have an internal source. Although some psychologists (i.e., behaviorists) might argue that all client problems have an external source, most client problems are treated by psychologists as if they had an internal etiology.

Level of acculturation refers to the extent to which the client has adopted the culture of mainstream, dominant society. Recent immigrants are often low in acculturation, although even third and fourth generations after immigration may have avoided adopting dominant cultural values. Persons high in acculturation have adopted the attitudes, values, and behaviors of dominant society; they may have retained cultural values from their indigenous culture (and are therefore bicultural) or they may have lost most of their ancestral cultural values.

The goals of counseling also can be portrayed as a continuum ranging from preventative on one end to remedial on the other. Atkinson et al., (in press) suggest that counselors can determine the best role to use with an ethnic minority client by conceptualizing the etiology, acculturation, and goals continua as a cube, or three-dimensional model (see Figure 16.1). The intersections of these three continua form the corners of the cube and each corner is associated with one of eight roles a counselor might assume when working with a racial/ethnic minority client.

Atkinson et al. (in press) caution against using the three-dimensional model as a cookbook for making this determination; in reality, clients and their problems are seldom identified with the extremes of these continua and therefore no one single role is clearly most appropriate. They also express concern that counselors not interpret the model as justification for ignoring minority experiences when the client is highly acculturated. Highly acculturated individuals may still retain strong ties to their indigenous culture. Also, as racial/ethnic minorities they cannot escape the oppression and discrimination of a racist society. Given these caveats, however, the three-dimensional model can be a useful way to conceptualize racial/ethnic minority clients and their problems and can help counselors determine the best role or combination of roles to use when working with them.

Figure 16.1

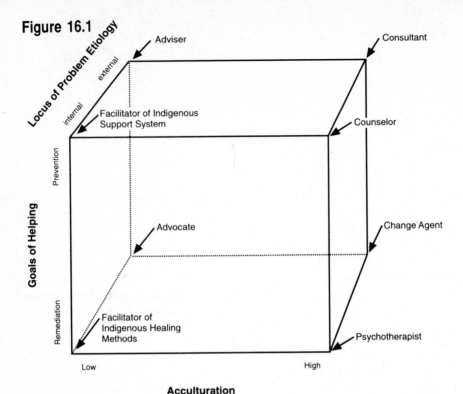

From Atkinson, D.R., Thompson, C.E., and Grant, S. (in press). A three-dimensional model for counseling racial/ethnic minorities. *The Counseling Psychologist.* Reprinted by permission of Sage Publications, Inc.

Helms' Interactional Model

Another model of cross-cultural counseling that emerged during the 1980s that has important implications for counseling practice in the future is Helms' Black/White Interaction Model (Helms, 1990). This model grew out of her work with Black Racial Identity Development (see Chapter 2) and White Racial Identity Development (Helms, 1984, 1990). Helms postulates that White racial identity is a two-phase developmental process in which:

> Phase 1, the abandonment of racism, begins with the Contact stage and ends with the Reintegration stage. Phase 2, defining a positive White identity, begins with the Pseudo-Independent stage and ends with the Autonomy stage. (p. 55)

Briefly, in the Contact stage the individual is oblivious to his/her own racial identity. This is followed by the Disintegration stage, in which the individual first acknowledges his/her White identity. The individual then moves to the Reintegration stage, in which he/she idealizes Whites and denigrates Blacks. In the subsequent Pseudo-Independent stage, the individual begins to question the attitude that Blacks are innately inferior to Whites. As the individual searches for a more positive attitude toward Whites, he/she enters the Immersion/Emersion stage and begins an honest appraisal of racism and what it means to be White. In the final stage, Autonomy, the individual assumes a multicultural identity and nonracist attitudes. (Helms, 1990, p. 51–52).

Although a full discussion of Helms' Black/White Interaction Model is beyond the scope of this text, a key concept is that the relationship between the counselor and client stages of racial identity development (rather than racial similarities or differences per se) are predictive of counseling outcome. Four types of relationships are possible for both same race and cross-race dyads: parallel, crossed, progressive, and regressive. In a parallel relationship, the counselor and client share similar racial attitudes about Blacks and Whites. In a crossed relationship, the counselor and client hold opposing racial attitudes about Blacks and Whites. ''A progressive relationship is one in which the counselor's stage of racial consciousness is at least one stage more advanced than the client's; a regressive relationship is one in which the client's stage of development is at least one stage more advanced than the counselor's'' (Helms, 1990, p. 141). Examples of each type of relationship are presented in Table 16.1 (numerous other combinations within each type are possible, however).

Although a few studies have been conducted on Helms' Black/White Interaction Model, more research is needed to determine its validity. Research is also needed to determine if the model can be generalized to racial/ethnic groups other than Blacks and Whites. Assuming that the Model is supported by future research, it will have important implications for the practice of counseling and the training of counselors (to be discussed in the next section). With respect to counseling practice, it is clear that for both ethnically similar and ethnically dissimilar counseling dyads, progressive relationships are likely to be most productive and regressive relationships likely to be least productive (and perhaps even harmful). This suggests that counselors should assess their own and their clients' racial identity development and refer the client to a more appropriate counselor in the case of a regressive counseling relationship. It also suggests that counselors, Black or White, at higher levels of racial identity development will be able to establish productive relationships with more clients than those at the Preencounter (Black counselor) or Contact (White counselor) stages of development.

Table 16.1
Examples of the Four Types of Counseling Relationships Based on Racial Identity Stages

Stages of Identity			Counseling Process		
Counselor's	Client's	Type of Relationship	Common Affective Issues	Counselor/Strategies	Counseling Outcome
Black Dyads					
1. Preencounter	Preencounter	Parallel	*Anger* about being assigned to a Black person. *Guilt* about negative feelings.	Both will use strategies designed to deny and avoid issues to reinterpret whatever happens in a manner consistent with perceived negative stereotypes.	Client terminates with little symptom remission. Counselor "pushes" client out of counseling.
2. Immersion	Preencounter	Crossed (Progressive)	Counselor may feel angry and *rejecting;* client feels *fearful* and *intimidated.*	General non-acceptance of one another; counselor may be low in empathy, use much advice giving; client is passive and tries not to become involved in the process.	If counselor can act as positive role model, client may develop positive feelings about Blackness; self-esteem is enhanced.
3. Preencounter	Immersion	Regressive (Crossed)	Counselor shares White society's *fear, weariness* and anxiety; client displaces *anger.*	Client attempts to *reform counselor;* counselor attempts to avoid issues.	Short relationships; client's anger may be *enhanced, counselor's* anxiety may be increased.
4. Encounter	Preencounter	Progressive	Counselor feels *excited* and *apprehensive* about working with Black client; client feels *angry* and *apprehensive* and *distrusting.*	Social discussion in which counselor tries to prove he/she is Black; client tries to prove he/she isn't.	Long relationships if counselor uses enthusiasm to engage client; limited symptom remission if counselor avoids doing therapy.

Table 16.1—*Continued.*

Examples of the Four Types of Counseling Relationships Based on Racial Identity Stages

Stages of Identity				Counseling Process	
Counselor's	Client's	Type of Relationship	Common Affective Issues	Counselor/Strategies	Counseling Outcome
			White Dyads		
1. Contact	Contact	Parallel	Counselor and client exhibit *curiosity* and *naivete* about racial issues.	Information sharing, avoidance of negative affect related to racial matters.	Discussion of racial issues is aborted because neither knows how to resolve them.
2. Contact	Reintegration	Crossed (Regression)	Mutual *dislike* because they don't empathize with one another's racial attitudes.	Argumentative attempts to reeducate each other.	Premature termination; client's symptoms may be aggravated because he/she doesn't respect counselor.
3. Autonomous	Disintegration	Progressive	Counselor may be *empathic* and *accepting;* client needs to deal with *self-concept* issues and confused feelings.	Counselor attempts to encourage self-awareness and understanding of racial dynamics.	Potential for client insight and knowledge acquisition is good.
4. Disintegration	Autonomous	Regressive	*Friction;* low levels of *empathy* and *understanding.*	Counselor attempts to protect and nurture client inappropriately.	Premature termination; client perceives counselor as inexpert.

Table 16.1—Continued.
Examples of the Four Types of Counseling Relationships Based on Racial Identity Stages

	Stages of Identity			Counseling Process	
Counselor's	Client's	Type of Relationship	Common Affective Issues	Counselor/Strategies	Counseling Outcome
			Mixed Dyads		
1. Preencounter	Reintegration	Parallel	Mutual *anxiety*; counselor wants to prove competence; client displaces *anger* previously denied.	Abusive relationship; client tests and manipulates; counselor is unassertive and task oriented.	Relationship may be long-lasting because it reinforces stereotypes; little symptom remission.
2. Immersion	Reintegration	Crossed	Direct overt expression of *hostility* and *anger* by both.	Debates; refusal to become involved with one another.	Short-lived; leaves both feeling frustrated about original beliefs.
3. Internalization	Disintegration	Progressive	Client's *self-concept* issues, feelings of confusion, and helplessness are the focus.	Counselor attempts to model positive adjustment and to elicit denied feelings.	Potential for client cross-racial skill development and improved self-confidence is good.
4. Disintegration	Internalization	Regressive	Counselor experiences *pain* and/or *anxiety* about cross-racial issues.	Counselor interacts with undue reserve, uneasiness, and incongruence; client senses counselor's discomfort.	Premature termination; client will seek counselor more in tune with her/his needs.

Counselor Education
Underrepresentation of Ethnic Minorities in Psychology

It is probably safe to say that very few professional psychology and counselor education programs have intentionally discriminated against minority applicants in their admission's policies and procedures over the past ten years. Yet, racial/ethnic minority representation in psychology programs and counselor education programs has not improved since the 1970s. Surveys of psychology departments and American Psychological Association (APA) members in the 1970s consistently revealed that racial/ethnic minorities were underrepresented in the profession (Kennedy & Wagner, 1979; Padilla, Boxley, & Wagner, 1973; Parham & Moreland, 1981; Russo, Olmedo, Stapp, & Fulcher, 1981; Strong & Peele, 1977). The situation had not improved by 1980. According to Russo et al. (1981), ethnic minorities made up 3.1 percent of all APA members, 5 percent of all graduate faculty in psychology, approximately 8 percent of those awarded Ph.D.s in psychology in 1980, and approximately 10 percent of those enrolled in graduate psychology programs in 1981. An article in the December 1990 issue of the *APA Monitor* suggests that these figures probably did not change in the decade of the 1980s; "only about 10 percent of psychology Ph.D. recipients are minorities, and that number hasn't increased in a decade" (Moses, 1990, p. 39).

Underrepresentation of racial/ethnic minorities also has been documented in counselor-education programs in the last decade. Atkinson (1983a) surveyed education programs and found that Asian Americans were underrepresented as faculty and that Blacks and Hispanics were underrepresented as both students and faculty. A more recent survey of racial/ethnic minority representation among counselor education faculty revealed that the situation has gotten worse, not better. Young, Chamley, and Withers (1990) found that Asian American representation in the general population was 1.9 times higher than their representation on counselor education faculty, Black representation in the general population was 2.7 times higher than on counselor education faculty, and Hispanic representation in the population at large was 4.3 times higher than on counselor education faculty.

These data and data from other mental health fields prompted organizations like the National Institute of Mental Health, the American Psychological Association Council of Representatives, and the Presidential Commission on Mental Health to call for an increase in the number of minority mental health professionals (Ridley, 1985; Young, Chamley, & Withers, 1990). Korchin (1981) has identified five reasons, paraphrased below, why the underrepresentation of racial/ethnic minorities in the mental health professions must be eliminated:

1. It is morally right to do so.
2. Minority mental health workers are better able than are their nonminority colleagues to understand minority clients.
3. Minority mental health workers are more motivated than are their nonminority colleagues to work with minority clients.
4. Minority mental health workers are needed as identification figures for minority clients.
5. Minority mental health workers can enrich the knowledge of their nonminority colleagues by sharing their knowledge of human diversity.

After two decades of nondiscrimination and affirmative action, ethnic parity in professional psychology remains an elusive goal. In our opinion, drastic steps are needed if ethnic parity is to be achieved among psychology students and faculty in the foreseeable future.

Recruiting, Admitting, and Supporting Minority Counselor Trainees

According to APA, ''there are only about 15 or 20 programs that really have been proactive in developing training and in recruitment and retaining of minority students in psychology'' (Moses, 1990). One reason that psychology departments and counselor education programs have not enrolled significant numbers of racial/ethnic minority students in the past is that they fail to recognize counselor-trainee selection as a three-phase process involving recruitment, admissions, and support (Atkinson, 1981). Even an admission policy designed to increase minority enrollment will be unsuccessful if the applicant pool includes only a few ethnically diverse applicants. Further, as victims of oppression, racial/ethnic minorities often need economic, social, and emotional support that nonminorities may not need in order to complete a degree in counseling.

In a survey of a representative sample of counselor-education programs, Atkinson and Wampold (1981) found that 57 percent of the respondents stated an interest in enrolling racial/ethnic minorities in the literature describing their program. Slightly fewer than half (49 percent) indicated that someone from their campus had been identified as an affirmative action recruiter for their program, and only 31 percent said their affirmative action recruiter travels to other colleges or universities to recruit ethnic minorities. Fewer than three out of ten programs (29 percent) responding to the survey said that they send applications to eligible racial/ethnic minorities without request.

Bernal, Barron, and Leary (1983) examined the application packets of 105 graduate clinical psychology programs to determine their potential for recruitment of racial/ethnic minority students. They found a definite relationship between the proportions of students enrolled in the programs and the availability of minority-related information in the application packet. Further, they found that two pieces of information, description of minority training opportunities and use of special admissions criteria, accounted for most of the variance in minority student proportions.

Affirmative action recruitment efforts should be designed to identify and solicit applications not only from those minority individuals who already have definite plans to enroll in a counselor training program, but also from those individuals who have ruled out graduate education in counseling for reasons unrelated to their qualifications (e.g., lack of knowledge about financial support available to them). Such a recruitment effort is affirmative in the true sense of the word. It reaches out to those who might settle for a less appealing vocation because their oppressive experience has conditioned them to settle for less than what they actually desire. It includes recruitment literature that identifies: (a) the counselor-education faculty's commitment to enroll a diversified student population, (b) racial/ethnic minority faculty members, (c) the numbers or proportions of racial/ethnic minority students, (d) aspects of the training program (e.g., course content, field-work settings, research focus) that provide a multicultural experience, and (e) support services (e.g., tutorial, financial, social) that are available to minorities. It includes active recruitment by students and faculty at college career days, at professional conventions, and in day-to-day encounters. It also includes personal contacts with interested minority persons by department heads and individual faculty to communicate a real interest in enrolling racial/ethnic minorities.

With regard to admission criteria, the Atkinson and Wampold (1981) survey found that fewer than half (42 percent) of the responding programs give credit for ethnicity as part of the selection process. Approximately four out of ten (39 percent) of the respondents indicated that credit is given to applicants who have prior experience working with members of a racial/ethnic minority. Only 34 percent of the respondents used racial/ethnic minority persons to review application materials and only 31 percent used minority interviewers when they interviewed applicants.

Counselor training programs need to develop admission policies and procedures that will admit as many minority applicants as is legally, morally, and ethnically possible in order to eliminate the current underrepresentation of minorities in the field of counseling. Traditional admission criteria of undergraduate GPA and graduate aptitude test scores have been found to discriminate against racial/ethnic minorities (Bernal, 1980) and to be unreliable predictors of counseling performance (Rowe, Murphy, & DeCsipkas, 1975). New and/or additional criteria need to be identified by counselor education programs that will insure minorities are adequately represented in their student populations.

As most counselor educators are aware, the famous U.S. Supreme Court decision in *Bakke vs. Regents of the University of California* ruled out the use of quotas as a means of ensuring minority admissions. What tends to be overlooked, however, was the court's approval of some admission's procedures designed to ensure minority representation. Citing the Harvard undergraduate admission policy as an example, the court held that a "representational" admission policy designed to ensure representation from diverse groups was acceptable as long as it did not involve quotas.

An alternative to the "representational" admission policy has been described by Atkinson, Staso, and Hosford (1978); it seeks to identify counseling-related strengths held by minorities and include them as admission criteria. Briefly, the selection process involves three equally weighted criteria: academic index, experiential background, and personal interview. The traditional criteria of undergraduate GPA and graduate aptitude test are included in the academic index but their negative impact on minority applicants is lessened by using only the higher of the two scores (GPA or test score) relative to other applicants and restricting the weight to one-third of the total criteria. Experiential background is measured by a background questionnaire and points are awarded to applicants with multicultural experiences and goals that include working with ethnic minorities. For the personal interview criterion, applicants are asked to respond to videotaped counseling scenarios that involve minority clients and are offered an opportunity to conduct their interview in a second language. The combined effect of this process is to admit increased numbers of minority applicants by structuring the admission criteria around multicultural strengths that anyone may have, but which minorities are more likely to possess than nonminorities.

In the area of support, the Atkinson and Wampold (1981) survey found that over half of the respondents (57 percent) offered support groups for racial/ethnic minorities. However, only 39 percent reserved special fellowship, teaching assistantships, or other intramural sources of financial assistance exclusively for racial/ethnic minorities, and only 28 percent provided special tutorial services for these groups. Fewer than four out of ten respondents (37 percent) provided special advising services for minorities.

A variety of support services are needed to ensure that racial/ethnic minorities, once admitted, are able to complete their graduate education in counseling. Special fellowship funds need to be developed and administered for underrepresented groups that could not otherwise attend graduate school (Bernal, 1980). Whenever feasible, racial/ethnic minorities should be employed as research and teaching assistants, since these positions involve not only a financial remuneration but serve as apprenticeships for skills needed as a professional counselor and/or researcher. In addition to financial support, counselor training programs should provide tutorial support to those individuals who may have experienced an inferior education due to their minority status.

Since role models for racial/ethnic minorities are often missing from counselor education faculties, nonminority faculty need to expand their advising role for minority students to include the functions of mentor (Walton, 1979). The results of a recent study suggest that European American psychology faculty can serve successfully as mentors for racial/ethnic minority graduate students (Atkinson, Neville, & Casas, 1991). As a minority-student mentor, the faculty member attempts to minimize the trauma of graduate education and maximize the supportive services for each minority advisee. For emotional/psychological support, many counseling programs have arranged to have support groups offered for their minority students.

In summary, counselor-trainee selection involves recruitment, admission, and support. If counseling programs are to reduce the underrepresentation of racial/ethnic minorities in the counseling profession, expanded effort in all three areas will be needed in the future.

Rationale for Training in Cross-Cultural Counseling

In addition to training more ethnically diverse counselors and psychologists, all mental-health practitioners, regardless of their ethnicity, need to be trained to work with culturally diverse clients. In view of the multicultural makeup of American society, it seems highly unlikely that counselors being trained today (especially those being trained for educational settings) will escape contact with culturally different clients. It is imperative, therefore, that counselors of all cultural backgrounds be at least minimally prepared to work with clients who differ culturally from themselves.

The need to train counselors and psychologists to work with culturally diverse clients has been recognized by the Association of Counseling and Development (AACD) and the American Psychological Association (APA). Both of these professional organizations have developed training standards that include education in cultural diversity as an important component. In order to be accredited by the Council for Accreditation of Counseling and Related Educational Programs (CACREP, the accrediting arm of AACD), a counseling program's goals must reflect (a) ''current knowledge . . . concerning the counseling and human development needs of a multicultural society'' and (b) ''the present and projected needs of a multicultural society for which specialized counseling and human development activities have been developed'' (Accreditation procedures, 1988, p. 25). Further, in order to be accredited by CACREP, the curriculum of a counselor training program must provide knowledge and skill in human growth and development ''within cultural contexts'' and in social and cultural foundations of "societal subgroups" (Accreditation procedures, 1988, p. 25).

Similarly, the APA accreditation manual includes cultural and individual difference as one of the major criteria (criterion II) for approval of a psychology training program.

> . . . social responsibilities and respect for cultural and individual differences and attitudes . . . must be reflected in all phases of the program's operation: faculty recruitment and promotion, student recruitment and evaluation, curriculum, and field training. . . . Programs must develop knowledge and skills in their students relevant to human diversity, such as people with handicapping conditions; of differing ages, genders, ethnic and racial backgrounds; religions, and life-styles; and from differing social and individual backgrounds. (Committee on Accreditation, 1980).

Issues in Defining and Teaching Cross-Cultural Counseling

Need for Defining Competencies

As suggested in Chapter 3, however, these accreditation requirements have not been translated into specific competencies that counseling and psychology trainees are expected to acquire. Very few counselor training programs to date have developed and offered systematic training in multicultural counseling (Bales, 1985; Bryson & Bardo, 1975; Moses, 1990). According to Moses (1990, "there is little agreement on what organized psychology can and should do to help programs improve their records [with respect to cultural sensitivity training]" p. 39.

In spring 1990, the APA Committee on Accreditation created a subcommittee on Cultural and Individual Differences in order to review criterion II of the APA "Criteria for Accreditation." The subcommittee came up with a number of recommendations but stopped short of defining content that programs need to teach. "The Committee [on Accreditation] respects differences among programs in terms of their goals and methods to achieve those goals" (*The Nature Scope,* 1991, p. 5).

However, several authors have attempted to specify the goals and competencies of a cross-cultural training program. S. Sue, Akutsu, and Higashi (1985) have identified three important elements of any cross-cultural counseling training program. According to these authors, training in cross-cultural counseling should include knowledge of various cultural groups and history of their treatment in this country, experience counseling clients of various racial/ethnic groups, and training in devising innovative treatment strategies. Copeland (1983) listed four components of a cross-cultural training program: a conscious-raising component, a cognitive understanding component, an affective component, and a skills component (p. 13). Similarly, Bernal (quoted in Bales, 1985) stated that a multicultural training program for psychologists should have the following goals:

> Understanding the social, historical, and cultural background and characteristics of minority groups; conveying a positive attitude toward these groups and a desire to learn from them, gaining theoretical knowledge and expertise in the scientific study of sociocultural variables, as well as in culturally appropriate intervention strategies; and communicating fluently in the appropriate language (p. 7).

According to Bernal and Padilla (1982), a multicultural approach to training psychologists includes certain important components and a particular training philosophy.

> The components include a concern for cultural sensitivity, a better understanding of racism and its consequences for mental health, knowledge about the merits and dangers of customs of different cultures as they affect their members in terms of universal standards of mental health, an increase in opportunities for students to work with clients of ethnically similar and dissimilar backgrounds, and enlargements of the numbers of minority students and faculty. The multicultural training philosophy acknowledges that it is vital for trainees to have a broad-based historical and cultural understanding of minority groups, to develop positive attitudes toward them, to gain theoretical knowledge and expertise in the scientific study of sociocultural variables, to become experienced in the application of primary, secondary, and tertiary preventative strategies that are culturally appropriate, and to be able to communicate fluently in their client's language (Bernal & Padilla, 1982, p. 786).

One of the most explicit descriptions of cross-cultural counseling competencies to date was offered by the Educational and Training Committee of Division 17, American Psychological Association. In their position paper, the committee identified consciousness raising (attitudes and beliefs), knowledge, and skills as three important curriculum areas for a cross-cultural counseling program. Under attitudes and beliefs they list four competencies that a cross-cultural counselor would have. The culturally skilled counseling psychologist:

1. is one who has moved from being culturally unaware to being aware and sensitive to his/her own cultural heritage and to valuing and respecting differences.
2. is aware of his/her own values and biases and how they may affect minority clients.
3. is one who is comfortable with differences that exist between the counselor and client in terms of race and beliefs.
4. is sensitive to circumstances that may dictate referral of the minority client to a member of his/her own race/culture.

The committee also identified four types of knowledge a cross-cultural counselor should have. The culturally skilled counseling psychologist:

1. will have a good understanding of the sociopolitical systems operation in the United States with respect to its treatment of minorities.
2. must possess specific knowledge and information about the particular group he/she is working with.
3. must have a clear and explicit knowledge and understanding of the generic characteristics of counseling and therapy.
4. is aware of institutional barriers that prevent minorities from using mental health services.

Finally, the committee identified three skills that a cross-cultural counselor should have:

1. must be able to generate a wide variety of verbal and nonverbal responses.
2. must be able to send and receive both verbal and nonverbal messages accurately and "appropriately."
3. is able to exercise institutional skills on behalf of his/her client when appropriate. (D. W. Sue et al., 1982).

More recently, the Professional Standards Committee of the Association for Multicultural Counseling and Development (a division of the American Association for Counseling and Development) published a position paper that proposes 31 multicultural counseling strategies (D. W. Sue, Arredondo, & McDavis, 1992). We consider this document to be extremely important to the counseling profession and we have reprinted it in the Appendix.

Curriculum Controversy

In addition to lack of consensus about the cross-cultural counseling competencies that need to be taught, there is some controversy about how best to integrate training in cross-cultural counseling into existing curricula. Copeland (1982) has identified four curriculum models that have been employed by cross-cultural counseling programs. The four curriculum models are: (a) separate course, (b) interdisciplinary, (c) integrated, and (d) area of concentration. Briefly, in the separate-course and interdisciplinary models, students are encouraged to take courses in ethnic studies and human-service-oriented fields in order to sensitize them to the needs of ethnic and other minority groups. Under the integrated model, the goals of cross-cultural training are integrated into all the counseling courses. And under the area of concentration model, the training program offers several courses that focus on one or several minority groups.

Each of these models has certain strengths and weaknesses. The separate course model is easy to employ but may be viewed as ancillary to the core training program (Copeland, 1982). Margolis and Rungta (1986) have argued against the inclusion of an indefinite number of specialized courses in the counseling curriculum. Their criticisms include: (a) budget restraints make it impractical to cover all groups, (b) accenting subgroup differences may lead to the advocation of a separate set of standards and strategies (leading to a new form of racism), (c) focus on one characteristic (e.g., being Latino) may result in a failure to understand the person's total experience, (d) counselors who specialize too much may limit their employability as graduate counselors, (e) choosing which groups will receive special courses could be divisive for a counseling program, and (f) focus on separate groups could limit counselors' ability to transfer their learning from one group to another.

Margolis and Rungta (1986) suggest that, ideally, attention to the needs of diverse groups should be infused in all aspects of a counselor-education program. Unfortunately, this is probably an unrealistic goal for the near future since it would require that all faculty members have knowledge and skills for which they have not received training. Instead, these authors argue for a course that:

> would include the examination of common client issues associated with membership in a special population, as well as difficulties of counselors in working with populations different from themselves. Opportunities for role play or actual counseling sessions with a variety of clients would be provided. The integrated nature of the course would allow counselors to formulate guidelines that would help them deal effectively with any unfamiliar populations with which they might work in the future (pp. 643–644).

While the differences among ethnically diverse groups must not be ignored, they do share the common experience of oppression. As a result, many clients from ethnically diverse groups also face the common issues in counseling of identity crisis, poor self-esteem, a need for validation of personal experience, and a need for empowerment (Margolis & Rungta, 1986, p. 643). The area of concentration and interdisciplinary models provide for an in-depth study of one or several ethnic groups but may not result in the kind of generalized understanding of ethnic and other minority groups that is the goal of cross-cultural training. The integration model meets all the goals of cross-cultural training but may be the most difficult to achieve because it requires that all the counseling faculty be sensitive to cross-cultural issues that relate to the courses they teach and be willing to incorporate these issues into their course content.

We feel that, ideally, cross-cultural issues should be integrated into all counselor training courses. We are aware, however, that most counseling faculty members have never received any training in cross-cultural counseling and that it therefore may be unrealistic to assume that the integrated model can be successful at this time. We therefore advocate that training programs employ a combination of the separate course model and a pseudo-integrated model while working toward a fully integrated model.

We feel a separate course can cover some of the important common experiences of ethnic and other oppressed groups. One of the major objectives of a cross-cultural counseling class should be to acquaint the student with etic and emic qualities of favored counseling approaches. For instance, it seems clear that rapport is a culturally generalizable element basic to all counseling interaction (Vontress, 1971, 1973, 1974, 1979). Techniques to establish rapport, however, may be culturally specific and not capable of generalization. Nondirective techniques presently taught in many training programs as rapport-building responses may actually antagonize some minorities or seem meaningless to others (D. W. Sue & S. Sue, 1972). As Bryson and Bardo (1975) point out, "... it can no longer be assumed that techniques and strategies that are successful with one group of clients will work effectively with another group" (p. 14). Yet it would be a serious error to assume that all concepts associated with counseling theory developed to date must be discarded when working with a minority client. For instance, the learning theory principles upon which behavioral counseling is predicted presumably hold true in any culture. It seems axiomatic that operant conditioning, classical conditioning, and vicarious learning concepts apply to one culture as well as another. The ways in which these principles may manifest themselves in a variety of cultures may differ, however, and what may be a reinforcing stimulus in one culture may prove to be aversive in another.

Existing and Proposed Training Models

A number of models for training counselors in cross-cultural counseling have appeared in the professional literature since 1970. Most of these models have described simulation exercises, fieldwork experiences, training workshops, or courses that can be used to prepare counselors to work with ethnic minorities. More recently, developmental training models have been proposed. Examples of each will be presented.

Several authors have proposed that prior to direct experience in a cross-cultural setting, counselors in training should be exposed to simulated cross-cultural encounters. Bryson, Renzaglia, and Danish (1974) describe a simulation-training procedure designed "... to assist counselors in training and other human service workers to function successfully with Black citizens" (p. 219), which might be adapted to other cross-cultural situations. A counselor-trainee group is shown a number of videotaped or filmed vignettes in which actors portray the emotions associated with rejection, fear of rejection, intimacy given, and fear of intimacy. The trainees are asked to think of the role player as a client and to respond affectively and empathicly. The trainees as a group then discuss their reactions to the simulated situation. During the discussion, trainees are asked to (a) identify the role-played emotion, (b) identify their own emotional reaction, and (c) suggest alternative responses to the role-played emotion.

An intriguing simulation procedure referred to as the Triad Model has been described by Pedersen (1977), who views counseling as a power struggle between client and counselor and the problem. Counselor trainees are divided into teams of three in which one trainee portrays the counselor, one the client, and one the "anticounselor." The client and "anticounselor" are matched with respect to cultural factors as closely as possible and the "anticounselor's" role is to use ". . . cultural similarity with the client in order to disrupt the counselor-client cross-cultural coalition" (Pedersen, 1977, p. 95). The "anticounselor" may attempt to build a coalition with the client by privately supplying negative feedback to the client about the counselor, or may attempt to destroy a client-counselor coalition by joining the counseling interaction and attacking the counselor openly. Pedersen (1978) has also identified four skill areas (articulate the problems, anticipate resistance, diminish defensiveness, and recovery skills) covered by the Triad Model. He reports that this procedure has been successfully employed with both prepracticum training and inservice workshops (Pedersen, 1977, 1978). Pedersen and his associates (Pedersen, Holwill, & Shapiro, 1978) and others (Neimeyer, Fukuyama, Bingham, Hall, & Mussenden, 1986) have provided research evidence that counselors who participate in triad training increase their ability to interact empathicly, genuinely, and with understanding of affective communication. A one-hour videotape consisting of four triad interviews and a training manual have been developed for use in any counselor-training program. One concern we have with the Triad Model is that it seems to infer that barriers to counseling relationships reside in the client, not the counselor. This might be corrected by adding an "anti-client" role to the simulation.

Vontress (1974) has suggested that, "although a course in counseling racial and ethnic minorities may be another exciting and rewarding cognitive exposure, needed most are affective experiences designed to humanize counselors" (p. 164). The experiences that he and other authors suggest are needed are those designed to increase counselor understanding in two areas: first, to understand themselves and their previous unrecognized biases; second, to gain appreciation for the experiences of someone who is culturally different and to become open to divergent life-styles (Calia, 1966). In order to achieve these goals, "sensitive training," in which the counselor lives and works in the minority community to experience it first-hand, is recommended (Vontress, 1971).

Lewis and Lewis (1970) propose a training model in which beginning counselors-in-training are paired with experienced counselors and placed as teams in inner-city schools to work as full-time counselors. While on-the-job experience working with disadvantaged youth would serve as the basic core of this program, didactic course work taught in participating public schools would bridge theory and practice requirements. A major objective of this training model would be to develop counselors ". . . skilled in the processes of consultation and change and group and individual counseling" (Lewis & Lewis, 1970, p. 37).

Mitchell (1971) describes a counselor training program that is similar to the Lewis-Lewis (1970) model. The program is designed to provide for a Black perspective but includes several features that could be generalized to cross-cultural situations. For instance, in implementing the new program, internships were developed in predominantly minority-attended schools. Also, in addition to developing new courses aimed at understanding the Black experience, core guidance and counseling courses were designed to include minority-relevant materials. This could conceivably be done in any counselor education program. Most programs, for instance, include the equivalent of such courses as Introduction to Guidance/Counseling, Tests and Measurements, and Vocational and Education Information. The introduction course could include a discussion of how the promise of guidance has fallen short for minority students (Russell, 1970). The testing class could devote considerable attention to cultural test biases as well as to problems of validity and reliability (Barnes, 1972). And the vocational class could focus on the special problems of minorities in obtaining and retaining jobs (Miller & Oetting, 1977).

Merta, Stringham, and Ponterotto (1988) describe a bipartite learning exercise designed to increase counselor trainees' sensitivity to cultural differences. Although the exercise is based on theories of culture shock developed through work with international students, the authors contend it can be extended to U.S. racial/ethnic minorities as well.

Parker and his associates have described several courses and/or workshops that combine simulation and experience. One method for increasing counselors' understanding of themselves and their previously unrecognized biases is the Awareness Group Experience (AGE) described by Parker and McDavis (1979). AGE is a one-day structured workshop for minority and nonminority counselors (the authors recommend fifteen members from each group) consisting of five sessions. Session one, *Becoming Aware*, provides for dyadic and large-group sharing of individual cross-cultural experiences. Session two, *Eliminating Stereotypes*, involves a role-played social gathering with each participant wearing an ethnic stereotypic label on his/her back followed by a group processing of the experience. In session three, *Ethnic Lunch*, participants eat together at an ethnic restaurant followed by a tour of an ethnic community. Session four,

Minority Student Perceptions of Counselors, is designed to make counselors aware of how they are viewed by ethnic minority students. Seven to ten students are interviewed by the group leaders in a "fishbowl" procedure with the participants seated around them. In session five, *Action Plan,* the participants are divided into groups of five to develop plans for changing their negative attitudes toward ethnic minorities.

McDavis and Parker (1977) have described a course designed to help counselor-education students become aware of their attitudes toward ethnic minorities that includes AGE as one component. Other topics/experiences covered are *Facilitating Interracial Groups, Minority Student Panels, Counseling Ethnic Minorities Individually, Class Projects,* and *Ethnic Dinner.* In addition to increasing self-awareness of ethnic biases, the course is designed to help students learn to build rapport and counsel ethnic minorities individually and in groups.

The most recent cross-cultural training program developed by Parker and his associates is called the Ethnic Student Training Group (ESTG; Parker, Bingham, & Fukuyama, 1985). The ESTG is a service and training experience offered for counseling center psychologists, intern trainees, and practicum students to improve their ability to understand and counsel ethnically diverse students. The ESTG meets for one-hour sessions bimonthly and includes the following activities: (a) intercultural interaction; (b) case presentations; (c) panel presentations; (d) ethnic student walk-in; and (e) supervision.

Mio and Morris (1990) describe a cross-cultural course taught at Washington State University that includes three major components: (a) general issues in cross-cultural psychology; (b) discussion of four general minority groups; and (c) student paper presentations. The course also focuses on current events related to race relations and includes discussion of segments from contemporary documentaries on racial issues.

Developmental models for teaching cross-cultural competencies have only recently made their appearance. Carney and Kahn (1984) were the first authors to propose a developmental model of training in cross-cultural counseling. Their model consists of five stages. Counselor trainee characteristics and appropriate learning environments are identified and described for each stage. In stage 1, the trainee has limited knowledge about other cultural groups and feels conflicted by the disparity between his/her own ethnocentrism and the egalitarian values of the counseling profession. At this stage, the trainer provides information on the history of America's cultural groups. In stage 2, the trainee begins to become aware of his/her own ethnocentric attitudes and behavior but still employs ethnocentric counseling approaches. The trainer at this stage provides information about barriers to cross-cultural counseling, ethnocentrism in counseling, and alternative world views. In stage 3, the trainee feels guilty and responsible for injustices and espouses an attitude of "colorblindness."

The trainer at this stage encourages self-review and exploration of the colorblindness. In stage 4, the trainee begins to identify as a cross-cultural change agent and attempts to blend new cross-cultural knowledge, attitudes, and skills with his/her indigenous attitudes and behavior. In this stage, the trainer places the trainee in direct counseling experiences in multicultural settings and acts as a supervisor. In stage 5, the trainee "assumes a self-directed activist posture in expanding own cross-cultural knowledge, attitudes, and skills, and in promoting cultural pluralism in society at large" (p. 113). The trainer in stage 5 acts as a peer consultant to help the trainee reach his/her goals.

Lopez et al. (1989) also suggest that training for cultural sensitivity is a developmental process, but consisting of only four stages. In the first stage, unawareness of cultural issues, the counselor does not entertain cultural hypotheses (i.e., does not recognize the potential for cultural interpretations of the client's problem). Participation in a cross-cultural counseling course, coursework, supervision, or personal experience "may serve as an impetus for therapists to begin valuing the cultural context of their clients' lives" (p. 372). At this point the counselor moves into the second stage of development, the heightened awareness of culture stage. In this stage the counselor is aware of how important cultural factors are in fully understanding clients but feels unprepared to work with culturally different clients. The authors suggest that "with proper supervision, student-therapists can learn that they have the capability of understanding and helping someone from a distinct cultural group" (p. 373). However, after working with several ethnic minority clients, counselors then move into the third, or burden of considering culture, stage. In this stage the counselor becomes hypervigilant about cultural factors and their clinical effectiveness may be diminished because they feel they must be constantly on the alert for cultural issues. In order to move supervisees on to the fourth stage, supervisors must "provide a supportive atmosphere and allow student-therapists to voice their sense of feeling burdened" (p. 374). In the fourth stage, toward cultural sensitivity, counselors are able to entertain cultural hypotheses and to test these hypotheses before accepting cultural explanations.

The concept of White racial identity development (WRID) that emerged in the counseling literature in the mid-1980s has important implications for training nonminority counselors to be culturally sensitive. Ostensibly, WRID models describe stages of development that Whites go through as they become more racially conscious. Perhaps the most parsimonious training model based on WRID presented in the professional literature to date is that described by Sabnani, Ponterotto, and Borodovsky (1991). Sabnani et al. examined the Hardiman (1982), Helms (1984), and Ponterotto (1988) models and integrated the common themes into a six-stage model.

Stage 1: Lack of awareness of self as a racial being

Stage 2: Interaction with members of other cultures

Stage 3: Breakdown of former knowledge regarding racial matters; conflict

Stage 4: Prominority stance

Stage 5: Pro-White, antiminority stance

Stage 6: Internalization (Sabnani et al., 1991, p. 82)

Sabnani et al. propose that the training of White counselors for cross-cultural counseling should involve a matching of goals and tasks to the first five stages of WRID. They define the goals and tasks for each stage under three headings used by Sue et al. (1982): Beliefs/attitudes; knowledge; and skills. Table 16.2 summarizes the key points of their model.

Although Sabnani et al. (1991) can be criticized for advancing a training model based on a WRID before the stages of White racial consciousness have been empirically verified (Rowe & Hill, 1992), there is considerable merit in the concept of linking cross-cultural training goals and tasks to the counselor trainee's existing racial attitudes. Intrinsically it is more appealing than earlier training programs that prescribe a common experience for all counselor trainees.

Several counselor training programs have gained recognition for their efforts to provide training in cross-cultural counseling. Arredondo (1985) describes three types of cross-cultural training programs that have been implemented in American universities: (a) specifically funded projects, (b) specializations integral to existing counseling-psychology programs, and (c) continuing-education conferences. She lists the DISC (Developing Interculturally Skilled Counselors) program at the University of Hawaii as an example of the first type. For existing counseling-psychology programs that have integrated a cross-cultural focus, she lists: Boston University; Teachers College, Columbia University; the University of California, Santa Barbara; California State University, Northridge; Syracuse University; the University of Massachusetts at Amherst; and Western Washington University at Bellingham. For universities sponsoring continuing-education conferences on cross-cultural counseling, she lists Teachers College, Columbia University, and Boston University.

As part of their Delphi survey of fifty-three experts in cross-cultural counseling, Heath, Neimeyer, and Pedersen (1988) asked respondents to identify the top cross-cultural counseling programs in the United States. The top five programs in this survey were Syracuse University, University of Hawaii, Teachers College, Columbia, University of California, Santa Barbara, and Western Washington University. Ponterotto and Casas (1987) surveyed eighteen "leading multicultural counseling specialists" to

Table 16.2
Cross-Cultural Counseling Training Goals and Tasks

	Beliefs/Attitudes		Knowledge		Skills	
	Goals	*Tasks*	*Goals*	*Tasks*	*Goals*	*Tasks*
Stage 1 Preexposure/ Precontact	Awareness of one's own cultural heritage Awareness of the cultural heritage of minority groups	Awareness group experience[ab] "Ethnic dinners"[b] Tours/exhibits of other cultures' crafts/areas Intercultural sharing[c] Multicultural action planning (low level of active involvement)[c] Free drawing test[h] Public and private self-awareness exercise[g] Value statements exercise[h] Decision awareness exercise[g]	Knowledge of the cultural heritage of other minority groups	Research into the history of other cultures Intercultural sharing[c] Multicultural action planning (low level of active involvement)[c] Ethic literature reviews Field trips Case studies[c] Culture assimilator[jik]	Beginning development of counseling skills	Regular counselor training tasks (microskills training)[def]

Table 16.2—*Continued.*

Cross-Cultural Counseling Training Goals and Tasks

	Beliefs/Attitudes		Knowledge		Skills	
	Goals	*Tasks*	*Goals*	*Tasks*	*Goals*	*Tasks*
Stage 2 Conflict	Awareness of one's stereotypes and prejudicial attitudes and the impact of these on minorities Awareness of the conflict between wanting to conform to White norms while upholding humanitarian values Dealing with feelings of guilt and depression or anger	Critical incidents exercise[h] Implicit assumptions checklist exercise[h] We and you exercises[h] Exercise for experiencing stereotypes[c] Stereotypes awareness exercise[g] Less structured cross-cultural encounter groups	More extensive knowledge of other cultures Knowledge of the concepts and prejudice and racism Knowledge of the impact of racism on minorities and the privileges of being White	MAP-investigative[e] Tours to other communities Research on racism in the past and present Classes in multicultural issues presenting survey data on minorities Films	Develop more client-specific methods of intervention	Critical incidents method[l] Role-playing exercise[h] Role-playing a problem in a group[h]

Table 16.2—Continued.
Cross-Cultural Counseling Training Goals and Tasks

	Beliefs/Attitudes		Knowledge		Skills	
	Goals	Tasks	Goals	Tasks	Goals	Tasks
Stage 3 Prominority/ Antiracism	Awareness of overidentification and of paternalistic attitudes, and the impact of these on minorities	Interracial encounters[m] Cross-cultural encounter groups Responsible feedback exercise[h] Anonymous feedback from the group exercise[h]	Further immersion into other cultures	Guided self-study Exposure to audiovisual presentations[g] Interviews with consultants and experts[g] Lectures Minority student panels[b] Research into the impact of race on counseling	Continue developing culturally emic and etic approaches to counseling	Role-playing exercises Communication skills training Facilitating interracial groups (FIG)[b] Counseling ethnic minorities (CEM)[b]
Stage 4 Retreat into White Culture	Awareness of and dealing with one's own fear and anger	Cross-cultural encounter groups Lump sum[h]	Knowledge of the development of minority identity and White identity	Research into minority identity development models Research into White identity development models	Building culturally etic (transcendent) approaches	Microskills training Ponterotto and Benesch (1988)

Table 16.2—Continued.

Cross-Cultural Counseling Training Goals and Tasks

	Beliefs/Attitudes		Knowledge		Skills	
	Goals	*Tasks*	*Goals*	*Tasks*	*Goals*	*Tasks*
Stage 5 Redefinition and Integration	Develop an identity which claims Whiteness as a part of it	Feedback-related exercises (see Stage 3)	Expand knowledge on racism in the real world Expand knowledge on counseling methods more appropriate to minorities	Visits to communities with large minority populations Research on ways to transform White-based counseling methods to one more credible to minorities	Deepen more culturally emic approaches Face more challenging cross-cultural counseling interactions	Facilitating interracial groups (FIG)[b] Counseling ethnic minorities individually (CEMI)[b] Triad model[g] Cross-cultural practica

Note: References for exercises suggested in Table 16.2 are indicated by letters, as follows: a. Parker & McDavis, 1979; b. McDavis & Parker, 1977; c. Parker, 1988; d. Ivey & Authier, 1978; e. Egan, 1982; f. Carkhuff & Anthony, 1979; g. Pedersen, 1988; h. Weeks et al., 1977; i. Brislin et al., 1986; j. Albert, 1983; k. Merta, Stringham & Ponterotto, 1988; l. Sue, 1981; m. Katz & Ivey, 1977. From "White racial identity development and cross-cultural counselor training," by Sabnani, H. B., Ponterotto, J. G., & Borodovsky, L. G. (1991) *The Counseling Psychologist*, 1991, *19*, 76–102. Copyright 1991 by Sage Publications, Inc. Reprinted by permission.

determine their rankings of leading cross-cultural training programs. In order of nominations received, the five leading programs were housed at Syracuse University, Boston University, Western Washington University, University of Hawaii, and University of California, Santa Barbara. The common core-elements shared by these five programs were: (a) at least one faculty member seriously committed to cross-cultural counseling research and/or training, (b) at least one course on multicultural issues is offered, and (c) more racial-ethnic diversity on the faculty and student body than is typical at most training programs.

In summary, although the accreditation committee of the APA and other professional counseling associations have yet to define specific competencies that all counselors should have, there is general agreement that counselors do need training in cross-cultural knowledge, skills, and attitudes and number of training models have been developed. Furthermore, position papers by the Educational Training Committee of APA Division 17 and the Professional Standards Committee of the AMCD have identified cross-cultural counseling competencies that could be taught in counselor training programs. Although they are in need of empirical validation, training models based on developmental stages of racial awareness appear to offer the most promise for the future.

Counseling Research

Sattler reviewed the research concerned with the effect of experimenter race on experimentation, testing, interviewing, and psychology in 1970, and found only three studies related to counselor-client interaction. While a number of studies have been carried out since Sattler completed his review (see subsequent reviews by Abramowitz & Murray, 1983; Atkinson, 1983b, 1985; Casas, 1984, 1985; Harrison, 1975; Leong, 1986; Ponterotto, 1988; Sattler, 1977), only a small proportion of studies being published in the counseling journals include race/ethnicity or culture as an independent variable. For example, in his review of articles published in the *Journal of Counseling Psychology* from 1976 to 1986 (inclusive), Ponterotto (1988) found that only 5.7 percent focused on racial/ethnic minority variables.

There are several hypotheses for the relatively low percentage of counseling studies that examine race/ethnicity or culture as an independent variable. One possibility is that a majority-controlled counseling research establishment has simply not viewed race/ethnicity or culture as important factors in counseling. Counselor educators and researchers who espouse an etic counseling approach may feel cultural factors in counseling play a subordinate role to counseling techniques in affecting counseling outcome.

Another reason may be that majority researchers believe that the topic is a highly controversial issue and prefer to conduct research on less controversial subjects. As Gardner (1971) points out, ". . . many blacks have called for a moratorium on all further efforts by white investigators to study and explain the psychological and social characteristics of blacks" (p. 78). Similar requests have been made by other minority professionals who believe that forays by majority researchers into minority cultures have resulted in reinforced stereotypes rather than enlightened understanding. While aimed primarily at researchers in sociology and psychology who have attempted to explain minority behavior in terms of deviance from majority norms, the attitude that the majority researcher-minority subject combination is destined to produce distorted, biased results has obviously become generalized to counseling psychology. This same theme was sounded recently in response to an APA symposium on the role of White researchers in ethnic minority research (Ponterotto et al., 1990).

Furthermore, individual members of various minority groups have grown increasingly resistant to participating in research as subjects (Sue & Sue, 1972b). African American males are understandably reluctant to participate in any activity that smacks of experimentation. Perhaps the most tragic violation of human rights to occur under the auspices of a research project in this country involved Black men in Macon County, Alabama (Jones, 1981). The study, which came to be known as The Tuskegee Study, was initiated in 1932 by the United States Public Health Service. A total of 399 syphilitic Black men in the late stage of the disease were examined but their condition not treated over a forty-year period (despite the availability of penicillin in the 1940s) so that the progress of the disease could be tracked (European studies in the late 1890s had already documented the course of the disease). As an incentive to participate in the study, the men received free physical examinations, free transportation to the clinics, free treatment for other minor ailments, hot meals the days they were examined, and a guarantee that their survivors would receive a burial stipend when they died. At least forty-eight of these men died (some estimates range as high as 100) and numerous others were permanently maimed as a direct result of the disease. A number of other studies with potentially harmful effects have been conducted on inmates (a majority of whom are members of racial/ethnic minorities) in federal and state prisons either without the subject's knowledge or with direct or indirect coercion.

Whatever the reasons for the relatively low percentage of studies that examine race/ethnicity or culture as an independent variable, it is clear that more research is needed. In challenging APA members to advance psychology's role in minority issues, Jones (1990) listed as a top priority the needs to "aggressively and effectively expand the publication of ethnic minority relevant material in APA journals."

Proposed Research Model for Minority Group/Cross-Cultural Research

The suggestion has been made that the impacts of the preconceptions or prejudices of the experimenter on cross-cultural counseling research can be minimized when the researcher feels "comfortably polycultural" (Vontress, 1976, p. 2). We feel that the danger of cultural bias on the part of a single researcher, no matter what his/her race, socioeconomic background, sex, sexual orientation, etc., is unavoidable. It seems unlikely that any researcher has totally escaped the impact of cultural stereotyping that may be present as unrecognized bias in the design, implementation, and/or data analysis of a research project.

The possibility of unrecognized bias can be reduced, however, when research teams are composed of at least one representative from each cultural group included in the study. We are proposing, in effect, that whenever two or more cultural groups are represented in a research design, each group have an advocate from their group on the research team. Objectivity might also be enhanced if the research team included a person whose cultural background was not directly related to the variables under study. Thus, a research team examining the effectiveness of Black or White counselors with Black or White clients might include a Latino researcher as well as African American and European American investigators.

The American Psychological Association hosted a conference on professional training at Vail, Colorado, in 1973; one recommendation developed at the conference was that ". . . counseling of persons of culturally diverse backgrounds by persons who are not trained or competent to work with such groups should be regarded as unethical" (Pedersen, 1976, p. 35). We would like to recommend that a similar ethical restriction be placed on minority group/cross-cultural researchers.

Other steps that can be taken to reduce cultural bias in cross-cultural counseling research include having a member(s) of the ethnic group(s) to be studied on the human subjects committee that reviews the research, the funding review committee if it is a funded study, and the journal editorial board if the study description is submitted for publication. When members of the group(s) being studied do not already sit on these reviewing agencies, the reviewing agency should be required to appoint ad hoc members for the review of cross-cultural studies.

The Need for Theory-Based Research

Reviews of cross-cultural counseling research have found that: (a) racial/ethnic minorities underutilize voluntary mental health services (Leong, 1986; Sattler, 1977); (b) African Americans prefer African American counselors over Caucasian American counselors (Atkinson, 1983; Harrison, 1975; Sattler 1977); (c) findings are equivocal regarding racial/ethnic a bias in clinical diagnosis and treatment (Abramowitz & Murray, 1983; Sattler, 1977); and (d) racial/ethnic minorities are underrepresented as faculty and students in counseling and clinical psychology (Bernal & Padilla, 1982; Russo, Olmedo, Stapp, & Fulcher, 1981).

These reviews also identified a number of methodological shortcomings of the cross-cultural counseling research to date. Some of the criticisms are using designs in which client and therapist race or ethnicity are not fully crossed (Sue, 1988), using measures that are not applicable to counseling (Atkinson, 1985), failing to take intra-group differences into account (Atkinson, 1983, 1985; Casas, 1985), and selecting subjects on the basis of accessibility rather than representation (Abramowitz & Murray, 1983; Casas, 1985). A majority of cross-cultural studies to date have also failed to link their hypotheses to an adequate theoretical base. Ponterotto (1988) analyzed the cross-cultural counseling studies published in the *Journal of Counseling Psychology* between 1976 and 1986 and found that fewer than one-third of them tied their research hypotheses to theory.

After examining the cross-cultural counseling research published in the 1980s, Atkinson and Thompson (in press) concluded that racial identity development, acculturation, and social influence theories were being used as the bases of some studies. They also point out, however, that theory was lacking from many studies of racial/ethnic/cultural variables in counseling, despite the fact that a number of current psychological theories appear to have relevance to cross-cultural issues. Atkinson and Thompson suggest that with regard to within-group variability, some of the personality constructs that may be a function of oppression experienced by racial/ethnic minorities, as well as those hypothesized to be a function of culture should be examined. As examples of the former, they cite cultural mistrust (Terrell & Terrell, 1981, 1984) and self-efficacy (Bandura, 1982). As examples of the latter they identify field dependence/independence (Witkin, 1962) and locus of control (Rotter, 1966). Other theoretical constructs that they judge to have relevance for cross-cultural counseling research included social cognitive theory (Bandura, 1986), balance theory (Heider, 1958), cognitive dissonance theory (Festinger, 1957), the Elaboration Likelihood Model (ELM, Petty & Cacioppo, 1986a, 1986b), and attribution theory (Kelley, 1973).

We believe that attribution theory deserves special attention. Parham and McDavis (1987) recently suggested that although many problems experienced by Black men can be attributed to external sources, it is very important that counselors promote an attribution of internal responsibility for solving the problem. Brickman et al. (1982) define this as the "compensatory" model of helping and hypothesize that "many of the problems characterizing relationships between help givers and help recipients arise from the fact that the two parties are applying [attribution] models that are out of phase with one another'' (p. 375). Brickman et al. have identified four models of helping (moral, medical, compensatory, enlightenment) based on attributions people make regarding responsibility for a problem and responsibility for solving the problem. How important is it that counselors offer their ethnically similar and dissimilar clients models of helping that are consistent with the client's model? What role does culture play in shaping attributions about the responsibility of a problem and the responsibility for solving it? These are questions that cross-cultural counseling researchers might address.

A closely related topic has to do with the attributions clients and counselors make about the causes of psychological problems. Medical anthropologists have concluded that shared beliefs between a healer and patient about the etiology of the patient's health problem play a major role in the healing relationship (Kleinman, 1980; Torrey, 1972). Torrey (1972) provides a graphic example of this point:

> A psychoanalyst trying to cure a patient who does not believe in oedipal conflicts and a witchdoctor trying to cure a patient who does not believe in spirit possession will be equally ineffective unless they can persuade the patient to accept their theory of causation. (p. 21)

Future research might examine the role that culture plays in determining etiology attributions and how these attributions affect counseling process and outcome.

Finally, research is needed to assess the effectiveness of activist counseling roles when dealing with minority clientele. Are counselors who serve as advocates, change agents, etc., actually perceived by minority clients as more helpful than counselors who function in a more conventional role? More important, what is the actual impact of counselors functioning in these roles?

Heath et al. (1988) surveyed fifty-three cross-cultural counseling experts and asked them to indicate the areas in which they expect increased or decreased publications over the next ten years. Publication of empirical work was expected to increase almost as much as theoretical work (37 percent and 40 percent, respectively). Panelists indicated that they expected a 50 percent increase in publications related to Hispanics, 45 percent increase in publications related to Asians, a 35 percent increase in publications related to refugees, a 32 percent increase in publications related to Blacks, and a 25 percent increase in publications related to Native Americans. They also predicted increases in publications related to being bicultural (35 percent), acculturation (32 percent), racial identity development (30 percent), and social political factors affecting the psychosocial development of minorities. Publication of work related to counselor responses and to the impact of training on counseling process and outcome were both expected to increase by 30 percent. Publications related to counselor-client matching was expected to increase by only 20 percent.

If this book helps to stimulate research activity in these and other areas related to minority group/cross-cultural counseling, it will have served an important purpose. We remain optimistic that the barriers to cross-cultural counseling can be bridged.

References

Abramowitz, S. I., & Murray, J. (1983). Race effects in psychotherapy. In J. Murray & P. R. Abramson (Eds.), *Bias in psychotherapy* (pp. 215–255). New York: Praeger.

Accreditation procedures manual and application. (1988). Alexandria, VA: Council for Accreditation of Counseling and Related Educational Programs.

Arredondo, P. (1985). Cross-cultural counselor education and training. In P. Pedersen (Ed.), *Handbook of cross-cultural counseling and therapy.* (pp. 281–290). Westport, CT: Greenwood Press.

Atkinson, D. R. (1981). Selection and training for human rights counseling. *Counselor Education and Supervision, 21,* 101–108.

Atkinson, D. R. (1983). Ethnic minority representation in counselor education. *Counselor Education and Supervision, 23,* 7–19, (a).

Atkinson, D. R. (1983). Ethnic similarity in counseling psychology: A review of research. *The Counseling Psychologist, 11* (3), 79–92 (b).

Atkinson, D. R. (1985). A meta-review of research on cross-cultural counseling and psychotherapy. *Journal of Multicultural Counseling and Development, 13,* 138–153.

Atkinson, D. R., Neville, H., & Casas, A. (1991). The mentorship of ethnic minorities in professional psychology. *Professional Psychology: Research and Practice, 22,* 336–338.

Atkinson, D. R., Staso, D., & Hosford, R. (1978). Selecting counselor trainees with multicultural strengths: A solution to the Bakke decision crisis. *Personnel and Guidance Journal, 56,* 546–549.

Atkinson, D. R., & Thompson, C. E. (in press). Racial, ethnic, and cultural variables in counseling. In S. D. Brown & R. W. Lent (Eds.), *Handbook of Counseling Psychology* (2nd edition) New York: John Wiley.

Atkinson, D. R., Thompson, C. E., & Grant, S. K. (in press). A three-dimensional model for counseling racial/ethnic minorities. *The Counseling Psychologist.*

Atkinson, D. R., & Wampold, B. (1981). Affirmative action efforts of counselor education programs. *Counselor Education and Supervision, 20,* 262–272.

Bales, J. (1985). Minority training falls short. *APA Monitor, 16* (11), 7.

Bandura, A. (1982). Self-efficacy mechanism in human agency. *American Psychologist, 37,* 122–147.

Bandura, A. (1986). *Social foundations of thought and action: A social cognitive theory.* Englewood Cliffs, NJ: Prentice-Hall.

Barnes, E. J. (1972). Cultural retardation or shortcomings of assessment techniques? In R. L. Jones (Ed.), *Black psychology.* New York: Harper & Row.

Bernal, M. E. (1980). Hispanic issues in psychology: Curricula and training. *Hispanic Journal of Behavioral Sciences, 2,* 129–146.

Bernal, M. E., Barron, B. M., & Leary, C. (1983). Use of application materials for recruitment of ethnic minority students in psychology. *Professional Psychology: Research and Practice, 14,* 817–829.

Bernal, M. E., & Padilla, A. M. (1982). Status of minority curricula and training in clinical psychology. *American Psychologist, 37,* 780–787.

Berthold, S. M. (1989). Spiritualism as a form of psychotherapy: Implications for social work practice. *Social Casework: The Journal of Contemporary Social Work. 70,* 502–509.

Brickman, P., Rabinowitz, V. C., Karuza, J. Jr., Coates, D., Cohn, E., & Kidder, L. (1982). Models of helping and coping. *American Psychologist, 37,* 368–384.

Bryson, S., & Bardo, H. (1975). Race and the counseling process: An overview. *Journal of Non-White Concerns in Personnel and Guidance, 4,* 5–15.

Bryson, S., Renzaglia, G. A., & Danish, S. (1974). Training counselors through simulated racial encounters. *Journal of Non-White Concerns in Personnel and Guidance, 3,* 218–223.

Calia, V. F. (1966). The culturally deprived client: A re-formulation of the counselor's role. *Journal of Counseling Psychology, 13,* 100–105.

Carney, C. G., & Kahn, K. B. (1984). Building competencies for effective cross-cultural counseling: A developmental view. *The Counseling Psychologist, 12,* 111–119.

Casas, J. M. (1984). Policy, training and research in counseling psychology: The racial/ethnic minority perspective. In S. Brown & R. Lent (Eds.), *Handbook of counseling psychology* (pp. 785–831). New York: John Wiley.

Casas, J. M. (1985). A reflection of the status of racial/ethnic minority research. *Counseling Psychologist, 13* (4), 581–598.

Cayleff, S. E. (1986). Ethical issues in counseling gender, race, and culturally distinct groups. *Journal of Counseling and Development, 64,* 345–347.

Cayleff, S. E. (1986). Ethical issues in counseling gender, race and culturally distinct groups. *Journal of Counseling and Development,* 345–347.

Committee on Accreditation. (1980). *Accreditation handbook.* Washington, DC: American Psychological Association.

Copeland, E. J. (1982). Minority populations and traditional counseling programs: Some alternatives. *Counselor Education and Supervision, 21,* 187–193.

Copeland, E. J. (1983). Cross-cultural counseling and psychotherapy: A historical perspective, implications for research and training. *Personnel and Guidance Journal, 62,* 10–15.

Education and Training Committee of Division 17 (1984). *"What is a counseling psychologist?"* (Available from the American Psychological Association, 1200 Seventeenth Street, N.W., Washington, DC 20036).

Egan, G. (1985). *Change agent skills in helping and human service settings.* Monterey, CA: Brooks/Cole Publishing Co.

Esquivel, G. B., & Keitel, M. A. (1990). Counseling immigrant children in the schools. *Elementary School Guidance and Counseling, 24,* 213–221.

Festinger, L. (1957). *A theory of cognitive dissonance.* Stanford, CA: Stanford University Press.

Gardner, L. H. (1971). The therapeutic relationship under varying conditions of race. *Psychotherapy: Theory, Research and Practice, 8* (1), 78–87.

Grevious, C. (1985). The role of the family therapist with low-income Black families. *Family Therapy, 12,* 115–122.

Haettenschwiller, D. L. (1971). Counseling black college students in special programs. *Personnel & Guidance Journal, 50,* 29–35.

Hansen, J. C., Himes, B. S., & Meier, S. (1990). *Consultation: Concepts and Practice.* Engelwood Cliffs, NJ: Prentice Hall.

Hardiman, R. (1982). White identity development: A process oriented model for describing the racial consciousness of White Americans. *Dissertation Abstracts International, 43,* 104A. (University Microfilms No. 82–10330).

Harrison, D. K. (1975). Race as a counselor-client variable in counseling and psychotherapy: A review of the research. *The Counseling Psychologist, 5* (1), 124–133.

Heath, A. E., Neimeyer, G. J., & Pedersen, P. B. (1988). The future of cross-cultural counseling: A delphi poll. *Journal of Counseling and Development, 67,* 27–30.

Heider, F. (1984). *The psychology of interpersonal relations.* New York: John Wiley.

Helms, J. E. (1984). Toward a theoretical explanation of the effects of race on counseling: A Black and White model. *The Counseling Psychologist, 12,* 153–165.

Helms, J. E. (1990). *Black and White racial identity: Theory, research, and practice.* Westport, CT: Greenwood Press.

Ivey, A. E. (1976). *Counseling psychology, the psychoeducator model and the future.* Paper prepared for APA Division 17 Professional Affairs Committee.

Jones, J. H. (1981). *Bad blood: The Tuskegee syphilis experiment.* New York: The Free Press.

Jones, J. M. (1990). A call to advance psychology's role in minority issues. *APA Monitor, 21* (6), 23.

Katz, J. H., & Ivey, A. (1977). White awareness: The frontier of racism awareness training. *Personnel and Guidance Journal, 55,* 485–489.

Kelley, H. H. (1973). The process of causal attribution. *American Psychologist, 28,* 107–128.

Kennedy, C. D., & Wagner, N. N. (1979). Psychology and affirmative action: 1977. *Professional Psychology, 10,* 234–243.

Kleinman, A. (1980). *Patients and healers in the context of culture.* Berkeley, CA: University of California Press.

Korchin, S. J. (1981). Clinical psychology and minority problems. *American Psychologist, 35,* 262–269.

LaFromboise, T. D., & Rowe, W. (1983). Skills training for bicultural competence: Rationale and application. *Journal of Counseling Psychology, 30,* 589–595.

Leong, F. T. L. (1986). Counseling and psychotherapy with Asian-Americans: Review of the literature. *Journal of Counseling Psychology, 33,* 196–206.

Lewis, M. D., & Lewis, J. A. (1970). Relevant training for relevant roles: A model for educating inner-city counselors. *Counselor Education and Supervision, 10,* 31–38.

Lewis, M. D., & Lewis, J. A. (1977). The counselor's impact on community environments. *Personnel and Guidance Journal, 55,* 356–358.

Lopez, S. R., Grover, K. P., Holland, D., Johnson, M. J., Kain, C. D., Kanel, K., Mellins, C. A., & Rhyne, M. C. (1989). Development of culturally sensitive psychotherapists. *Professional Psychology: Research and Practice, 20,* 369–376.

Maes, W. R., & Rinaldi, J. R. (1974). Counseling the Chicano child. *Elementary School Guidance and Counseling, 9,* 279–284.

Margolis, R. L., & Rungta, S. A. (1986). Training counselors for work with special populations: A second look. *Journal of Counseling and Development, 64,* 642–644.

McDavis, R. J., & Parker, W. M. (1977). A course on counseling ethnic minorities: A model. *Counselor Education and Supervision, 17,* 146–148.

Merta, R. J., Stringham, E. M., & Ponterotto, J. G. (1988). Simulating culture shock in counselor trainees: An experiential exercise for cross-cultural training. *Journal of Counseling and Development, 66,* 242–245.

Miller, C. D., & Oetting, G. (1977). Barriers to employment and the disadvantaged. *Personnel and Guidance Journal, 56,* 89–93.

Mio, J. S., & Morris, D. R. (1990). Cross-cultural issues in psychology training programs: An invitation for discussion. *Professional Psychology: Research and Practice, 21,* 434–441.

Mitchell, H. (1971). Counseling black students: A model in response to the need for relevant counselor training programs. *The Counseling Psychologist, 2* (4), 117–122(a).

Mitchell, H. (1971). The black experience in higher education. *The Counseling Psychologist, 2* (1), 30–36, (b).

Moses, S. (1990, December). Sensitivity to culture may be hard to teach. *APA Monitor,* p. 39.

National Coalition of Advocates for Students. (1988). *New voices: Immigrant students in U.S. public schools.* Boston: Author. (ERIC Document Reproduction Service No. ED 297 063).

Neimeyer, G. J., Fukuyama, M. A., Bingham, R. P., Hall, L. E., & Mussenden, M. E. (1986). Training cross-cultural counselors: A comparison of the pre-counselor and anti-counselor triad models. *Journal of Counseling and Development, 64,* 437–439.

Padilla, E. R., Boxley, R., & Wagner, N. (1973). The desegregation of clinical psychology training. *Professional Psychology, 4,* 259–265.

Parham, W., & Moreland, J. R. (1981). Nonwhite students in counseling psychology: A closer look. *Professional Psychology, 12,* 499–507.

Parker, W. M., Bingham, R. P., & Fukuyama, M. (1985). Improving cross-cultural effectiveness of counselor trainees. *Counselor Education and Supervision, 24,* 349–352.

Parker, W. M., & McDavis, R. J. (1979). An awareness experience: Toward counseling minorities. *Counselor Education and Supervision, 18,* 312–317.

Pedersen, P. B. (1976). The field of intercultural counseling. In P. Pedersen, W. J. Lonner, & J. G. Draguns (Eds.), *Counseling across cultures.* Honolulu: The University of Hawaii Press.

Pedersen, P. B. (1977). The triad model of cross-cultural training. *Personnel and Guidance Journal, 56,* 94–100.

Pedersen, P. B. (1978). Four dimensions of cross-cultural skill in counselor training. *Personnel and Guidance Journal, 56,* 480–484.

Pedersen, P. B., Holwill, C. F., & Shapiro, J. (1978). A cross-cultural training procedure for classes in counselor education. *Counselor Education and Supervision, 1978, 17,* 233–237.

Petty, R. E., & Cacioppo, J. T. (1986a). *Communication and persuasion: Central and peripheral routes to attitude change.* New York: Springer-Verlag.

Petty, R. E., & Cacioppo, J. T. (1986b). The elaboration likelihood model of persuasion. In L. Berkowitz (Ed.), *Advances in experimental social psychology* (Vol. 19, pp. 123–205). New York: Academic Press.

Pine, G. J. (1972). Counseling minority groups: A review of the literature. *Counseling and Values, 17,* 35–44.

Ponterotto, J. G. (1987). Counseling Mexican Americans: A multimodel approach. *Journal of Counseling and Development, 65,* 308–312.

Ponterotto, J. G. (1988). Racial consciousness development among white counselor trainees: A stage model. *Journal of Counseling and Development, 16,* 146–156.

Ponterotto, J. G. (Chair), Casas, J. M., Helms, J. E., Ivey, A. E., Pedersen, P. B., & Sue, D. W. (1990, August). *The white American researcher in multicultural counseling: Significance and challenges.* Symposium presented at the 98th Annual Convention of the American Psychological Association, Boston, MA.

Ponterotto, J. G., & Casas, J. M. (1987). In search of multicultural competence within counselor education programs. *Journal of Counseling and Development, 65,* 430–434.

Ridley, C. R. (1985). Imperatives for ethnic and cultural relevance in psychology training programs. *Professional Psychology: Research and Practice, 16,* 611–622.

Rotter, J. B. (1966). Generalized expectancies for internal versus external locus of reinforcement. *Psychological Monographs, 80,* 1–28.

Rowe, W., & Hill, T. L. (1992). On carts and horses: The status of white racial identity attitude research. *The Counseling Psychologist, 20,* 189–190.

Rowe, W., Murphy, H. B., & De Csipkes, R. A. (1975). The relationship of counselor characteristics and counseling effectiveness. *Review of Educational Research, 45,* 231–246.

Russell, R. D. (1970). Black perception of guidance. *Personnel and Guidance Journal, 48,* 721–728.

Russo, N. F., Olmedo, E. L., Stapp, J., & Fulcher, R. (1981). Women and minorities in psychology. *American Psychologist, 36,* 1315–1363.

Sabnani, H. B., Ponterotto, J. G., & Borodovsky, L. G. (1991). White racial identity development and cross-cultural counselor training. *The Counseling Psychologist, 19,* 76–102.

Sattler, J. M. (1970). Racial experimenter effects in experimentation, testing, interviewing and psychotherapy. *Psychological Bulletin, 73,* 137–160.

Sattler, J. M. (1977). The effects of therapist-client racial similarity. In A. S. Burman & A. M. Razin (Eds.), *Effective psychotherapy* (pp. 252–290). New York: Pergamon Press.

Smith, E. M. J. (1985). Ethnic minorities: Life stress, social support, and mental health issues. *The Counseling Psychologist, 13,* 537–579.

Strong, D. J., & Peele, D. (1977). The status of minorities in psychology. In E. L. Olmedo & S. Lopez (Eds.), *Hispanic mental health professionals.* Los Angeles: Spanish Speaking Mental Health Research Center.

Sue, D. W., Arredondo, P., & McDavis, R. J. (1992). Multicultural counseling competencies/standards: A call to the profession. *Journal of Counseling and Development, 70,* 477–486.

Sue, D. W., Bernier, J. E., Durran, A., Feinberg, L., Pedersen, P., Smith, E. J., & Vasquez-Nuttal, E. (1982). Position paper: Cross-cultural counseling competencies. *The Counseling Psychologist, 10*(2), 45–52.

Sue, D. W., & Sue, S. (1972). *Counseling Chinese-Americans. Personnel and Guidance Journal, 50,* 637–644. (a)

Sue, D. W., & Sue, S. (1972). Ethnic minorities: Resistance to being researched. *Professional Psychology, 3,* 11–17. (b)

Sue, S. (1988). Psychotherapeutic services for ethnic minorities: Two decades of research findings. *American Psychologist, 43,* 301–308.

Sue, S., Akutsu, P. D., & Higashi, C. (1985). Training issues in conducting therapy with ethnic-minority-group clients. In P. Pedersen (Ed.), *Handbook of cross-cultural counseling and therapy.* Westport, CT: Greenwood Press.

Sue, S., & Zane, N. (1987). The role of culture and cultural techniques in psychotherapy: A critique and reformulation. *American Psychologist, 42,* 37–45.

Terrell, F., & Terrell, S. L. (1981). An inventory to measure cultural mistrust among Blacks. *The Western Journal of Black Studies, 5,* 180–184.

Terrell, F., & Terrell, S. L. (1984). Race of counselor, client sex, cultural mistrust level, and premature termination from counseling among black clients. *Journal of Counseling Psychology, 31,* 371–375.

The nature, scope, and implementation of criterion II: Cultural and individual differences (1991, Summer). *APA CAPSULE,* 1–5.

Torrey, E. F. (1970). Mental health services for American Indians and Eskimos. *Community Mental Health Journal, 6,* 455–463.

Torrey, E. F. (1972). *The mind game: Witch doctors and psychiatrists.* New York: Emerson-Hall.

Tseng, W. S., & McDermott, J. F., Jr. (1975). Psychotherapy: Historical roots, universal elements, and cultural variations. *American Journal of Psychiatry, 132,* 378–384.

Tyler, L. E. (1961). *The work of the counselor* (2nd Edition). New York: Appleton-Century-Crofts.

Vontress, C. E. (1971). Racial differences: Impediments to rapport. *Journal of Counseling Psychology, 18* (1), 7–13.

Vontress, C. E. (1973). Counseling: Racial and ethnic factors. *Focus on Guidance, 5,* 1–10.

Vontress, C. E. (1974). Barriers in cross-cultural counseling. *Counseling and Values, 18* (3), 160–165.

Vontress, C. E. (1976). Racial and ethnic barriers in counseling. In P. B. Pedersen, W. J. Lonner, & J. G. Draguns (Eds.), *Counseling across cultures.* Honolulu: The University of Hawaii Press.

Vontress, C. E. (1979). Cross-cultural counseling: An existential approach. *Personnel and Guidance Journal, 58,* 117–122.

Walton, J. M. (1979). Retention, role modeling, and academic readiness: A perspective on the ethnic minority student in higher education. *Personnel and Guidance Journal, 58,* 125–127.

Waltz, G. R., & Benjamin, L. (1977). *On becoming a change agent.* Ann Arbor: Eric Counseling and Personnel Services Information Center.

Williams, R. L., & Kirkland, J. (1971). The white counselor and the black client. *The Counseling Psychologist, 2,* 114–116.

Wilson, W., & Calhoun, J. F. (1974). Behavior therapy and the minority client. *Psychotherapy: Theory, Research and Practice, 11,* 317–325.

Witkin, H. A. (1962). A cognitive-style approach to cross-cultural research. *International Journal of Psychology, 2,* 233–250.

Wood, P. S., & Mallinckrodt, B. (1990). Culturally sensitive assertiveness training for ethnic minority clients. *Professional Psychology: Research and Practice, 21,* 5–11.

Woods, E. (1977). Counseling minority students: A program model. *Personnel and Guidance Journal, 55,* 416–418.

Young, R. L., Chamley, J. D., & Withers, C. (1990). Minority faculty representation and hiring practices in counselor education programs. *Counselor Education and Supervision, 29,* 148–154.

APPENDIX A

Multicultural Competencies/Standards:
A Pressing Need

Rationale and Description

Derald Wing Sue, Patricia Arredondo, & Roderick J. McDavis

Despite the long history of warnings and recommendations concerning the need to develop a multicultural perspective in the counseling profession, and the need to develop multicultural competencies and standards, it is ironic that the Association for Multicultural Counseling and Development finds itself continuing to justify these concerns. Numerous conferences held by the American Association for Counseling and Development, the American Psychological Association, and other governmental-sponsored events have noted the serious lack and inadequacy of training programs in dealing with racial/ethnic/cultural matters (ACES Commission on Non-White Concerns [McFadden, Quinn, & Sweeney, 1978]; Austin Conference 1975, Dulles Conference 1978, National Conference on Graduate Education in Psychology 1978, and President's Commission on Mental Health 1978 [D. W. Sue, 1990; D. W. Sue, 1991]; Vail Conference [Korman, 1973]).

Since the early 1970s, it has been gratifying to witness the increase in both literature and graduate training programs addressing the need to develop multicultural awareness, knowledge, and skills. For example, an early curriculum survey (McFadden & Wilson, 1977) of graduate education programs revealed that less than 1 percent of the respondents reported instructional requirements for the study of racial/ethnic minority groups. Subsequent surveys (Arredondo-Dowd & Gonzales, 1980; Arredondo & McFadden, 1986; Ibrahim, Stadler, Arredondo, & McFadden, 1986; Wyatt & Parham, 1985) reveal an increasing emphasis in this area. The most recent survey to be published shortly (Hills & Strozier, 1991), reveals that 89 percent of counseling psychology programs now offer a multiculturally-focused course. These surveys fail, however, to give us any indication as to (a) their integration in the overall counseling curriculum, (b) the multicultural perspective of the courses, and (c) the degree of

Reprinted from *Journal of Counseling and Development*, 70 (4), 1992, pp. 477–486. © AACD. Reprinted with permission. No further reproduction authorized without written permission of American Association for Counseling and Development.

commitment by the department to multicultural issues. Indeed, one of the greatest fears among multicultural specialists is that programs continue to see multicultural courses as less legitimate than other counseling requirements, that they are taught primarily by junior level faculty and/or adjuncts, that they are haphazard and fragmented, without a strong conceptual framework linked to specific competencies, and that they tend to deal with cultural differences from a purely intellectual perspective without reference to the sociopolitical ramifications of counseling (oppression, discrimination, and racism) (Ponterotto & Casas, 1991; D. W. Sue, 1990; D. W. Sue & D. Sue, 1990; D. W. Sue, Bernier, Durran, Feinberg, Pedersen, Smith, & Vasquez-Nuttal, 1982). In reality, most counselors do not have enough practical experience in training, nor in their daily lives with racial/ethnic minorities.

The purpose of this paper is threefold. First, we explore the need and rationale for a multicultural perspective in our society, particularly in counseling and education. We advocate the need for a multicultural approach to assessment, practice, training, and research. Secondly, we propose specific multicultural standards and competencies which should become a part of what can be defined as a culturally competent counselor. Last, we advocate specific strategies and issue a call for action regarding the implementation of multicultural standards in the American Association for Counseling and Development.

The multicultural competencies and standards proposed in this report refer primarily to four groups in our society: African Americans, American Indians, Asian Americans, and Hispanics/Latinos. Many of these standards, however, have been seen to have useful relevance to other oppressed groups as well. Before we continue, it is imperative to clarify some terms and issues likely to be raised in this report. One of these is the controversy surrounding the inclusiveness or exclusiveness of the term multicultural counseling (Fukuyama, 1990; Lee & Richardson, 1991; Locke, 1990). There are those who would like to define culture broadly to include race, ethnicity, class, affectional orientation, class, religion, gender, age, etc. As such, multicultural counseling would not only include racial/ethnic minorities, but women, gays and lesbians, and other special populations as well. There are those who prefer to limit the discussion of multicultural counseling to what has been referred to as "Visible Racial Ethnic Minority Groups" (VREG): African Americans, American Indians, Asian Americans, and Hispanics/Latinos. Those who hold this point of view acknowledge that to some extent all counseling is cross-cultural, but that the term can be defined so broadly that it dilutes the focus on racial/ethnic concerns (a primary one being racism) and allows the profession to avoid and omit dealing with the four major minority groups in our society.

We believe that the "universal" and "focused" multicultural approaches are not necessarily contradictory. Both offer legitimate issues and views that can enrich our understanding of multicultural counseling. On the one hand, we believe strongly that all forms of counseling are cross-cultural, that cultural issues need to be seen as central to cross-cultural counseling (not ancillary), and that by focusing just on ethnic minority issues, we may be "ghettoizing" the problem. Yet, we believe that multicultural counseling is a specialty area as well. While all of us are racial, ethnic, and cultural beings, belonging to a particular group does not endow a person with the competencies and skills necessary to be a culturally skilled counselor. After all, does a person who is born and raised in a family make that individual a competent family counselor?

The Rationale and Need for a Multicultural Perspective

Multiculturalism has been referred to as psychology's "Fourth Force" (Pedersen, 1989; 1990) and is seen as "the hottest topic" in the counseling profession (Lee, 1989; Lee & Richardson, 1991). Much of this is driven by our recognition that we are fast becoming a multiracial, multicultural, and multilingual society (D. W. Sue, 1991; D. W. Sue & D. Sue, 1990). In the past, society has operated primarily within a monocultural and monolingual perspective reflected in what has been referred to as the "encapsulated counselor" (Wrenn, 1962). The changing "complexion of our society" and the "diversification of America (U.S.) " as reflected in the 1990 U.S. Census makes it imperative for the counseling profession to take a proactive stance on cultural diversity.

The Diversification of America (U.S.)

The 1990 U.S. Census reveals that the United States is fast undergoing some very radical demographic changes. Projections show that by the year 2000, over one-third of the population will be racial/ethnic minorities with even higher numbers (45 percent) in our public schools. By the year 2010, less than twenty years from now, racial ethnic minorities will become a numerical majority with white Americans constituting approximately 48 percent of the population (D. W. Sue, in press). The current population trend can be referred to as the "diversification of America" and is the result of two notable trends: (a) current immigration patterns, and (b) differential birth rates among the White and racial/ethnic minority populations (Atkinson, Morten, & Sue, in press).

1. The current immigration rates (documented immigrants, undocumented immigrants, and refugees) are the largest in U.S. history. Unlike their earlier European counterparts who are oriented more toward assimilation, the current wave consists of primarily Asian (34 percent), Latino (34 percent), and other visible racial/ethnic groups. These groups are not readily assimilated, as many prefer to retain their cultural heritage. For example, the Asian American population is the fastest growing group in the United States (nearly an 80 percent increase in the 1980s) due to the large increase of Indochinese refugees since the 1965 changes in immigration laws. The Latino population will reach 55 million by the year 2000, and they will constitute the largest group by the year 2025.
2. Along with becoming an aging population (the mortality rate of whites is declining and people are living longer), white Americans are experiencing a declining fertility and birthrate (1.7 children per mother). This is in marked contrast to racial/ethnic minorities who are also showing birth declines, but continue to have a much higher rate (African Americans = 2.4, Mexican Americans = 2.9, Vietnamese = 3.4, Laotians = 4.6, Cambodians = 7.4, and Hmongs = 11.9 per mother).

The implications concerning the dramatic increase in the non-White population are immense. Already 75 percent of the entering labor force is racial/ethnic minorities and women. By the time the so-called ''baby boomers'' retire (those born between 1946 and 1961), the majority of people contributing to the social security and pension plans will be racial/ethnic minorities. Business and industry already recognize that the USA minority marketplace equals the GNP of Canada, and projections are that it will become immense as the shift in demographics continue. To remain economically competitive, businesses now recognize that they must learn how to fully utilize a diverse workforce.

Likewise, counselors and teachers in our schools have already encountered these demographic forces in their work. Educational institutions are most likely to be first affected by the changing student population. In California, for example, the number of white students has already dropped below 50 percent enrollment. Last year, one in every four students in California lived in a home in which English was not spoken. One in every six students was foreign-born (Atkinson, Morten, & Sue, in press). Increasingly, working with minority constituents will become the norm rather than the exception. To be fully competent in working with minority populations or those clients culturally different from ourselves, it is imperative that the Association for Counseling and Development (AACD) take a proactive stance in incorporating standards of practice which reflect the diversity of our society.

Monocultural Nature of Training

A body of literature exists which documents the widespread ineffectiveness of traditional counseling approaches and techniques when applied to racial/ethnic minority populations (Bernal & Padilla, 1982; Casas, 1982; Casas, Ponterotto & Gutierrez, 1986; Ibrahim & Arredondo, 1986; President's Commission on Mental Health, 1978; Smith, 1982; D. W. Sue, 1990; D. W. Sue & D. Sue, 1990; D. W. Sue, et al., 1982). It is apparent that the major reason for therapeutic ineffectiveness lies in the training of mental health professionals (S. Sue, Akutsu, & Higashi, 1985). Even in graduate programs where a course or courses on multicultural counseling exist, it is often still treated as ancillary and not an integral part of counseling (Arredondo-Dowd & Gawelek, 1982). The counseling profession needs to recognize that race, culture, and ethnicity are functions of each and every one of us and not limited to "just minorities" (D. W. Sue & D. Sue, 1990). For example, a review of the AACD Ethnical Standards (1988) and the AACD Bylaws (1989) by this Committee leads us to three conclusions: (a) Not much, if anything is said about multicultural/cross-cultural issues; (b) Not a single statement about multicultural/cross-cultural courses or preparation is included under Section H: Preparation Standards in the Ethnical Standards; and (c) Multicultural/cross-cultural competence is still seen in isolation (and unnecessary) from the overall standards of the profession. Likewise, the American Psychological Association ethical guidelines has been severely criticized by Pedersen (1989) who states:

> . . . existing (APA) guidelines suggest that competence in the cultures of persons being studied or served should be included "when necessary." As long as that phrase is allowed to stand, cultural factors and the expertise in being responsive to them rest with the complainant, not the psychologist. In view of the present state of our knowledge about the presence of cultural factors in all forms of psychological functioning, we conclude that psychologists individually and collectively cannot justify the inclusion of the conditional phrase "when necessary". (p. 649)

There are hopeful signs, however, that APA has begun the process of revising the bylaws and ethical principles to reflect an affirmation of cultural diversity. In the spring of 1990, a subcommittee on Cultural and Individual Differences was created in order to review Criterion II of the APA "Criteria for Accreditation." A number of recommendations were proposed with new phrases "must be imparted," "must be developed," and "in all phases of the program's operation" (APA CAPSULE, 1991).

Sociopolitical Reality

Another important factor which we need to recognize is that the profession of counseling oftentimes reflects the values of the larger society (Katz, 1985; D. W. Sue & D. Sue, 1990). References to counseling as "the handmaiden of the status quo" and "transmitters of society's values" indicate the potential sociopolitical nature of counseling. There are two political realities that our profession must acknowledge and address.

First, the world view of both the counselor and client is ultimately linked to the historical and current experiences of racism and oppression in the United States (Atkinson, Morten, & Sue, 1989; Helms, 1990; Parham, 1989; Sabnani, Brodsvy, & Ponterotto, 1991). For the minority client, he/she is likely to approach counseling with a great deal of healthy suspicion as to the counselor's conscious and unconscious motives in a cross-cultural context. For the white counselor or helping professional, he/she is likely to inherit the racial and cultural biases of his/her forebears (Corvin & Wiggins, 1989; White & Parham, 1990). In all cases, the counselor, client, and counseling process are influenced by the state of race relations in the larger society. That the counselor is "supposed to help" or that counseling is supposed to encompass values and assumptions that reflect democratic ideals such as "equal access to opportunity," "liberty and justice for all," and "pursuit of happiness" may not be realistically reflected in the actual practice of counseling. Indeed, these lofty goals have often been translated into support for the status quo. When used to restrict rather than enhance the well-being and development of individuals from ethnic and racial minority groups, it may entail overt and covert forms of prejudice and discrimination (D. W. Sue & D. Sue, 1990).

Second, the counseling profession needs to recognize that counseling does not occur in isolation from larger events in our society. All of us have a responsibility in understanding the political forces and events that affect not only our personal but professional lives as well. For example, the changing demographics cited earlier are having a major impact upon our educational, economic, social, political, legal and cultural systems (D. W. Sue, 1991). With the increased visibility of racial/ethnic minorities in the United States, it appears that racial intolerance is on the rise. The increase in so-called "hate crimes" (murder, physical attacks, threats, racial epithets, destruction of property, etc.) against minority groups are well documented. These reports are even more disturbing in light of the apparent erosion of the nation's civil rights law and President Bush's vetoing of the Civil Rights Act of 1990 and his opposition of the Democratic version of the 1991 proposal.

Likewise, the "English-only movement" appears to have major political ramifications on the nature of race relations in the United States, and directly to education and counseling. In a perceptive article concerning the "English-only movement" and language use, specialists (Padilla, Lindholm, Chen, Duran, Hakuta, Lambert & Tucker, 1991) conclude that (a) linguistic assimilation is already occurring rapidly among racial/ethnic minorities; (b) promoting second language learning for English speakers fosters positive interethnic relations; (c) maintaining bilingualism enhances positive identity; (d) high-quality bilingual education programs can promote higher levels of academic achievement and language proficiency; and (e) the movement contains a strong racist flavor. These authors conclude further that the "English-only movement" can have negative consequences for the delivery of psychological, educational, psychometric, and health services for linguistic minorities. Promoting bilingualism rather than monolingualism should be a major goal to the provision of mental health services; it is an expression of personal freedom and pluralism.

Multicultural Conceptualizations and Research

White middle-class value systems are often reflected in counseling and social psychological research regarding racial/ethnic minorities. Historically, three very harmful models have been used to guide and conceptualize research on racial and linguistic minorities (Casas, 1985; Ponterotto, 1988; Katz, 1985; D. W. Sue & D. Sue, 1990). The first of these is the inferiority or pathological model. The basic premise was that minorities are lower in the evolutionary scale (more primitive) than their white counterparts and, thus, more inherently pathological. The second assumed that blacks and other racial/ethnic minorities were deficient in desirable genes and that differences between whites and minorities were the reflection of biological/genetic inferiority (genetically deficient model). The culturally deprived (deficient) model blamed the culture for the "minority problem." Ironically, it was well-intentioned white social scientists who were attempting to reject the genetically deficient model who talked about "cultural deprivation." Unfortunately, these social scientists were as much prisoners of their own cultural conditioning as those of an earlier decade (D. W. Sue & D. Sue, 1990). For instead of blaming genes, they blamed the culture. The cultural deficit notion does not make sense because everyone inherits a culture. What proponents of this view were really saying was that racial/ethnic minorities do not possess "the right culture." Thus the underlying data and research base regarding racial/ethnic minorities have (a) perpetuated a view that minorities are inherently pathological, (b) perpetuated racist research and counseling practices, and (c) provided an excuse for the profession not to take social action to rectify inequities in the system (Baratz & Baratz, 1970; Katz, 1985; D. W. Sue & D. Sue, 1990; Thomas & Sillen, 1972).

Within the last ten years a new and conceptually different model has emerged in the literature. Oftentimes referred to as the "culturally different model" (D. W. Sue, 1981; Katz, 1985), multicultural model (Johnson, 1990), culturally pluralistic or culturally diverse model (Ponterotto & Casas, 1991), it makes several assumptions. First and foremost is the explicit belief that to be culturally different does not equate with "deviancy," "pathology," or "inferiority." Second, there is strong acknowledgment that racial/ethnic minorities are bicultural and function in at least two different cultural contexts. Third, biculturality is seen as a positive and desirable quality which enhances the full range of human potential. Last, individuals are viewed in relationship to their environment, and the larger social forces (racism, oppression, discrimination, etc.) may be the obstacles rather than the individual or minority group.

If AACD and other professional organizations were to take a strong stand in adopting the above model and all its implicit assumptions, then research and counseling may become a proactive means in correcting many of the inadequacies and problems which have plagued us for ages. For example, adoption of such a model would mean that (a) graduate programs could no longer present a predominately white Anglo-Saxon Protestant orientation, (b) racial/ethnic minority issues would become an integral part of the curriculum and internship requirement, (c) research would become a powerful means of combating stereotypes and correcting biased studies, (d) studies would begin to focus on the positive attributes and characteristics of minorities as well as biculturalism, (e) recruitment, retention, and promotion of racial/ethnic minorities in counseling would increase, (f) interracial and interethnic relations would be positively enhanced, and (g) we would refocus research and practice toward the environment via systems intervention.

Ethical Issues

The provision of professional services to persons of culturally diverse backgrounds by persons not competent in understanding and providing professional services to such groups shall be considered unethical. (Korman, 1973, p. 105) A serious moral vacuum exists in the delivery of cross-cultural counseling and therapy services because the values of a dominant culture have been imposed on the culturally different consumer. Cultural differences complicate the definition of guidelines even for the conscientious and well-intentioned counselor and therapist. (Pedersen & Marsella, 1982, p. 498)

Both these quotes make it clear that professionals without training or competence in working with clients from diverse cultural backgrounds are unethical, potentially harmful, and borders on a violation of human rights. In 1981, both the American Association for Counseling and Development (1981) and the American Psychological Association (1981) published ethical guidelines making it imperative for counselors/therapists to have some sort of formal training on cultural differences. Yet, declarations such as these do not automatically enhance counselor sensitivity and effectiveness, nor does it mean that training programs will on their own volition infuse cross-cultural concepts into the curriculum (Ibrahim & Arredondo, 1986; 1990). Too often, lip service is given to multicultural concerns without the commitment to translate them into ethical standards and see that they become part of the accreditation criteria. If we truly believe that multiculturalism is central to our definition of a competent counselor, then monoculturalism can be seen as a form of maladjustment in a pluralistic society (Szapocznik, Santisteban, Kurtines, Perez-Vidal, & Hervis, 1983).

It appears that a major obstacle in getting our profession to understand the negative implications of monoculturalism is that white culture is such a dominant norm that it acts as an invisible veil that prevents people from seeing counseling as a potentially biased system (Katz, 1985). Counselors who are unaware of the basis for differences that occur between them and their culturally different clients are likely to impute negative characteristics. What is needed for counselors are for them to become culturally aware, to act on the basis of a critical analysis and understanding of their own conditioning, the conditioning of their clients, and the sociopolitical system of which they are both a part. Without such awareness, the counselor who works with a culturally different client may be engaging in cultural oppression via unethical and harmful practices.

Cross-Cultural Competencies and Standards

It is clear to us that the need for multiculturalism in the counseling profession is urgent, necessary for ethical practice, and an integral part of our professional work. These realities and philosophies should underlie AACD's mission and purpose. Yet, a study of AACD's Bylaws (1989) and the Ethical Standards (1988) reveal serious shortcomings and casts doubt upon the organization's awareness and commitment to the concepts of multiculturalism. Reviews of the Ethical Principles of AACD have continued to indicate that it falls short in addressing racial/ethnic matters across all professional activities (Casas, Ponterotto, Gutierrez, 1986; Cayleff, 1986; Ibrahim & Arredondo, 1986; Ponterotto & Casas, 1991). Our critical analysis of the Bylaws, for instance, indicates only one place in which reference to racial/ethnic groups is made (ARTICLE XIV - Nondiscrimination). The Ethical Standards contain nothing in the Preamble regarding multiculturalism and mentions racial, ethnic, national origin, and/or minority groups only four times (one under Section B: Counseling

Relationship, article 19; two under Section C: Measurement & Evaluation, articles 1 and 12; and one under Section G: Personnel Administration, article 11). Sections on General, Research and Publication, Consulting, Private Practice and *Preparation Standards* contain nothing on multiculturalism! Omissions in the Preparation Standards, in our eyes, is inexcusable and represents a powerful statement of the low priority and lack of commitment to cultural diversity.

Furthermore, we find it difficult to accept two prevailing reasons given for the lack of multicultural statements in the standards and guidelines. The first is that additions and revisions of the standards would make the document too cumbersome and lengthy. The second explanation is that while there is a failure to address minority groups explicitly, they do so implicitly (Ponterotto & Casas, 1991). Behind this last statement is the belief that the standards are developed from a universal humanistic perspective and underscores the dignity and worth of all persons. The first reason suffers from structural bias in that it considers racial/cultural statements less worthy than other statements. The issue of length is a convenient excuse not to make needed changes. Furthermore, we are not recommending simple changes in the standards that would tack on more articles to the Ethical Principles. What needs to occur is a philosophical change in the premise of counseling which incorporates a movement toward inclusiveness, altruism, community, care and justice (Hillerbrand, 1987; Ivey, 1987; LaFromboise & Foster, 1989; Ponterotto & Casas, 1991). The second reason is simply another form of ''universalism'' in which ''people are people'' and ''should be treated the same.'' Such beliefs are ethnocentric and have been documented to be highly destructive to racial/ethnic minority constituents (D. W. Sue & D. Sue, 1990).

Cross-Cultural Counselor Competencies

While the AACD Ethical Standards (1988) make reference to counselors not claiming professional qualifications exceeding those they possess and recognizing their boundaries of competence (Section A: General, articles 4 and 9, respectively), it fails to define competence in the multicultural sense. We believe this represents one of the major shortcomings of our profession. While many individual authors and groups have proposed cross-cultural counseling guidelines, skills, and competencies, AACD and its numerous Divisions have failed to enact such standards. The only formal statement adopted by a Division of AACD is seen in the position paper: ACES Commission on Non-White Concerns (McFadden, Quinn, & Sweeney, 1978). As a result of these glaring deficiencies, the Association for Multicultural Counseling and Development (AMCD), under the presidency of Dr. Thomas Parham requested the Professional Standards Committee to (a) outline multicultural issues facing our profession,

(b) develop tentative minimal cross-cultural counseling competencies for adoption by AMCD and AACD, and (c) explore means of implementing these standards into official documents of AACD and in the accreditation process.

In developing cross-cultural competencies, we have relied heavily upon the works of the Division of Counseling Psychology - *Position Paper: Cross-cultural Counseling Competencies* (D. W. Sue, et al., 1981) and the *Guideline for Providers of Psychological Services to Ethnic and Culturally Diverse Populations* (American Psychological Association, 1991). These competencies and standards have been widely endorsed and currently represent the best various groups and organizations have to offer. If these principles are to be adopted by AACD, they need to be appropriately translated into meaningful statements for the profession. At the present time, attempts to add to and/or refine them would require massive investment of time and energy. Because of time constraints, we have chosen to (a) provide a conceptual framework from which these competencies can be organized/developed and (b) leave the task of tangible translations for future urgent work.

The Culturally Competent Counselor

In their review of the literature dealing with characteristics of the culturally skilled counselor, D. W. Sue and D. Sue (1990) have been able to organize these characteristics along three dimensions. *First, a culturally skilled counselor is one who is actively in the process of becoming aware of his/her own assumptions about human behavior, values, biases, preconceived notions, personal limitations, etc.* They understand their own world views, how they are the product of their cultural conditioning, and how it may be reflected in their counseling and work with racial/ethnic minorities. The old adage "counselor, know thyself" is important in not allowing one's biases, values, or "hang-up" to interfere with his/her ability to work with clients. Prevention of ethnocentrism is a key ingredient to effective cross-cultural counseling.

Second, a culturally skilled counselor is one who actively attempts to understand the world view of his/her culturally different client without negative judgments. It is crucial that counselors understand and can share the world views of their culturally different clients with respect and appreciation. This statement does not imply that counselors have to hold the world views as their own, but can accept them as another legitimate perspective.

Third, a culturally skilled counselor is one who is in the process of actively developing and practicing appropriate, relevant, and sensitive intervention strategies/skills in working with his or her culturally different clients. Studies consistently reveal that counseling effectiveness is enhanced when counselors use modalities and defines goals consistent with the life experiences/cultural values of clients. It recognizes that extrapsychic as well as intrapsychic approaches may be more appropriate and that differential helping strategies may be called for.

In summarizing these three characteristics, D. W. Sue & D. Sue (1990) state,

> These three goals stress the fact that becoming culturally skilled is an *active process*, that it is ongoing, and that it is a process that *never reaches an end point*. Implicit is recognition of the complexity and diversity of the client and client populations, and acknowledgment of our own personal limitations and the need to always improve. (p. 146)

Dimensions of Cultural Competency

Most attempts to identify specific cross-cultural counseling competencies have divided them up into three dimensions: (a) beliefs/attitudes; (b) knowledges; and (c) skills (Carney & Kahn, 1984; D. W. Sue, et al., 1982). The first deals with counselors' attitudes and beliefs about racial/ethnic minorities, and need to check biases and stereotypes, developing a positive orientation toward multiculturalism, and how his/her values and biases may hinder effective cross-cultural counseling. The second recognizes that the culturally skilled counselor has good knowledge and understanding of his/her own world view, has specific knowledge of the cultural groups he/she works with, and understands sociopolitical influences. The last deals with specific skills (intervention techniques and strategies) needed in working with minority groups (it includes both individual and institutional competencies). A more thorough description of these three dimensions can be found in the above two cited references.

Cross-Cultural Counseling Competencies: A Conceptual Framework

Given the above discussion of cross-cultural counseling competencies, it is possible to develop a 3 (Characteristics) X 3 (Dimensions) matrix in which most of the cross-cultural skills can either be organized or developed. For example, the characteristics: (a) counselor awareness of own assumptions, values and biases, (b) understanding the world view of the culturally different client, and (c) developing appropriate intervention strategies and techniques, would each be described as having three dimensions: (a) beliefs/attitudes, (b) knowledges, and (c) skills. Thus, a total of nine competency areas are identified in Table A.1. We tentatively offer what we believe to be important competencies under each area.

Table A.1
Proposed Cross-Cultural Competencies/Objectives

	Counselor Awareness of Own Cultural Values and Biases
Attitudes/ Beliefs	a. Culturally skilled counselors have moved from being culturally unaware to being aware and sensitive to his/her own cultural heritage and to valuing and respecting differences. b. Culturally skilled counselors are aware of how their own cultural background/experiences, attitudes, values, and biases influence psychological processes. c. Culturally skilled counselors are able to recognize the limits of their competencies and expertise. d. Culturally skilled counselors are comfortable with differences that exist between themselves and clients in terms of race, ethnicity, culture, and beliefs.
Knowledges	a. Culturally skilled counselors have specific knowledge about their own racial/cultural heritage and how it personally and professionally affects their definitions of normality-abnormality and the process of counseling. b. Culturally skilled counselors possess knowledge and understanding about how oppression, racism, discrimination, and stereotyping affects them personally and in their work. This allows them to acknowledge their own racist attitudes, beliefs, and feelings. While this standard applies to all groups, for white counselors it may seem that they understand how they may have directly or indirectly benefited from individual, institutional, and cultural racism (White Identity Development Models). c. Culturally skilled counselors possess knowledge about their social impact upon others. They are knowledgeable about communication style differences, how their style may clash or facilitate the counseling process with minority clients, and how to anticipate the impact it may have on others.
Skills	a. Culturally skilled counselors seek out educational, consultative, and training experience to enhance their understanding and effectiveness in working with culturally different populations. Being able to recognize the limits of their competencies, they (a) seek consultation, (b) seek further training or education, and/or (c) refer out to more qualified individuals or resources. b. Culturally-skilled counselors are constantly seeking to understand themselves as racial/cultural beings and are actively seeking a nonracist identity.

Table A.1—*Continued.*
Proposed Cross-Cultural Competencies/Objectives

	Counselor Awareness of Client's World View
Attitudes/ Beliefs	a. Culturally skilled counselors are aware of their negative emotional reactions toward other racial/ethnic groups which may prove detrimental to their clients in counseling. They are willing to contrast their own beliefs and attitudes with those of their culturally-different clients in a nonjudgmental fashion. b. Culturally skilled counselors are aware of their stereotypes and preconceived notions which they may hold toward other racial/ethnic minority groups.
Knowledges	a. Culturally skilled counselors possess specific knowledge and information about the particular group he/she is working with. They are aware of the life experiences, cultural heritage, historical background of their culturally different clients. This particular competency is strongly linked to the "minority identity development models" available in the literature. b. Culturally skilled counselors understand how race, culture, ethnicity, etc. may affect personality formation, vocational choices, manifestation of psychological disorders, help-seeking behavior, and the appropriateness or inappropriateness of counseling approaches. c. Culturally skilled counselors understand and have knowledge about sociopolitical influences that impinge upon the life of racial/ethnic minorities. Immigration issues, poverty, racism, stereotyping, and powerlessness all leave major scars which may influence the counseling process.
Skills	a. Culturally skilled counselors familiarize themselves with relevant research and latest findings regarding mental health and mental disorders of various ethnic/racial groups. As in competency 3a, they actively seek out educational experiences which enhance their knowledge, understanding, and cross-cultural skills. b. Culturally skilled counselors become actively involved with minority individuals outside of the counseling setting (community events, social/political functions, celebrations, friendships, neighborhood groups, etc.) so that their perspective of minorities is more than an academic or helping exercise.

Table A.1—*Continued.*
Proposed Cross-Cultural Competencies/Objectives

	Culturally Appropriate Intervention Strategies
Attitudes/ Beliefs	a. Culturally skilled counselors respect clients' religious and/or spiritual beliefs and values, including attributions and taboos, since they affect world view, psychosocial functioning, and expressions of distress. b. Culturally skilled counselors respect indigenous helping practices and respect minority community intrinsic help-giving networks. c. Culturally skilled counselors value bilingualism and do not view another language as an impediment to counseling (monolingualism may be the culprit).
Knowledges	a. Culturally skilled counselors have a clear and explicit knowledge and understanding of the generic characteristics of counseling/therapy (culture-bound, class-bound, and monolingual) and how they may clash with the cultural values of various minority groups. b. Culturally skilled counselors are aware of institutional barriers which prevent minorities from using mental health services. c. Culturally skilled counselors have knowledge of the potential bias in assessment instruments and use procedures and interpret findings keeping in mind the cultural and linguistic characteristics of the clients. d. Culturally skilled counselors have knowledge of minority family structures, hierarchies, values, and beliefs. They are knowledgeable about the community characteristics and the resources in the community as well as the family. e. Culturally skilled counselors are aware of relevant discriminatory practices at the social and community level that may be affecting the psychological welfare of the population being served.
Skills	a. Culturally skilled counselors are able to engage in a variety of verbal/nonverbal helping responses. They are able to *send* and *receive* both *verbal* and *nonverbal* messages *accurately* and *appropriately*. They are not tied down to only one method or approach to helping, but recognize that helping styles and approaches may be culture-bound. When they sense that their helping style is limited and potentially inappropriate, they can anticipate and ameliorate it's negative impact.

Table A.1—*Continued.*

Proposed Cross-Cultural Competencies/Objectives

	Culturally Appropriate Intervention Strategies
Skills	b. Culturally skilled counselors are able to exercise institutional intervention skills on behalf of their clients. They can help clients determine whether a "problem" stems from racism or bias in others (the concept of health paranoia) so that clients do not inappropriately personalize problems. c. Culturally skilled counselors are not adverse to seeking consultation with and/or including traditional healers, religious/spiritual leaders/practitioners in the treatment of culturally-different clients when appropriate. d. Culturally skilled counselors take responsibility for interacting in the language requested by the client and, if not feasible, to make appropriate referral. A serious problem arises when the linguistic skills of a counselor do not match the language of the client. If not possible, counselors should (a) seek a translator with cultural knowledge and appropriate professional background, and (b) refer to a knowledgeable and competent bilingual counselor. e. Culturally skilled counselors have training and expertise in the use of traditional assessment and testing instruments. They not only understand the technical aspects of the instruments, but are aware of the cultural limitations. This allows them to use test instruments for the welfare of the diverse clients. f. Culturally skilled counselors attend to, as well as work to eliminate, biases, prejudices, and discriminatory practices. They should be cognizant of sociopolitical contexts in conducting evaluation and providing interventions; and develop sensitivity to issues of oppression, sexism, elitism, and racism. g. Culturally skilled counselors take responsibility in educating their clients to the processes of psychological intervention, such as goals, expectations, legal rights, and the counselor's orientation.

Counselor Awareness of Own Assumptions, Values, and Biases

Beliefs/Attitudes

A. Culturally skilled counselors have moved from being culturally unaware to being aware and sensitive to his/her own cultural heritage and to valuing and respecting differences.

B. Culturally skilled counselor's are aware of how their own cultural background/experiences, attitudes, values and biases influence psychological processes.

C. Culturally skilled counselors are able to recognize the limits of their competencies and expertise.

D. Culturally skilled counselors are comfortable with differences that exist between themselves and clients in terms of race, ethnicity, culture and beliefs.

Knowledges

A. Culturally skilled counselors have specific knowledge about their own racial/cultural heritage and how it personally and professionally affects their definitions and biases of normality-abnormality and the process of counseling.

B. Culturally skilled counselors possess knowledge and understanding about how oppression, racism, discrimination and stereotyping affects them personally and in their work. This allows them to acknowledge their own racist attitudes, beliefs, and feelings. While this standard applies to all groups, for white counselors it may mean that they understand how they may have directly or indirectly benefitted from individual, institutional, and cultural racism (White Identity Development Models).

C. Culturally skilled counselors possess knowledge about their social impact upon others. They are knowledgeable about communication style differences, how their style may clash or facilitate the counseling process with minority clients, and how to anticipate the impact it may have on others.

Skills

A. Culturally skilled counselors seek out educational, consultative and training experiences to enhance their understanding and effectiveness in working with culturally different populations. Being able to recognize the limits of their competencies, they (a) seek consultation, (b) seek further training or education, and/or (c) refer out to more qualified individuals or resources.
B. Culturally skilled counselors are constantly seeking to understand themselves as racial/cultural beings and are actively seeking a nonracist identity.

Understanding the World View of the Culturally Different Client

Beliefs/Attitudes

A. Culturally skilled counselors are aware of their negative emotional reactions toward other racial/ethnic groups which may prove detrimental to their clients in counseling. They are willing to contrast their own beliefs and attitudes with those of their culturally different clients in a nonjudgmental fashion.
B. Culturally skilled counselors are aware of their stereotypes and preconceived notions which they may hold toward other racial/ethnic minority groups.

Knowledges

A. Culturally skilled counselors possess specific knowledge and information about the particular group he/she is working with. They are aware of the life experiences, cultural heritage, historical background of their culturally different clients. This particular competency is strongly linked to the ''minority identity development models'' available in the literature.
B. Culturally skilled counselors understand how race, culture, ethnicity, etc. may affect personality formation, vocational choices, manifestation of psychological disorders, help-seeking behavior, and the appropriateness or inappropriateness of counseling approaches.

C. Culturally skilled counselors understand and have knowledge about sociopolitical influences that impinge upon the life of racial/ethnic minorities. Immigration issues, poverty, racism, stereotyping, and powerlessness all leave major scars which may influence the counseling process.

Skills

A. Culturally skilled counselors should familiarize themselves with relevant research and latest findings regarding mental health and mental disorders of various ethnic/racial groups. They actively seek out educational experiences which enhance their knowledge, understanding, and cross-cultural skills.
B. Culturally skilled counselors become actively involved with minority individuals outside the counseling setting (community events, social/political functions, celebrations, friendships, neighborhood groups, etc.) so that their perspective of minorities is more than an academic or helping exercise.

Developing Appropriate Intervention Strategies and Techniques

Attitudes/Beliefs

A. Culturally skilled counselors respect clients' religious and/or spiritual beliefs and values about physical and mental functioning.
B. Culturally skilled counselors respect indigenous helping practices and respect minority community intrinsic help-giving networks.
C. Culturally skilled counselors value bilingualism and do not view another language as an impediment to counseling (monolingualism may be the culprit).

Knowledges

A. Culturally skilled counselors have a clear and explicit knowledge and understanding of the generic characteristics of counseling/therapy (culture-bound, class-bound, and monolingual) and how they may clash with the cultural values of various minority groups.
B. Culturally skilled counselors are aware of institutional barriers which prevent minorities from using mental health services.

C. Culturally skilled counselors have knowledge of the potential bias in assessment instruments and use procedures and interpret findings keeping in mind the cultural and linguistic characteristics of the clients.
D. Culturally skilled counselors have knowledge of minority family structures, hierarchies, values, and beliefs. They are knowledgeable about the community characteristics and the resources in the community as well as the family.
E. Culturally skilled counselors are aware of relevant discriminatory practices at the social and community level that may be affecting the psychological welfare of the population being served.

Skills

A. Culturally skilled counselors are able to engage in a variety of verbal/nonverbal helping responses. They are able to *send* and *receive* both *verbal* and *nonverbal* messages *accurately* and *appropriately*. They are not tied down to only one method or approach to helping but recognize that helping styles and approaches may be culture-bound. When they sense that their helping style is limited and potentially inappropriate, they can anticipate and ameliorate it's negative impact.
B. Culturally skilled counselors are able to exercise institutional intervention skills on behalf of their clients. They can help clients determine whether a "problem" stems from racism or bias in others (the concept of healthy paranoia) so that clients do not inappropriately blame themselves.
C. Culturally skilled counselors are not adverse to seeking consultation with and/or including traditional healers, religious/spiritual leaders/practitioners in the treatment of culturally different clients when appropriate.
D. Culturally skilled counselors take responsibility for interacting in the language requested by the client; this may mean appropriate referral to outside resources. A serious problem arises when the linguistic skills of the counselor do not match the language of the client. This being the case, counselors should (a) seek a translator with cultural knowledge and appropriate professional background, or (b) refer to a knowledgeable and competent bilingual counselor.
E. Culturally skilled counselors have training and expertise in the use of traditional assessment and testing instruments. They not only understand the technical aspects of the instruments, but are aware of the cultural limitations. This allows them to use test instruments for the welfare of the diverse clients.
F. Culturally skilled counselors attend to, as well as work to eliminate, biases, prejudices, and discriminatory practices. They are cognizant of sociopolitical contexts in conducting evaluations and providing

interventions; and develop sensitivity to issues of oppression, sexism, and racism.

G. Culturally skilled counselors take responsibility in educating their clients to the processes of psychological intervention, such as goals, expectations, legal rights, and the counselor's orientation.

We believe that these cross-cultural competencies represent AMCD's first formal attempt to define those attributes of a culturally skilled counselor. They are not meant to be "the final word" in establishing cross-cultural standards for the profession; rather, they represent what we consider to be very important criteria for counselor practice in working with racial/ethnic minorities. Many will, no doubt, undergo further revision and other new competencies will be added. We propose these competencies in the spirit of open inquiry and, hopefully, eventual adoption into the counseling standards of the profession.

A Call for Action

In light of the foregoing analysis and discussion, the Professional Standards Committee of the Association of Multicultural Counseling and Development makes the following recommendations and requests the following actions.

1. In keeping with Goal II: Professional Standards, Objective C: "To promote and encourage the highest standards of ethical and professional conduct for multicultural counseling and development." (Strategic Plan for the Association for Multicultural Counseling and Development, 1990, p. 6), we propose that the Executive Committee of AMCD immediately appoint an ad hoc committee to review, advocate, and work to implement a major change in the AACD Bylaws (1989) and Ethical Standards (1988). The direction of these changes should be consistent with the position and analysis outlined in this paper and other detailed recommendations found elsewhere (Cayleff, 1986; Casas, Ponterotto, & Gutierrez, 1986; Ibrahim & Arredondo, 1986; 1990; Ponterotto & Casas, 1991; D. W. Sue & D. Sue, 1990). We believe that enough analysis and discussion has taken place and that the time for action is *now*!

2. We ask that the AACD Governance and leadership actively endorse the spirit of the proposed competencies with the knowledge that further refinement, revisions, and extensions will occur. These competencies can serve to pace the movement of the profession because they are grounded in the realities of our culturally diverse populations.

3. We further propose that AMCD and AACD immediately set up a mechanism which will advocate the adoption of these competencies in accreditation criteria, and eventually become a standard for curriculum reform in graduate schools of counseling and other helping professions. Perhaps a mini-conference devoted towards developing strategies for implementation of the standards/competencies would be helpful.

4. A change in the bylaws and ethical standards may be meaningless unless the goals of multiculturalism are operationalized. Strong (1986) has defined a multicultural organization as,

> . . . one which is genuinely committed to diverse representation of its membership; is sensitive to maintaining an open, supportive, and responsive environment; is working toward and purposefully including elements of diverse cultures in its ongoing operations; and one which is authentic in its response to issues confronting it. (p. 7)

We propose that AMCD should serve a proactive role in doing a critical analysis of how AACD can become a more multicultural organization. This may entail altering the structure of the organization. We are aware, however, of the difficulty inherent in this task, but believe such actions well worth the effort.

In closing, we urgently appeal to the leadership of AACD and all its Divisions to consider the infusion of multiculturalism throughout their organizations. This commitment will, hopefully, be reflected in the education, training, research, and practice of counselors everywhere. Multiculturalism is inclusive of all persons and groups. Continuing to deny its broad influence and importance is to deny social reality.

References

American Association for Counseling and Development. (1988). *Ethical standards.* Alexandria, VA: Author.

American Association for Counseling and Development. (1981). *Ethical principles.* Alexandria, VA: Author.

American Association for Counseling and Development. (1989). *Bylaws.* Alexandria, VA: Author.

American Psychological Association. (1991, July). *CAPSULE.* Washington, DC: Author.

American Psychological Association. (1981). Ethical principles of psychologists. *American Psychologist, 36,* 633–681.

American Psychological Association. (1991). *Guidelines for providers of psychological services to ethnic, linguistic, and culturally diverse populations.* Washington, DC: Author.

Arredondo-Dowd, P., & Gawelek, M. (Eds.) (1982). *Human rights training manual.* Boston: Association for Counselor Education and Supervision.

Arredondo-Dowd, P. M., & Gonzales, J. (1980). Preparing culturally effective counselors. *Personnel and Guidance Journal, 58,* 657–662.

Atkinson, D., Morten, G., Sue, D. W. (1989). *Counseling American minorities: A cross-cultural perspective.* Dubuque, IA: W. C. Brown.

Atkinson, D., Morten, G., Sue, D. W. (in press). *Counseling American minorities: A cross-cultural perspective.* Dubuque, IA: W. C. Brown.

Baratz, S., & Baratz, J. (1970). Early childhood intervention: The social sciences base of institutional racism. *Harvard Educational Review, 40,* 29–50.

Bernal, M. E., & Padilla, A. M. (1982). Status of minority curricula and training in clinical psychology. *American Psychologist, 37,* 780–787.

Carney, C. G., & Kahn, K. B. (1984). Building competencies for effective cross-cultural counseling: A developmental view. *The Counseling Psychologist, 12,* 111–119.

Casas, J. M. (1985) A reflection on the status of racial/ethnic minority research. *The Counseling Psychologist, 13,* 581–598.

Casas, J. M. (1982). Counseling psychology in the marketplace: The status of ethnic minorities. *The Counseling Psychologist, 37,* 780–787.

Casas, J. M., Ponterotto, J. G., Gutierrez, J. M. (1986). An ethical indictment of counseling research and training: The cross-cultural perspective. *Journal of Counseling and Development, 64,* 347, 349.

Cayleff, S. E. (1986). Ethical issues in counseling gender, race and culturally distinct groups. *Journal of Counseling and Development, 64,* 345–347.

Corvin, S., & Wiggins, F. (1989). An antiracism training model for white professionals. *Journal of Multicultural Counseling and Development, 17,* 105–114.

Fukuyama, M. A. (1990). Taking a universal approach to multicultural counseling. *Counselor education and supervision, 30,* 6–17.

Helms, J. (1990). *White identity development.* New York: Greenwood Press.

Hillerbrand, E. (1987). Philosophical tensions influencing psychology and social action. *American Psychologist, 42,* 111–118.

Hills, H. I., & Strozier, A. L. (1991). Multicultural training in APA-approved counseling psychology programs: A survey. *Professional Psychology,* in press.

Ibrahim, F. A., & Arredondo, P. M. (1990). Ethical issues in multicultural counseling. In B. Herlihy & L. Golden (Eds.) *Ethical standards casebook.* Alexandria, VA.: American Association for Counseling and Development.

Ibrahim, F. A., & Arredondo, P. M. (1986). Ethical standards for cross-cultural counseling: Counselor preparation, practice, assessment, and research. *Journal of Counseling and Development, 64,* 349–352.

Ibrahim, F. A., Stadler, H. A., Arredondo, P., & McFadden, J. (1986). *Status of human rights in counselor education: A national survey.* Paper presented at the American Association for Counseling and Development. Los Angeles, CA.

Ivey, A. E. (1987). The multicultural practice of therapy: Ethics, empathy, and dialectics. *Journal of Social and Clinical Psychology, 5,* 195–204.

Johnson, S. D. (1990). Toward clarifying culture, race, and ethnicity in the context of multicultural counseling. *Journal of Multicultural Counseling and Development, 18,* 41–50.

Katz, J. (1985). The sociopolitical nature of counseling. *The Counseling Psychologist, 13,* 615–624.

Korman, M. (1974). National conference on levels and patterns of professional training in psychology: Major themes. *American Psychologist*, *29*, 301–313.

LaFromboise, T. D., & Foster, S. L. (1989). Ethics in multicultural counseling. In P. B. Pedersen, W. J. Lonner, & J. E. Trimble (Eds.), *Counseling across cultures* (3rd ed.), (pp. 115–136). Honolulu, HI: University of Hawaii Press.

Lee, C. (1989). Editorial: Who speaks for multicultural counseling? *Journal of Multicultural Counseling and Development*, *17*, 1–3.

Lee, C., & Richardson, B. L. (1991). *Multicultural issues in counseling: New approaches to diversity*. Alexandria, VA.: American Association for Counseling and Development.

Locke, D. C. (1990). A not-so-provincial view of multicultural counseling. *Counselor Education and Supervision*, *30*, 18–25.

McFadden, J., Quinn, J. R., & Sweeney, T. J. (1978). *Position paper: Commission on non-white concerns*. Washington, DC: ACES.

McFadden, J., Wilson, T. (1977). Non-white academic training with counselor education rehabilitation counseling, and student personnel programs. Unpublished research.

Padilla, A. M., Lindholm, K. J., Chen, A., Duran, R., Hakuta, K., Lambert, W., & Tucker, G. R. (1991). The English-only movement: Myths, reality, and implications for psychology. *American Psychologist*, *46*, 120–130.

Parham, T. A. (1989). Cycles of psychological nigrescense. *The Counseling Psychologist*, *17*, 187–226.

Pedersen, P. (1989). Developing multicultural ethical guidelines for psychology. *International Journal of Psychology*, *24*, 643–652.

Pedersen, P. B. (1988). *A handbook for development of multicultural awareness*. Alexandria, VA: American Association for Counseling and Development.

Pedersen, P. B. (1990). The constructs of complexity and balance in multicultural counseling theory and practice. *Journal of Counseling and Development*, *68*, 550–554.

Pedersen, P. B., & Marsella, A. J. (1982). The ethical crisis for cross-cultural counseling and therapy. *Professional Psychology*, *13*, 492–500.

Ponterotto, J. G. (1988). Racial/ethnic minority research in the *Journal of Counseling Psychology*: A content analysis and methodological critique. *Journal of Counseling Psychology*, *35*, 410–418.

Ponterotto, J., & Casas, M. (1991). *Handbook of racial/ethnic minority counseling research*. Springfield, IL: Charles C. Thomas.

President's Commission on Mental Health. (1979). *Report from the President's Commission on Mental Health*. Washington, DC: U.S. Government Printing Office.

Sabnani, H. B., Ponterotto, J. G., Borodovsky, L. G. (1991). White racial identity development and cross-cultural training. *The Counseling Psychologist*, *19*, 76–102.

Smith, E. J. (1982). Counseling psychology in the marketplace: The status of ethnic minorities. *The Counseling Psychologist*, *10*, 61–67.

Strong, L. J. (1986). Race relations for personal and organizational effectiveness. Unpublished manuscript.

Sue, D. W. (1991). A conceptual model for cultural diversity training. *Journal of Counseling and Development*, in press.

Sue, D. W. (1990). Culture specific strategies in counseling: A conceptual framework. *Professional Psychology, 24,* 424–433.

Sue, D. W., Bernier, Y., Durran, A., Feinberg, L., Pedersen, P. B., Smith, E. J., & Vasquez-Nuttal, E. (1982). Position Paper: Cross-cultural counseling competencies. *The Counseling Psychologist, 10,* 45–52.

Sue, D. W. (1991). *Counseling the culturally different: Theory and practice.* New York: John Wiley.

Sue, D. W., & Sue, D. (1990). *Counseling the culturally different: Theory and practice.* New York: John Wiley.

Sue, S., Akutsu, P. D., & Higashi, C. (1985). Training issues in conducting therapy with ethnic-minority clients. In P. B. Pedersen (Ed.), *Handbook in cross-cultural counseling and therapy* (pp. 275–280). Westport, CT: Greenwood Press.

Szapocznik, J., Santisteban, D., Kurtines, W., Perez-Vidal, A., & Hervis, O. L. (1983, November). Bicultural effectiveness training: A treatment for enhancing intercultural adjustment in Cuban American families. Paper presented at the Ethnicity, Acculturation, and Mental Health among Hispanics Conference, Albuquerque, New Mexico.

Thomas, A., & Sillen, S. (1972). *Racism and psychiatry.* New York: Brunner/Mazel.

White, J. L., & Parham, T. A. (1990). *The psychology of Blacks.* Englewood Cliffs, NJ: Prentice-Hall.

Wrenn, C. G. (1962). The culturally encapsulated counselor. *Harvard Educational Review, 32,* 444–449.

Wyatt, G. G., Parham, W. D. (1985). The inclusion of culturally sensitive course materials in graduate school and training programs. *Psychotherapy, 22,* 461–468.

AUTHOR INDEX

Manson, S., 127, 131, 140, 146, 166, 173, 174, 179, 180, 182, 185, 228, 229, 233
Manson, S. M., 123, 125, 127, 129, 132, 142, 144, 146, 147, 148, 168, 170, 172, 176, 178, 179, 185
Manson, V. G., 124, 142
Marcos, L., 272, 277
Marcos, L. R., 257, 261, 287, 292, 293
Margolis, R. L., 323, 342
Margullis, C., 45, 46, 68
Marsella, A., 205, 209
Marsella, A. J., 354, 370
Marshal, M., 127, 128, 143, 147, 169
Martin, E. P., 81, 86
Martin, J., 81, 86
Martinez, C., 252, 261, 268, 277
Maruyama, M., 51, 53, 64
Masuda, 200
Matheson, L., 180, 181, 185
Matsui, S., 51, 53, 64
Matsumoto, 200
Matsushita, Y. J., 53, 64
Mayes, B., 105, 110
Mayovich, M. H., 25, 38
McAdoo, H., 104, 108, 111
McBee, S., 195, 197
McCarty, T. L., 155, 168
McCauley, C., 11, 17
McDavis, R. J., 54, 57, 73, 322, 326, 327, 333, 337, 342, 343
McDermott, J. F. Jr., 305, 344
McDonald, P. R., 124, 142
McFadden, J., 46, 55, 66, 329, 339, 347, 356, 369, 370
McFee, M., 155, 168
McKinney, H., 42, 68, 211, 212, 216, 224
McLemore, S. D., 10, 17
McLeod, B., 195, 197, 206, 209
McQuiston, J. M., 123, 139
McShane, D., 138, 142
Medicine, B., 127, 132, 142, 144, 146, 170, 174, 186
Meier, S., 303, 341
Melgoza, B., 256, 260
Mellins, C. A., 56, 66, 328, 341
Memmi, A., 86
Mercado, P., 62, 151, 165
Meredith, C. W., 200, 205, 209
Meredith, G. M., 199, 205, 209
Merta, R. J., 326, 333, 342
Meyer, G. G., 135, 142, 182, 186
Milazzo-Sayre, L. J., 42, 67
Miller, C. D., 326, 342

Miller, J. D. B., 13, 17
Miller, N. B., 179, 186
Miller, S. I., 149, 169
Miller, W., 156, 166
Mindel, C., 101, 110
Minerbrook, S., 72, 73
Minuchin, S., 103, 107, 111
Mio, J. S., 47, 55, 56, 66, 327, 342
Mirabla, D., 179, 182, 186
Mirowsky, J., 250, 262
Mitchell, H., 301, 326, 342
Mitchell, M., 138, 140
Mizokawa, D. T., 204, 209
Mohatt, G. V., 130, 135, 142, 147, 168
Molesky, J., 285, 293
Moncher, M. S., 156, 169
Monelli, C., 285, 292
Montoya, V., 168
Moon, A., 227, 228, 233
Moore, B. M., 4, 5, 17
Moore, J., 251, 261
Morales, A., 254, 262, 267, 277
Moreland, J. R., 50, 66, 315, 342
Morishima, J. K., 68, 199, 204, 209, 210, 212, 215, 216, 223, 224
Morokvasic, M., 279, 291
Morris, D. R., 47, 55, 56, 66, 327, 342
Morten, G., 36, 38, 151, 161, 164, 165, 349, 350, 352, 369
Moscicki, E. K., 253, 261
Moses, L. G., 155, 168
Moses, S., 50, 51, 55, 56, 66, 315, 316, 320, 342
Moskos, C., 94, 98
Munoz, F. U., 216, 223
Murphy, H. B., 317, 343
Murray, J., 48, 52, 64, 334, 337, 339
Mussenden, M. E., 325, 342
Myers, L. J., 25, 38

Naparstek, A. J., 137, 139
Naron, N., 267, 277
National Coalition of Advocates for Students, 4, 17, 301, 342
National Conference on Graduate Education in Psychology, 347
National Urban League, 76, 86
Neider, J., 203, 210
Neidert, L. J., 22, 38
Neihardt, J., 119, 121
Neimeyer, G. J., 20, 21 37, 325, 329, 338, 341, 342
Neliegh, G., 146, 168

Wu, I. H., 51, 68
Wyatt, G. G., 347, 371

Yamamoto, J., 216, 224, 228, 233, 251, 259
Young, C., 77, 86
Young, R. L., 50, 68, 315, 345
Youngman, G., 175, 181, 187
Yu, K. H., 216, 224

Zanden, J. V., 79, 86
Zane, N., 8, 17, 48, 53, 68, 308, 344
Zane, W. S., 199, 210
Zayas, L. H., 156, 169
Zell, P., 126
Zuckerman, M., 5, 6, 8, 17

SUBJECT INDEX

Acculturation defined, 10, 21, 22, 23, 204, 251, 252, 280–81
Ad Hoc Committee on Equal Opportunity in Psychology, 47
Adviser role, 304
Advocate role, 301
Alloplastic adaption, 57
American Association for Counseling and Development, 46, 55, 56, 95, 319, 322, 347, 348, 350, 354, 355, 356, 357, 367, 368
American Indian Religious Freedom Act, 147
Americanize, 10
American Psychological Association, 46, 55, 56, 126, 161, 319, 336, 347, 351, 354, 357
Anticounselor, 325
Assimilation, 10, 19, 22
Association for Counselor Education and Supervision, 356
Association for Multicultural Counseling and Development, 46, 56, 322, 356, 357, 367, 368
Association for Non-White Concerns in Personnel and Guidance, 47
Austin Conference, 47, 347
Autonomy stage, 311, 313
Autoplastic adaption, 57

Bakke vs. Regents of the University of California, 317, 318
Biculturalism, 155
Bicultural socialization model, 23
Black pathology, 16
Black Racial Identity Attitude Scale, 27
Black Racial Identity Development, 27, 104, 310
Black Student Psychological Association, 47
Black/White Interaction Model of Counseling, 63, 310–14
Board of Ethnic Minority Affairs, 47

Board of Social and Ethical Responsibility for Psychology, 47
Bureau of Indian Affairs, 119, 124, 128, 129, 163, 172

Change agent role, 302–3
Chinese Exclusion Act, 9, 202
Civil Rights Act of 1990, 352
Coalition of the Hispanic Health and Human Services Organization, 246
Committee on Accreditation, 55, 320
Committee on Equality of Opportunity in Psychology, 47
Compensatory model of helping, 337
Conformity stage, 28–30, 33, 34, 35
Consultant role, 303–4
Contact stage, 310, 311, 313
Conventional counseling role, 307
Conventional psychotherapy role, 307
Council for Accreditation of Counseling and Related Educational Programs, 319
Cross-cultural counseling competency, 358–68
Cross-cultural counseling defined, 15
Cross-cultural psychology defined, 15
Cuento, 274, 275
Cultural commitment, 24
Cultural fatalism, 250
Cultural insensitivity, 4
Cultural pluralism, 10
Cultural sensitivity, 4, 24, 62, 265–76, 321, 328
Culturally competent counselor, 357–68
Culturally deprived, 8, 353
Culturally different, 9
Culturally disadvantaged, 8, 9
Culturally distinct, 9
Culture-blind, 24, 49, 62
Culture conflict, 203
Culture defined, 5
Culture-sensitive, 49, 62
Culturocentrism, 31, 32

385

Vail Conference, 47, 55, 135, 336
VREG defined, 13

White Identity Development, 52, 310, 328–33
Wido-Ako-Dode-Win Program, 131
World View, 364

Yellow peril, 202
Yin-yan, 228